The Other Saudis

Toby Matthiesen traces the politics of the Shia in the Eastern Province of Saudi Arabia from the nineteenth century until the present day. This book outlines the difficult experiences of being Shia in a Wahhabi state, and casts new light on how the Shia have mobilised politically to change their position. Shia petitioned the rulers, joined secular opposition parties, and founded Islamist movements. Most Saudi Shia opposition activists profited from an amnesty in 1993 and subsequently found a place in civil society and the public sphere. But since 2011 a new Shia protest movement has again challenged the state. *The Other Saudis* shows how exclusionary state practices created an internal Other and how sectarian discrimination has strengthened Shia communal identities. The book is based on little-known Arabic sources, extensive fieldwork in Saudi Arabia, and interviews with key activists. Of immense geopolitical importance, the oil-rich Eastern Province is a crucial but little known factor in regional politics and Gulf security.

Toby Matthiesen is a Research Fellow in Islamic and Middle Eastern Studies at Pembroke College, University of Cambridge.

Cambridge Middle East Studies

Editorial Board

Cambridge Middle East Studies has been established to publish books on the nineteenth- to twenty-first-century Middle East and North Africa. The series offers new and original interpretations of aspects of Middle Eastern societies and their histories. To achieve disciplinary diversity, books are solicited from authors writing in a wide range of fields including history, sociology, anthropology, political science, and political economy. The emphasis is on producing books affording an original approach along theoretical and empirical lines. The series is intended for students and academics, but the more accessible and wide-ranging studies will also appeal to the interested general reader.

Other titles in the series can be found after the index.

The Other Saudis

Shiism, Dissent and Sectarianism

TOBY MATTHIESEN

University of Cambridge

CAMBRIDGE
UNIVERSITY PRESS

CAMBRIDGE
UNIVERSITY PRESS

University Printing House, Cambridge CB2 8BS, United Kingdom

One Liberty Plaza, 20th Floor, New York, NY 10006, USA

477 Williamstown Road, Port Melbourne, VIC 3207, Australia

314-321, 3rd Floor, Plot 3, Splendor Forum, Jasola District Centre, New Delhi - 110025, India

79 Anson Road, #06-04/06, Singapore 079906

Cambridge University Press is part of the University of Cambridge.

It furthers the University's mission by disseminating knowledge in the pursuit of education, learning and research at the highest international levels of excellence.

www.cambridge.org
Information on this title: www.cambridge.org/9781107618237

© Toby Matthiesen 2015

First published 2015
Reprinted 2016

A catalogue record for this publication is available from the British Library

Library of Congress Cataloging in Publication data
Matthiesen, Toby, 1984–
The other Saudis : Shiism, dissent and sectarianism / Toby Matthiesen.
    pages   cm. – (Cambridge Middle East studies ; 46)
Includes bibliographical references and index.
ISBN 978-1-107-04304-6 (hardback) – ISBN 978-1-107-61823-7 (paperback)
1. Sharqiyah (Saudi Arabia : Province) – Politics and government.   2. Sharqiyah
(Saudi Arabia : Province) – Religion.   3. Shi'ah – Relations – Sunnites.
4. Sunnites – Relations – Shi'ah.   5. Shiites – Political activity – Saudi Arabia –
Sharqiyah (Province) – History.   6. Islam and politics – Saudi Arabia – Sharqiyah
(Province) – History.   7. Dissenters – Saudi Arabia – Sharqiyah (Province) – History.
8. Sects – Political aspects – Saudi Arabia – Sharqiyah (Province) – History.   I. Title.
DS247.9.S52M38   2014
305.6'978209538–dc23   2014016638

ISBN 978-1-107-04304-6 Hardback
ISBN 978-1-107-61823-7 Paperback

To my parents

Contents

Maps and Pictures

Acknowledgements

This book is the product of countless conversations, extensive fieldwork and a close reading of textual sources. During my main period of fieldwork in Saudi Arabia, in 2008, discussing the histories and contemporary manifestations of being Shia in Saudi Arabia was possible in a way that it would not be for much longer. The mid-2000s were characterised by national dialogues and a public recognition on the part of King Abdullah that the Shia are an integral part of Saudi Arabia. Unlike in previous decades, particularly the most confrontational phase between 1979 and 1993, the history of Shia dissent, and of discrimination against them, was a topic that some Saudis were willing to discuss. When I finished the doctorate on which this book is based in 2011, what is often simplistically called 'the Shia question' in Saudi Arabia was framed very differently, however. Shia in the Eastern Province had staged mass protests for more rights, which undermined the notion that Saudi Arabia was somehow exempt from the fallout of the Arab uprisings. Research on Saudi Arabia, and particularly on a sensitive issue such as Shia politics, is extremely difficult and sources are hard to come by. While I had the opportunity to carry out fieldwork across Saudi Arabia, including in various cities and villages of the Eastern Province, I broadened the geographical scope of my fieldwork considerably. I interviewed Saudi Shia, opposition activists but also clerics, intellectuals, journalists and less politically active people in Europe, the United States, Bahrain, Kuwait, Syria and Lebanon. Across these countries I also searched for opposition publications and local historiographical books on Saudi Shia history. I found some on the outdoor book market in the Eastern Province city of Qatif, where one can buy books that are banned in Saudi Arabia for discussing Shia religious beliefs or promoting historical narratives that contradict those of the rulers. I found them in Bahraini village bookshops; the owner of one of these bookshops has since been tortured to death as part of the crackdown on the 2011 uprising. I found them in the bustling alleys that lead up to the Shia shrine of Sayyida Zeinab outside of Damascus, then still a preferred holiday location for Gulf Shia and now a site of fierce fighting. I found some of the books in the Shia libraries in Kuwait, in the vast second-hand bookshops off of Beirut's cosmopolitan Hamra Street and in the Shia publishing houses of Beirut's southern suburbs, where most Saudi Shia historical books are published. I found them on London's Edgware Road, and in libraries and private archives in Britain and the United States. I have written about some of the fieldwork trips that led to this book elsewhere, particularly in *Sectarian Gulf*.[1] In many ways, the two books complement each other, *The Other Saudis* outlining the historical struggle of the Shia in Saudi Arabia, and *Sectarian Gulf* detailing the protest movements and sectarian politics across the Gulf since 2011.

Many people have made this research possible; this list will inevitably be incomplete. Some of the Saudis and other Khalijis who shared their memories with me asked to remain anonymous but I hope they will recognise their voices in the book. Charles Tripp, the supervisor of my doctoral dissertation, and Laleh Khalili, my second supervisor, have been a tremendous source of support. In Saudi Arabia, I am indebted to Awad al-Badi, Sadiq al-Jubran, Habib Al Jumayʿ, Kamil al-Khatti, Jaʿfar al-Shayib and many others. Several friends and colleagues have commented on earlier versions of this manuscript, and have in some cases read it several times. Their comments have significantly improved this book, and I am beholden to them: Khalid Abdallah, Safa Al Ahmad, Khadija von Zinnenburg Carroll, Werner Ende, Thomas Hegghammer, Claudia Honegger, Laurence Louër, Laetitia Nanquette, James Piscatori, Anees Alqudaihi, Siavush Randjbar-Daemi, Glen Rangwala, Madawi al-Rasheed, Adrian Ruprecht, Tawfiq al-Sayf, Roger Tomkys, Kristian Coates Ulrichsen, Marc Valeri, Max Weiss and Alice Wilson, as well as the Cambridge reviewers. Louis Allday deserves a special mention for coining the term that became the title of this book, and for reading this manuscript over and over again. ʿAli al-Ahmad, Hamza al-Hasan,

---

[1] Toby Matthiesen, *Sectarian Gulf: Bahrain, Saudi Arabia, and the Arab Spring That Wasn't* (Stanford, CA: Stanford University Press, 2013). On Sayyida Zeinab see also Toby Matthiesen, "Syria: Inventing a Religious War", *New York Review of Books Blog*, 12 June, 2013.

Fu'ad Ibrahim, Toby Jones, and Guido Steinberg have shared their private archives and libraries with me and have been very generous with their time. In addition, I would like to thank 'Abd al-Nabi al-'Akri, Atef Alshaer, Rochana Bajpai, Matthias Determann, Nelida Fuccaro, Ulrike Freitag, Robert Gleave, Arshad Hadjirin, Kai Hafez, Bernard Haykel, Steffen Hertog, Ghanim Jawad, Gilles Kepel, Ubay al-Khunayzi, Gudrun Krämer, Stéphane Lacroix, Marc Lynch, Phebe Marr, Kai Matthiesen, J.E. Peterson, Amélie Le Renard and Reinhard Schulze.

I have presented parts of this book at various research seminars. I would particularly like to thank the organisers and participants of seminars at the Berlin Graduate School Muslim Cultures and Societies, BRISMES, George Washington University, the Middle East Study Group, MESA, Princeton University, SOAS and the University of Cambridge. I would also like to thank Robert Gleave and the participants of the 'Clerical Authority in Shi'ite Islam' project sponsored by the British Academy, which also provided funding for research trips that contributed to this book.

My doctoral research at SOAS was funded by the German Academic Exchange Service and the Swiss National Science Foundation. Additional fieldwork assistance was provided by the British Institute for the Study of Iraq and the London School of Economics and Political Science (LSE). The staff at the American University of Beirut, the Arab World Documentation Unit at the University of Exeter, the British Library, Cambridge University Library, the Centre for Arab Unity Studies in Beirut, Georgetown University Library, King Fahd National Library in Riyadh, the Library of Congress, SOAS Library and the Zentrum Moderner Orient were most helpful in locating sources. Post-doctoral fellowships at Pembroke College, University of Cambridge and the LSE granted me the time to rewrite my dissertation while the old Arab order was unravelling before our eyes. What will replace this old order is not yet clear, but a historical understanding of how and why sectarian politics emerges and what role it plays in key Middle Eastern states is as important as ever.

A Note on Conventions

This book largely uses the transliteration guide of the *International Journal of Middle East Studies* (IJMES). Names and places that have a common English spelling will be spelled accordingly and no diacritic marks added (such as King Abdullah, Al Saud, Shia). Al refers to the larger family of someone, as in Al Saud, and is therefore transliterated differently from the common al- in front of last names. Arabic names are transcribed according to the IJMES system and the article is dropped before common place names unless a different transcription is dominant in English (e.g. Tarut not Tarout, Qatif not al-Qatif, Khobar not al-Khubar, al-Ahsa not al-Hasa or Hasa, Riyadh not al-Riyadh, Awwamiyya not al-ʿAwwamiyya, Hufuf not Hofuf or al-Hufuf, Saihat not Seihat). Arabic words are not capitalised, except if they refer to places, names and publications (*hawza* not *Hawza*, *qadi* not *Qadi*). For Iranian names and places I largely use the Persian transliteration.

In some instances there are disagreements about the dating of a particular incident or the birth or death of a prominent figure. Often, the birth and death dates of historical figures are only roughly given in the Islamic (AH) calendar, which means that the date can often be in two separate years in the Gregorian calendar. Therefore, I have chosen sometimes to put both possibilities in the text, such as 1842/3.

The various Web sites cited in this book were last accessed in September 2013 (in some cases also in early 2014) and stored electronically by the author. Therefore, consultation dates of Internet sources have been omitted. The Internet archive was used to retrieve earlier versions of defunct Web sites and can be used in the future to retrieve Web sites cited in this book (http://web.archive.org). Full URLs are only provided in cases where the title of a Web page is not mentioned in the footnotes. The typing of an English title into a search engine should allow the reader to find the article. In the case of Arabic or Persian Web sites, the titles have been transliterated and translated into English. Using the transliteration, readers familiar with these languages can retrieve the article or a copy thereof even after the original Web site has changed its URL or has closed down by typing the title into a search engine.

Glossary

This is based on the glossary in Meir Litvak, *Shi'i Scholars of Nineteenth-Century Iraq: The 'Ulama' of Najaf and Karbala'* (Cambridge: Cambridge University Press, 1998), 235–237.

'alim, pl. 'ulama'	'learned man', cleric
Akhbari, Akhbariyya	the Shia school of jurisprudence that rejects deductive methodology in the study of law and requires unmitigated adherence to the limited meaning of the *akhbar*, the traditions (words and deeds) of the Prophet and the Shia Imams as transmitted by chains of narrators
Al	the house of/the clan of
Amir	governor
Ashura	tenth day of the month of Muharram; commemoration of the martyrdom of Hussayn, the Prophet Muhammad's grandson and third Imam in Shia Islam, in 680
ayatallah	lit. sign of God, title for a senior *mujtahid*
diwaniyya, pl. diwaniyyat	lit. salon, semi-public discussion forum or gathering
Hasawi	from al-Ahsa (Hasa)
hawza 'ilmiyya	lit. territory of learning, refers to a community of learning in a specific location and encompasses the actual sites of learning

	but also the social bonds, the organisation and the finances in a specific *hawza*: while the main Shia *hawzat* are in Najaf, Karbala and Qom, the religious schools of Qatif, al-Ahsa, Kuwait, Tehran and Sayyida Zaynab are also referred to as *hawzat*
hussainiyya, pl. hussainiyyat	Shia mourning house for the commemoration of the martyrdom of Hussayn, also community centres
ijtihad	the process of arriving at independent legal judgment in matters of religious law by using the principles of jurisprudence (*usul al-fiqh*)
Imam	one of the twelve recognised hereditary successors of the Prophet Muhammad in Twelver Shia Islam
intifada	lit. uprising, refers here to the uprising of Saudi Shia in the Eastern Province in 1979/80
khums	religious tax, while it was originally paid to the Prophet, and by Shia Muslims to the Imam, Shia Muslims now pay these taxes to the *marjiʿ al-taqlid* in his capacity as representative of the Imam, and at the local level to the representative (*wakil*) of the *marjiʿ*
leftist	here used as a term describing all broadly left-leaning and secular Saudi opposition groups
Majlis al-Shura	Consultative Council
marjiʿ al-taqlid, pl. marajiʿ	lit. reference point for emulation, someone who is qualified through his learning and probity to be followed in all points of religious practice and law by the generality of Shia Muslims
marjiʿiyya	authority, the institution of *marjiʿ al-taqlid*
mujtahid, pl. mujtahidun	an *ʿalim* that reached the level of competence and scholarship necessary to perform *ijtihad*

mutasarrif	governor of a *sanjak* (Ottoman sub-province)
nakhawila	name for the indigenous Shia community in Medina
qadi	judge
qaimaqam	governor of an Ottoman provincial district (*kaza*)
al-qalʿa	lit. castle, Old city of Qatif
Qatifi	from Qatif
Shaykhi, Shaykhiyya	followers of Ahmad al-Ahsaʾi (1753–1826), esoteric strand of Shia Islam, sometimes deemed heretical by other Twelver Shia scholars
shirazi, shiraziyya, pl. shiraziyyun	transnational Shia political network, whose name derives from its spiritual leader, Muhammad al-Shirazi (1928–2001)
taqlid	the process of following and emulating the practices and pronouncements of a *mujtahid* in matters relating to religious law and practices
Usuli, Usuliyya	the school of jurisprudence that emphasizes the use of reason in the study of the principles of jurisprudence (*usul al-fiqh*)
Wahhabi, Wahhabiyya	followers of Muhammad ibn ʿAbd al-Wahhab (1703–92), whose teachings centered on the oneness of God (*tawhid*) and who wanted to purify Islam from innovations; official form of religious interpretation in Saudi Arabia
wakil, pl. wukalaʾ	local representative of a *marjiʿ al-taqlid*
waqf, pl. awqaf	religious endowment

Abbreviations

al-daʿwa	Islamic al-Daʿwa Party (*hizb al-daʿwa al-islamiyya*)
ANLF	Arab National Liberation Front (*jabhat al-taharrur al-watani al-ʿarabiyya*)
Baath Party	Arab Socialist Baath Party in Saudi (*hizb al-baʿth al-ʿarabi al-ishtiraki fi al-suʿudiyya*)
CDLR	Committee for the Defence of Legitimate Rights (*lajnat al-difaʿ ʿan al-huquq al-shariʿiyya*)
hizb al-ʿamal	Arab Socialist Action Party in the Arabian Peninsula (*hizb al-ʿamal al-ishtiraki al-ʿarabi: al-jazira al-ʿarabiyya*)
IAO	Islamic Action Organisation in Iraq (*munazzamat al-ʿamal al-islami fi al-ʿIraq*), Iraqi wing of MVM
IFLB	Islamic Front for the Liberation of Bahrain (*al-jabha al-islamiyya li-tahrir al-Bahrayn*), Bahraini wing of MVM
IRGC	Islamic Revolutionary Guard Corps
MAN	Movement of Arab Nationalists (*harakat al-qawmiyyin al-ʿarab*)
MVM	Movement of Vanguards' Missionaries (*harakat al-risaliyyin al-talaʿ*)
OIRAP	Organisation for the Islamic Revolution in the Arabian Peninsula (*munazzamat al-thawra al-islamiyya fi al-jazira al-ʿarabiyya*), Saudi wing of MVM
PDPAP	Popular Democratic Party in the Arabian Peninsula (*al-hizb al-dimuqrati al-shaʿbi fi al-jazira al-ʿarabiyya*)
RMS	Reformist Movement in Saudi (*al-haraka al-islahiyya fi al-suʿudiyya*)

MAP 1. Map of Saudi Arabia.

Introduction

The stigmatisation of Shia Muslims as Saudi Arabia's internal Other fulfills an important function in Saudi religious nationalism. At times of crisis the 'Shia threat' is used to rally the rest of the population, most of whom are Sunnis of different persuasions, around the ruling family. Shia in Saudi Arabia are confronted with a religious establishment that promotes the Wahhabi interpretation of Islam, the religious police, and a state apparatus from which they are often barred. Yet, when they travel abroad they are doing so on a Saudi passport, and are often confronted with the same stereotypes that people all over the world have of "the Saudis". Indeed, they are an important if often misunderstood factor in Saudi domestic and regional policies. And their history in the country that is home to the two holy places of Islam – Mecca and Medina – is relevant to Muslims beyond Saudi Arabia's borders. Shia Muslims all over the world are interested in the fate of their co-religionists in the Kingdom. Some Sunni Muslims, on the other hand, particularly those with *salafi* and anti-Shia leanings, consider their mere existence, and any political claims by Saudi Shia, to be anathema. Together with the fact that Shia live on top of some of Saudi Arabia's largest oil fields, their history and political mobilisation, therefore, have ramifications far beyond Saudi Arabia.

IN THE SHADOW OF THE WAHHABIYYA

Saudi Arabia is often portrayed as a largely Hanbali- and Wahhabi-dominated country, but a variety of Islamic traditions and all four schools of Sunni religious law can be found across the country. The Eastern oasis of al-Ahsa has strong Maliki, Hanafi and Shafi'i traditions. For most of modern Saudi history, these schools were largely excluded from official religious institutions. Only in 2009 were non-Wahhabi Sunni scholars appointed to the highest religious body, the Council of the Committee of Senior 'Ulama'.[1] Shia clerics have unsuccessfully demanded to be appointed to this body and have equally unsuccessfully pushed for the recognition of a higher body of Shia clerics.

Sufis, who make up a large part of the population in the Hijaz, also face supression of their religious beliefs and rituals. But they have been able to continue their religious traditions through their organisation in semi-clandestine Sufi orders.[2]

The southern region of Najran near the border with Yemen is home to a substantial Ismaili community. The Ismailis are mainly from the powerful Yam tribe and many of them carry the last name al-Yami. They are led religiously by local religious scholars, the *da'is* from the al-Makrami family. They also face harrassment by the religious police. At the same time, however, their socio-political structures differ from the Eastern Province Shia and they have historically had better relations with the Saudi state. This is partly due to their integration into the tribal system and because the Yam tribe was an important ally of the Al Saud in the conquest of the southern parts of the country.[3]

Significant numbers of Ismailis moved to the Eastern Province in the twentieth century to find work in the oil industry and some became active in the labour movement there. In the Eastern Province, they faced similar religious discrimination to the local Shia, with whom they inter-

---

[1] This included Qays bin Muhammad bin 'Abd al-Latif Al Mubarak, a Maliki scholar from al-Ahsa. Roel Meijer, "Reform in Saudi Arabia: The Gender Segregation Debate," *Middle East Policy* 17, no. 4 (Winter 2010), 80–100.

[2] Interview with a Sufi leader from the Hijaz, Cairo, 2013. Identity in possession of the author (this comment will not be repeated in subsequent footnotes where interviewees are cited without names). Mark J. R. Sedgwick, "Saudi Sufis: Compromise in the Hijaz, 1925–40," *Die Welt des Islams* 37, no. 3 (1997), 349–68; *al-tasawwuf fi al-su'udiyya wa-l-khalij* (Sufism in Saudi and the Gulf) (Dubai: Markaz al-Misbar li-l-Dirasat wa-l-Buhuth, 2011).

[3] John R. Bradley, *Saudi Arabia Exposed: Inside a Kingdom in Crisis* (New York: Palgrave Macmillan, 2006), 73–6; Farhad Daftary, *The Ismailis: Their History and Doctrines*, 2nd ed. (Cambridge: Cambridge University Press, 2007), 295–8; Fuad Hamza, "Najran," *Journal of The Royal Central Asian Society* 22, no. 4 (1935), 631–40; Guido Steinberg, *Religion und Staat in Saudi-Arabien: Die wahhabitischen Gelehrten 1902–1953* (Würzburg: Ergon Verlag, 2002), 484.

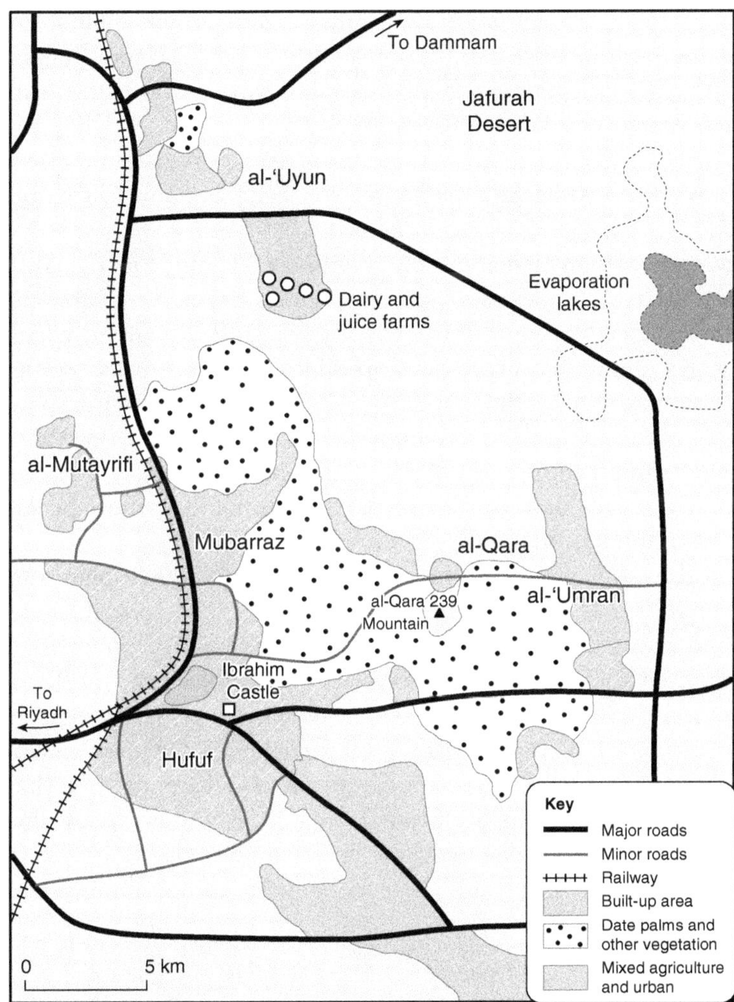

MAP 2. Map of al-Ahsa Oasis.

acted and shared their experiences. Any attempt to organise politically as Ismailis or Najranis has been suppressed harshly.[4]

The Twelver Shia are mainly concentrated in and around the two old population centres of al-Ahsa and Qatif in the Eastern Province, but there is also a small Twelver Shia community in Medina called *nakhawila*. Unlike the Shia in the Eastern Province, the *nakhawila* are partly tribally organised and are members of key Hijazi tribes. While intermarriage and

[4] Interview with 'Ali al-Yami, Washington, October 2013.

religious links exist between *nakhawila* and Eastern Province Shia, the *nakhawila* are more quietist and did not join Shia political movements. Before the oil era, many *nakhawila* were hired to work as agriculturalists on fields belonging to local Sunnis and many Hijazis still associate the *nakhawila* with this.[5] They also face significant sectarian discrimination, which, like with the Ismailis, is facilitated by their common last name, al-Nakhli.[6]

Al-Ahsa is an oasis located about 140 kilometres inland from the Gulf. Around 180 square kilometres of gardens, palm trees and villages surround its two main towns, Hufuf (see Picture 0.1) and Mubarraz, which throughout the twentieth century developed into one single urban settlement. Al-Ahsa was used as the name for the whole province until 1953, when it was renamed Eastern Province (*al-mintaqa al-sharqiyya*) and the provincial capital moved from Hufuf to Dammam. Thereafter, the name al-Ahsa was only used for the oasis, which is made up more or less equally of both Sunnis and Shia (see map of al-Ahsa).

Qatif, on the other hand, is an almost exclusively Twelver Shia port town on the shores of the Gulf (see map of Qatif). The coastal towns Safwa to the north and Saihat to the south have become suburbs of Qatif. Connected to Qatif via two causeways lies the island of Tarut (see Picture 0.2), which has four Shia quarters and one Sunni quarter. Population estimates of these areas, and particularly the numbers of Shia, are a constant source of politically inspired debate, as there has never been a census detailing sectarian affiliation. The number of Shia in al-Ahsa and Qatif totalled somewhere between 30,000 and 40,000 in the early nineteenth century[7] and grew to between 50,000 and 60,000

---

[5] Mishary Abdalrahman al-Nuaim, *State Building in a Non-Capitalist Social Formation: The Dialectics of Two Modes of Production and the Role of the Merchant Class, Saudi Arabia 1902–1932* (PhD, University of California, 1987), 133, 143f.; Werner Ende, "The Nakhawila, a Shiʿite Community in Medina, Past and Present," *Die Welt des Islams* 37, no. 3 (1997), 264–348; al-Shaykh Salih al-Jadʿan, *Ayatallah al-Shaykh Muhammad ʿAli al-ʿAmri: sira wa-ʿita*ʾ (n.p.: n.p., 2011); Yousif al-Khoei, "The Marja and the Survival of a Community: The Shia of Medina," in *The Most Learned of the Shia: The Institution of the Marjaʿ Taqlid*, ed. Linda Walbridge (Oxford: Oxford University Press, 2001), 247–50, 249f.; Hasan bin Marzuq Rijaʾ al-Sharimi al-Nakhli, *al-nakhawila (al-nakhliyyun) fi al-Madina al-Munawwara: al-takwin al-ijtimaʿi wa-l-thaqafi* (The Nakhawila in Medina: The Social and Cultural Formation) (Beirut: Muʾassasat al-Intishar al-ʿArabi, 2012).

[6] Unlike in the Eastern Province, there is no Shia court in Medina. Interview with Shia from Medina, Riyadh, October 2008; U.S. Department of State, Bureau of Democracy, Human Rights, and Labor, *International Religious Freedom Report: Saudi Arabia* (July–December 2010).

[7] Report by Major Colebrook about the Persian Gulf littoral, 10. 9. 1820, quoted in Jerome Anthony Saldanha, and C. H. Gabriel, *The Persian Gulf Précis*, 8 vols., vol. 5: Jerome

PICTURE O.1. Market and Ottoman fort in Hufuf.
Source: Nestor Sander Collection/Saudi Aramco World/SAWDIA.

towards the end of the century.[8] By the second half of the twentieth century these figures rose to several hundred thousand and estimates in the early 1980s varied between 300,000 and 440,000.[9] At the beginning of

Anthony Saldanha, *Précis of Turkish Expansion on the Arab Littoral of the Persian Gulf and Hasa and Katif Affairs* (Simla: 1904, reprinted Gerrards Cross: Archive Editions, 1986), 2. In 1865, the population of al-Ahsa was estimated at 20,000 and was said to provide 270,000 MT$ (Maria Theresa dollars) while Qatif, with a population of 6,000, was said to provide 130,000 MT$ of a total revenue of 692,000 MT$ of all realms under Saudi control. L. Pelly, *Report on a Journey to Riyadh in Central Arabia 1865* (Cambridge: Oleander Press, reprinted 1978).

[8] Lorimer estimates the Shia population of al-Ahsa and Qatif as 56,000 as part of an overall population of 284,000 on the eastern side of the Gulf. John Gordon Lorimer, *Gazetteer of the Persian Gulf, 'Oman, and Central Arabia*, 2 vols. (Calcutta: Superintendent Government Printing, 1908–15), vol. 1, Appendix R, 2. In the 1920s, the Secretary of the Saudi Palace put the figure of Shia in al-Ahsa, which at the time referred to the whole Eastern Province, at 30,000 when asked by the Lebanese traveller and writer Ameen Rihani. This probably underestimates their size. Ameen Fares Rihani, *Ibn Sa'oud of Arabia: His People and His Land* (London: Constable, 1928), 235.

[9] Gary Anderson, *Differential Urban Growth in the Eastern Province of Saudi Arabia: A Study of the Historical Interaction of Economic Development and Socio-Political Change* (PhD, Johns Hopkins University, 1984), 302–31; Ghassane Salameh and Vivian Steir, "Political Power and the Saudi State," *MERIP Reports* 91 (1980), 5–22, 21; Abdulla Mansour al-Shuaiby, *The Development of the Eastern Province with Particular Reference to Urban Settlement and Evolution in Eastern Saudi Arabia* (PhD, University of Durham,

PICTURE O.2. Tarut Island.
Source: Dorothy Miller/Saudi Aramco World/SAWDIA.

the twenty-first century, consultants for the Saudi government put the figure of Shia in the Eastern Province at around 1 million with the overall number of native Shia reaching around 1.5 million in Saudi Arabia, including an Ismaili population in Najran of around 250,000.[10] Figures provided by Shia activists are significantly higher and range between two and three million native Shia including the Ismailis, or between 10 and 15 percent of the Saudi citizen population.[11]

   1976); Peter N. Woodward, *Oil and Labor in the Middle East: Saudi Arabia and the Oil Boom* (New York: Praeger, 1988), 93.

[10] They estimate that Saudi Arabia had 1,319,541 native Shia in 2005–6. Email correspondence with Nawaf Obaid, May 2010.

[11] Various interviews with Saudi Shia, 2007–11.

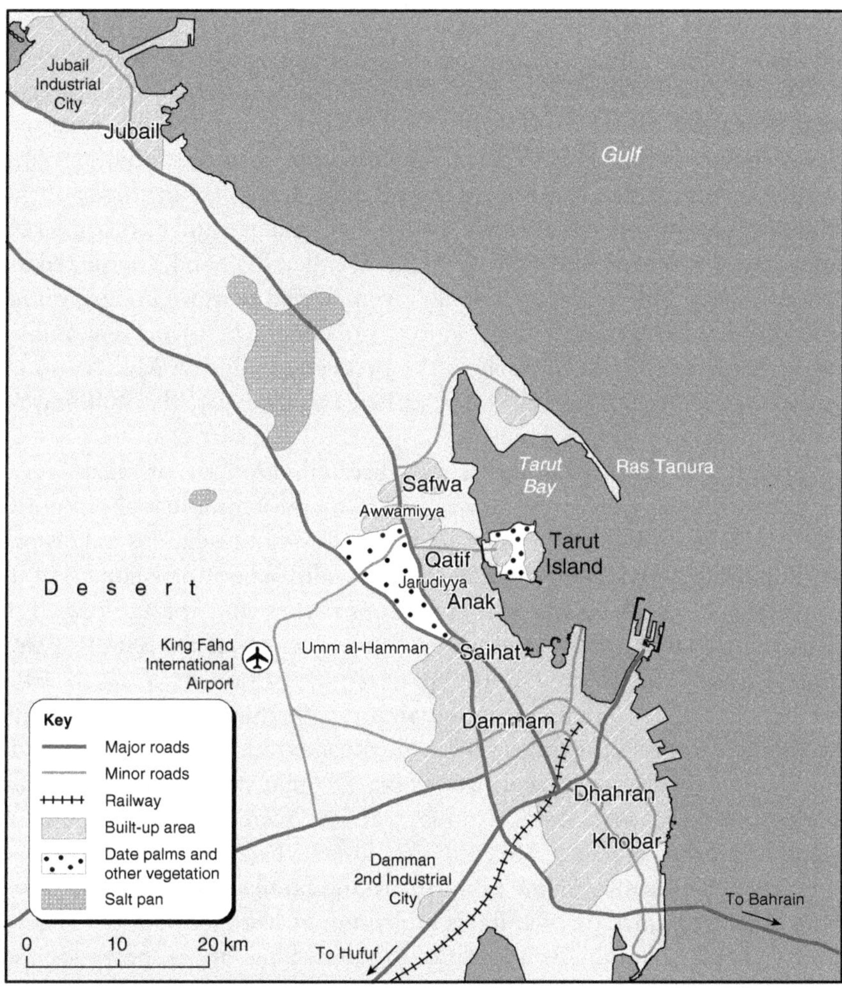

MAP 3. Map of the coastal areas of the Eastern Province.

The inhabitants of the oases of Qatif and al-Ahsa have been sedentary for centuries and largely engaged in agriculture, trade, fishing and pearl diving. Politics often amounted to ensuring the safety, economic wellbeing and survival of the community in a hostile environment. Some members of the urban notable elite were integrated into the Ottoman bureaucracy in the late nineteenth and early twentieth centuries. But since the Saudi conquests of the Eastern Province in 1913 the Shia of al-Ahsa and Qatif have been subjects of a political entity that does not treat Shia Muslims as equal citizens. Shia from all backgrounds have prospered comparatively less than others.

The Wahhabi clergy has from the mid-eighteenth century onwards seen Shia Islam as one of its main, if not *the* main, enemy. While relations between Shia political leaders and individual members of the Saudi ruling family have fluctuated, and have improved at times, the attitudes of the Wahhabi clergy towards Shia Muslims did not change and have remained adversarial.[12] When 'Abd al-'Aziz Al Saud, called Ibn Saud, conquered al-Ahsa in 1913, Shia religious practices were forced to move underground, and Wahhabi clerics and the religious police sought to prevent public displays of the Shia faith, such as the processions during Muharram or gatherings in mourning houses, so-called *hussainiyyat*, the building of which was also officially banned.

Contrary to other cases of sectarian discrimination, the problems associated with being Shia in Saudi Arabia are therefore not just about political economy or identity politics, they are also about religious beliefs per se. For the acceptance of Shia Islam as a valid school of Islamic law is anathema to the Wahhabi clerics. In 1927, they and the *ikhwan* even demanded that Ibn Saud ensure the conversion of all the Shia in Qatif and al-Ahsa. The ruling family has tried to position itself as an arbiter between the Wahhabis and the Shia. To the Shia, the ruling family implicitly promised protection from the most extreme Wahhabi demands for the conversion or execution of Shia. To placate the Wahhabis, the bargain ensured that Shia religious practices were kept largely out of sight, at most tolerated in Shia majority areas where Sunnis could not be "molested". This also implied that the ruling family would not accede to Shia demands, since the Wahhabis are certainly stronger than the Shia in this triangular bargain. As a result of this, anti-Shia fatwas, polemics and books have been tolerated if not openly supported by the ruling family for a century. Under Crown Prince and then King Abdullah this practice eased slightly as Shia were invited to a National Dialogue that acknowledged religious difference in the country. From 2009 onwards, however, there has been a marked resurgence of sectarian writings and statements by Wahhabi clerics. Anti-Shia incitement is also given space in Saudi-owned media, especially at times of crisis and when tensions with the local Shia flare up, such as after 1979 and since 2009.[13]

[12] Raihan Ismail, "The Saudi Ulema and the Shi'a of Saudi Arabia," *Journal of Shi'a Islamic Studies* 5, no. 4 (2012), 403–22, 404.

[13] See, for example, Werner Ende, "Sunni Polemical Writings on the Shi'a and the Iranian Revolution," in *The Iranian Revolution and the Muslim World*, ed. David Menashri

Anti-Shia treatises by Saudi scholars (not to mention those by foreign Sunni clerics residing in Saudi Arabia) are too numerous to be discussed here in detail. Many of these texts focus on the refutation of religious beliefs and practices of Shia Muslims per se, and on a historical rejection of Shia Islam. But some specifically attack Shia Muslims in Saudi Arabia. *The Situation of the Rejectionists in the Lands of Monotheism* by the prominent salafi cleric Nasir al-'Umar is one of the most notorious anti-Shia pamphlets. Written in 1993, it aims to analyse the politics and religious rituals of Shia Muslims in Saudi Arabia, and brands them as infidels and a danger to the nation and the Islamic umma. One of al-'Umar's main aims is to identify and name prominent Shia in business, education, and the administration in order to prove that the Shia are proselytising and taking over key sectors of the country.[14]

Similar polemics also target the Shia in Medina. Sunni authors accuse them of seclusion, of despising Sunnis, and make recommendations about how to confront them.[15] The Ismailis in Najran are described in equally derogatory terms.[16] The former Grand Mufti of Saudi Arabia, 'Abd al-'Aziz bin Baz ('Ibn Baz') (1910–99), issued numerous statements and fatwas against Shia religious pratices and Saudi Shia clerics.[17] In 2008, a fatwa forbidding the sale of properties to Shia by another scholar was published in Saudi newspapers.[18] These anti-Shia views of the religious establishment are perpetuated in the media and in schooling, together with historical narratives that centre on the ruling family and leave out

---

(Boulder, CO: Westview Press, 1990), 219–32; Guido Steinberg, "Jihadi-Salafism and the Shi'is: Remarks about the Intellectual Roots of Anti-Shi'ism," in *Global Salafism: Islam's New Religious Movement*, ed. Roel Meijer (London: Hurst, 2009), 107–25; Guido Steinberg, "The Wahhabiyya and Shi'ism, from 1744/45 to 2008," in *The Sunna and Shi'a in History: Division and Ecumenism in the Muslim Middle East*, ed. Ofra Bengio and Meir Litvak (New York: Palgrave Macmillan, 2011), 163–82.

[14] Nasir ibn Sulayman al-'Umar, *waqi' al-rafida fi bilad al-tawhid* (The Situation of the Rejectionists in the Lands of Monotheism), http://ar.islamway.net/book/3165.

[15] Abu 'Abdallah al-Athari, *"bahth tafsili 'an rafidat al-madina al-nakhawila"* (A Detailed Study on the Nakhawila Rejectionists of Medina), http://ar.islamway.net/book/99. For more examples see Ismail, "The Saudi Ulema," 411–13.

[16] *"'Indama absartu al-haqiqa: haqa'iq la yasa' ahl najran jahlaha"* (When I Saw the Truth: Facts Can not Help the People of Najran from their Ignorance), http://maktabah.com/site/itemfiles/AndmaAbsartALhagigah.pdf.

[17] Fouad Ibrahim, *The Shi'is of Saudi Arabia* (London: Saqi Books, 2006), 35–41; Ismail, "The Saudi Ulema," 416.

[18] Ibid., 417.

the agency and socio-political make up of people in peripheral regions such as the Eastern Province.[19]

Partly as a result of these anti-Shia narratives, some Sunnis fear that an empowerment of the Shia in the Eastern Province could encourage them to try to secede with the help of Iran and deprive the country of its oil income. However unrealistic that scenario may be, it is a recurrent theme in conversations with Sunnis of various political persuasions and decision makers in Saudi Arabia and the Arab Gulf states.

Wherever a Shia goes in Saudi Arabia, he will be recognised after a while because of his name, his place of birth, his accent, and his religious practices. Shia are largely absent from top positions in the bureaucracy as well as in the private sector. There has never been a Shia minister and only one Shia ambassador.[20] Shia find it harder to reach the top management of state-owned companies, large Saudi conglomerates and even Saudi branches of multinational companies.

Saudi Shia sought to redress this situation and embraced various revolutionary ideologies throughout the twentieth century. From communism to Khomeinism, Shia have tried most political ideologies in the Middle East but to no avail: The opposition movements failed to change the inferior status of Saudi Shia fundamentally. Many came to realise that the Saudi Shia are too weak to transform Saudi politics single-handedly. At the same time, however, they are too numerous and live in a too strategically important region to be politically quiescent.

THE SHIA IN HISTORIOGRAPHY

Some of the best books on the Shia in al-Ahsa and Qatif are written by Saudi Shia themselves, including by long-time opposition activists such as Hamza al-Hasan[21] and Fu'ad Ibrahim. Ibrahim's book is the only other monograph on Saudi Shia in English and mainly recounts the history

---

[19] Eleanor Abdella Doumato, "Manning the Barricades: Islam According to Saudi Arabia's School Texts," *Middle East Journal* 57, no. 2 (2003), 230–47; Michaela Prokop, "The War of Ideas: Education in Saudi Arabia," in *Saudi Arabia in the Balance: Political Economy, Society, Foreign Affairs*, ed. Paul Aarts and Gerd Nonneman (New York: New York University Press, 2005), 57–81; Center for Religious Freedom of Freedom House/Institute for Gulf Affairs, *Saudi Arabia's Curriculum of Intolerance: With Excerpts from Saudi Ministry of Education Textbooks for Islamic Studies* (Washington, DC: 2006).

[20] Jamil al-Jishi served as ambassador to Iran from 1999 to 2003.

[21] Hamza al-Hasan, *al-shi'a fi al-mamlaka al-'arabiyya al-su'udiyya* (The Shia in the Kingdom of Saudi Arabia), 2 vols. (Beirut: Mu'assasat al-Baqi' li-Ihya' al-Turath, 1993).

of the *shiraziyyun*, a transnational Shia political movement whose name derives from its spiritual leader, Muhammad al-Shirazi (1928–2001).[22]

These books are part of an effort by Saudi Shia activists and historians to write the Shia back into Saudi history, to preserve manuscripts, and to create historical narratives for the people of the Eastern Province. They emphasise histories of sedentarisation, trade, scholarship and religious learning, and instances of resistance to rulers they perceive as being unjust. These local historiographies are reactions to state-sponsored narratives that largely ignore the very existence of Shia Muslims in Saudi Arabia. This local historical scholarship constitutes a key source for this book.[23] A number of memoirs of Saudi Shia opposition activists have also been published.[24] A book written by two young Saudi Shia not affiliated with the *shiraziyyun* challenges the view that the *shirazi* movement was the main force amongst Saudi Shia and also focusses on other Shia Islamist groups such as Khat al-Imam.[25] Clerical dictionaries, which outline the biographies of important scholars, are another key source for Shia intellectual history.[26] The Qatifi scholar Faraj al-ʿUmran (1322–98,

---

[22] Ibrahim, *Shiʿis*. See also his essayistic reflection on the current position of Saudi Shia: Fuʾad Ibrahim, *al-shiʿa fi al-suʿudiyya* (The Shia in Saudi) (Beirut: Dar al-Saqi, 2007).

[23] For a detailed analysis and extensive bibliography of Saudi Shia local historiography see Toby Matthiesen, *The Shia of Saudi Arabia: Identity Politics, Sectarianism and the Saudi State* (PhD, SOAS, 2011), 56–107; Toby Matthiesen, "Shiʿi Historians in a Wahhabi State: Identity Entrepreneurs and the Politics of Local Historiography in Saudi Arabia," *International Journal of Middle East Studies* 47, no. 1 (2015). See also Madawi al-Rasheed, "The Shia of Saudi Arabia: A Minority in Search of Cultural Authenticity," *British Journal of Middle Eastern Studies* 25, no. 1 (1998), 121–38; Jörg Matthias Determann, *Historiography in Saudi Arabia: Globalization and the State in the Middle East* (London: I.B. Tauris, 2014), 167–175; Yitzhak Nakash, *Reaching for Power: The Shiʿa in the Modern Arab World* (Princeton, NJ: Princeton University Press, 2006), 16–41.

[24] Sayyid ʿAli al-Sayyid Baqir al-ʿAwwami, *al-haraka al-wataniyya fi al-suʿudiyya 1953–1973* (The National Movement in Saudi 1953–1973), 2 vols. (Beirut: Riyyad al-Rayyis li-l-Kutub wa-l-Nashr, 2012); ʿAdil al-Labad, *al-inqilab: bayʿ al-wahm ʿala al-dhat* (The Coup: The Selling of the Illusion to the Self) (Beirut: Dar al-Jamal li-l-Tibaʿa wa-l-Nashr, 2009).

[25] Interestingly, al-Ibrahim and al-Sadiq are close to the circle of Sunni Islamic reformist activists in Riyadh and also publish in one of the publishing houses associated with this trend. Badr al-Ibrahim and Muhammad al-Sadiq, *al-hirak al-shiʿi fi al-suʿudiyya: tasyis al-madhhab wa-madhhabat al-siyasa* (The Shia Movement in Saudi: The Politicisation of Confession and the Confessionalisation of Politics) (Beirut: al-Shabaka al-ʿArabiyya li-l-Abhath wa-l-Nashr, 2013). For more on Khat al-Imam see Toby Matthiesen, "Hizbullah al-Hijaz: A History of the Most Radical Saudi Shiʿa Opposition Group," *The Middle East Journal* 64, no. 2 (Spring 2010), 179–97.

[26] Saudi Shia clerics are discussed in several classical clerical dictionaries: Muhammad ʿAli bin Ahmad bin ʿAbbas al-Tajir al-Bahrani, *muntazim al-darrayn fi tarajim ʿulamaʾ wa-udabaʾ al-Ahsaʾ wa-l-Qatif wa-l-Bahrayn (tahqiq Dayaʾ Badr Al Sunbal)* (A

1904–78), for example, wrote a monumental chronicle of day-to-day events in mid-twentieth century Qatif and recorded oral histories that intersected with biographies of clerics from Qatif.[27] Another key work focusses on the Shia clerics of al-Ahsa.[28] One history written by a Sunni journalist has also been published.[29]

In terms of Western secondary literature, Toby Jones has outlined how residents of the Eastern Province came to experience the state through policies of development, particularly through the oil industry and large-scale irrigation projects, which increased the state's grip over the population.[30] Jones also published widely on key events in Saudi Shia history and on anti-Shia polemics.[31] Saudi Shia politics are given some attention

Dictonary of the Pearls amongst the Biographies of the Clerics and Writers from al-Ahsa, Qatif and Bahrain), 3 vols. (Qum/Beirut: Mu'assasa Tayyiba li-Ihya' al-Turath, 2009); 'Ali al-Biladi al-Bahrani, *anwar al-badrayn fi tarajim 'ulama' al-Qatif wa-l-Ahsa' wa-l-Bahrayn* (The Lights of the Two Moons in the Biographies of the Scholars of Qatif, al-Ahsa and Bahrain) (Beirut: Dar al-Murtada, 1991); Yusuf bin Ahmad al-Bahrani, *lu'lu'at al-Bahrayn fi al-ijazat wa-tarajim rijal al-hadith* (The Pearl of Bahrain in the Licences and Biographies of the Men of Hadith) (Najaf: Matba'a al-'Uthman, 1966). On 'Ali al-Biladi see also Hasan al-Saffar, *al-shaykh 'Ali al-Biladi al-Qudayhi* (Beirut: Mu'assasat al-Baqi' li-Ihya' al-Turath, 1990).

[27] Faraj al-'Umran, *al-azhar al-arajiyya fi al-athar al-farajiyya* (The Aroma Blossoms of the Faraji Legacy), 2nd ed., 6 vols. (Beirut: Manshurat Dar Hajar, 2008). The first edition had been published by Matba'at al-Najaf in Najaf in 1383 A.H. (1963/4). See also Faraj al-'Umran, *majmu'a mu'allafat al-shaykh Faraj al-'Umran* (A Collection of Writings of Shaykh Faraj al-'Umran), vol. 1 (Beirut: Mu'assasat al-Khutt li-l-Tahqiq wa-l-Nashr, 2010).

[28] It was written by a former leader of Khat al-Imam: Hashim Muhammad al-Shakhs, *a'lam hajar min al-madiyyin wa-l-mu'asirin* (Symbols of al-Ahsa from Past and Present), 4 vols. (Beirut: Mu'assasat Umm al-Qura li-l-Tahqiq wa-l-Nashr, 1996–2006).

[29] Ibrahim al-Hatlani, *al-shi'a al-su'udiyyun: qira'a tarikhiyya wa-siyasiyya li-namadhij matlabiyya* (The Saudi Shia: A Historical and Political Reading of Sample Claims) (Beirut: Riyyad al-Rayyis li-l-Kutub wa-l-Nashr, 2009).

[30] Toby Craig Jones, *The Dogma of Development: Technopolitics and the Making of Saudi Arabia 1950–1980* (PhD, Stanford University, 2006); Toby Craig Jones, *Desert Kingdom: How Oil and Water Forged Modern Saudi Arabia* (Cambridge, MA: Harvard University Press, 2010).

[31] Toby Jones, "Violence and the Illusion of Reform in Saudi Arabia," *Middle East Report Online*, November 13, 2003; Toby Jones, "Seeking a 'Social Contract' for Saudi Arabia," *Middle East Report* 228 (2003), 42–8; Toby Jones, "The Iraq Effect in Saudi Arabia," *Middle East Report* 237 (2005), 20–5; Toby Jones, "Rebellion on the Saudi Periphery: Modernity, Marginalization, and the Shi'a Uprising of 1979," *International Journal of Middle East Studies* 38 (2006), 213–33; Toby Jones, "Saudi Arabia's Not So New Anti-Shi'ism," *Middle East Report* 242 (2007), 29–32; Toby Jones, *Embattled in Arabia: Shi'is and the Politics of Confrontation in Saudi Arabia* (Combating Terrorism Center at West Point, 2009).

in works on Arab Shia[32] and Shia in the Gulf.[33] Some study Shia Islamist movements as part of the wider Saudi Islamist opposition,[34] and many emphasise the influence of the Iranian Revolution on Saudi Shia.[35] Others focus on the development of a discourse of inclusive Saudi nationalism and citizenship amongst Saudi Shia intellectuals after 1993, and on their rapprochement with the state.[36] Comparatively little has been written on the notable families,[37] the Shia judiciary or Shia in leftist groups. Federico Vidal, an anthropologist who worked for the Arabian American Oil Company (ARAMCO) in the 1950s, provided the most detailed study of social, religious, and geographical conditions in the al-Ahsa oasis.[38]

But this is the first book that tells the political history of the Shia in Qatif and al-Ahsa since the late nineteenth century and is based on both

[32] Graham E. Fuller and Rend Rahim Francke, *The Arab Shiʿa: The Forgotten Muslims* (New York: St. Martin's Press, 1999); Nakash, *Reaching.*

[33] Joseph Kostiner, "Shiʿi Unrest in the Gulf," in *Shiʿism, Resistance, and Revolution,* ed. Martin Kramer (Boulder, CO: Westview Press, 1987), 173–86; Laurence Louër, *Transnational Shiite Politics: Religious and Political Networks in the Gulf* (London: Hurst, 2008); Frederic M. Wehrey, *Sectarian Politics in the Gulf: From the Iraq War to the Arab Uprisings* (New York: Columbia University Press, 2014).

[34] Mamoun Fandy, *Saudi Arabia and the Politics of Dissent* (Basingstoke: Palgrave, 1999), 195–228; Joshua Teitelbaum, *Holier than Thou: Saudi Arabia's Islamic Opposition* (Washington, DC: Washington Institute for Near East Policy, 2000).

[35] David E. Long, "The Impact of the Iranian Revolution on the Arabian Peninsula and the Gulf States," in *The Iranian Revolution: Its Global Impact,* ed. John L. Esposito (Miami: Florida International University Press, 1990), 100–15; Christin Marschall, *Iran's Persian Gulf Policy: From Khomeini to Khatami* (London: RoutledgeCurzon, 2003), 26–45; R. K. Ramazani, "Shiʿism in the Persian Gulf," in *Shiʿism and Social Protest,* ed. Juan R. I. Cole and Nikki R. Keddie (New Haven, CT: Yale University Press, 1986), 30–54; R. K. Ramazani, "Iran's Export of the Revolution: Politics, Ends, and Means," in *The Iranian Revolution: Its Global Impact,* ed. John L. Esposito (Miami: Florida International University Press, 1990), 40–62; Rouhollah K. Ramazani, *Revolutionary Iran: Challenge and Response in the Middle East* (Baltimore, MD: Johns Hopkins University Press, 1988).

[36] Mamoun Fandy, "From Confrontation to Creative Resistance: The Shia's Oppositional Discourse in Saudi Arabia," *Critique: Critical Middle Eastern Studies* 5, no. 9 (1996), 1–27; Laurence Louër, "Shiʿi Identity Politics in Saudi Arabia," in *Religious Minorities in the Middle East: Domination, Self-Empowerment, Accommodation* ed. Anh Nga Longva and Anne Sofie Roald (Leiden: Brill, 2012), 221–43; Roel Meijer and Joas Wagemakers, "The Struggle for Citizenship of the Shiites of Saudi Arabia," in *The Dynamics of Sunni-Shia Relationships: Doctrine, Transnationalism, Intellectuals and the Media,* ed. Brigitte Maréchal and Sami Zemni (London: Hurst, 2013), 117–38.

[37] Guido Steinberg, "The Shiites in the Eastern Province of Saudi Arabia (al-Ahsa') 1913–1953," in *The Twelver Shia in Modern Times: Religious Culture & Political History,* ed. Rainer Brunner and Werner Ende (Leiden: Brill, 2001), 236–54.

[38] F. S. Vidal, *The Oasis of al-Hasa* (n.p.: Arabian American Oil Company, 1955). See also the following work, which is based heavily on Vidal: Hans-Jürgen Philipp, *Geschichte und Entwicklung der Oase al-Hasa (Saudi Arabien)* (Saarbrücken: Breitenbach, 1976).

written sources and fieldwork. Apart from local historiography, this book also uses British and American diplomatic records, private archives and a plethora of publications by various Saudi opposition groups. Many of these hitherto unexamined sources were collected during fieldwork trips to Saudi Arabia and other Middle Eastern states between 2007 and 2013 and around sixty in-depth interviews in Arabic and English with Saudi Shia activists. They were designed to get to know the field and identify key issues and personalities. Most were narrative interviews, in which I gathered biographical data on social background, politicisation, identity formation and views on the development of the Shia opposition and the history of Saudi Shia. For the last two chapters, I have also used Web sites, social media discussions and online archives.

SECTARIANISM AND COMMUNAL POLITICS

This book uses the Shia in Saudi Arabia as a case study to gain insights into how and why people identify with a particular group, in this case a sect, in competition with other possible markers of identity. It narrates different aspects of Shia communal politics to rethink the usefulness of sectarianism as an analytical category. Considerable ambiguity surrounds the term *sectarianism*. What complicates academic discussions about sect and sectarianism is that in Western academia the concept originates in a Christian and largely European context. Sociology of religion has defined sect as distinct from church in the Christian context.[39]

With regard to Islam, where the split between Sunni and Shia Muslims occurred very early after the death of the Prophet Muhammad, many aspects of the Western sociology of sects are rendered void.[40] The development of Islamic sects is associated with their peripheral geographical and political location and their opposition to the often Sunni-dominated state.[41] An analysis of sectarianism in Islam should distinguish between historical processes leading to the creation of sects and political aspects of sectarianism. The term *confessionalism* is sometimes put forward as

---

[39] See for example: Meredith B. McGuire, *Religion, the Social Context*, 4th ed. (Belmont, CA: Wadsworth, 1997); Bryan R. Wilson, *Religion in Sociological Perspective* (Oxford: Oxford University Press, 1982); Max Weber, "Kirchen und Sekten," in *Schriften 1894–1922*, ed. Dirk Kaesler (Stuttgart: Alfred Kröner, 2002), 227–42, 234–36.

[40] Michael Cook, "Max Weber und islamische Sekten," in *Max Webers Sicht des Islams: Interpretation und Kritik*, ed. Wolfgang Schluchter (Frankfurt a. M.: Suhrkamp, 1987), 334–41.

[41] Fuad I. Khuri, *Imams and Emirs: State, Religion and Sects in Islam* (London: Saqi Books, 1990).

an alternative, even though it often signifies religious sectarianism. In a political context it refers particularly to the sharing of powers on a *confessional* basis.[42] The analytical value of the term sectarianism is further complicated by the fact that it has quite negative connotations in English, as has its equivalent in Arabic, *ta'ifiyya*.

The political aspects of sectarianism have frequently been studied with reference to Northern Ireland, Lebanon, Iraq, the Balkans, and South-East Asia. In the Indian context the term *communalism* is often used to describe Hindu-Muslim conflicts,[43] while *sectarianism* denotes Sunni-Shia conflicts.[44] Political sectarianism is an instrument for elites trying to maintain their privileges or for strategic groups trying to challenge the existing order. In Iraq, Lebanon, and Syria political sectarianism aided the development of Islamism amongst non-dominant groups.[45] Especially the influence of the international dimension and international actors in fuelling sectarian conflict needs to be kept in mind.[46]

The most fruitful approaches are those that take a historical perspective and focus on the social and political circumstances that led to the creation of modern political sectarianism, by looking at spaces and institutions of sectarian socialisation and identity formation, such as sport clubs[47] and courts.[48] Another important aspect is the legacy of Ottoman and Western colonial rulers, whose cooperation with certain religious groups together with the influx of modern ideologies of ethnic

---

[42] See the use of the term *confessionalism* in Kais M. Firro, *Inventing Lebanon: Nationalism and the State under the Mandate* (London: I. B. Tauris, 2003); Bodo Nischan, *Lutherans and Calvinists in the Age of Confessionalism* (Aldershot: Ashgate, 1999).

[43] See for example Sandria B. Freitag, *Collective Action and Community: Public Arenas and the Emergence of Communalism in North India* (Berkeley: University of California Press, 1989).

[44] See Justin Jones, *Shi'a Islam in Colonial India: Religion, Community and Sectarianism* (Cambridge: Cambridge University Press, 2012), 23.

[45] Ferhad Ibrahim, *Konfessionalismus und Politik in der arabischen Welt: Die Schiiten im Irak* (Münster: LIT-Verlag, 1997), 17–24.

[46] Samir Khalaf, *Civil and Uncivil Violence in Lebanon: A History of the Internationalization of Communal Conflict* (New York: Columbia University Press, 2002); Vali R. Nasr, "International Politics, Domestic Imperatives, and Identity Mobilization: Sectarianism in Pakistan, 1979–1998," *Comparative Politics* 32, no. 2 (2000), 171–90.

[47] Bill Murray, *The Old Firm: Sectarianism, Sport, and Society in Scotland* (Edinburgh: John Donald, 1984); John Peter Sugden and Alan Bairner, *Sport, Sectarianism and Society in a Divided Ireland* (Leicester: Leicester University Press, 1993); Danyel Reiche, "War Minus the Shooting? The Politics of Sport in Lebanon as a Unique Case in Comparative Politics," *Third World Quarterly* 32, no. 2 (2011), 261–77.

[48] Max Weiss, *In the Shadow of Sectarianism: Law, Shi'ism, and the Making of Modern Lebanon* (Cambridge, MA: Harvard University Press, 2010).

nationalism were crucial for the development of political sectarianism.[49] Sectarian belonging becomes particularly salient if sect overlaps with class, as in Northern Ireland,[50] or if one sectarian group dominates key sectors of the state apparatus, as in Syria.[51]

On the Arab side of the Gulf, political elites have long kept Shia out of political decision making and worked to keep political institutions unrepresentative. In addition, Shia are excluded from nationalist re-enactments that glorify Arab, Sunni and tribal identities. This has led to a strengthening of sectarian political identities amongst Gulf Shia. This is reinforced by the fact that in Bahrain and the Eastern Province Sunni and Shia often live in more or less segregated residential areas.[52] The division of urban settings according to sect can lead to 'segregated lives'. This is particularly so if quarter identities are based on sect and little interaction between sects occurs during schooling or leisure. In such segregated contexts, cross-sectarian contacts can lead to conflicts or refresh memories of past sectarian violence.[53]

Sectarian identities are only relevant at certain times in history. External influences, such as the Iranian Revolution; struggles over scarce resources, i.e. political economy; as well as competing myth-symbol complexes such as debates and polemics about religious rituals contribute to the salience of sectarian identities.[54] These factors determine whether a sectarian identity is passive and politically irrelevant, or whether, at times of crisis or when the sect is under threat, this identity becomes assertive.[55] Since the invasion of Iraq in 2003, the term sectarianism has become a catchall phrase in politics, media and academia. Culturalist explanations of Middle East politics dominate much of the media coverage and

[49] Ussama Samir Makdisi, *The Culture of Sectarianism: Community, History, and Violence in Nineteenth-Century Ottoman Lebanon* (Berkeley: University of California Press, 2000); Bruce Masters, *Christians and Jews in the Ottoman Arab World: The Roots of Sectarianism* (Cambridge: Cambridge University Press, 2001).

[50] Henry Patterson, *Class Conflict and Sectarianism: The Protestant Working Class and the Belfast Labour Movement 1868–1920* (Belfast: Blackstaff Press, 1980).

[51] Nikolaos Van Dam, *The Struggle for Power in Syria: Sectarianism, Regionalism and Tribalism in Politics 1961–1978* (London: Croom Helm, 1979).

[52] Justin J. Gengler, "Understanding Sectarianism in the Persian Gulf," in *Sectarian Politics in the Persian Gulf*, ed. Lawrence G. Potter (London: Hurst, 2013), 31–66.

[53] Jennifer Hamilton, Ulf Hansson, John Bell et. al., *Segregated Lives: Social Division, Sectarianism and Everyday Life in Northern Ireland* (Belfast: Institute for Conflict Research, 2008); Peter Shirlow and Brendan Murtagh, *Belfast: Segregation, Violence and the City* (London: Pluto Press, 2006).

[54] Another factor in the Iraqi case is a 'contested ownership of the nation'. Fanar Haddad, *Sectarianism in Iraq: Antagonistic Visions of Unity* (London: Hurst, 2011), 10.

[55] Ibid. 25–9.

the ways in which some decision makers in the Middle East view their actions. Conflicts between Sunni and Shia have led some to speak of a 'sectarian substructure that runs beneath Middle East politics'.[56] But "Sunni" and "Shia" should not be used as ascriptions of sociological or political categories. Other competing identities and factors such as class, profession, gender, nationality, ideology, religiosity and education will fragment any cultural group. So the profound socio-economic transformation, the exponential growth of the state apparatus, urbanisation, and the changing regional environment throughout the twentieth century form the backdrop for the political struggles outlined in this book.

To explain when these political categories become salient, this book will use a historically grounded approach to the study of communal politics that is empirical and mainly focusses at the micro level. At the same time, this book will, following Seyla Benhabib, keep in view the macro level, 'the functional/structural imperatives of material systems of action like the economy, bureaucracy, and various social technologies on the one hand, and the symbolic-representative imperatives of systems of cultural signification on the other.'[57] The goal is to understand the role of structures, while keeping in mind the use of political culture by elites.

This book also tries to account for the agency of subaltern groups, whose political creativity and opposition can at times transcend the boundaries set by power structures. Saudi Shia tried to change their subaltern status and fought against the limitations and constraints imposed on them by the state. At the same time, Saudi Shia society is highly stratified, and some of the Shia elites became integrated into the Saudi political economy, even though they, too, never reached the top echelons of business and politics.

The Saudi Shia case shows that religious and institutional discrimination can lead to the reinforcement of religiously based communal boundaries. Recognition as a group by an outside observer is key, argues Seyla Benhabib, as it imposes 'together with local elites, unity and coherence on cultures as observed entities.' A culture can only be seen from the outside as a delineable whole: 'From within, a culture need not appear as a whole, rather, it forms a horizon that recedes each time one approaches it.'[58] Such experiences reinforce certain elements of collective identities at

56 Vali Nasr, *The Shia Revival: How Conflicts within Islam Will Shape the Future* (London: W. W. Norton, 2007), 26.
57 Seyla Benhabib, *The Claims of Culture: Equality and Diversity in the Global Era* (Princeton, NJ: Princeton University Press, 2002), 11.
58 Ibid., 5.

the expense of other, competing, markers. In many cases of cultural politics this outside observer is the state.[59]

But there are also actors from within the Shia community that aim to strengthen communal identities. I refer to some Saudi Shia activists as identity entrepreneurs, as I analyse their ways of creating and politicising collective identities. The notion of the entrepreneur who capitalises on certain forms of identity is taken from the instrumentalist study of ethnicity, which argues that collective identities can be used as a political resource by competing interest groups. Brass points out that collective identities based on ethnicity and nationalism 'are creations of elites, who draw upon, distort, and sometimes fabricate materials from the cultures of the groups they wish to represent in order to protect their well-being or existence or to gain political and economic advantage for their groups as well as for themselves'.[60] Ethnic activists or 'entrepreneurs' in ethnic groups and nationalist movements, such as those described by Barth, work on projects to construct difference and reinforce boundaries towards other groups.[61] Barth further argues that ethnic groups are 'a form of social organization' and he puts emphasis on the 'ethnic boundaries'.[62]

Applying Barth's notion of the 'entrepreneur' to the Lebanese case, Shaery-Eisenlohr has defined 'Shia ethnic entrepreneurs' as clerics and lay activists with some religious education who seek 'to establish the previously marginalized Shi'ites as part of the Lebanese nation'.[63] While these entrepreneurs might run businesses, they are not per se businessmen; they can also be religious activists, or activists in charities and schools. In the Saudi Shia case, some of those that I identify as identity entrepreneurs are also engaged in debates about history and have written local histories.[64] Saudi Shia identity entrepreneurs all want that the Saudi Shia strengthen their collective identities and try to represent their interests as a group, rather than as individuals or members of other collectives.

[59] Charles Taylor and Amy Gutmann, eds., *Multiculturalism: Examining the Politics of Recognition* (Princeton, NJ: Princeton University Press, 1994).

[60] Paul R. Brass, *Ethnicity and Nationalism: Theory and Comparison* (London: Sage, 1991), 8.

[61] Fredrik Barth, *Models of Social Organization* (London: Royal Anthropological Institute, 1966).

[62] Fredrik Barth, *Ethnic Groups and Boundaries: The Social Organization of Culture Difference* (Prospect Heights, IL: Waveland Press, 1998 [1st ed., 1969]), 11–15.

[63] Roschanack Shaery-Eisenlohr, *Shi'ite Lebanon: Transnational Religion and the Making of National Identities* (New York: Columbia University Press, 2008), 6.

[64] See Matthiesen, "Shi'i Historians in a Wahhabi State".

STRUCTURE OF THE BOOK

The first chapter is a history of the old Saudi Shia elites and of the institutions they shaped. The notables in Qatif and al-Ahsa form a status group that became quite powerful and wealthy, particularly under Ottoman rule from 1871 onwards. After the Saudi conquest in 1913 they became the main interlocutors with a state that was openly hostile towards the Shia. The socio-political standing of these families derived from clerical authority, the position of judge (*qadi*), control over large areas of agricultural land and the pearl trade. Analytically, this chapter shows how local politics in Saudi Arabia was carried out through a class of intermediaries and how the state operated in provincial towns and villages. Clerics from the notable families dominated the Shia judiciary. Through an analysis of Shia courts in Qatif and al-Ahsa, this chapter highlights the importance of institutions in fostering collective identities.

A close reading of the history of Shia elite families shows how the Saudi rentier state can buy off certain segments of society while antagonising others. The chapter emphasises the localised nature of patronage and state-society relations. The Saudi Shia case illustrates through which channels a local elite was able to gain limited authority and independence, as well as how it was used by the state in a larger political struggle to achieve acceptance and legitimacy within its borders. The state needed these families' cooperation to maintain its rule over the East. But contrary to other urban notables or tribal leaders in Saudi Arabia, the Shia notables were never integrated into high-level Saudi politics the way prominent Sunni families were. The main reason for this was the fact that they were Shia. Therefore, this chapter is also a story of relative decline, as it outlines how, from being local governors under the Ottomans, the notables became increasingly sidelined. They faced the almost impossible task of trying to secure benefits for their constituencies from a state that deliberately marginalised the Shia, while ensuring political acquiescence in their regions.

When oil extraction started in earnest in the 1940s, many notables, but also many others who moved to the East to work in the oil camps, became inspired by Arab nationalism and leftist ideologies. In a bid to improve the working conditions in the labour camps, large strikes were held throughout the 1950s. Leftists also participated in municipal elections and won seats across the Eastern Province. After a ban on strikes, demonstrations and any form of open political organisation, many activists moved underground or into exile, a story that is the subject of chapter two. Saudi Shia became active in communist, Nasserist, Baathist, and other secular opposition movements.

The failures of Arab nationalism and the weakening appeal of leftist ideologies at a regional and global level, facilitated the rise of Islamist movements. The emergence of Islamist opposition movements in the Eastern Province is the topic of the third chapter, which explains how the Iraqi Shia Islamist movement known as the *shiraziyya* started to spread down the Gulf coast in the 1970s. The leaders of the *shirazi* movement took up residence in Kuwait, where young Saudi Shia students were encouraged to form a movement of their own. The *shirazi* political networks were key in organising the Shia uprising, or *intifada*, of 1979/1980, in the Eastern Province. But the intifada was crushed and scores went into exile.

The historical narrative presented in these two chapters contradicts claims that political opposition has been almost absent in Saudi Arabia. Such arguments often make use of rentier state theory, the dominant political economy approach in Gulf studies, to explain the persistence of authoritarian monarchies. The main part of the economy in rentier states is based on commodity revenue, which the state distributes to different layers of rent recipients. Rentier state theory generally sees society as passive and argues that 'democracy is not a problem for allocation states' and that economically motivated parties or political opposition groups do not exist: 'Parties will develop only to represent cultural or ideological orientation' such as 'Islamic fundamentalism'.[65] According to the model, just a few are engaged in the production of wealth 'the majority being only involved in the distribution or utilisation of it',[66] and a large part of the bourgeoisie is dependent on the state.[67] Workers with fewer rights such as expatriates or minorities are carrying out much of the actual work.

Since the discovery of oil Saudi Shia have been involved in its extraction but have benefitted less than other groups in the Kingdom from the wealth it brings. Their opposition is therefore also a response to

---

[65] Giacomo Luciani, "Allocation vs. Production States: A Theoretical Framework," in *The Rentier State*, ed. Giacomo Luciani and Hazem Beblawi (London: Croom Helm, 1987), 65–84, 74–6.

[66] Hazem Beblawi, "The Rentier State in the Arab World," in *The Rentier State*, ed. Giacomo Luciani and Hazem Beblawi (London: Croom Helm, 1987), 49–62.

[67] Hootan Shambayati, "The Rentier State, Interest Groups, and the Paradox of Autonomy: State and Business in Turkey and Iran," *Comparative Politics* 26, no. 3 (1994), 307–31; Theda Skocpol, "Rentier State and Shi'a Islam in the Iranian Revolution," *Theory and Society* 11, no. 3 (1982), 265–83.

governmental spending policies. Okruhlik, for example, argues that allocation states, far from just gaining society's acquiescence through the distribution of rent, accrue their own opposition through spending policies.[68] But rentier state theory is of limited use to explain the forms of opposition, its timing and its impact on local communities. More recent studies have started to reject the notion of state autonomy that is implicit in many of these approaches and argue that some groups are more able to influence the state than others. These include 'the royal family, the bureaucratic elite, and the neo-bourgeoisie'.[69] These groups distribute oil wealth according to 'Islamic familialism',[70] 'Asabiyya capitalism'[71] or 'segmented clientelism'. It is therefore 'less distribution as such, than the structures of ties and groups involved in distribution which determines political action'.[72]

It is the virtual exclusion from the groups that determine rent distribution that has led to the marginalisation of the Shia in the Saudi political economy and in Saudi institution building. The leftist activism described in chapter two shows that at least a certain mobilisation capability along class lines, and across sectarian divides, existed in the 1950s, even though it had largely disappeared by the 1970s. From the 1970s onwards, the fusion of an under-class sentiment with the vocabulary of Islamism and the political reinterpretation of Shia historical symbols managed to mobilise many Shia. Factors such as ideology, religious discrimination and regional dynamics are as important for an understanding of Shia dissent as the distributive policies of the rentier state.

The fourth chapter describes how the Saudi Shia opposition moved into exile in the 1980s and how it fared in Iran, in Syria, and elsewhere. Post-revolutionary Iran was initially a haven for Saudi Shia opposition activists, but as the revolutionary spirit in Iran became increasingly overshadowed

---

[68] Gwenn Okruhlik, "Rentier Wealth, Unruly Law, and the Rise of Opposition: The Political Economy of Oil States," *Comparative Politics* 31, no. 3 (1999), 295–315, 300.

[69] Rayed Khalid Krimly, *The Political Economy of Rentier States: A Case Study of Saudi Arabia in the Oil Era 1950–1990* (PhD, George Washington University, 1993), 398.

[70] Mamoun Fandy, *Saudi Arabia and the Politics of Dissent* (Basingstoke: Palgrave, 1999), 26–31.

[71] Daryl Champion, *The Paradoxical Kingdom: Saudi Arabia and the Momentum of Reform* (London: Hurst, 2003).

[72] Steffen Hertog, "Segmented Clientelism: The Political Economy of Saudi Economic Reform Efforts," in *Saudi Arabia in the Balance: Political Economy, Society, Foreign Affairs*, ed. Paul Aarts and Gerd Nonneman (New York: New York University Press, 2005), 111–43, 128.

by geo-political realities and factionalism within the regime, many Saudis left Iran again. Throughout the 1980s, the *shirazi* movement was challenged by a group of Saudi Shia Islamists who favoured the *marji'iyya* of Ruhollah Khomeini. This group would come to form a loose political movement, Khat al-Imam, and a militant organisation set up with Iranian help in order to attack Saudi interests, Hizbullah al-Hijaz. This militarisation in the late 1980s elevated the conflict between the Shia and the state to another level and fragmented the Shia Islamist opposition.

But the opposition activists eventually had to come to terms with the logic of the state both in Iran and in Saudi Arabia. The fifth chapter explains why the state and the Saudi Shia opposition decided to negotiate a general amnesty and the return of the Shia opposition in 1993. These negotiations occurred in the wake of the Gulf War and the mass deployment of American troops on Saudi soil. This led to a strong Sunni Islamist opposition and a petitions campaign that profoundly challenged the ruling family's grip on power. The chapter also highlights debates within the Shia opposition and divisions resulting from the negotiations with the government, divisions that shaped Shia politics post 1993. Those who did oppose the negotiations continued to voice criticism at home or remained active in the militant movement Hizbullah al-Hijaz, which was blamed for the 1996 bombings of the Khobar Towers U.S. military housing complex.

Since 1993, some Shia have been integrated into newly created institutions of the Saudi state such as the Majlis al-Shura. The returning activists focussed on activism in the public sphere and civil society and Shia politicians won seats in municipal elections. The clerics who returned set up religious institutions such as hawzat, *hussainiyyas* and mosques, often in a legal grey area. Cultural journals, local news websites, and social media gave Saudi Shia a public voice they had hitherto lacked. And the National Dialogue sessions sponsored by Crown Prince and later King Abdullah gave Shia public intellectuals a space to communicate with the ruling family and wider Saudi society. This marginal recognition under Abdullah is the topic of chapter six.

When Arab dictators were ousted across the region in 2011, Saudi Shia went out into the streets, thrilled by the wave of pro-democracy protests and in support of the uprising in Bahrain. Small protests in early 2011 turned to mass demonstrations from November 2011 onwards. The seventh and final chapter explores how the major conflict lines between the Shia and the state, as well as amongst the different Shia political groups, have been recalibrated through the largest protest movement Saudi Arabia has witnessed since 1979. The state reacted with repression and killed twenty young Shia. Accompanied by an intensified anti-Shia rhetoric, the partial integration of the Shia was largely reversed. The Shia were once again cast as the enemy within, as the *Other Saudis*.

Politics of Notables

> Are we not Muslims? And if we are not Muslims ... then are we not citizens?
>
> Letter by Shia notables to King Fahd, 5 January 1992

SHIA ISLAM IN EASTERN ARABIA

Several histories of the Shia of al-Ahsa, Qatif and Bahrain trace their lineage to the partially Christian tribe ʿAbd al-Qays that entered Bahrain and Qatif in the sixth century.[1] Branches of the ʿAbd al-Qays participated in the conquests of the Muslim forces and espoused the cause of ʿAli.[2] The Qarmatians, a Sevener Shia Ismaili movement, ruled Eastern Arabia from 899 until the late eleventh century. This contributed to a distinct sense of religious identity that differed from that of the interior of the Arabian Peninsula. Twentieth century Shia identity entrepreneurs depict this period of 'ancient Bahrain' as the golden age of the Shia of Eastern Arabia, effectively formulating a 'Bahrani nativism'.[3] *Bahrani* is a term that refers to the native, mainly Arab Shia, inhabitants of Bahrain, Qatif,

---

[1] Fuʾad al-Ahmad, *al-shaykh Hasan ʿAli Al Badr al-Qatifi* (Beirut: Muʾassasat al-Baqiʿ li-Ihyaʾ al-Turath, 1991), 44–53; al-Hasan, *al-shiʿa*, vol. 1, 17, 27; Muhammad Saʿid al-Muslim, *sahil al-dhahab al-aswad: dirasa tarikhiyya insaniyya li-mintaqat al-khalij al-ʿarabi* (Coast of Black Gold: A Historical-Humanitarian Study of the Arabian Gulf Region), 2nd ed. (Beirut: Manshurat Dar Maktabat al-Haya, 1962), 93–5; al-Shakhs, *aʿlam*, vol. 2, 124–79; Ibrahim, *Shiʿis*, 172.

[2] W. Caskel, "ʿAbd al-Qays," *Encyclopedia of Islam*, 2nd. ed., ed. P. Bearman, Th. Bianquis, C. E. Bosworth, E. van Donzel and W. P. Heinrichs (Leiden: Brill Online), hereafter *EI2*; Louër, *Transnational*, 13; Nakash, *Reaching*, 22.

[3] Louër, *Transnational*, 23.

and to a lesser extent al-Ahsa. An early 20th century British source, for example, uses the term *Bahrani* to describe Shia of Qatif, but the term has become less common in al-Ahsa and Qatif, while it remains widely used in Bahrain.[4]

The political union between Qatif, al-Ahsa and the islands of Bahrain, which is key to the idea of an 'ancient Bahrain', existed for most of the time between the ninth and the fifteenth century.[5] After the Qarmatians, from the late eleventh to the middle of the sixteenth century, local tribal dynasties ruled the lands of Bahrain and had their capitals at times on the island of Bahrain and at times in Qatif or al-Ahsa. Until the early fourteenth century, the tribal dynasties in al-Ahsa were Sunni, and thereafter Shia. In 1515, the Portuguese took Hormuz and five years later a joint Portuguese-Hormuzi naval force conquered Qatif and Bahrain.[6]

While Bahrain came under Safavid rule, which further strengthened Shia Islam on the island, the Shia of Qatif and al-Ahsa faced Christian rulers who were hostile towards their religious beliefs.[7] The Qatifis sought refuge under the Ottomans and a delegation from Qatif swore allegiance to the Ottoman Sultan "Suleiman the Magnificent" in 1534. Around 1550, the Ottomans took over control in Qatif and al-Ahsa.[8] Eastern Arabia became an arena in the power struggle between the Ottomans and the Safavids (along with the Portuguese, who were aligned with the Safavids). The Ottomans, who ruled over al-Ahsa and Qatif until 1670,

---

[4] IOR/L/PS/10/134: From Captain A. P. Trevor, First Assistant Resident, Bushire, to S. H. Butler, Secretary to the Government of India in the Foreign Department, Simla, 9 August 1908.

[5] Muhammad Al ʿAbd al-Qadir al-Ansari al-Ahsaʾi, *tuhfat al-mustafid bi-tarikh al-Ahsaʾ fi al-qadim wa-l-jadid* (A Beneficial Masterpiece about the Old and New History of al-Ahsa), 2 vols., vol. 1 (Riyadh: Matabiʿ al-Riyyad, 1960), 4–45; Muhammad Mahmud Khalil, *tarikh al-khalij wa-sharq al-jazira al-ʿarabiyya al-musamma iqlim bilad al-Bahrayn fi zill hukm al-duwaylat al-ʿarabiyya 469–963A.H./1076–1555* (History of the Gulf and the East of the Arabian Peninsula Called 'Lands of Bahrain' Region in the Shadow of the Rule of Arab States 1076–1555) (Cairo: Maktaba Madbuli, 2006).

[6] ʿAli bin Ibrahim al-Darura, *tarikh al-ihtilal al-burtughali li-l-Qatif 1521–1572* (The History of the Portuguese Occupation of Qatif 1521–1572) (Abu Dhabi: Majmaʿ al-Thaqafi, 2001); Abdul Aziz M. Awad, "The Gulf in the Seventeenth Century," *Bulletin (British Society for Middle Eastern Studies)* 12, no. 2 (1985), 123–34; Werner Caskel, "Eine "unbekannte" Dynastie in Arabien," *Oriens* 2, no. 1 (1949), 66–71; Juan R. I. Cole, "Rival Empires of Trade and Imami Shiism in Eastern Arabia, 1300–1800," *International Journal of Middle East Studies* 19, no. 2 (1987), 177–203, 182f.

[7] Louër, *Transnational*, 15.

[8] G. Rentz, "al-Qatif," *EI2*; al-Darura, *tarikh*.

regarded the local Shia populations with suspicion and feared they could be agents of the Shia Safavids.[9]

Sixteenth century Qatif was an important port town with substantial tax revenue.[10] But under Ottoman rule landholding patterns changed drastically and land was expropriated, leading some Shia to emigrate to Bahrain. The sizeable landholdings of a wealthy merchant from Qatif residing in Bahrain, for example, were confiscated by the Ottoman governor and resold. Many properties became tax farms for Ottoman officials and soldiers.[11] Declining revenues from the port and from the pearl trade resulted in fewer funds for mosques and Shia mourning houses (*hussainiyya*, pl. *hussainiyyat*) and for the support of the clerical class. The Ottomans also closed the trans-Arabian pilgrimage and trade route from Qatif to Mecca from the 1550s until at least 1591. One of the main reasons for this was fear of infiltration by Shia and Safavid pilgrims. This economic, political and religious marginalisation of Eastern Arabia probably led many locals to support the revolt of the Bani Khalid tribe, which succeeded in driving the Ottomans out in 1670.[12] Thereafter, the Bani Khalid started raids on Bedouins roaming between al-Ahsa and Najd and even attacked areas of Najd.[13]

Shia authors argue that religious life under the Bani Khalid was relatively good, and that some members of the tribe converted to Shia Islam.[14] The Bani Khalid conferred some stability on al-Ahsa and the nomads of Najd were able to exchange their animals and animal products for agricultural products, manufactured goods and imports in the markets of Qatif and Hufuf (see Picture 1.1).[15] Yet, tribal rule proved to be fragile.

---

[9] Jon E. Mandaville, "The Ottoman Province of al-Hasa in the Sixteenth and Seventeenth Centuries," *Journal of the American Oriental Society* 90, no. 3 (1970), 486–513, 496–9. See also Mehmet Mehdi Ilhan, "The Katif District (Liva) during the First Few Years of Ottoman Rule: A Study of the 1551 Ottoman Cadastral Survey," *Belleten (Türk Tarih Kurumu)* 51, no. 200 (1987), 780–98.

[10] Salih Özbaran, "Ottomans and the India Trade in the Sixteenth Century: Some New Data and Reconsiderations," *Oriente Moderno* 25, no. 86 (2006), 173–9, 174–6.

[11] Mandaville, "Ottoman Province," 504–6.

[12] Ibid., 498f.

[13] Alexei Vassiliev, *The History of Saudi Arabia* (London: Saqi, 2000), 60f.

[14] Al-Hasan, *al-shi'a*, vol. 1, 27; Nakash, *Reaching*, 22.

[15] Hala Fattah, *The Politics of Regional Trade in Iraq, Arabia, and the Gulf 1745–1900* (Albany: State University of New York Press, 1997), 66–8; Madawi Al Rasheed, *A History of Saudi Arabia* (Cambridge: Cambridge University Press, 2002), 34–7; Horst Reichert, *Die Verstädterung der Eastern Province von Saudi Arabien und ihre Konsequenzen für die Regional- und Stadtentwicklung* (Stuttgart: Krämer, 1980), 228–44.

PICTURE I.I. Market in Hufuf.
Source: J. W. "Soak" Hoover/Saudi Aramco World/SAWDIA.

In 1722/23, a struggle amongst the nobility of the Bani Khalid weakened the tribal confederation.[16]

In 1744/45 Muhammad ibn Saud struck an alliance in Najd with Muhammad ibn ʿAbd al-Wahhab, the founder of the religious doctrine that later became known as the Wahhabiyya. The followers of the Wahhabiyya propagated the oneness of God (*tawhid*). They aimed at "purifying" the Islam of the nomadic and sedentary populations of Arabia. In the middle of the eighteenth century, Muhammad ibn ʿAbd al-Wahhab and many of

---

[16] Vassiliev, *The History*, 60f. For more on the Bani Khalid see ʿAbd al-Karim bin ʿAbdallah al-Munif al-Wahbi, *banu Khalid wa-ʿalaqatuhum bi-Najd 1669–1794* (Bani Khalid and their Relationship with Najd 1669–1794) (n.p.: Dar Thaqif li-l-Nashr wa-l-Taʾlif, 1989); al-Shaykh Ahmad al-ʿAmari al-Nasiri, *qabilat bani Khalid fi al-tarikh* (The Bani Khalid Tribe in History) (Beirut: Dar al-Rafidayn li-l-Tibaʿa wa-l-Nashr wa-l-Tawziʿ, 2009).

his followers moved to al-Dir'iyya, the stronghold of the Al Saud. The Wahhabiyya became the ideological backbone of the religious-political movement that led to what in official Saudi historiography is called the first Saudi state.[17] Political power was the realm of the Al Saud, while religious, moral and educational authority became the domain of Ibn 'Abd al-Wahhab and his descendants, the Al al-Shaykh.[18] The Saudi-Wahhabi alliance was different from earlier tribal alliances because it was based on missionary zeal. The Wahhabis saw Shia religious practices as *shirk* (polytheism) and their preferred targets were the Shia Muslims in the East and the Hijaz.[19]

Over the coming century, political rule over al-Ahsa was contested amongst different regional powers. The Saudi forces, Eastern tribes like the Bani Khalid, the Egyptians under Muhammad Ali and the Ottomans all conquered the area.[20] For much of this period, al-Ahsa and Qatif were integrated into the Saudi realm.[21] The political insecurity in the eighteenth and nineteenth centuries led to frequent battles and raids on the settlements in the East, and the Saudi-Wahhabi forces repeatedly destroyed Shia places of worship.[22] The Al Saud appointed Sunni rulers, sometimes former black slaves, to govern Qatif and al-Ahsa. They also worked with local notable families such as the al-Ghanim from Qatif, who for a period became representatives of the Al Saud. Their status, however, remained precarious. In the mid-nineteenth century a Saudi official even killed 'Ali bin 'Abdallah bin Ghanim, the former leader of Qatif.[23]

---

[17] Vassiliev, *The History*, 83–6.

[18] John S. Habib, "Wahhabi Origins of the Contemporary Saudi State," in *Religion and Politics in Saudi Arabia: Wahhabism and the State*, ed. Mohammed Ayoob and Hasan Kosebalaban (London: Lynne Rienner, 2008), 57–73, 58.

[19] Jacob Goldberg, "The Shi'i Minority in Saudi Arabia," in *Shi'ism and Social Protest*, ed. Juan R. I. Cole and Nikki R. Keddie (New Haven, CT: Yale University Press, 1986), 230–46, 231f.

[20] Abdul-Wahab S. Babeair, *Ottoman Penetration of the Eastern Region of the Arabian Peninsula, 1814–1841* (PhD, Indiana University, 1985), 70–4, 90–94, 121–123; George Forster Sadlier and Patrick Ryan, *Diary of a Journey across Arabia from el Khatif in the Persian Gulf, to Yambo in the Red Sea, during the Year 1819* (Bombay: Education Society's Press, Byculla, 1866), 26–32. For al-Ahsa and Qatif in the nineteenth century see also P. J. L. Frankl and K. Jopp, "Lieutenant Jopp's Report on a Visit to Hufuf, 1257/1841," *New Arabian Studies* 1 (1993), 215–27; Lorimer, *Gazetteer*, vol. 1, 947–99; Rentz, "al-Qatif".

[21] For more on this period see Maryam bint Khalaf al-'Utaybi, *al-Ahsa' wa-l-Qatif fi 'ahd al-dawla al-su'udiyya al-thaniyya (1245–1288 AH)* (al-Ahsa and Qatif in the Era of the Second Saudi State 1830–1871) (Beirut: Jadawel, 2012); 'Abdallah al-Salih al-'Uthaymin, *tarikh al-mamlaka al-'arabiyya al-su'udiyya* (The History of the Kingdom of Saudi Arabia), 9th ed., 2 vols. (Riyadh: Obeikan, 1998), vol. 1, 117–23.

[22] Steinberg, *Religion*, 490f.; Vassiliev, *The History*, 88–91.

[23] Al-Hasan, *al-shi'a*, vol. 1, 110f. According to Philby he was killed 'for being a Shia and having intelligence with Bahrain' and according to Winder for his cooperation with the Ottomans. H. St John Philby, *Sa'udi Arabia* (London: Benn, 1955), 197; R. Bayly

In the late eighteenth and the first half of the nineteenth century, the Saudi-Wahhabi forces used the judiciary to implement Wahhabi teachings on social and religious matters as well as to establish the sovereignty of nascent Saudi rule. In al-Ahsa, the Wahhabiyya was confronted with the fact that the Sunni Muslims living there followed all four Sunni schools of jurisprudence. Sunni Hasawi clerics had been amongst the earliest critics of Muhammad Ibn ʿAbd al-Wahhab. The relations between them and the Najdi *ʿulama*', who were advocating the strict teachings of Muhammad Ibn ʿAbd al-Wahhab, were often far from easy.[24] The Wahhabi *ʿulama*' ensured that posts in the local judiciary were filled with pro-Wahhabi clerics whose families were often from Najd.[25] The judge of Hufuf became the de facto judge over the whole of al-Ahsa, while non-Hanbali judges continued to rule on matters of personal status law but were nominally under his control. Wahhabi judges were also appointed in Qatif.[26]

AN IMPERIAL FRONTIER

Yet, the changing political circumstances in the second half of the nineteenth century and the Ottoman conquests led to a reversal of Wahhabi policies. In 1871, the Ottomans, who wanted to counter British influence in Arabia and restore some sense of order on the Gulf coast, profited from a power struggle within the Al Saud and conquered al-Ahsa.[27] From 1871 to 1913, the province of al-Ahsa formed part of the Ottoman

Winder, *Saudi Arabia in the Nineteenth Century* (London: Macmillan, 1965), 151f. See also William Gifford Palgrave, *Personal Narrative of a Journey through Central Arabia* (London: Macmillan, 1868), 349–78.

[24] Muhammad A. al-Zekri, *The Religious Encounter between Sufis and Salafis of East Arabia: Issue of Identity* (PhD, University of Exeter, 2004); Esther Peskes, *Muhammad b. ʿAbdalwahhab (1703–92) im Widerstreit: Untersuchungen zur Rekonstruktion der Frühgeschichte der Wahhabiya* (Beirut: Orient-Institut, 1993), 54–8.

[25] This was the case of the al-Wuhaybi family, who had family links to the Al al-Shaykh and became judges of Hufuf. Steinberg, *Religion*, 475f.

[26] Goldberg writes that Muhammad al-Farisi, whose last name (*nasab*) means 'the Persian', was Shia and appointed *qadi* of al-Ahsa. He interprets this move as a concession to the Shia. Goldberg, "Shiʿi Minority," 233. Winder argues that he was appointed *qadi* of Qatif and that the appointment of a Shia should be seen as an example of Turki's 'relatively tolerant attitude toward the Shiite inhabitants'. Winder, *Saudi Arabia*, 77. Al-Hasan, however, states that although al-Farisi was Persian he was not Shia and he was *qadi* of Qatif and not of al-Ahsa. Al-Hasan, *al-shiʿa*, vol. 1, 129. Steinberg argues that although al-Farisi was Persian, he was Sunni and a supporter of the Wahhabiyya. Steinberg, *Religion*, 475.

[27] Frederick F. Anscombe, *The Ottoman Gulf: The Creation of Kuwait, Saudi Arabia, and Qatar* (New York: Columbia University Press, 1997), 16–25.

Empire.[28] In this period, the Ottomans instituted wide-reaching political and administrative reforms across the Empire amidst increasing tensions with Western colonial powers. So in the period of Ottoman rule al-Ahsa experienced developments akin to those in other Ottoman provinces.

Midhat Pasha, one of the leading figures of the *tanzimat* reforms in the Ottoman Empire and governor of Baghdad, was determined to implement reforms in al-Ahsa similar to those in Iraq. He carried out a large-scale survey of al-Ahsa and planned a system of local administration that was supposed to draw Eastern Arabia firmly within the Ottoman Porte's reach. But not much of the plan was implemented, as Midhat was recalled to Istanbul in 1872.[29]

In the Gulf the competition with the British was particularly pronounced, and the Shia of Qatif and al-Ahsa lived at the frontier of this larger imperial struggle. The British effectively ruled in Bahrain, just a short boat ride away from Qatif and home to many relatives of Shia from Qatif, and so the Shia on the mainland often compared their situation with Bahrain.

Given the strained resources of the empire, the Ottomans had to make use of the powerful men at the periphery of their empire such as traders, landowners and religious and tribal leaders in order to consolidate their authority.[30] Especially in late nineteenth century Qatif, one can discern a 'politics of notables' that was not unlike that in other provinces of the Ottoman Empire. As Albert Hourani has shown, these notables arose under three conditions: Firstly, 'when society is ordered according to relations of personal dependence', for example, when the peasant in the countryside produces mainly for the landowner; secondly, if the

[28] Many Ottoman documents relating to the history of al-Ahsa were published and translated in the Saudi Shia historiographical journals *al-Waha* and *al-Sahil*, as well as in the following works: Faysal 'Abdallah al-Kandari, *al-hamla al-'uthmaniyya 'ala al-Ahsa' 'am 1871 min khilal al-watha'iq al-'uthmaniyya* (The Ottoman Campaign on al-Ahsa in the Year 1871 according to Ottoman Documents) (Kuwait: Markaz Dirasat al-Khalij wa-l-Jazira al-'Arabiyya, 2003); Zakariyya Kurshun and Muhammad Musa al-Qarini, *sawahil Najd "al-Ahsa'" fi al-arshif al-'uthmani: Jabal Shammar – al-Qasim – al-Riyyad – al-Qatif – al-Kuwayt – al-Bahrayn – Qatar – Masqat* (The Oases of Najd "al-Ahsa" in the Ottoman Archives: Jabal Shammar – Qasim – Riyadh – Qatif – Kuwait – Bahrain – Qatar – Musqat) (Beirut: al-Dar al-'Arabiyya li-l-Mawsu'at, 2005); Suhayl Saban, *min watha'iq al-Ahsa' fi al-arshif al-'uthmani 1871–1913* (Some Documents on al-Ahsa in the Ottoman Archives) (al-Ahsa': Nadi al-Ahsa' al-Adabi, 2009); Suhayl Saban, *aradi al-Ahsa' wa-mazari'ha al-miriyya fi sajl al-khazna al-khasa raqm 4125 min sajalat al-arshif al-'uthmani* (The Landholdings of al-Ahsa and its Agricultural Miri Gardens in the Special Register No 4125 of the Ottoman Archives) (al-Ahsa': Nadi al-Ahsa' al-Adabi, 2010).

[29] Anscombe, *Ottoman Gulf*, 35.

[30] Ibid., 55.

PICTURE I.2. Fishermen in Dammam.
Source: T. F. Walters/Saudi Aramco World/SAWDIA.

urban notables reside mainly in the city and because of their position there dominate a rural hinterland; and thirdly, if the notables are able to exercise influence vis-à-vis a monarchical power.[31]

In the case of Qatif and to a lesser extent al-Ahsa, the first two components were given. The main economic activities such as overland trade and date farming allowed for the emergence of rich and influential merchants and landowners, who controlled the local market and interacted with foreign traders. Fishing and the capital intensive pearl trade also constituted important parts of the economy in the coastal areas until the late 1920s (see Picture I.2).[32]

---

[31] Albert Hourani, "Ottoman Reform and the Politics of Notables," in *The Modern Middle East: A Reader*, ed. Albert Hourani, Philip S. Khoury, and Mary C. Wilson (London: I. B. Tauris, 2004), 83–110, 87.

[32] Hussayn bin Hasan bin Makki Al Sulham, *Sayhat wa-l-bahr: bahth tarikhi li-l-haraka al-milahiyya fi madinat Sayhat* (Saihat and the Sea: A Historical Study of Seafaring in

The inhabitants of the villages around Qatif were dependent on the owners of date gardens resident in Qatif or Bahrain. A local historian calls the landholding class the 'aristocracy in society and it is from their midst that the notables *(wujaha')* emerge' that deal with the authority of the state *(al-sulta)*. One of the distinctive features of this status group was intermarriage. People from the Old Town *(al-qal'a)* of Qatif or from the notable families in the villages largely refrained from marrying into non-notable families.[33]

The oldest member of an extended family decided on family matters such as marriage.[34] Marriage amongst first cousins and other close relatives was common, not just amongst notable families. These marriage patterns only started to change at the end of the twentieth century.[35] Extended families related through intermarriage would often settle in similar villages or urban quarters leading to extended clans occupying whole quarters.[36] In addition to the urban centres of Qatif and al-Ahsa, the villages and small towns such as Awwamiyya, Saihat, Safwa and Tarut also developed a group of local notable families.

After the Ottoman conquest in 1871, Hufuf became the administrative seat of the sub province *(sanjak)* of Najd (see Picture 1.3). The *sanjak* of Najd was divided into five disctricts *(kazas)*: Hufuf, Qatif, Mubarraz, Qatar and Najd. While the governor *(mutasarrif)*, his administration, a sharia court judge, a court of appeal and an administrative council were located in Hufuf, the districts were headed by a *qaimaqam* supported by a treasurer, a sharia court judge and a claims tribunal. Initially, the administration was often staffed with Arabic speaking Ottoman officials, who had gained experience in the Arab provinces.[37] But by 1874, the Ottomans

the City of Saihat) (Beirut: Dar al-Mahajja al-Bayda', 2000); Richard LeBaron Bowen, "Marine Industries of Eastern Arabia," *Geographical Review* 41, no. 3 (1951), 384–400; Richard LeBaron Bowen, "The Pearl Fisheries of the Persian Gulf," *The Middle East Journal* 5, no. 2 (1951), 161–80; Robert Carter, "The History and Prehistory of Pearling in the Persian Gulf," *Journal of the Economic and Social History of the Orient* 48, no. 2 (2005), 139–209; F. S. Vidal, "Date Culture in the Oasis of al-Hasa," *The Middle East Journal* 8 (1954), 417–28.

33 Muhammad Sa'id al-Muslim, *al-Qatif waha 'ala difaf al-khalij* (Qatif: An Oasis on the Shores of the Gulf), 2nd ed. (Riyadh: Matabi' al-Farazdaq, 1991), 106f.

34 Ibid., 108f.

35 Interviews with various Sunni and Shia Saudis, October and November 2008, Saudi Arabia.

36 See the study written by Malcolm Quint: Arabian Affairs Division, *Home and Family in Qatif Oasis*, November 1960, Box 3, Folder 5, William E. Mulligan Papers, Georgetown University, Washington, D.C. Hereafter called Mulligan Papers.

37 Anscombe, *Ottoman Gulf*, 49f.

PICTURE I.3. Street scene in the Old City of Hufuf.
Source: Dorothy Miller/Saudi Aramco World/SAWDIA.

started to shift administration to local staff and appointed a Shaykh of
the Bani Khalid first as *qaimaqam* of Qatif and then as *mutasarrif* of
al-Ahsa.[38] This shift led to the appointment of the Shia notable Ahmad
bin Mahdi bin Nasrallah as *qaimaqam* of Qatif in 1875. His dismissal
in 1878 was due to a reversal of this policy, and thereafter no local was
appointed to this post either in Qatif or in al-Ahsa.[39] Nevertheless, Shia

[38] 'Abdallah ibn Nasir al-Subay'i, *al-hukm wa-l-idara fi al-Ahsa' wa-l-Qatif wa-Qatar
athna' al-hukm al-'uthmani al-thani 1871–1913* (Government and Administration in al-
Ahsa, Qatif and Qatar during the Second Period of Ottoman Rule 1871–1913) (Riyadh:
Matabi' al-Jum'a al-Iliktruniyya, 1999), 65f., 190.

[39] Muhammad al-'Awwami, *al-za'im Ahmad bin Mahdi Nasrallah: hayatuhu wa-shi'ruhu*
(The Leader Ahmad bin Mahdi Nasrallah: His Life and His Poetry) (London: Dar al-
Jazira li-l-Nashr wa-l-Tawzi', n.d.); Muhammad Musa al-Qarini, *al-idara al-'uthmaniyya*

notables became wealthy and influential under the Ottomans, particularly in Qatif.

Initially, an agricultural council was set up in Qatif composed of the *qaimaqam* Ibrahim Bek, Ahmad bin Mahdi bin Nasrallah, Ahmad al-Hussayn and another Qatifi merchant in order to organise tax collection.[40] It seems that Nasrallah and a number of other Shia notables controlled much of the administration in Qatif, principally tax collection and the administration of government land. The introduction of tax farming (*iltizam*), which involved the selling of the right to collect agricultural, excise and customs duties to locals, empowered the local notables but also enabled abuse. Where taxes were not farmed out, the village headmen had to collect them, strengthening the rural notables in the villages.[41] As many people's relations with the Ottoman state were limited to the paying of taxes and, if involved in legal issues, appearance in court, many Qatifis and Hasawis, despite being under Ottoman rule, dealt almost exclusively with their own elite.[42]

As members of the Qatifi Civil Administration Council they had access to and some degree of influence over the Ottoman governor. In Qatif, for example, the *qaimaqam* headed this council with the assistance of a local leader. The aforementioned Ahmad bin Mahdi bin Nasrallah filled this post until his death in 1888 and was then replaced by Mansur bin Jum'a.[43] The influence of the Shia notables stemmed from the weakness of the empire at its periphery, and from the fact that Qatif was an important port city. It should not be misread as a sign of religious tolerance by the Ottoman rulers. While the Ottoman Empire ruled over large Shia populations in Mesopotamia and the Levant, the Ottomans regarded their Shia subjects as potentially disloyal.[44]

---

fi mutasarrifiyyat al-Ahsa' 1288–1331/1871–1913 (The Ottoman Administration in the al-Ahsa District 1871–1913) (Riyadh: Darat al-Malik 'Abd al-'Aziz, 2005), 142; al-Subay'i, *al-hukm*, 184, 190.

[40] 'Abdallah ibn Nasir al-Subay'i, *iqtisad al-Ahsa' wa-l-Qatif wa-Qatar athna' al-hukm al-'uthmani al-thani 1871–1913* (The Economy of al-Ahsa, Qatif and Qatar during the Second Period of Ottoman Rule 1871–1913) (Riyadh: Matabi' al-Jum'a al-Iliktruniyya, 1999), 213.

[41] Al-Subay'i, *al-hukm*, 225–34; Anscombe, *Ottoman Gulf*, 58.

[42] Ibid., 55.

[43] Al-Hasan, *al-shi'a*, vol. 1, 194.

[44] Gökhan Cetinsaya, "The Ottoman View of the Shiite Community of Iraq in the Late Nineteenth Century," in *The Other Shiites: From the Mediterranean to Central Asia*, ed. Alessandro Monsutti, Silvia Naef, and Farian Sabahi (New York: Peter Lang, 2008), 19–40.

But the Ottomans were wary of acquiescing to British pressures in the Gulf and sought to protect Shia notables from claims in British courts. In 1886, a case developed between Ahmad bin Mahdi bin Nasrallah and Shaykh Ahmad bin ʿAli Al Khalifa, the brother of the ruler of Bahrain. The Ottomans refused to recognise the Shaykh's right to British protection and argued that the matter should be brought before an Ottoman court. The case could have caused an international crisis if both men had not died in 1888, thus settling the case.[45]

At the periphery of the multi-ethnic and multi-religious Ottoman Empire, the different religious groups of al-Ahsa were often able to use their own informal courts. This was especially the case in Shia areas of al-Ahsa. The Ottomans established formal courts that followed the Hanafi code of law in Hufuf and Qatif. In Qatif, the claims tribunal was made up of two local citizens and was attached to the Ottoman court. Even though the Ottoman courts were the highest judicial authority, non-Hanafi Sunni and Shia scholars acted as local judges in al-Ahsa for the followers of their religious schools. As these judges were not appointed directly by the state they had a certain degree of autonomy in their rulings. The Shia judges ruled on matters of personal status law, inheritance and *awqaf*.[46] Yet, their rulings were not binding. If one was not content with the rulings of the Shia *qadi*, one could take a matter to the official Ottoman court.[47]

The integration into the Ottoman Empire also gave al-Ahsa an increasingly cosmopolitan flavour. Some Jews and probably some Christians lived in Hufuf, Ottoman officials from all over the empire arrived and several dozen Indian merchants resided in Qatif.[48] From 1864 onwards, Indian trading houses and independent merchants established close trade relations with Qatif, and 'they controlled the greater portion of the trade

---

[45] James Onley, *The Arabian Frontier of the British Raj: Merchants, Rulers, and the British in the Nineteenth-Century Gulf* (Oxford: Oxford University Press, 2007), 165f.

[46] Muhsin al-Amin, *mustadrakat aʿyan al-shiʿa: haqqaqahu wa-akhrajahu Hasan al-Amin* (Amelioration of Outstanding Men of the Shia: Checked and Published by Hasan al-Amin), 11 vols. (Beirut: Dar al-Taʿarruf li-l-Matbuʿat, 1986), vol. 8, 298f.; Steinberg, *Religion*, 474–7; ʿAbdallah ibn Nasir al-Subayʿi, *al-qadaʾ wa-l-awqaf fi al-Ahsaʾ wa-l-Qatif wa-Qatar athnaʾ al-hukm al-ʿuthmani al-thani 1871–1913* (Judiciary and Religious Endowments in al-Ahsa, Qatif and Qatar during the Second Period of Ottoman Rule 1871–1913) (Riyadh: Matabiʿ al-Jumʿa al-Iliktruniyya, 1999), 38–40, 77, 85.

[47] Muhammad al-Hirz, "al-qadaʾ al-jaʿfari fi al-Ahsaʾ," (Shia Jurisprudence in al-Ahsa) *al-Waha* 20 (2001), 19–38, 23.

[48] Frederick F. Anscombe, "An Anational Society: Eastern Arabia in the Ottoman Period," in *Transnational Connections and the Arab Gulf*, ed. Madawi al-Rasheed (London: Routledge, 2004), 21–38.

which was principally in rice, cotton goods, sugar, coffee, spices, metals, and hardware imported from India via Bahrein, and pearls, dates and hides exported to the same country'.[49]

There were between seventy and eighty Indian merchants in Qatif but their numbers gradually declined in the 1890s after their businesses suffered from heavy taxation. As British subjects, the Indian merchants were at an advantage vis-a-vis the local Shia merchants in the overseas trade with Bahrain and India. But a Turkish Custom House with a system of farming out the revenues was established, and 'wealthy Katif [*sic*] merchants' with 'seats in the local Government Council' such as Mansur bin Jum'a (see Picture 1.4) were accused in British documents of influencing Ottoman officials to demand higher taxes from Indian merchants.[50]

This alliance with the Ottomans, however, also meant that Qatifi notables did not develop the same kind of links with the British, the other major colonial power in the Gulf, as most of Qatif's neighbours did. At the same time, the relationship with the Ottomans was far from easy. Mansur bin Jum'a was not more powerful than Ottoman governors of al-Ahsa such as Thalib Pasha, who had assumed the post in 1901. A British source reported in 1903:

One of the principal merchants of Katif is Mansur Pasha, the local representative of the Civil List. He is very rich, and Thalib Pasha soon saw in him a suitable subject for blackmail. Mansur, however, declined to accede to the Mutesarrif's extortion, and fled to Basrah, and thence to Baghdad. Soon after, at the end of January Thalib Pasha made a descent on Mansur's house, and imprisoned his brother, Abdul Hussain, carrying off property, including pearls, in which Mansur trades, to a very considerable amount [*sic*].[51]

As an excuse, Thalib Pasha argued that rifles as well as a number of 'seditious newspapers' had been found in Mansur's home. The British source suggests that these newspapers had been placed in the home by Thalib Pasha's men, hinting at a sectarian undertone to the conflict: 'Mansur Pasha is a Shiah, which will tell in the Thalib's favour at Constantinople but is likely to embitter local feeling at Katif, where the Shiahs are numerous and influential.' Pirates also repeatedly attacked Indian merchants,

[49] Saldanha, *Précis*, 73–7.
[50] Ibid.
[51] Report by Colonel Wratislam, 10. 3. 1903, cited in Saldanha, *Précis*, 61.

PICTURE 1.4. Mansur bin Jum'a.
Source: al-Sahil Archive.

inspiring unsuccessful attempts to establish a British Consular officer in Qatif.[52]

POLITICAL ECONOMY OF PIETY

The Shia notables were in close contact with Ottoman officials in al-Ahsa and Basra, the rulers of Kuwait and Bahrain, and British officials in Bahrain and Bushehr. But, according to Hourani, notables also need to have some social power that is not dependent on their access to the political authorities.[53] The social power of the Shia notables rested mainly on landownership, trade and religious credentials. Most notable families had produced at least one well-known cleric and had through him received *awqaf* and some form of historical legitimacy. Although the

[52] Ibid.
[53] Hourani, "Ottoman Reform," 87.

notable families were not initially forced to register their land with the government, they were affected by the Ottoman reorganisation of the system of *awqaf*. In 1871, Midhat Pasha had promised to keep taxation low and wanted social services to be funded by charitable endowments. His report, however, stated that the *waqf* system was unregulated and inefficient and had fuelled corruption. So Midhat instituted a new system of state oversight over *waqf* land in al-Ahsa, which was being introduced throughout the empire.[54]

It is, however, not entirely clear to what extent the Shia *awqaf* were included in these Ottoman registries, as they would usually be administered by the semi-official Shia judges themselves. People often kept their documents at home rather than deposit them in a central registry.[55] Yet, the case of one of the largest Shia *awqaf* in Saudi Arabia, called al-Ramis, is illustrative. Al-Ramis is a vast agricultural area between the village of Awwamiyya and the Gulf. Shia authors argue that a notable from Awwamiyya, Salman al-Faraj, bought it from the Ottomans in 1881/2 for 20,000 Rupees and donated it to the residents of Awwamiyya. While the al-Faraj family had hitherto administered the *waqf*, Shia authors argue that when the *waqf* was registered with the Saudi authorities in 1941 only a small proportion of the original *waqf* bought from the Ottomans remained part of the *waqf* and the rest was confiscated.[56]

Awqaf were destined to give the clerics a degree of financial autonomy and to pay for charitable institutions and religious festivities. The administrator officially received a fee of 10 percent of the income yielded from the mainly agricultural property.[57] The Shia judge could appoint relatives or associates to administer the *awqaf*. Many notable families had received their *awqaf* at a time when a prominent cleric or judge was head of the family. After the death of ʿAli Abu ʿAbd al-Karim al-Khunayzi (1868–1943), for example, the *awqaf*, some of whom he had inherited from his father and grandfather, were distributed to his relatives and his

---

[54] Anscombe, *Ottoman Gulf*, 51f.

[55] A detailed study of *awqaf* in al-Ahsa by a Saudi historian only describes *awqaf* by Ottomans and Sunni clerical families. The reason for this could be that they might not have been registered in the Ottoman *awqaf* registry or that the author did not obtain *awqaf* certificates from Shia families. Al-Subayʿi, *al-qadaʾ*, 85.

[56] Zaki ʿAli al-Salih, *al-ʿAwwamiyya: tarikh wa-turath* (Awwamiyya: History and Heritage), 2nd ed. (Beirut: Dar al-Kunuz al-Adabiyya, 1998), 295–300. For a history of the al-Faraj family see Suʿud ʿAbd al-Karim al-Faraj, *al-ʿAwwamiyya bayn ʿaraqat al-ams wa-ibdaʿ al-yawm* (Awwamiyya: Between the Deep-Rootedness in the Past and the Creation of Today) (n.p.: n.p., 2008).

[57] Email correspondence with Kamil al-Khatti al-Khunayzi, June 2009.

successors as *qadi* of Qatif: ʿAli Abu al-Hasan al-Khunayzi (1874–1944), Muhammad ʿAli al-Khunayzi and Muhammad al-Mubarak.[58]

Revenue from *awqaf* continues to be among the main sources of income for the notable families. In the second half of the twentieth century, the urban areas around Qatif grew towards the former agricultural areas to form an urban cluster incorporating Saihat, Anak, Safwa, Tarut and other surrounding villages.[59] Many new residential and commercial properties lie within the endowments of the notable families, yielding even higher revenue.[60] *Awqaf* were probably more important for the Shia clergy than the *khums* in the pre-oil era because the region was much less prosperous and less people could afford to pay large amounts of *khums*.[61]

The *khums* tax is a duty for every Shia who can afford it. It amounts to one fifth of someone's annual surplus income. Historically, it was designated for God and the hidden Imam as well as the poor. In the absence of the hidden Imam, the clerics have argued that it is up to them to administer the funds from the *khums*.[62] The *khums* has a certain democratic function because the believer can choose which *marji* he wants to support. After the decline of the local *marji ʿiyya* in the Gulf in the first half of the twentieth century it represented a transnational link to the Shia spiritual guides, be they in Iraq, Iran or Kuwait. The establishment of this *khums* system went hand in hand with the centralisation of the *marji ʿiyya* in Najaf and Karbala in the nineteenth century.[63] *Awqaf* and *khums* continue to finance *hussainiyyat*, which play a central role in the social and religious lives of al-Ahsa and Qatif and have become actual community centres.[64] This is similar to Bahrain, where merchant families,

[58] Email correspondence with a member of the al-Khunayzi family, July 2009. Muhammad al-Mubarak was also closely related to the al-Khunayzi by marriage.

[59] For a detailed analysis of urbanisation in the Qatif area see Faez Saad Al-Shihri, *Sustainable Development and Strategic Environmental Assessment (Sea) in the Planning Process: The Case of Al-Qatif Oasis and Its Settlements* (PhD, University of Newcastle upon Tyne, 2001), 250–348.

[60] Email correspondence with Kamil al-Khatti al-Khunayzi, June 2009.

[61] Interview with Muhammad Saʿid al-Shaykh ʿAli al-Khunayzi, Eastern Province, November 2008.

[62] Robert Gleave, "Khums," *EI2*; Heinz Halm, *Die Schiiten* (München: C. H. Beck, 2005), 58–61.

[63] Meir Litvak, *Shiʿi Scholars of Nineteenth-Century Iraq: The ʿUlamaʾ of Najaf and Karbalaʾ* (Cambridge: Cambridge University Press, 1998); Meir Litvak, "The Finances of the Ulama Communities of Najaf and Karbala, 1796–1904," *Die Welt des Islams* 40, no. 1 (2000), 41–66.

[64] Vidal, *Oasis*, 35–7.

some of them migrants from al-Ahsa, have funded *hussainiyyat* since the late nineteenth century in order to foster patronage networks.[65]

Theoretically, it has been forbidden to build *hussainiyyat* in Saudi Arabia since 1927, when Wahhabi missionaries destroyed some *hussainiyyat* in the East. Thereafter, many Shia converted actual *hussainiyyat* into 'normal' houses and houses into *hussainiyyat* to circumvent this ban.[66] The issue of the official ban on *hussainiyyat* is a topic that can be found in the petitions of Shia notables throughout the twentieth century. And yet, many of the old *hussainiyyat* remained in place and new ones were built without official permission. Most notable families in al-Ahsa and Qatif established their own *hussainiyyat* and mosques. The main Qatifi notable families such as the al-Khunayzi, al-ʿAwwami, al-Jishi and others still have a *hussainiyya* in the old city of Qatif. Some Qatifi clerics also built *hussainiyyat* in the villages.[67] They are used for religious festivities, for mourning the dead and for weddings. For these families, the *hussainiyya* serves as a link to popular religious practices, even after the sons of the notable families stopped becoming clerics. It is also the place where a preacher (*khatib*) and not necessarily a cleric (*ʿalim*) reads the prayers and where popular religiosity and community building overlap.

THE SHAYKHIYYA AND CLERICAL NETWORKS

Before the nineteenth century local *marajiʿ* would often reside amongst their followers rather than in the shrine cities. The most popular *marajiʿ* of the region would also work as judges, establish religious schools and own extensive landholdings. Shia *ʿulamaʾ* families in Qatif, such as the al-Khunayzi, became part of the political elite of the city. But in al-Ahsa, the situation was different. Sunni families dominated politics and were the largest landowners.[68]

The Shia *ʿulamaʾ* families were crucial for the affairs of the Shia, but not so much for the politics of the oasis as a whole. In late nineteenth century al-Ahsa there were three local Shia *marajiʿ* and judges: Muhammad

---

[65] Nelida Fuccaro, *Histories of City and State in the Persian Gulf: Manama since 1800* (Cambridge: Cambridge University Press, 2009), 107; Fuad I. Khuri, *Tribe and State in Bahrain: The Transformation of Social and Political Authority in an Arab State* (Chicago: University of Chicago Press, 1980), 154–60; ʿAbdallah Sayf, *al-maʾtam fi al-Bahrayn: dirasa tawthiqiyya* (The Maʾtam in Bahrain: A Documented Study) (Bahrain: al-Matbaʿ al-Sharqiyya, 1995), 119–23.

[66] Steinberg, *Religion*, 501.

[67] Abu ʿAbd al-Karim al-Khunayzi, for example, opened a *hussainiyya* in Awwamiyya in 1940. Al-Salih, *al-ʿAwwamiyya*, 81.

[68] Steinberg, "Shiites," 239; Vidal, *Oasis*, 37.

Abu Khamsin, Hashim al-Salman al-Musawi and Muhammad Al ʿIthan. From the nineteenth century onwards, the religious trends in al-Ahsa, Qatif and Bahrain became more closely intertwined with and influenced by developments in the shrine cities. But in previous centuries, Eastern Arabia gave rise to Shia schools of thought and jurisprudence that had a real impact on intellectual developments in the wider Shia worlds.

The Gulf was a centre of the Akhbariyya, and Yusuf al-Bahrani (1695–1772), a prominent scholar from Bahrain, was key in the reinterpretation and propagation of the Akhbariyya. The Akhbari school of Shia jurisprudence rejects deductive methodology in the study of law and requires unmitigated adherence to the limited meanings of the *akhbar*, the traditions (words and deeds) of the Prophet and the Shia Imams as transmitted by chains of narrators. It is opposed to the Usuliyya, which throughout the nineteenth century became the dominant form of Twelver Shia jurisprudence. The Usuliyya emphasises the use of reason in the study of the principles of jurisprudence *(usul al-fiqh)*. Contrary to the Usulis, Akhbaris generally do not emulate a living *marjiʿ*. Al-Bahrani's school of thought that spread on the island of Bahrain in the early eighteenth century also had an influence on the mainland, and he frequently moved back and forth to Qatif.[69] While the Akhbariyya has almost disappeared today, pockets of Akhbari adherence in Eastern Arabia continue to exist, particularly in Bahrain and in the village of Awwamiyya.[70]

The other main local form of Shia Islam was the Shaykhiyya, which derives its name from Shaykh Ahmad al-Ahsaʾi (1753–1826). Born in Mutayrifi, a village in al-Ahsa, he rose to fame only after he travelled to Iraq and then Iran, where he became the leader of a mystical Shia

---

[69] Robert Gleave, *Akhbari Shii Jurisprudence in the Writings of Yusuf B. Ahmad al-Bahrani (d.1186/1772)* (PhD, University of Manchester 1996).

[70] Habib Al Jumayʿ, *muʿjam al-muʾallafat al-shiʿiyya fi al-jazira al-ʿarabiyya* (Bibliography of Shia Writings in the Arabian Peninsula), 3 vols. (Beirut: Dar al-Mahajja al-Baydaʾ/ Muʾassasat al-Baqiʿ li-Ihyaʾ al-Turath, vol. 1, 1997), 282–4; al-Ahmad, *al-shaykh Hasan*, 97–101; Cole, "Rival Empires," 195f.; Fuʾad Ibrahim, *al-faqih wa-l-dawla: tatawwur al-fikr al-siyasi al-shiʿi* (Cleric and State: The Development of Shia Political Thought) (Beirut: Dar al-Kunuz al-Adabiyya, 1998); ʿAbd al-ʿAzim al-Mushaykhas, *al-Qatif wa-mula-haqatuha: abʿad wa-tatallaʿat* (Qatif and its Surroundings: Dimensions and Outlooks), 2 vols., (Beirut: Sharikat al-Shaykh li-l-Tahqiq wa-l-Nashr, 2002), vol. 1, 515–38, 551–73; Ahmad al-ʿAli, *shaʿb al-Qatif fi al-qarn al-hadi wa-l-ʿashrin: dirasa tahliliyya li-hadir wa-mustaqbal al-mujtamaʿ al-islami al-shiʿi fi al-alfiyya al-thalitha* (The People of Qatif in the 21st Century: An Analytical Study of Present and Future of Shia Islamic Society in the Third Millenium) (n.p.: Dar al-ʿArab, 2007), 257–65; Jihad al-Khunayzi, *maʿalim marjiʿiyyat al-imam al-Shirazi fi al-Qatif wa-adwaʾ ʿala tarikh al-ʿulamaʾ wa-l-marjiʿiyya fi al-Qatif* (Signposts of the Marjiʿiyya of Imam Shirazi in Qatif and Lights on the History of the Clerics and the Marjiʿiyya in Qatif) (Beirut: Dar al-Waha li-l-Tibaʿa wa-l-Nashr wa-l-Tawziʿ/Dar al-ʿUlum li-l-Tahqiq wa-l-Tibaʿa wa-l-Nashr wa-l-Tawziʿ, 2002), 26f.

movement that sought to revolutionise Shia jurisprudence and scholarship, later termed the Shaykhiyya. But most mainstream Shia scholars in the centres of learning in Iraq, who at that time already followed the Usuli school of Shia jurisprudence, regarded his teachings as heretical.[71]

But the Shaykhiyya retained support in al-Ahsa and amongst Hasawi migrants in Kuwait and Basra. Several scholars from al-Ahsa studied with Kazim al-Rashti (d. 1844), al-Ahsa'i's successor as leader of the Shaykhiyya. Thereafter, they returned to al-Ahsa and set up religious schools and seminaries to spread Shaykhi teachings. The Abu Khamsin family was key in transmitting Shaykhi teachings back to al-Ahsa, and acted as a link to the Shaykhi leadership that resided in Iraq and Iran.

The family, which also has branches in Basra, Kuwait and Dammam, traces its genealogy back to Muhammad Abu Khamsin al-Kabir (d.1774/5), who founded the Fawaris mosque and the *hussainiyyat Abu Khamsin* in al-Ahsa. His grandson Hussayn Abu Khamsin (1170 or 1190–1263/5, 1756/7 or 1776–1847/9) studied at the *hawza* of Ahmad al-Ahsa'i, and Hussayn's son Muhammad (1210–1316, 1795/96–1898/99) became an important local Shaykhi *marji*. He studied in Najaf and received the permission to perform *ijtihad* from Kazim al-Rashti.[72] After his return from Iraq in 1843, Muhammad Abu Khamsin founded a *hawza* in Hufuf and started to receive people in his *majlis* and settle their disputes. Some even claim that Muhammad Abu Khamsin ruled according to both Sunni and Shia law and the Ottomans respected his rulings but did not officially appoint him *qadi*.[73]

---

[71] See amongst others Mangol Bayat, *Mysticism and Dissent: Socioreligious Thought in Qajar Iran* (Syracuse, NY: Syracuse University Press, 1982); Denis MacEoin, *From Shaykhism to Babism: A Study in Charismatic Renewal in Shi'i Islam* (PhD, Cambridge University, 1979), 75–81; Litvak, *Shi'i Scholars*. For more on his teachings see Juan R. I. Cole, "Casting Away the Self: The Mysticism of Shaykh Ahmad al-Ahsa'i," in *The Twelver Shia in Modern Times: Religious Culture and Political History*, ed. Rainer Brunner and Werner Ende (Leiden: Brill, 2001), 25–37.

[72] Muhammad Hasan Al al-Talaqani, *al-shaykhiyya: nash'atha wa-tatawwurha wa-masadir dirasatha* (The Shaykhiyya: Its Emergence, Development and Sources of Studies) (Beirut: al-Amal li-l-Matbu'at, 1999), 117–73; al-Bahrani, *anwar*, 331; Muhammad al-Hirz, *al-shaykh Baqir Abu Khamsin: 'ilm wa-'ata' wa-adab* (Shaykh Baqir Abu Khamsin: Knowledge, Giftedness and Literature) (Beirut: Dar al-Khalij al-'Arabi li-l-Tiba'a wa-l-Nashr, 1999); al-Shakhs, *a'lam*, vol. 1, 352–70, vol. 3, 514f., vol. 4, 35–119.

[73] Al-Hirz, "al-qada'." This claim has to be treated with care. Al-Shakhs, *a'lam*, vol. 4, 67. In a personal interview, a member of the Abu Khamsin family has made similar claims, especially that Muhammad Abu Khamsin had ruled amongst both Sunnis and Shia. Interview with a member of the Abu Khamsin family, London, 2008.

PICTURE 1.5. Rock mountain and the village of al-Qara, al-Ahsa oasis.
Source: Tor Eigeland/Saudi Aramco World/SAWDIA.

The other local Shaykhi *marji'* Hashim al-Salman al-Musawi (d. 1891) also worked as a *qadi* after his studies with Muhammad Baqir al-Usku'i (d. 1883/84) in Karbala.[74] His family operated the *hawzat al-Salman al-'ilmiyya* in Mubarraz, which was initially attached to a mosque and a *hussainiyya* that were funded by *awqaf* donated around 1887/8 by, amongst others, Mansur Bin Jum'a, the main notable of Qatif at the time.[75] Muhammad Al 'Ithan (1844–1912/3) became a judge after the death of Muhammad Abu Khamsin and took over the *marji'iyya*. He was a Shaykhi from the village of al-Qara (see Picture 1.5) and had followers in other regions of the Gulf, including Qatif.[76] Contemporary Shaykhi

[74] Al-Amin, *a'yan al-shi'a*, vol. 10, 237; al-Bahrani, *anwar*, 331f.; al-Hirz, "al-qada'," 21; Ahmad Sadr Hajj Javadi, Kamran Fani, and Baha' al-Din Khorramshahi (eds.), *dayerat al-ma'arif-i tashayyu'* (Encyclopedia of Shiism), 12 vols. (Tehran: Nashr-i Shahid Sa'id Muhibbi, 1988–2007), vol. 1, 503.

[75] Muhammad al-Hirz, "al-hawzat wa-l-madaris al-'ilmiyya fi al-Ahsa' (The Hawzas and Religious Schools in al-Ahsa)," *Rasid* (11 August 2005); al-Shakhs, *a'lam*, vol. 1, 542–4, vol. 4, 147–50.

[76] Al-Bahrani, *anwar*, 332; al-Hasan, *al-shi'a*, vol. 1, 242f.; al-Shakhs, *a'lam*, vol. 4, 61, 437–78; Abu Bakr Muhammad 'Abdallah Ibrahim al-Shammari, *al-fihrist al-mufid fi tarajim a'lam al-khalij, al-halaqa al-ula* (The Useful List of Biographies of Scholars of the Gulf: Part One) (Khobar: al-Dar al-Wataniyya al-Jadida li-l-Nashr wa-l-Tawzi', 1992/1993), 155. See also these two at times contradictory biographies: Ahmad 'Abd

clerics argue that Qatif was overwhelmingly Shaykhi in the nineteenth century, but many Usulis see this differently.[77] Qatif was probably mainly Usuli at that point and this limited the interaction between the regions, as most Usuli scholars saw the Shaykhiyya as a heresy. But the Shaykhiyya was the dominant form of Shia Islam in nineteenth century al-Ahsa.[78]

Local *maraji* were also revered in Qatif. ʿAli Abu ʿAbd al-Karim al-Khunayzi returned from Najaf to Qatif in 1905/6, and briefly was the sole *mujtahid* in Qatif. The Ottomans apparently accepted him as the first *qadi* for the Shia of Qatif. According to Shia sources, the Shia judge under the Ottomans dealt with personal status law, legislating for both Sunnis and Shia.[79] His work was complementary to the work of the main judge, who was appointed from Iraq and ruled over all other matters.[80] Before his appointment different clerics, who were not *mujtahids*, jointly carried out this function.[81]

Clerics also taught in local religious schools, giving semi-formal Quran and Arabic lessons. Until the mid-twentieth century education remained the realm of the *ʿulama*, providing them with a source of income and social authority.[82] The first modern elementary schools were introduced

al-Muhsin al-Badr, *shams al-shumus: ustadh al-maraji ayatallah al-ʿuzma al-shaykh Muhammad al-ʿIthan al-Ahsaʾi* (The Greatest Sun: The Teacher of Maraji Grand Ayatallah Shaykh Muhammad al-ʿIthan al-Ahsaʾi) (Beirut: Dar al-Mahajja al-Bayda, 2011); Hasan al-Shaykh, *al-raʾis al-ʿIthan: tarjuma li-l-shaykh Muhammad al-ʿIthan bi-munasibat al-dhikra al-miʾawiyya al-ula ʿala rahilihi* (The Leader al-ʿIthan: A Biography of Shaykh Muhammad al-ʿIthan on the Occasion of the Remembrance of His Hundredth Deathday) (n.p.: Dar al-Mahajja al-Bayda/Dar Kumayl, 2010).

[77] Interview with Tawfiq al-Bu ʿAli, Kuwait, February 2012.

[78] For more on the *shaykhiyya* in Qatif see Al al-Talaqani, *al-shaykhiyya*; Ahmad ʿAbd al-Hadi al-Muhammad Salih, *aʿlam madrasat al-shaykh al-awhad fi al-qarn al-thalith ʿashr al-hijri* (Scholars of the School of the Unique Shaykh in the 13th Century A.H.) (Beirut: Dar al-Mahajja al-Bayda, 2006); al-Mushaykhas, *al-Qatif*, vol. 1, 538–51. For a more detailed account of the history of the Shaykhiyya in the Gulf see Toby Matthiesen, "Mysticism, Migration and Clerical Networks: Ahmad al-Ahsaʾi and the Shaykhis of al-Ahsa, Kuwait and Basra," *Journal of Muslim Minority Affairs* 34, no. 4 (2014).

[79] ʿAbd al-ʿAli Al Sayf, "qarn min tarikh al-qadaʾ fi al-Qatif" (A Century of the History of Jurisprudence in Qatif), *al-Waha* 20 (2001), 14–18, 14.

[80] Al-Amin, *aʿyan al-shiʿa*, vol. 8, 298f.

[81] The most important of them was ʿAbdallah Nasrallah, who gave up his post after the appointment of Abu ʿAbd al-Karim al-Khunayzi. Luʾi Muhammad Shawqi Al Sunbal, *al-shaykh al-Khunayzi: ʿaliman wa-zaʾiman* (Shaykh al-Khunayzi: Cleric and Leader) (n.p.: Manshurat Dar Wahi al-Qalam, 2004), 61; Muhammad al-Nimr, "qudat al-Qatif" (Judges of Qatif), *al-Waha* 21 (2001), 41–4, 41f.; ʿAli Baqir ʿAli al-ʿAwwami, "al-shaykh Abu ʿAbd al-Karim al-Khunayzi," *al-Waha* 20 (2001), 53–66, 54f.

[82] Muhammad al-Hirz, *al-taʿlim al-taqlidi al-mutawwaʿ fi al-Ahsa* (The Traditional "Mutawwa" Education in al-Ahsa) (Beirut: Dar al-Mahajja al-Bayda, 2001); Vidal, *Oasis*, 96.

in al-Ahsa in the early 1930s and ARAMCO played an important role in the expansion of education in the area.[83] In comparison to Najd and the Hijaz, the Eastern Province had far fewer schools, teachers and students until at least the 1970s.[84] The local *maraji'* operated local *hawzat* and had their own circle of students. Since 1913, however, and especially since 1927 the local *hawzat* declined and many closed down. The Qatifi cleric Mansur al-Marhun's (1877–1943) attempt to establish a *hawza* in the 1940s even led to his imprisonment.[85]

IBN SAUD'S CONQUEST OF AL-AHSA AND QATIF

In the early twentieth century, Ibn Saud strove to conquer al-Ahsa and Qatif, and he may have encouraged tribes to raid Shia settlements as early as 1908.[86] Because they feared tribal raids and the Saudi forces, and because they felt neglected by the Ottomans, several Shia notables petitioned the British in Bahrain to take the people of Qatif and Saihat under their protection. Shortly before Ibn Saud's move towards al-Ahsa and Qatif, the Shaykh of Saihat, Hussayn bin Nasir, approached the British authorities in Bahrain seeking 'to be under the protection of the British with his people under him who are 1500 his object being that if he gets any trouble from Turks, or Bedous [*sic*] or others, the British will help him.'[87] After Ibn Saud conquered Qatif, Hussayn bin Nasir reaffirmed his request in a formal letter, arguing that he and his people were caught up

---

[83] 'Abd al-Rahman bin 'Abdallah Thamir al-Ahmari, *dawr sharikat al-zayt al-'arabiyya al-amrikiyya (Aramku) fi tanmiyyat al-mintaqa al-sharqiyya min al-mamlaka al-'arabiyya al-su'udiyya: dirasa fi tarikh al-tanmiyya 1363–1384 AH/1944-1964* (The Role of the Arabian American Petroleum Company (Aramco) in the Development of the Eastern Province of the Kingdom of Saudi Arabia: A Study in the History of Development 1944–1964) (Riyadh: n.p., 2007), 269–321; Muhammad bin 'Abd al-Latif bin Muhammad Al Mulham, *kanat ashbah bi-l-jami'a: qissat al-ta'lim fi muqata'at al-Ahsa' fi 'ahd al-malik 'Abd al-'Aziz* (It Was Like a University: The Story of Education in the al-Ahsa District in the Era of King 'Abd al-'Aziz) (Riyadh: Darat al-Duktur Al Mulham li-l-Nashr wa-l-Tawzi', 1999); 'Abdallah ibn Nasir al-Subay'i, *al-haya al-'ilmiyya wa-l-thaqafiyya wa-l-fikriyya fi al-mintaqa al-sharqiyya 1930–1960* (The Scholarly, Cultural and Intellectual Life in the Eastern Province 1930–1960) (Riyadh: al-Dar al-Wataniyya al-Jadida, 1987).

[84] Ibrahim Mohamed al-Awaji, *Bureaucracy and Society in Saudi Arabia* (PhD, University of Virginia, 1971), 47f., 236–42.

[85] Al-Ahmad, *al-shaykh Hasan*, 76–9; Steinberg, *Religion*, 504f.

[86] IOR/L/PS/10/134: From Captain A. P. Trevor, Assistant Resident, Bushire, to S. H. Butler, Secretary to the Government of India in the Foreign Department, Simla, 7 September 1908.

[87] IOR: R/15/2/31: Yousuf bin Ahmed Kanoo to Major Trevor, Bahrain, 18 April 1913.

in 'absolute danger between the two sides' (the Ottomans and the Saudi forces). He also lamented the 'non-defence by our Ottoman Government for us'. In addition, he appealed to the common descent of people from the coast and Bahrain: 'You know of course the territory I am in, is Saihat and most of her inhabitants belong to Bahrein, and most of them are pearlers and pearl merchants and most of their trade is with Bahrein people [*sic*].'[88] Thereafter, in July 1913, 'Abd al-Hussayn bin Jum'a, the leader of the Shia in Qatif, also approached the British agent in Bahrain and asked to be under British protection.[89] The British declined all requests, arguing that they remained neutral in this dispute because the towns on the mainland were Ottoman territory.[90]

The British had at that point already implicitly accepted that Ibn Saud was going to incorporate al-Ahsa and Qatif into his realm. In May 1913, Ibn Saud moved with his armed forces to the East. He conquered Hufuf without fighting, after assembling the village headmen and tribal leaders outside the town and gaining their support.[91] Soon, the Turkish garrison surrendered and Ibn Saud sent Hasawi notables to the *mutasarrif*, who convinced him to admit defeat.[92] Shia sources claim that in 1913, an agreement was worked out between Ibn Saud and local Shia leaders, both in al-Ahsa and Qatif. The al-Ahsa agreement was made in a house of the Al Mulla, a local Sunni Hanafi notable family. The two Shia *maraji'*, Musa Abu Khamsin and Nasir al-Asha'i, were the representatives of the Shia of al-Ahsa in the negotiations with Ibn Saud.[93] The third *marji'* of al-Ahsa, Muhammad Al 'Ithan, had died a couple of months before the Saudi conquest.[94] Some also argue that Shia businessmen from al-Ahsa

---

[88] IOR: R/15/2/31: Translation of a letter dated 19 Jamadi II. 1331 (=26 May 1913) from Sheikh Husein bin Nasir of Saihat to Major A. P. Trevor, Political Agent, Bahrain.

[89] IOR: R/15/2/31: Political Agency, Bahrain to Lt. Colonel Sir Percy Cox, Political Resident in the Persian Gulf, 14 July 1913.

[90] IOR: R/15/2/31: Political Agency, Bahrain, to Lt. Colonel Sir Percy Cox, Political Resident in the Persian Gulf, 27 May 1913.

[91] Jacob Goldberg, "The 1913 Saudi Occupation of Hasa Reconsidered," *Middle Eastern Studies* 18, no. 1 (1982), 21–9; Steinberg, "Shiites;" Vassiliev, *The History*, 231–4.

[92] IOR: R/15/5/28: Political Agency Kuwait to the Political Resident, Bushire, 20 May 1913.

[93] *Al-Mawsim* 9–10 (1991), 461–75; al-Hasan, *al-shi'a*, vol. 1, 238f., 248; al-Hasan, *al-shi'a*, vol. 2, 12; Ibrahim, *Shi'is*, 25; Javadi et al., *dayerat al-ma'arif-i tashayyu'*, vol. 1, 503; 'Abd al-Rahman bin 'Uthman Al Mulla, *tarikh hajar: dirasa shamila fi ahwal al-juz' al-sharqi min shibh al-jazira al-'arabiyya: al-Ahsa', al-Bahrayn, al-Kuwayt wa-Qatar* (History of Hajar: A Comprehensive Study on the Situation of the Eastern Part of the Arabian Peninsula: al-Ahsa', Bahrain, Kuwait and Qatar), 2. vols. (Hufuf: Maktabat al-Ta'awun al-Thaqafi, 1990), vol. 1, 773–80; Steinberg, *Religion*, 495f.

[94] Al-Hasan, *al-shi'a*, vol. 1, 250.

may have supported Ibn Saud even before his capture of al-Ahsa because they suffered from frequent tribal raids.[95]

Thereafter, letters and delegations of Hasawi Shia notables were sent to Qatif to urge them and the Ottoman officials to accept Ibn Saud.[96] In Qatif, the Shia notables and clerics were divided over their stance towards the Saudi forces. At that time the notables of Qatif had not yet agreed upon a successor to the former leader of Qatif, Mansur bin Jum'a, who had died in 1912. The majority, amongst them 'Ali Abu 'Abd al-Karim al-Khunayzi, thought that resistance to the Saudis would not bear fruit. They urged the Ottoman garrison in Qatif not to resist Ibn Saud.[97] Hussayn bin Nasir, the Shaykh of Saihat who had earlier asked for British protection, also played a role in the negotiations between the Ottoman governor of Qatif and Ibn Saud's emissaries. This led the British to doubt his intentions even more.[98]

On the other hand, notables such as 'Abd al-Hussayn bin Jum'a and clerics such as Hasan 'Ali al-Badr (1861/2-1925/6) were advocating armed resistance against the Saudi forces.[99] 'Ali Abu al-Hasan al-Khunayzi, who was one of the most renowned scholars in Qatif, might also have been critical towards the Saudi forces. 'Ali Abu al-Hasan, called Abu al-Hasan, and 'Ali Abu 'Abd al-Karim al-Khunayzi, called Abu 'Abd al-Karim (see Picture 1.6), were two of probably five *mujtahids* in Qatif at the time. While Abu 'Abd al-Karim had been involved in social and political matters, Abu al-Hasan had focussed more on spiritual and religious issues. Although Abu 'Abd al-Karim was older than Abu al-Hasan, he was the latter's nephew.[100] Local historians disagree about which Qatifi scholars

---

[95] Al-Nuaim further argues that 'big Shi'i merchants have always maintained good or working relationships with the state'. Yet, Sunni merchants such as the al-Qusaybi were more important creditors of Ibn Saud and, in return, benefitted much more after 1913. Al-Nuaim, *State*, 309f.

[96] A British source suggests that 'messengers were also sent to Katif accompanied by Shiah notables and the chief Shiah Mujtahid in Hasa with a letter from the Mutaserif to the Kaimakam ordering him to surrender'. IOR: R/15/5/28: Political Agency Kuwait to the Political Resident, Bushire, 20 May 1913. See also al-Hasan, *al-shi'a*, vol. 2, 13.

[97] Al-'Awwami, "al-shaykh Abu 'Abd al-Karim," 56f.

[98] IOR: R/15/2/31: From Lt. Colonel Sir Percy Cox, Political Resident in the Persian Gulf to Major A. P. Trevor, Political Agent, Bahrain, 30 May 1913. See also IOR: R/15/2/31: Translation of a letter from the Shaikh of Saihat to Yusuf bin Ahmed Kanoo, Bahrain, 11th Jemadi II. 1331 (8 May 1913).

[99] Steinberg, *Religion*, 492f.

[100] Al-Amin, *a'yan al-shi'a*, vol. 8, 295–8; al-Bahrani, *anwar*, 302; al-Hasan, *al-shi'a*, vol. 1, 232; al-Shammari, *al-fihrist*, 124f.; Ibrahim, *Shi'is*, 264. In the historiography of the al-Khunayzi family, Abu 'Abd al-Karim is remembered as leader (*za'im*) al-Khunayzi, while

PICTURE 1.6. ʿAli Abu ʿAbd al-Karim al-Khunayzi.
Source: al-Sahil Archive.

were *mujtahids* at the time. They debate this point because a ruling by a *mujtahid* is seen as more authoritative than a ruling by a cleric who has not reached the rank of *mujtahid*.[101]

> Abu al-Hasan is remembered as Imam al-Khunayzi, emphasising his religious credentials. ʿAbdallah al-Khunayzi, *dhikra al-imam al-Khunayzi* (Remembrance of Imam Khunayzi), 2nd ed. (Beirut: al-Muʾassasa al-ʿAlamiyya li-l-Kitab, 1998), 241; Muhammad Saʿid al-Shaykh ʿAli al-Khunayzi, *al-ʿabqariyyu al-maghmur* (The Unknown Genius) (Beirut: Muʾassasat al-Balagh li-l-Tibaʿa wa-l-Nashr wa-l-Tawziʿ, 2003).

[101] This affects the importance of the opinions of different clerics regarding Saudi rule. Al-ʿUmran refers to Majid al-ʿAwwami, ʿAbdallah al-Maʿtuq and Hasan ʿAli al-Badr as the other *mujtahids* of Qatif. Al-Hasan mentions a number of other *mujtahids* such as Muhammad al-Nimr and ʿAli al-Jishi (1859/60–1956/7). Al-Mushaykhas also mentions ʿAli al-Jishi as a *mujtahid*. Al Sunbal mentions that Hasan ʿAli al-Badr acted as a *marjiʿ* before the return of Abu al-Hasan al-Khunayzi, to whom he directed his followers after the latter's return. Finally, al-Ahmad even argues that Hasan ʿAli al-Badr urged the people of Qatif to accept Abu al-Hasan al-Khunayzi as a *marjiʿ*, possibly to be more united in resistance to the Saudi forces. Luʾi Muhammad Shawqi Al Sunbal, *al-ʿallama al-Khatti: taʾrikh mushriq* (The Most Learned al-Khatti: Shining History) (n.p.: n.p., 1998), 142f.; al-Ahmad, *al-shaykh Hasan*, 101–4; al-Hasan, *al-shiʿa*, vol. 1, 232; al-Mushaykhas, *al-Qatif*, vol. 1, 591; al-ʿAwwami, "al-shaykh Abu ʿAbd al-Karim,"

But the advocates of resistance towards Ibn Saud did not manage to gain the upper hand and several hundred Shia emigrated, mainly to Bahrain and Iraq, amongst them Hasan 'Ali al-Badr.[102] 'Abd al-Hussayn bin Jum'a became a casualty of the changing times. After having asked the British for protection in mid-1913 he clashed with the new Amir of Qatif, who took over a coffee shop in Qatif that belonged to bin Jum'a in December 1913. In January 1914, a merchant from Karachi sent a representative to Bahrain to claim 19,000 Rials, which bin Jum'a allegedly owed him. Moreover, it seems that bin Jum'a and thirteen other notables of al-Ahsa had written to the Ottomans and urged them to reconquer the region. But Ibn Saud was sent these letters by a supporter and had bin Jum'a arrested in February 1914. Bin Jum'a remained in prison and Ibn Saud's troops started using his houses. In April 1914, Ibn Saud went to Qatif to meet the 'Nobles to whom he said that unless they gave him security that Turks will not make any trouble he would bring them the head of Abdul Hussayn bin Juma [*sic*], and if they gave the security he would release him.' In addition, 'Abdallah bin Jiluwi (d. 1938), the Amir of al-Ahsa resident in Hufuf, where bin Jum'a was imprisoned, asked him to pay the amount he owed to the Karachi trader. A Hasawi notable from the Al al-Sayyid Salman family, 'a man who counselled peace to people in Katif as they were against bin Saood when he took the place', sent the money to the Amir of al-Ahsa. Thereafter, the notable had to collect another 13,000 Rials in Qatif but bin Jum'a was still not released.[103]

These attempts at saving bin Jum'a demonstrate a certain solidarity and cooperation amongst the notables of Qatif and al-Ahsa. Nonetheless, bin Jum'a was publicly executed and all of his belongings confiscated by Ibn Saud. One of his gardens was given to the Amir of Qatif and another one, together with a significant amount of pearls, to 'Abdallah bin Hasan al-Qusaybi.[104] The descendants of the bin Jum'a family tried for more than a decade to get their properties back through various means. They, for example, sent petitions to Shaykh Khazal of Muhammara in Southern Iran, asking him for help as he was a fellow Shia and had good relations

---

63; al-'Umran, *al-azhar*, vol. 1, 79–89, 213–23, 335–45, 400f. For more on the clerics of the traditionalist trend in Qatif see 'Abdallah al-Khunayzi, *al-harakat al-fikriyya fi al-Qatif* (The Intellectual Movements in Qatif), 3 vols. (Beirut: Mu'assasat al-Balagh li-l-Tiba'a wa-l-Nashr wa-l-Tawzi', 2002), vol. 3.

[102] Steinberg, *Religion*, 495f.

[103] IOR: R/15/2/31: Report of Yusuf bin Ahmed Kanoo regarding Bin Saud's treatment of Abdul Hussain bin Juma.

[104] Ibid.

with the British.[105] In early 1923, notables from Bahrain asked the British authorities to intervene with Ibn Saud on behalf of the descendants of Mansur and 'Abd al-Hussayn bin Jum'a. They argued that the two had been 'of the town of Bahrein but residing at Katiff' and 'had immense properties at Katiff and Mesopotamia, and had also many charitable institutions'. The petition aims to speak in the name of the 'people of Katiff and Hassa (who through fear of being prosecuted by the Sultan of Nejd cannot openly join us in our appeal)' and states that 'the people of Bahrein Katiff Hass and Mesopotamia and Mujtahids (High Priests) [*sic*] from big and small' are urging the British government to take up this matter. The statement shows the influence and wealth of Qatifi merchants before 1913, as well as their links to Bahrain, the *marji'iyya* and their funding of *awqaf*.[106] Later in the same year, a suit was filed in the Joint Court in Bahrain to retrieve a house in Qatif that belonged to Mansur bin Jum'a.[107]

While the first decade of Saudi rule was difficult for Shia in Qatif and al-Ahsa, the worst period for them came in the late 1920s. In 1926, participants at a conference of the *ikhwan*, the tribal forces that had been the backbone of Ibn Saud's army, criticised Ibn Saud for not converting the Shia of al-Ahsa and Qatif. In early 1927, Ibn Saud met the leaders of the *ikhwan* in Riyadh in order to ease tensions with them. At the end of the meeting a fatwa was issued by the *'ulama'* that took into consideration key aspects of the *ikhwan*'s demands. The fatwa proscribed that the *'rafida'* of the al-Ahsa oasis had to convert to 'true Islam'. *Rafida*, which literally means rejectionist, is a derogatory but widely used term to describe Shia. The fatwa also demanded that their houses of worship be destroyed and that Wahhabi clerics be sent to the region. The fatwa was slightly less detailed on the treatment of the Shia of Qatif, but stated that they too should be enlightened by preachers sent into their districts and villages. Ibn Saud then implemented the fatwa and the Shia notables of al-Ahsa were forced to convert and pledge that they would hold their

---

[105] IOR: R/15/2/31: Extract of news report by Yusuf bin Ahmad Kanoo, 15 August 1914.

[106] IOR: L/P.S/11/232: To the Secretary of State for India, Bahrain 1. 3. 1923, 'Petition against the alleged ill treatment by Ibn Saud of certain residents in Qatif and Hasa'; the original of this letter with the signatures can be found at IOR: R/15/1/334.

[107] IOR: R/15/1/334: Major I. A., Political Agent, Bahrain to Political Resident in the Persian Gulf, Bushire, 29 September 1923. In December 1929 a group of Shia Notables, mainly from villages surrounding Qatif, wrote a letter to the British stating that they had assigned Shaykh Muhammad Sa'id, the son of 'Abd al-Hussayn bin Jum'a, as their deputy in any future negotiations with Great Britain. IOR: R/15/1/334: Petition from Muhammad Ali Al Jishi, 27 December 1929.

religious rituals according to Wahhabi teachings.[108] Ibn Saud sent a letter
to Abu ʿAbd al-Karim al-Khunayzi demanding the same from the people
in Qatif. It is not exactly known what happened with the notables of
Qatif, but, as a letter translated by the British in Bahrain states, 'all the
inhabitants of Qatif are one and combined not to surrender to the matter
he (bin Saud) wants even if they were to be killed'. A group of notables
from Qatif also tried to speak with Ibn Saud about the matter.[109] These
policies remained in place for about a year, until Ibn Saud moved militarily against the *ikhwan*. This campaign severely weakened one of the main
groups that had lobbied for this especially harsh treatment of the Shia.

The developments of 1927 showed the problems that the Shia notables
were facing when engaging with the state. Even though the large-scale
conversion of Shia was not a top priority anymore, the economic burdens
on the Shia actually increased. In 1929, a special jihad tax was levied to
finance Ibn Saud's struggle with the *ikhwan*. Together with the decline
of the pearl trade due to the international economic depression, this led
to major difficulties.[110] Triggered by the activities of Wahhabi missionaries and the introduction of this tax, Muhammad al-Nimr (1277–1348,
1860/1-1929/30), a cleric from Awwamiyya, who had opposed the agreement with Ibn Saud in 1913, led a local uprising against Saudi rule in
1929/30.[111] The main Qatifi notables sought to mediate and the uprising
eventually stopped.[112] The Shia *mujtahids* including Abu ʿAbd al-Karim
al-Khunayzi even issued a fatwa 'decreeing that the Shiʿis in Qatif should

---

[108] David Commins, *The Wahhabi Mission and Saudi Arabia* (London: I. B. Tauris, 2006),
75f.; Goldberg, "Shiʿi Minority," 236; al-Hasan, *al-shiʿa*, vol. 2, 146–55; al-Hatlani,
al-shiʿa, 133–5; Ibrahim, *Shiʿis*, 25–7; Steinberg, *Religion*, 497–505. For more on this
period see B. D. Hakken, "Sunni-Shia Discord in Eastern Arabia," *The Moslem World*
23 (1933), 302–5.

[109] They included ʿAbdallah bin Nasrallah, ʿAbdallah bin Rashid, Muhammad bin Hussayn
al-Faraj and Shaykh Mansur of Tarut. See IOR: R/15/2/1859: Abdallah bin Muhammad
Husain, Tarut, to Hajj Ahmad son of Hajj Ali bin Khamis, Sinabis (April 1927).

[110] Al-ʿAwwami, "al-shaykh Abu ʿAbd al-Karim," 57f. The British intercepted communications about an increase of the jihad tax in 1936. Anita L. P. Burdett, ed., *Saudi Arabia:
Secret Intelligence Records 1926–1939*, 8 vols. (Slough: Archive Editions, 2003), vol. 6:
1935–6, 711–30.

[111] Muhammad al-ʿAwwami, *thaʾir min ajl al-din: malamih min hayat al-ʿallama al-mujahid al-shaykh Muhammad bin Nasir al-Nimr* (A Revolutionary for the Sake of Religion:
Features of the Life of the Learned Fighting Shaykh Muhammad bin Nasir al-Nimr)
(London: Dar al-Jazira li-l-Nashr, 1987); *al-Thawra al-Islamiyya* 57 (January 1985),
38f.; Steinberg, *Religion*, 503.

[112] al-Hasan, *al-shiʿa*, vol. 2, 261; Steinberg, *Religion*, 503.

obey King Abdul Aziz and that the use of force against them [the Wahhabi missionaries] be prohibited'.[113]

Ibn Saud continued to employ a number of Ottoman officials, particularly those who were in charge of the Sultan's land (*amlak saniyya*) and some policemen. ʿAbdallah bin Jiluwi, the governor of al-Ahsa, had the Ottoman landholding registries translated into Arabic. The Ottoman system of tax farming, whereby the right to collect taxes for a certain period from a given area was sold to the highest bidder, remained in place for at least two decades. The nascent Saudi administration took over the Sultan's landholdings in Qatif and al-Ahsa and started to lease them out.[114] Some wealthy Shia benefitted from this system until it was reorganised. According to Hafiz Wahba, Ibn Saud had little experience of customs dues before he occupied al-Ahsa and so the customs revenues from Qatif were initially sold to 'a wealthy man in Qatif for £40,000' and in 1920 for £72,000.[115]

Theoretically, the Shia notables were in terms of social status the local equivalents of urban or tribal nobility in other areas of Arabia. In the first decades after 1913, 'state-society relations revolved around personalised contacts with the King and other senior members of the royal lineage'.[116] The Shia notables tried to maintain these contacts. They were the ones who met with and delivered petitions to the king and the governor. And yet, they were rarely appointed to important posts in the emerging bureaucracy. Notwithstanding some prominent exceptions, even Sunni Hasawis were less prominent in the bureaucracy than people from Najd and Hijaz.[117] Ibn Saud, who married many women from Arabian tribal nobility, including Eastern Arabian tribes such as the Bani Khalid, never married a Shia woman.[118] The role of the Shia notable families then diminished throughout the twentieth century as the expanding

---

[113] Ibrahim, *Shiʿis*, 28.

[114] Al-Subayʿi, *iqtisad*, 120; Hassan Hamza Hajrah, *Public Land Distribution in Saudi Arabia* (London: Longman, 1982), 20, 50; J. B. Mackie, "Hasa: An Arabian Oasis," *The Geographical Journal* 63, no. 3 (1924), 189–207, 192; Herbert Pritzke, *Bedouin Doctor: The Adventures of a German in the Middle East* (London: Weidenfeld and Nicolson, 1957), 213f.

[115] Al-Nuaim, *State*, 101; Hafiz Wahba, *Arabian Days* (London: Arthur Barker, 1964), 67.

[116] Al-Rasheed, *A History*, 86

[117] Al-Awaji, *Bureaucracy*, 52, 236–42. See also Muhammad bin Sunaytan, *al-nukhab al-suʿudiyya: dirasa fi al-tahawwulat wa-l-ikhfaqat* (The Saudi Elites: A Study of Transformations and Failures), 2nd ed. (Beirut: Markaz Dirasat al-Wahda al-ʿArabiyya, 2005), 70–3, 93, 140.

[118] Al-Rasheed, *A History*, 75–80.

bureaucracy took on many of their responsibilities.[119] While religion was the main obstacle for the Shia, their lack of tribal lineage contributed to their socio-political marginalisation.[120]

Saudi Arabia was initially made up of four main territories, later called districts, ruled by a governor (*amir*) directly responsible to the King: Najd, al-Ahsa, Hijaz, and Asir. Each city in al-Ahsa was ruled by a representative of the district governor.[121] The governors were usually trusted companions of Ibn Saud from Najd. 'Abdallah bin Jiluwi was after 1913 rewarded with the governorship of al-Ahsa (see Picture 1.7). He was a cousin and close associate of Ibn Saud and had played a key role in the capture of Riyadh in 1902. He remained district governor of al-Ahsa from 1913 until 1935 and was succeeded by his son, Sa'ud, who ruled until 1967. 'Abdallah dealt with internal security independently, ruled in disputes according to customary tribal law, and only took orders directly from the king.[122] This only changed in the late 1950s, when the administration became increasingly centralised.[123]

'Abd al-Rahman al-Suwaylim had led the forces that conquered Qatif in 1913 and was subsequently made governor of Qatif. Four other members of his family later succeeded him in the post.[124] It appeared that the post would become hereditary but in the aftermath of the rebellion in Awwamiyya in 1929/30, petitions by Ahmad al-Khunayzi and residents of Awwamiyya and Safwa led Ibn Saud to depose 'Abd al-'Aziz al-Suwaylim and his family as governors of Qatif in 1931.[125] Thereafter,

---

[119] Al-Awaji, *Bureaucracy*, 122f.; Hamza al-Hasan, *al-'amal al-matlabi fi mi'a 'am: tajribat 'amal wujaha' al-shi'a fi al-su'udiyya* (Hundred Years of Petitions: The Experience of Shia Notables' Work in Saudi) (n.p.: Dar al-Multaqa, 2010).

[120] Anderson, *Differential Urban Growth*, 264.

[121] Sa'ad al-Saud, *The Evolution of Local Government in the Kingdom of Saudi Arabia with Special Reference to the 1992 Reforms* (PhD, University of Reading, 2005), 76f.

[122] K. E. Evans, ed., *U.S. Records on Saudi Affairs 1945–1959*, 8 vols. (Slough: Archive Editions, 1997), vol. 3: Defense Affairs 1950–1954, 237; Mackie, "Hasa," 196. For a hagiography of 'Abdallah bin Jiluwi by a family member see Jawahir bint 'Abd al-Muhsin bin Jiluwi Al Su'ud, *al-amir 'Abdallah bin Jiluwi Al Su'ud wa-dawruhu fi ta'sis al-dawla al-su'udiyya al-thalitha* (Prince 'Abdallah bin Jiluwi Al Saud and His Role in the Foundation of the Third Saudi State) (Dammam: Matabi' al-Nimri, n.d.).

[123] Al-Awaji, *Bureaucracy*, 43–51; Evans, *U.S. Records*, vol. 5: Internal and Foreign Affairs 1955–1959, 537; Steffen Hertog, *Princes, Brokers, and Bureaucrats: Oil and the State in Saudi Arabia* (Ithaca, NY: Cornell University Press, 2010), 62.

[124] Philby, *Sa'udi*, 268; Muhammad 'Ali Salih al-Shurafa', *al-mintaqa al-sharqiyya min al-mamlaka al-'arabiyya al-su'udiyya: hadara wa-tarikh* (The Eastern Province of the Kingdom of Saudi Arabia: Civilization and History) (Dammam: Matabi' al-Madukhl, 1992), 313–15.

[125] Burdett, *Saudi Arabia: Secret*, vol. 1: 1926–1931, 419–21; al-Hatlani, *al-shi'a*, 138; Steinberg, *Religion*, 503.

PICTURE 1.7. Ottoman fort and palace of the governor of al-Ahsa, Hufuf.
Source: Dorothy Miller/Saudi Aramco World/SAWDIA.

members of important tribes and families from other areas, mainly Najd, held the post.[126]

THE SHIA COURT IN QATIF

With the influx of oil revenues, the creation of new oil towns, and the emergence of the Eastern Province as the economic powerhouse of Saudi Arabia in the 1950s, new courts were established and the court in Dhahran/Dammam became the highest court in the Eastern Province.[127] After 1913, it was decreed that courts in civil transactions should

[126] Al-Shurafa', *al-mintaqa*, 313–15.
[127] Steinberg, *Religion*, 505–9.

comply with the precepts of Hanbali sources, although the other three Sunni schools of law could also be consulted. There are major differences between Sunnis and Shia in how judicial opinions or rulings are inferred from the sources of jurisprudence. Shia jurisprudence is not generally accepted as a source of law in Saudi Arabia.[128] It is unclear whether Shia judges were officially appointed in the first decades of Saudi rule or whether they only operated with tacit approval of Ibn Saud and the governor of al-Ahsa, bin Jiluwi. Especially in al-Ahsa with its mixed Sunni-Shia population, it is likely that Sunni judges had even wider jurisdiction over the Shia population than in Qatif.

Nevertheless, Shia judges continued to rule amongst the Shia. Ibn Saud seems to have accepted Abu ʿAbd al-Karim al-Khunayzi as the Shia judge of Qatif. This was in line with Ibn Saud's policies in other parts of the country, where he would leave in charge the local leaders who did not oppose his rule. Al-Khunayzi remained the sole judge for Qatif Shia until 1925/26, when the Saudi rulers established the main court of Qatif and appointed Sayyid Ibrahim from the Sunni quarter of Tarut island, Darin, as head judge. They thereby maintained and institutionalised the dichotomy of powers between Shia and Sunni courts.[129] After the death of Abu ʿAbd al-Karim in 1943, Abu al-Hasan al-Khunayzi became *qadi* for around a year until he died in 1944. Many suggested that the *mujtahid* Majid al-ʿAwwami (1862/3-1947/8) should become the next *qadi*. But he declined because of bad health and encouraged Muhammad ʿAli al-Khunayzi to take over. Yet, al-Khunayzi was not a *mujtahid* and only remained *qadi* until 1947/8, when he was succeeded by the *mujtahid* ʿAli al-Jishi.[130] The latter had lived, studied and taught in Iraq for almost fifty years until he was encouraged to return to Qatif to become *qadi*.[131]

The al-Jishi family was also a notable and clerical family from *al-qalʿa* with marital bonds to other notable families such as the al-Khunayzi. Its wealth mainly stemmed from the pearl trade, in which the lay members of the family such as Muhammad Hasan al-Jishi (d.1921/22) and Mansur al-Jishi (d. 1941) engaged. They spent part of

---

[128] For background on the Saudi judicial system see Soliman A. Solaim, *Constitutional and Judicial Organization in Saudi Arabia* (PhD, Johns Hopkins University, 1970); Frank E. Vogel, *Islamic Law and Legal System: Studies of Saudi Arabia* (Leiden: Brill, 2000).

[129] Al-ʿAwwami, "al-shaykh Abu ʿAbd al-Karim," 56. Other sources say the *mahkamat al-shariʿiyya al-kubra* was founded in 1931. Al-Shurafaʾ, *al-mintaqa*, 335.

[130] Al Sunbal, *al-ʿallama al-khatti*, 33, 130; al-Shammari, *al-fihrist*, 147f.; al-ʿUmran, *al-azhar*, vol. 1, 258f.

[131] Al-Shammari, *al-fihrist*, 123f.; al-ʿUmran, *al-azhar*, vol. 2, 401–4.

PICTURE 1.8. Entrance to the Old City of Qatif.
Source: Dorothy Miller/Saudi Aramco World/SAWDIA.

their income on Shia religious festivities and the maintenance of students in Najaf. Their standing in the religious sphere was established through a number of clerics such as the *qadi* ʿAli al-Jishi as well as Muhammad ʿAli al-Jishi (1882/3-1942). The latter held a weekly *majlis* for the clerics and poets of Qatif and was in charge of the family's *awqaf* in Qatif.[132]

In response to pressure by Wahhabi *ʿulama*ʾ to downgrade the authority of the Shia court after the death of the two al-Khunayzi, Qatif Shia pressed for the institutionalisation of the Shia court.[133] This aim was achieved to a certain extent under Muhammad al-Mubarak, who was *qadi*

---

[132] Al-Mushaykhas, *al-Qatif*, vol. 1, 590–3; al-ʿUmran, *al-azhar*, vol. 5, 338–60.
[133] Al-Hasan, *al-shiʿa*, vol. 2, 337.

from 1956 until 1974.[134] Al-Mubarak was born in Safwa around 1900 and had studied in Iraq, where he became a *mujtahid*. Upon his return he led Friday prayers in the Rashid mosque in Safwa. Exemplifying the inter-marriage amongst Shia notable families, he married a daughter of Abu 'Abd al-Karim al-Khunayzi, the former *qadi* of Qatif.[135] The al-Mubarak family had a standing in Safwa similar to that of the notable families in Qatif. Unlike the Qatifi notable families, who were largely opposed to the Shia Islamist movements, however, a member of this family – Ja'far al-Mubarak – became a leader of the militant Islamist movement Hizbullah al-Hijaz in the late 1980s.[136] In 1963, a royal decree officially allowed Shia judges to rule on matters of inheritance and endowments amongst Shia.[137] Rulings were signed by the Ja'fari Sharia Court (*al-mahkama al-shari'iyya al-ja'fariyya*).[138] But when Muhammad al-Mubarak died in 1974, a new royal decree effectively reversed these policies and tried to transfer most of the competencies from the Shia court to ordinary courts.[139]

The Shia court once again became a major issue in discussions between Shia notables and the government. Because the judiciary in Saudi Arabia has traditionally been the realm of Wahhabi *'ulama'* and many of them view Shia courts as heretical, the issue of jurisdiction is crucial. Tensions between Shia and Wahhabi *'ulama'* become clearly visible in discussions over the Shia courts. In 1975 many prominent clerics and notables from Qatif sent a letter to Interior Minister and Crown Prince Fahd. The letter begins with the usual polite references and portrays the people of Qatif as part of the 'glorious Saudi people'. It recalls the early era of Saudi rule when the Shia judges could adjudicate amongst the Shia and when Ibn Saud had promised the Shia independence in their religious affairs. The

[134] Hasan al-'Awwami, "al-qada' al-shi'i fi al-Qatif: al-waqi' wa-l-tumuh," (Shia Jurisprudence in Qatif: Reality and Future) *al-Waha* 20 (2001), 43–6.

[135] Interview with a member of the al-Khunayzi family, London, July 2009. Al-Shammari, *al-fihrist*, 163. Muhammad Sa'id al-Khunayzi, however, disputes that al-Mubarak had studied in Iraq and argues that all his studies were completed in Qatif. He writes that his main teachers were 'Ali Abu al-Hasan al-Khunayzi and 'Ali Abu 'Abd al-Karim al-Khunayzi. He specifically refers to the book by al-Shammari and says that it does not mention sources to prove the claim that al-Mubarak studied abroad. See Muhammad Sa'id al-Shaykh 'Ali al-Khunayzi, *khuyut min al-shams: qissa wa-tarikh* (Strands of the Sun: Story and History) 2 vols. (Beirut: Mu'assasat al-Balagh li-l-Tiba'a wa-l-Nashr wa-l-Tawzi', 1999), vol. 2, 97–9.

[136] Matthiesen, "Hizbullah," 191.

[137] Al-Hasan, *al-shi'a*, vol. 2, 337; Ibrahim, *Shi'is*, 38.

[138] Al-'Awwami, "al-quda'."

[139] Al-Hasan, *al-shi'a*, vol. 2, 338.

signatories contrast this with the current situation, where 'in the eyes of those who rule us, we now do not judge according to what God has delivered, something that has become clear in the new regulations concerning the reform of the Shia courts. (...) Is the Shia *qadi* not a *qadi* for the Shia? Or are the Shia not a part of this kingdom who have the right that their confession (*madhhab*) be respected?'[140] Another letter argues that the text of these regulations hurt the dignity of the Shia and that it was puzzling why documents issued by Shia judges for 63 years should suddenly not be valid anymore.[141]

It was also not easy to choose a new successor for the downgraded court, as the Shia of Qatif were divided between those favouring the Akhbari 'Abd al-Majid Abu al-Makarim and those advocating the Usuli 'Abd al-Hamid al-Khatti. This is significant because Abu al-Makarim was one of the leaders of the Akhbari trend in Qatif and the surrounding villages.[142] Yet, the Usuli scholar al-Khatti, the son of Abu al-Hasan al-Khunayzi, managed to gain the upper hand and was appointed *qadi* of Qatif in 1975 by the Amir of the Eastern Province, 'Abd al-Muhsin bin Jiluwi.[143] One problem was, however, that although al-Khatti had studied in Najaf he was no *mujtahid*. He overcame this obstacle by asking several of his teachers, amongst them the Iraqi *marji'* Muhammad Baqir al-Sadr (1935–80), to write him a licence to act as a judge. The latter decreed that 'in absence of a *mujtahid* in your land' lesser-ranking scholars such as al-Khatti could also perform this task.[144]

---

[140] The letter is signed by amongst others the new *qadi* of Qatif, 'Abd al-Hamid al-Khatti, as well as by Faraj al-'Umran and Hasan al-'Awwami and reprinted in al-Hasan, *al-shi'a*, vol. 2, 487–91.

[141] Letter by notables and clerics of Qatif to the interior minister, 1976, reprinted in al-Hasan, *al-shi'a*, vol. 2, 492f. Dozens of petitions were sent to the king, the crown prince, the minister of interior, the minister of justice, the minister of municipal and rural affairs, other ministers and the governor of the Eastern Province regarding the issue of the Shia courts.

[142] The Abu al-Makarim family, which produced several Akhbari *'ulama'* such as Ja'far Abu al-Makarim (1864/5-1923/4), stems from Awwamiyya. 'Abd al-'Azim al-Mushaykhas, *al-'Awwamiyya: majdun wa-a'lam* (Awwamiyya: Honour and Symbols) (Beirut: Dar al-Khalij al-'Arabi li-l-Tiba'a wa-l-Nashr, 1999), 116–60, 202–5; al-Salih, *al-'Awwamiyya*, 330. See also 'Uqayl al-Maskin, "al-shaykh Sa'id Abu al-Makarim ba'd nisf qarn min al-khitaba al-diniyya" (Shaykh Sa'id Abu al-Makarim after Half a Century of Religious Preaching), *al-Waha* 20 (2001), 142–59, 150–4; 'Abd al-Qadir al-Shaykh 'Ali Abu al-Makarim, *al-kisa' fi ma 'arif al-umma al-islamiyya* (The Cloak: On the Knowledge of the Islamic Umma) (Beirut: Dar al-'Ulum li-l-Tahqiq wa-l-Tiba'a wa-l-Nashr wa-l-Tawzi', 2007), 55–63, 163–87, 197–200.

[143] Al Sunbal, *al-'allama al-khatti*, 131.

[144] Muhammad Baqir al-Sadr issued this in 1975, the year that al-Khatti became judge. Al-Khatti apparently also received a similar permission by Abu al-Qasim al-Khu'i,

While the court regained some of its competencies over the following years, many Shia refused to have their documents, land and *awqaf* registered under the new system.[145] In 1979, the Minister of Justice, Ibrahim bin Muhammad Al al-Shaykh, decreed that the 1974 regulations should be replaced by new ones and that 'affairs of *awqaf* and inheritance should be left to the Shia' and their *qadi*.[146] It was in 1980, shortly after the intifada, that the Shia court was renamed Court for Endowments and Inheritance in Qatif *(mahkamat al-awqaf wa-l-mawarith fi al-Qatif)* and officially founded by a royal decree from King Khalid.[147] The new court was narrowly defined to deal with *awqaf* and inheritance, and the integration into the Ministry of Justice subjected it to scrutiny from the higher-ranking Court of Appeals in Riyadh. The latter does not recognise Shia jurisprudence and disputed rulings by the Shia *qadis*, sometimes in arbitration cases between Sunni and Shia.[148] Henceforth, rulings on Shia *awqaf* and inheritance had to be published in local newspapers.[149] Fu'ad Ibrahim suspects that 'the subsequent restrictions on the Shi'i judicial authority suggest that both the royal family and the religious establishment were inclined to abandon Shi'i courts altogether.'[150]

This led to a new round of petitions and letters sent to ministers and the king, in which the Shia notables argued that if the Court of Appeals in Riyadh has higher jurisdiction than the Shia court in Qatif, then a Shia cleric should be appointed to this body.[151] Another contentious issue was that the court was downgraded to a court of secondary importance

---

although this is not preserved in writing. Ibid., 135f.; Lu'i Muhammad Shawqi Al Sunbal, *dhikra al-'allama al-khatti* (Remembrance of the Most Learned al-Khatti) (Beirut: Dar al-Awlia' li-l-Tiba'a wa-l-Nashr wa-l-Tawzi', 2005), 420, 428.

[145] Letter by the Vice-President of the Council of Ministers to the Minister of Municipal and Rural Affairs, 1979. From a private collection of letters and petitions by Shia notables, Saudi Arabia.

[146] Letter by the Minister of Justice, Ibrahim bin Muhammad Al al-Shaykh to the Minister of Municipal and Rural Affairs, 1979. From a private collection of letters and petitions by Shia notables, Saudi Arabia.

[147] Al-Shurafa', *al-mintaqa*, 340f.

[148] Several letters sent by branches of the Ministry of Justice such as the appeals committee *(hay'a tamayyiz)* in 1981/2. Private collection of letters and petitions by Shia notables, Saudi Arabia. See also al-Hasan, *al-shi'a*, vol. 2, 338–40.

[149] Al-Hasan argues that the Shia opposed this, while Al Sunbal claims that this underlined the official nature of the rulings and documents. Al Sunbal, *al-'allama al-khatti*, 133; al-Hasan, *al-shi'a*, vol. 2, 338.

[150] Ibrahim, *Shi'is*, 38.

[151] One letter mentions the following clerics as possible candidates for this post: 'Abdallah al-Khalifa and Hussayn al-Khalifa from al-Ahsa and 'Ali al-Sayyid Nasir from Dammam. Al-Hasan, *al-shi'a*, vol. 2, 339, 495–500.

(daraja b).[152] Despite these many difficulties, al-Khatti became a charismatic figure, whose standing helped to prevent the closing of the Shia court. He also worked as one of the main representatives (*wakil*, pl. *wukala'*) for the Iraqi-based *maraji'* such as Muhsin al-Hakim (1889–1970), Muhammad Baqir al-Sadr, Abu al-Qasim al-Khu'i (1899–1992) and since 1993/4 'Ali al-Sistani.[153] The court expanded and several other assistant judges and aides were hired.

THE SHIA COURT IN AL-AHSA

In al-Ahsa, Ibn Saud also accepted Shia judges, if not officially then at least implicitly. Musa Abu Khamsin (1878/9-1934/5) was *qadi* and had become a *marji'* after the death of Al 'Ithan in 1912/13. Unlike his father, Musa was not a Shaykhi, reflecting the diminished number of Shaykhis in al-Ahsa and establishing the family in the Usuli domain.[154] Shia authors claim that he was respected both under the Ottomans and under nascent Saudi rule. The governor of al-Ahsa, 'Abdallah bin Jiluwi, had told him, 'Judge, oh Shaykh Musa, and send to me whoever opposes your rulings'.[155] At the same time Hussayn al-'Ali worked as a Shia judge in Mubarraz. This indicates that the Saudi conquest led to the institutionalisation of this post. Al-'Ali held the position of judge unofficially for around ten years, was appointed officially in 1913 and remained in the post until 1950.[156]

His son, Muhammad al-'Ali (1902–68), began his studies in al-Ahsa in the *hawza* of the family and studied the highest level of *hawza* teaching, *bahth al-kharij*, with his uncle, Nasir al-Ahsa'i (d. 1939), from whom he received permission to carry out *ijtihad*. This trajectory was rather unusual because most students studied *bahth al-kharij*, which must be taught by a *mujtahid*, in Najaf or Karbala. Nasir al-Ahsa'i was one of the last local *maraji'* and so one of the last who taught these classes in al-Ahsa. Muhammad al-'Ali was one of the candidates to take over the *marji'iyya* in al-Ahsa after the death of Nasir al-Ahsa'i in 1939.[157] Yet, it

---

[152] Letter by Shia notables to King Fahd, 1983. Private collection of letters and petitions by Shia notables, Saudi Arabia.

[153] Al Sunbal, *al-'allama al-khatti*, 137–40; Al Sunbal, *dhikra*, 419–41.

[154] Al-Hasan, *al-shi'a*, vol. 1, 238f.; al-Hirz, *al-shaykh*, 33–6; al-Shakhs, *a'lam*, vol. 4, 41.

[155] Al-Hirz, "al-qada'," 22. This quote has to be assessed critically because of bin Jiluwi's reputation as a harsh ruler.

[156] Ibid. 24; al-Shakhs, *a'lam*, vol. 1, 545.

[157] Al-Shakhs, *a'lam*, vol. 4, 150–2.

seems that he was not widely accepted, and consequently no leader could be found amongst the clerics in Hufuf. Therefore, most Shia of al-Ahsa started to follow Habib bin Qurayn (1858/9-1944), a Hasawi *marji'* resident in Basra. Bin Qurayn was already a *marji'* for the Hasawis in Kuwait and Basra, and after 1939 moved to al-Ahsa. Bin Qurayn was in effect the last local *marji'* and thereafter the Shia of al-Ahsa followed the *maraji'* in Najaf, Karbala, Kuwait or Qom, further strengthening their transnational ties to these centres of learning.[158] Muhammad al-'Ali first studied in al-Ahsa and then in Najaf until 1942, when his father urged him to return to al-Ahsa to assist him in the Shia court. After his father's death in 1949/50 the Shia notables proposed him as the next judge. The Saudi rulers accepted him as *qadi* of al-Ahsa, a position he retained until his death in 1968/9.[159] His successors as *qadi* of al-Ahsa, Baqir Abu Khamsin (1914/15-1992/3) and Muhammad bin 'Abdallah al-Luwaymi (1942–), were amongst his students.[160]

The Shaykhis, whose numbers gradually declined but who continued to make up a significant part of the Shia in al-Ahsa, started to follow the *marji'iyya* of one of the families associated with the Tabrizi branch of the Shaykhiyya, the al-Usku'i family from present-day Iranian Azerbaijan. The first al-Usku'i *marji'* was Mirza Muhammad Baqir al-Usku'i (d. 1883), who took over the *marji'yya* after the death of his teacher Hasan Jawhar (d. 1849/50).[161] Descendants of the al-Usku'i family at times also resided in al-Ahsa. After completing his studies, Mirza 'Ali b. Mirza Musa al-Ha'iri al-Ihqaqi al-Usku'i (1886/7–1966/7) travelled to al-Ahsa and to other areas of the Gulf such as Iran and Iraq to meet the followers of his father. When Musa Abu Khamsin died in 1934/5, Mirza 'Ali, who was in Bahrain at the time, moved to Hufuf. He took over the supervision and training of *hawza* students in Hufuf around 1940. He founded a Shaykhi *hawza*, which was first located in the grounds of the Abu Khamsin *hawza* inside the Fawaris mosque and later moved to a building nearby.[162] Yet, Mirza 'Ali was compelled to leave after a dispute with local Shia *'ulama'*, who considered Shaykhi teachings to be un-Islamic. He took up residency in Kuwait and while the Shaykhi *hawza* in al-Ahsa closed down

---

158 Salman bin Hussayn al-Hijji, *sirat ayatallah al-shaykh Muhammad bin Salman al-Hajari* (The Biography of Ayatallah Shaykh Muhammad bin Salman al-Hajari) (n.p.: n.p., 2005/2006), 22; al-Shakhs, *a'lam*, vol. 1, 422-39; Steinberg, *Religion*, 487f.

159 Al-Hirz, "al-qada'," 24f.; al-Shakhs, *a'lam*, vol. 4, 170f.

160 Al-Shakhs, *a'lam*, vol. 4, 162f.

161 Al al-Talaqani, *al-shaykhiyya*, 196.

162 Al-Hirz, "al-hawzat wa-l-madaris."

temporarily, the al-Usku'i *maraji'* received regular visits by followers from al-Ahsa and were represented in al-Ahsa by a main *wakil*.[163]

The decline of local *hawzat* and the local *marji'iyya* made the shrine cities even more important. There, young students from al-Ahsa would meet and discuss in *majalis* and *diwaniyyat*, which were often organised by more senior Saudi scholars such as Ahmad al-Tahir (b. 1908).[164] Another Hasawi *diwaniyya* in Najaf was held in the house of the brothers Jawad and Baqir Abu Khamsin (1914/15-1992/3). Baqir Abu Khamsin studied in Najaf for around thirty-five years with scholars from al-Ahsa as well as with the *maraji'* Muhsin al-Hakim and Abu al-Qasim al-Khu'i.[165] During this time he became a *mujtahid* and a prolific writer for different Shia magazines such as the Lebanese *al-'Irfan*.[166] He also founded the cultural journal *al-Nadwa* (The Forum).[167] He and other Saudi clerics were also influenced by the nascent Islamic al-Da'wa Party (*hizb al-da'wa al-islamiyya*: hereafter *al-da'wa*). Upon his return to al-Ahsa in the mid-1960s, he founded a new mosque and several *hussainiyyat* in al-Ahsa and supported the family businesses, amongst others the Abu Khamsin Investment Company.[168] He was then appointed a member of a recently established appeals committee *(hay'a tamayyiz)* to the Shia judge in al-Ahsa. This committee, which was made up of a group of Shia *'ulama'*, dealt with problems in the courts and could negotiate with the bureaucracy in the Eastern Province.[169]

After the death of the *qadi* Muhammad al-'Ali, the governor of the Eastern Province appointed Baqir Abu Khamsin as Shia *qadi* of al-Ahsa in 1968. During his time in office, which lasted until his resignation in 1991/2, the court in al-Ahsa was officially established along the lines outlined previously for the court in Qatif.[170] Abu Khamsin became one of the

---

[163] Louër, *Transnational*, 49; Al al-Talaqani, *al-shaykhiyya*, 199f. For more on the al-Usku'i family see Mirza 'Abd al-Rasul al-Ha'iri al-Ihqaqi, *qarnan min al-ijtihad wa-l-marji'iyya fi usrat al-Ihqaqi* (Two Centuries of Ijtihad and Marji'iyya in the al-Ihqaqi Family) (Kuwait: Maktabat al-Imam al-Sadiq al-'Amma, n.d.), 129, 167, 175, 509–19.

[164] Al-Shakhs, *a'lam*, vol. 1, 310–16.

[165] Al-Hirz writes that he was born in 1917/18. Al-Hirz, *al-shaykh*, 5; al-Shakhs, *a'lam*, vol. 3, 355.

[166] Al-Hirz, *al-shaykh*, 106.

[167] Seven issues of the journal were published around 1950/1. The managing editor of the magazine was 'Abd al-Hadi al-Fadli and the editor in chief 'Abd al-Amir al-Ghafari. Ibid., 81f.

[168] Ibid., 100.

[169] The other members were Sadiq al-Khalifa and Hussayn al-Shawaf. Al-Hijji, *sirat ayatallah*, 52f., al-Hirz, "al-qada'," 33f.

[170] Al-Hirz, *al-shaykh*, 90–5; al-Shakhs, *a'lam*, vol. 3, 354–449.

main interlocutors between the government and the Shia in al-Ahsa. He, for example, co-operated with the Prince Sultan Benevolent Society to distribute suburban land in the village of al-'Uyun.[171] He became integrated into the neo-patrimonial political economy in Saudi Arabia because of the importance of his family, his clerical rank, and his contacts with the ruling family. Yet, during his time in office the Shia judicial system lost an important institution. Although he had elected his own group of clerics to the appeals committee, it was dissolved shortly after the intifada of 1979 upon request of the Council of the Committee of Senior 'Ulama', the high-ranking religious body dominated by Wahhabi clerics.[172]

Although his son, Hasan, was expected to become his successor, Muhammad al-Hajari (1916/17-2004/5) became the next *qadi* in 1991/2.[173] His appointment came in response to a letter by Hasawi notables to King Fahd in this regard.[174] In his youth, he had studied in the Shaykhi *hawza* founded by Mirza 'Ali al-Ihqaqi in Hufuf.[175] Al-Hajari continued his studies in Karbala because of the strong links of the Hasawi Shaykhis to Karbala. In Karbala he attended classes of Hasawi *maraji'* such as 'Ali Al 'Ithan, the son of the former Shaykhi *marji'* in al-Ahsa, and studied Shaykhi teachings with Muhammad Hadi al-Milani. He also studied with Mahdi al-Shirazi and received permission to carry out *ijtihad* from Muhammad al-Shirazi, the spiritual leader of the *shirazi* movement.[176]

In return, many other important *shiraziyyun* such as Sadiq al-Shirazi, Hasan al-Shirazi, Muhammad Taqi al-Mudarrisi and Hadi al-Mudarrisi later studied with al-Hajari. Yet, al-Hajari was careful not to voice his support for the Shaykhiyya or the *shiraziyyun* publicly and argued that he did not support the separation of the Twelver Shia into different factions.[177] Arguably, al-Hajari could have become a local *marji'* and he did not become *wakil* of a major *marji'* until 1997/8, when he became *wakil* of 'Ali al-Sistani.[178] This is an indication that he considered himself

---

[171] Al-Hirz, *al-shaykh*, 100.

[172] The members of the Shia Appeals Committee during this time were the later *qadi* Muhammad al-Hajari, 'Abdallah al-Khalifa, 'Ali al-Sayyid Nasir and Muhammad 'Ali al-'Ali. Al-Hijji, *sirat ayatallah*, 52f.; al-Hirz, "al-qada'," 34.

[173] Al-Hijji, *sirat ayatallah*, 54f.

[174] The notables sign the letter with 'your sons'. Ibid., 55, 128.

[175] Ibid., 14; al-Hirz, "al-hawzat."

[176] Al-Hijji, *sirat ayatallah*, 17.

[177] Ibid., 24–26, 33–5.

[178] Ibid., 22f. For an interview with al-Hajari see Salman bin Hussayn al-Hijji, *hakadha wajadtuhum* (This Is how I Found them) (Beirut: Jawatha li-l-Nashr, 2008), 291–6.

capable to make his own rulings and some call him *ayatallah*.[179] He symbolises the closeness between the Shaykhiyya and the *shiraziyya*, which was fostered by the interaction between both groups in Kuwait and Saudi Arabia.[180]

CONCLUSION

By the nineteenth century a status group of Shia notables had developed in Qatif and al-Ahsa. At times, these notables wielded considerable influence, ruling the area together with Ottoman officials. The Ottomans accepted the Shia elite and left religious matters to Shia clerics. Through these policies, Ottoman rule fostered a sense of collective identities amongst Qatifis and Hasawis. These collective identities were then reinforced as distinctively religious identities in response to the repression of Shia religiosity after 1913. As in the Ottoman provinces of the Levant, the Shia courts under Ottoman rule were not formally recognised, and after 1913 there were constant debates over the jurisdiction of the Shia courts. Even though in the twentieth century their authority became largely confined to personal status law, these courts were crucial in the everyday construction of sectarian identities. As in Lebanon, therefore, the courts were key in galvanising Shia collective identities, which partly pre-dated the development of Shia Islamist movements with their Shia identity politics.[181]

Since 1913 the notables tried to work within the framework of the Saudi state. Their uneasy relationship with the state was exemplified in the institution of the Shia court, whose judges formed the core of the clerical and at times political leadership of the Shia areas. The debates about the Shia courts focus on the question whether the Saudi state, which bases much of its legitimacy on the Wahhabiyya and a Hanbali legal tradition, accepts the Shia school of jurisprudence as a valid form of *fiqh*. This question has repercussions for sectarian relations way beyond Saudi Arabia. As the judiciary is one of the key fields in which a state

---

[179] "Al-Ahsa' tahtafilu bi-iftitah hawzat ayatallah al-shaykh Muhammad al-Hajari li-l-'ulum al-diniyya" (Al-Ahsa Celebrates the Opening of the Hawza Ayatallah Shaykh Muhammad al-Hajari for Religious Sciences), *Rasid*, 18 March 2009.

[180] For a discussion of the rapprochement between the two schools see Rivka Azoulay, *Entre marchands, effendi et l'Etat: changement social et renouvellement des élites au sein de la communauté chiite koweitienne* (MA, Institute d'Etudes Politiques de Paris, 2009), 49f.

[181] Max Weiss, "Institutionalizing Sectarianism: The Lebanese Ja'fari Court and Shi'i Society under the French Mandate," *Islamic Law and Society* 15, no. 3 (2008), 371–407.

asserts its authority, the ruling family always found it difficult to justify the appointment of Shia judges to Wahhabi *'ulama'*. The issue of the Shia courts, then, became an early cornerstone of Shia identity politics, exemplified by the petitions of Shia notables. Through appointment to the courts, the state managed to strengthen a group of relatively loyal Shia clerics who accept the legitimacy of the state. These Shia judges and their families, some of whom were non-political Shaykhis and Akhbaris, became integrated into the patron-client relationships of the Saudi political economy. As one senior Saudi prince put it: 'These families became very rich, but there was a limit.'[182]

After the decline of the local *marji'iyya*, these notable-clerical families mainly followed the mainstream *maraji'*, which sought a spiritual role for the clergy rather than a political one. These *maraji'* usually refrained from involvement in local politics, thus giving their representatives considerable autonomy. It is this socio-political and religious setting, together with the rivalry amongst the *maraji'*, that turned the Shia Islamist movements against their own political elite as well as against the state. The Shia Islamists of the 1970s, then, became followers of Muhammad Mahdi al-Shirazi, while the ones that would form Khat al-Imam became followers of Muhammad Baqir al-Sadr and Ruhollah Khomeini. Many notables, on the other hand, became leftists, bureaucrats, and businessmen and abandoned clerical education. This opened up the clerical field to new groups, largely drawn from non-notable families. Therefore, the politics of Shia notables influenced who would become active in leftist movements and who would be drawn into Shia Islamist movements.

The view of the Shia as a religious group led by clerics, and their role as judges – effectively the only job reserved for a Shia in Saudi Arabia – also led to a strengthening of the clerical caste. Heightened religious anxiety and conflicts with the Wahhabi clerics also reinforced the Shia clerics' standing amongst their village- and quarter-based networks of piety and patronage. The clerics and notables then had an interest that Shia would define themselves as Shia, and that the state would continue to see them as such. Otherwise their role would become obsolete. So state policies strengthened sectarianism, both by discriminating against Shia Muslims on religious grounds as well as by dealing with them through their "traditional" elites.

---

[182] Interview with a senior member of the Saudi ruling family, United States, November 2009.

2

Oil and Dissent

> When I was a kid, Nasser's pictures were everywhere; I thought he was our king!
>
> Former Saudi opposition activist, Eastern Province,
> November 2008

American companies signed the first oil concession agreement with Saudi Arabia in 1933.[1] The subsequent discovery of oil in 1938 profoundly transformed the lives of the inhabitants of al-Ahsa and Qatif. It led to urbanisation, industrialisation, the disruption of traditional forms of livelihood, the influx of migrant workers and the integration of Saudi Arabia into the American sphere of influence.[2] The agricultural population decreased, as many people saw agriculture as a less profitable source of income. Date production, which was only labour intensive at certain times of the year, lost its dominant position in the economy of the Eastern Province. The date price collapsed between 1948 and 1952, not least because the local population started importing food from abroad. Even though prices slightly recovered after a ban on the export of dates imposed in 1940 was lifted in 1952, this trend could not be reversed.[3]

---

[1] The initial agreement was signed by Standard Oil Company of California, which shortly afterwards became the California Arabian Standard Oil Company and in 1944 was renamed the Arabian American Oil Company (ARAMCO). Jones, *Desert Kingdom*, 259.

[2] See, for example, 'Abdallah ibn Nasir al-Subay'i, *iktishaf al-naft wa-atharuhu 'ala al-haya al-ijtima'iyya fi al-mintaqa al-sharqiyya 1933–1960* (The Discovery of Oil and its Influence on Social Life in the Eastern Province 1933–1960) (Riyadh: al-Dar al-Watani-yya al-Jadida, 1987).

[3] Hajrah, *Public*, 183f.; Don E. Totten, *Erdöl in Sa'udi-Arabien* (Heidelberg: Keyser, 1959), 130–3; Vidal, *Oasis*, 192–6.

PICTURE 2.1. Date farmer in Qatif.
Source: Dorothy Miller/Saudi Aramco World/SAWDIA.

Owning a date garden remained important as a status symbol for notable families but no longer as a main source of economic revenue (see Picture 2.1).[4]

Together with these structural changes, ideas of revolutionary socialism, communism, Arab nationalism and a general sense of anticolonialism spread to Eastern Arabia. Migrant workers, students returning from abroad, and newspapers filled with Arab nationalist and leftist ideas created the basis for widespread political mobilisation. Radical ideas that had spread beyond the centres of empire in the late nineteenth and early twentieth centuries[5] interacted with the social structures and

---

[4] Vidal, "Date," 427.
[5] Ilham Khuri-Makdisi, *The Eastern Mediterranean and the Making of Global Radicalism, 1860–1914* (Berkeley: University of California Press, 2010).

sectarian make-up of the Gulf. Many of these ideas and publications arrived through the British protectorate island of Bahrain, which had had an earlier tradition of anti-colonial activism and where clandestine networks, civil society organisations, and a radical press flourished since the first half of the twentieth century.[6]

Major strikes at the Arabian American Oil Company (ARAMCO) involved thousands of manual laborers from the Eastern Province, as well as migrant workers from other areas of the Kingdom and abroad. Discourses and networks of Arab nationalism and communism in the region became related to the struggle of Saudi Shia against religious and political discrimination. Many members and cadres of the clandestine opposition groups that formed after these strikes consisted of natives from the Eastern Province.[7] Interestingly, it was from the local upper class of Shia notable families that many of these activists were drawn.

A SAUDI WORKERS MOVEMENT

From the mid-1930s onwards, Saudis started to work mainly as non-skilled labourers in the oil industry. Then, Saudis were educated in ARAMCO schools and given scholarships by ARAMCO and the government to study abroad. Many Shia later occupied medium-level technical and clerical positions in the company, although few reached top managerial positions.[8] While the American employment policies were segregationist along national lines, they did not distinguish between sects. A former chairman recalled that they were 'colour-blind' in their employment of Shia who did jobs the Bedouins refused to do.[9] That does not mean, however, that the company did not know who was Shia and who was Sunni. In fact, the Arabian Affairs Division, the research and intelligence gathering unit of the company, carried out several in-depth studies of Shia communities and was aware of religious discrimination and animosities

---

[6] Fuccaro, *Histories*, 151–90.

[7] Asad AbuKhalil, *The Battle for Saudi Arabia: Royalty, Fundamentalism, and Global Power* (New York: Seven Stories, 2004), 165. For a more detailed account of leftist and nationalist opposition groups in the Eastern Province see Toby Matthiesen, "Between Communism, Nationalism and Islam: Labour Movements and Opposition Groups in Saudi Arabia, 1950–1975," *International Review of Social History* 59, no. 3 (Autumn 2014).

[8] Mordechai Abir, *Saudi Arabia: Government, Society and the Gulf Crisis* (London: Routledge, 1993), 17; David Holden and Richard Johns, *The House of Saud* (London: Sidgwick and Jackson, 1981), 531; Ibrahim, *Shi'is*, 111–17.

[9] Michael Field, *The Merchants: The Big Business Families of Saudi Arabia and the Gulf States* (New York: Overlook Press, 1985), 211.

between members of the two sects. Workers had to state whether they were Sunni or Shia on forms of the company's medical center. Especially Shia employees were vehemently opposed to this practice since they felt it would make government discrimination against them easier. But they were also appalled that the company would ask for this kind of information, and one Shia employee complained, 'Why do these foreigners ask whether I am a Sunni or a Shi'i? I am a Muslim, as all believers are Muslims.'[10] From the 1960s onwards, Shia workers in ARAMCO became a new Shia 'petite bourgeoisie'.[11] Shia initially constituted at least a quarter of the Saudi workforce[12] and in 1979 made up more than half of the twenty-two thousand Saudi employees.[13]

Saudi politics in the 1950s and 1960s was characterised by rivalries within the ruling family. Saud took over the throne from his father in 1953 but was challenged by his half brother, Crown Prince Faysal. The latter became more powerful from 1958 onwards and finally ascended the throne in 1964 (and reigned until he was assassinated by a nephew in 1975).[14] As in other parts of the Arab world, the impact of the Egyptian Revolution of 1952 and the nationalisation of the Suez Canal in 1956 was strong. Members of the educated Shia elite, for example, wrote poems hailing 'Abd al-Hakim 'Amr, who was the Egyptian commander during the Suez Crisis in 1956: 'Oh 'Abd al-Hakim you Leader of the Arabs, lead us forward to the Battlefield'.[15] Nasser was popular amongst many Saudis, particularly in the Eastern Province and the Hijaz, and some Saudi activists started to adopt Nasserism as a political ideology.[16] Partly to stave off this challenge and to prevent republican and anti-colonial

[10] *Shi'ite Muslims, Eastern Province*, Dhahran, 11 October 1958, Box 2, Folder 61, Mulligan Papers.

[11] Abir, *Saudi Arabia: Government*, 17; Louër, *Transnational*, 42.

[12] Goldberg, "Shi'i Minority," 237.

[13] Salameh and Steir, "Political Power," 21.

[14] See Sarah Yisraeli, *The Remaking of Saudi Arabia: The Struggle between King Saud and Crown Prince Faysal, 1953–1962* (Tel Aviv: Moshe Dayan Center for Middle Eastern and African Studies, 1997).

[15] Poem by Hasan Faraj al-'Umran: *Sawt al-Tali'a* 7 (1974), 57.

[16] Ahmad 'Adnan, *al-sajin 32: ahlam Muhammad Sa'id Tayyib wa-haza'imhu* (Prisoner 32: The Dreams of Muhammad Sa'id Tayyib and his Defeats) (Beirut: Markaz al-Thaqafi al-'Arabi, 2011); Nur al-Din bin al-Habib Hajlawi, *ta'thir al-fikr al-nasiri 'ala al-khalij al-'arabi 1956–1971* (The Impact of Nasserist Thought on the Arabian Gulf 1956–1971) 2nd. ed. (Beirut: Markaz Dirasat al-Wahda al-'Arabiyya, 2010), 83–148; Yusuf Makki, "al-haraka al-nasiriyya fi al-'arabiyya al-su'udiyya" (The Nasserist Movement in Saudi Arabia), in *al-ahzab wa-l-harakat wa-l-tanzimat al-qawmiyya fi al-watan al-'arabi* (The Nationalist Parties, Movements and Organisations in the Arab Homeland), ed. Muhammad Jamal Barut (Beirut: Markaz Dirasat al-Wahda al-'Arabiyya, 2012), 672–80.

movements from spreading across the Arabian Peninsula, Saudi Arabia would in the 1960s fight a proxy war against Egypt in Yemen.[17]

Influenced by Nasserism and Arab nationalism, many workers in the Eastern Province came to see the U.S. presence, symbolised by the American airbase at Dhahran and by ARAMCO, as imperialism. As ARAMCO was the biggest employer in the Kingdom, workers' grievances started to be expressed there most vocally. American employees lived in what was called the 'American Camp' in Dhahran, which by 1950 had developed into a segregated town, separated by barbed wire from the 'Saudi Camp' for Saudi and Arab workers. While the American Camp had many amenities, the Saudi Camp was much less equipped and, in 1950, lacked water, power and sewers.[18]

While Saudi employees were initially mainly unskilled workers, Palestinians, Syrians, Egyptians, Lebanese, Italians, Indians and others immigrated to the Eastern Province to perform semi-skilled work. These expatriate workers intermingled with Saudis and introduced ideas of pan-Arabism, Nasserism and socialism. The major labour mobilisations at ARAMCO occurred in 1945, 1947, 1953 and 1956.[19] The strikes in the 1950s were organised by Saudis and Arab expatriates.[20] The support

---

[17] Saeed M. Badeeb, *The Saudi-Egyptian Conflict over North Yemen 1962–1970* (Boulder, CO: Westview Press, 1986).

[18] Robert Vitalis, *America's Kingdom: Mythmaking on the Saudi Oil Frontier*, 2nd ed. (London: Verso, 2009), 62–112.

[19] The strikes are widely discussed in James Buchan, "Secular and Religious Opposition in Saudi Arabia," in *State, Society and Economy in Saudi Arabia*, ed. Tim Niblock (London: Croom Helm, 1982), 106–124, 111–13; Michael Sheldon Cheney, *Big Oilman from Arabia* (London: Heinemann, 1958), 260–75; Evans, *U.S. Records*, vol. 4: Internal Affairs 1955–1958 (Slough: Archive Editions, 1997), 33–367; Robert L. Jarman, ed., *Political Diaries of the Arab World: Saudi Arabia 1919–1965*, 6 vols., vol. 6: *Periodic Despatches and Annual Reviews 1941–1965* (Slough: Archive Editions, 1998), 192f.; Tawfiq al-Shaykh, *al-batrul wa-l-siyasa fi al-mamlaka al-ʿarabiyya al-suʿudiyya* (Oil and Politics in the Kingdom of Saudi Arabia) (London: Dar al-Safa li-l-Nashr wa-l-Tawziʿ, 1988), 326–50; Penelope Tuson and Anita Burdett, eds., *Records of Saudi Arabia: Primary Documents 1902–1960*, 10 vols. (Slough: Archive Editions, 1992), vol. 8: 1946–1953, 735–53; Vassiliev, *The History*, 336–40; Vitalis, *America's Kingdom*, 92–8, 145–84. Tawfiq al-Shaykh is a pseudonym for Tawfiq al-Sayf.

[20] Nasir al-Saʿid, who was originally from Hail in the north of the country, was one of the leaders of the strikes and a founding member of the National Reform Front (*jabhat al-islah al-watani*). He escaped Saudi Arabia to Damascus after the 1956 strike and founded the Nasserist Union of People of the Arabian Peninsula (*ittihad shaʿb al-jazira al-ʿarabiyya*). In 1979 he claimed to have masterminded the takeover of the Grand Mosque in Mecca and disappeared in Beirut later the same year. Opposition accounts generally state that he was killed by Saudi intelligence with the help of an armed Palestinian group. Abir, *Saudi Arabia: Government*, 35f.; Nasir al-Saʿid, *tarikh Al*

PICTURE 2.2. Gas station in Qatif.
Source: Dorothy Miller/Saudi Aramco World/SAWDIA.

for the strikes was cross-sectarian.[21] Leftist and Shia Islamist opposition groups later hailed these events as 'popular revolutions and uprisings against the Al Saud'.[22]

Su'ud (The History of Al Saud) (Beirut: Ittihad Sha'b al-Jazira al-'Arabiyya, 1984); Nasir al-Sa'id, *haqa'iq 'an ... al-qahr al-su'udi* (Truths about ... Saudi Oppression) (London: al-Safa li-l-Nashr wa-l-Tawzi', 1988), 73–85, 151–3; Evans, *U.S. Records*, vol. 4, 661f.; J. E. Peterson, *Historical Dictionary of Saudi Arabia* (Metuchen, NJ: Scarecrow Press, 1993), 119f.; *al-Thawra al-Islamiyya* 34 (February 1983), 16f.

[21] Some scholars have overstated the Shia factor in the strikes: Fandy argues that 'most of this protest came from the Shi'a population of the Eastern Province', and Kechichian even calls the strikes 'Shia uprisings'. Fandy, *Saudi Arabia*, 44; Joseph A. Kechichian, *Succession in Saudi Arabia* (New York: Palgrave Macmillan, 2001), 97f.

[22] See this article in the OIRAP mouthpiece: *al-Thawra al-Islamiyya* 71 (February 1986), 20.

The distribution of 'communist inspired pamphlets'[23], informal study circles, libraries, and the establishment of newspapers and cultural journals led to a new atmosphere of political awareness in the Eastern Province. In the late 1940s, a number of educated Shia notables from Qatif such as Hasan al-Jishi, 'Abdallah al-Jishi and 'Abd al-Ra'uf al-Khunayzi decided to form *jami'iyyat al-'ilm li-l-nidal* (Knowledge Society for the Struggle). This secret organisation wanted to educate and build cadres and was known publicly as *lajnat tashji'a al-tullab* (Committee for the Advancement of Students). The committee opened a centre in Qatif with a library of 'progressive' literature, the first evening school in the area and a theatre. In these facilities *jami'iyyat al-'ilm li-l-nidal* tried to spread its ideas through gatherings, lectures and plays. Although the centre was shut down after just seven months, *jami'iyyat al-'ilm li-l-nidal* continued to operate secretly and was behind the Qatif public library that was periodically closed and reopened throughout the 1950s and 1960s.[24]

Jami'iyyat al-'ilm li-l-nidal started cooperating with young activists in Jubail in 1950, and they legally published a number of issues of *al-Fajr al-Jadid* (The New Dawn) in 1955. The paper was closed down after its editor, Yusuf al-Shaykh Ya'qub, had offended the interior minister.[25] Those behind *al-Fajr al-Jadid* also established the Dammam public library, for which they secured donations from ARAMCO, in 1955.[26] In 1953, one of those behind *jami'iyyat al-'ilm li-l-nidal* had wanted to establish a newspaper called *al-Jazira* (The Island) but was not allowed to do so by the authorities.[27] This was part of a relatively free, albeit short-lived press in the Eastern Province in the mid-1950s that also included *Akhbar al-Dhahran* (Dhahran News) and *al-Ish'a'* (The Shining Light), which was published in Khobar from 1955 to 1957.[28]

This press, particularly the cultural journal *al-Ish'a'*, was influenced by earlier publications in Bahrain such as *Sawt al-Bahrayn* (Voice of Bahrain). This journal, published from 1950 to 1954, had become a rallying point for Arab nationalist writers from the Gulf, including Saudi

[23] Evans, *U.S. Records*, vol. 2: *Internal and Foreign Affairs 1950–1954*, 621–25; Jarman, *Political Diaries*, vol. 6, 213.

[24] *Sawt al-Tali'a* 1 (1973), 23f.; 8 (1974), 52–62.

[25] Evans, *U.S. Records*, vol. 4, 250.

[26] H. C. Mueller, *The Dammam Public Library*, Dammam, 17 July 1955, Mulligan Papers, Box 2, Folder 48.

[27] *Sawt al-Tali'a* 1 (1973), 24.

[28] See the facsimile: *al-ish'a': majalla shahriyya adabiyya ijtima'iyya* (The Shining Light: A Social and Literary Monthly Magazine) (Riyadh: Dar al-Mufradat li-l-Nashr wa-l-Tawzi', 2010).

Shia authors such as Muhammad Sa'id al-Muslim and 'Abd al-Rasul ('Abdallah) al-Jishi. It was circulated throughout the Gulf and featured articles about the Eastern Province, including the labour mobilisation at ARAMCO.[29] *Sawt al-Bahrayn* served as a 'launching pad' for the cross-sectarian nationalist political movement in Bahrain, the High Executive Committee (*al-hay'a al-tanfidhiyya al-'uliya*). This committee became the driving force of popular protests in Bahrain, and it had a strong impact on the Saudi leftists. Indeed, the activists in Saudi closely followed political developments in Dubai, Kuwait, and Bahrain, where urban riots occurred, anti-colonial movements flourished and some pushed for the establishment of elected parliaments.[30] Bahrain also served as a base for the organisation of strikes and protests in the Eastern Province and the strengthening of clandestine networks.[31]

These newspapers were filled with letters and editorials discussing the Arab Nation and local grievances. The 'appropriation of Arab nationalism' increasingly became a 'framework for criticizing the Saudi state and critiques of development'.[32] These critiques included articles and letters written by Shia complaining about the neglect of their areas in comparison with the newly founded oil towns Dammam, Dhahran, and Khobar. As early explorations took place in areas remote from the established settlements, new settlements for expatriate and Saudi workers were built. When the administrative seat of the Eastern Province was moved from Hufuf to Dammam in 1953, Hufuf experienced a relative decline and many Hasawis moved to Dammam.[33] This was reinforced by the crisis of the date market, which had hitherto played an important role in the economic life of the region. In early January 1956, a delegation of Hasawi notables went to see King Saud to discuss the deteriorating economic situation in the al-Ahsa oasis due to the decline of the date market.[34] Over the coming decades, the three new towns Dammam, Dhahran and

[29] Muhammad 'Abd al-Rizzaq al-Qasha'mi, *al-kuttab al-su'udiyyun fi majallat (Sawt al-Bahrayn) 1369–1373* (The Saudi Writers in the Magazine (Voice of Bahrain) (Riyadh: Dar al-Mufradat li-l-Nashr wa-l-Tawzi', 2010). See the facsimile, *Sawt al-Bahrayn: majalla adabiyya ijtima'iyya* (The Voice of Bahrain: A Social and Literary Magazine), 4 vols. (Muharraq: Bayt 'Abdallah al-Zayid li-Turath al-Bahrayn al-Sahafi/Markaz al-Shaykh Ibrahim bin Muhammad Al Khalifa li-l-Turath wa-l-Buhuth, 2003).

[30] Al-'Awwami, *al-haraka al-wataniyya*, vol. 1, 18; Fuccaro, *Histories*, 179.

[31] Interview with 'Ali al-Yami, Washington, October 2013.

[32] Jones, *Dogma*, 170.

[33] Ibrahim S. Al-Abdullah Al-Elawy, *The Influence of Oil upon Settlement in Al-Hasa Oasis, Saudi Arabia* (PhD, University of Durham, 1976), 84–9.

[34] Evans, *U.S. Records*, vol. 4, 197, 340.

PICTURE 2.3. Street scene in Dammam.
Source: Dorothy Miller/Saudi Aramco World/SAWDIA.

Khobar became a metropolitan region in the Eastern Province, while the older settlements were neglected (see Picture 2.3).[35]

Thus, while the oil industry led to an economic boom and jobs for many, it also led to unequal development, the first labour movements and to debates about how oil revenue should be distributed. In the aftermath of the strikes, the leaders of the labour movement were imprisoned and demonstrations, unions and strikes were banned. In addition, the number of Saudi ARAMCO employees decreased from 21,858 in 1954 to 11,682 in 1959. Some operations were passed on to local contractors, while several labour-intensive infrastructure projects were completed.[36] The three

[35] Jones, *Desert Kingdom*; Reichert, *Verstädterung*.
[36] Mordechai Abir, *Saudi Arabia in the Oil Era: Regime and Elites, Conflict and Collaboration* (London: Croom Helm, 1988), 79; Krimly, *Political Economy*, 286.

critical newspapers were closed down and some of their editors briefly arrested. Even ARAMCO's own monthly *Qafilat al-Zayt* (Oil Caravan), which was hardly critical of the government, was temporarily banned in 1955. *Akhbar al-Dhahran* was closed in February 1956 and its editor, 'Abd al-Karim al-Juhayman, briefly arrested.[37]

After the strike of 1953, a number of activists decided to establish clandestine groups that would try to organise the workers in ARAMCO and mobilise against the Saudi monarchy. In 1954, they founded the National Reform Front (*jabhat al-islah al-watani*), which was renamed National Liberation Front (NLF) (*jabhat al-taharrur al-watani*) around 1957/8. It entered into various alliances, with amongst others the Arab National Liberation Front (ANLF) (*jabhat al-taharrur al-watani al-'arabiyya*) of the dissident Saudi prince Talal bin 'Abd al-'Aziz.[38] The NLF used the hajj in 1958 to distribute leaflets, which demanded not only the liberation of ARAMCO workers but also the equal treatment of Shia and Sunnis and the abolition of special levies on Shia Muslims.[39] One of its leaders was the Shia cleric 'Abd al-Karim al-Humud from Saihat. Although he was not an ARAMCO worker, he participated in the demonstrations of 1956, was briefly imprisoned, and left for Beirut the same year.[40] He stayed there for almost two decades, continuing his oppositional activities as well as his religious studies with leading Shia scholars. He was responsible for 'workers affairs' and a representative of the Shia in the party because of his origin and clerical education.[41] In Beirut he also worked together with Nasir al-Sa'id, and the Saudi government revoked his citizenship because of his oppositional activities.[42]

---

[37] Al-Subay'i, *al-haya*, 103–7; Evans, *U.S. Records*, vol. 4, 250f., 262–5, 331; Jones, *Dogma*, 170–219; Vassiliev, *The History*, 340.

[38] 'Abd al-Nabi al-'Akri, *al-tanzimat al-yasariyya fi al-jazira wa-l-khalij al-'arabi* (The Leftist Organisations in the Peninsula and the Arabian Gulf) (Beirut: Dar al-Kunuz al-Adabiyya, 2003), 39f.; Peterson, *Historical Dictionary*, 121.

[39] The pamphlet is translated in Evans, *U.S. Records*, vol. 4, 655–9.

[40] He has published his memoirs on the events in 1956 under the heading 'ARAMCO and the Workers: The Revolution of the Workers' in 'Adnan al-'Attar, *al-harakat al-taharruriyya fi al-Hijaz wa-Najd: 1901–1973* (The Liberation Movements in the Hijaz and Najd: 1901–1973) (n.p.: n.p., 1973), 56–68.

[41] In an opposition publication he is listed as one of the five most important leaders of the ANLF along with Prince Talal, Shaykh Ibrahim bin Taqiqa, 'Abd al-'Aziz al-Sunayd and 'Abdallah al-Tariqi. Ibid., 56, 151. Salameh probably refers to him, when he argues that some of the members of the ANLF were 'Shi'i religious leaders'. Salameh and Steir, "Political Power," 20.

[42] Al-'Awwami, *al-haraka al-wataniyya*, vol. 1, 250f.

Others such as Hasan Faraj al-'Umran also sought to reconcile their religious beliefs and upbringings with the pan-Arab utopia they longed for. Hasan was the son of the prominent Shia cleric and local historian Faraj al-'Umran and was therefore exposed early on to an extensive library and religious gatherings. Like many others at the time he studied in the semi-official *kuttab* schools in Qatif and in 1954 became secretary at the Shia court in Qatif under 'Ali al-Jishi. He started to lecture in mosques and *hussainiyyat* about the Arab Nation and the socialist heritage of the Qarmatians, the Ismaili movement that ruled al-Ahsa from the ninth to the eleventh century. He also published nationalist poems in *Akhbar al-Dhahran* and was involved in the Qatif public library that opened in 1952 and whose organisers were arrested in 1956. He personally financed a new public library in Qatif in 1958 and founded a number of football clubs. After working as an accountant at a trading firm he was eventually arrested in 1969 and subsequently died in prison.[43]

These Shia leftists were mostly well educated, had studied abroad and obtained mid-ranking jobs in the bureaucracy, at ARAMCO or in the private sector. They saw themselves as intellectuals and were influenced by pan-Arab, socialist and communist ideologies. Some of them maintained their role as local notables and tried to petition the ruling family. In 1953 a delegation from Qatif under the leadership of 'Abdallah bin Hussayn al-Nasr and 'Abdallah al-Jishi apparently delivered a petition to King Saud upon his accession in November 1953 that asked for the establishment of an elected Majlis al-Shura (Consultative Council), the independence of the judiciary and educational reform.[44]

LOCAL ELECTIONS

In the 1950s and early 1960s, municipal elections in Saudi Arabia became important arenas for political expression, and particularly so in the Eastern Province. There had been some sort of consultation with the local population in matters of local administration before. In Qatif, a

---

[43] *Sawt al-Tali'a* 1 (1973), 23f.; 7 (1974), 54–9.

[44] This source has to be treated with caution, especially as it claims that sixteen thousand citizens signed this petition. *Sawt al-Tali'a* 1 (1973), 22. But an al-Jishi family history mentions that 'Abdallah al-Jishi was part of the Qatifi delegation who went to express condolences to King Saud in Jeddah in 1953 after the death of King 'Abd al-'Aziz. Jamil bin 'Abdallah al-Jishi, *turath al-ajdad: dirasa fi watha'iq 'a'ilat al-Jishi fi al-Qatif wa-l-Bahrayn (1200–1350AH)* (Heritage of the Forefathers: A Study of the Documents of the al-Jishi Family in Qatif and Bahrain [1786–1931]) (Jeddah: Dar al-Su'udiyya li-l-Nashr wa-l-Tawzi', 2007), 328.

council made up of local notables was appointed in 1925 and petitioned Ibn Saud to ease the financial burden on the Shia and to release prisoners.[45] In 1927 the Amir of Qatif appointed a new municipal council.[46] In 1937/8, a new law officially reorganised the local administration, which thereafter consisted of a president of the municipality, a municipal council, an administrative council and a representative of the municipality.[47] But the elections in the 1950s and 1960s were different, and were in some cases preceded by active campaigns against unelected officials. And later on, the elected members often struggled with the vested interests of the appointed members such as the appointed director of the municipality. Left-wing activists won seats in these elections, particularly in Qatif, Dammam and Khobar.[48]

The first municipal elections in al-Ahsa in 1954 did not gain the Shia the representation they had hoped for, as only two of eleven elected members were Shia. The electoral system allowed for interference by the government and ensured that mainly candidates approved by the Amir would be elected. The election committee, which was appointed by the Amir, did not include a single Shia. The eight elected Sunni candidates all stemmed from families who had been established in al-Ahsa at least since the nineteenth century. In September 1960, the different villages and quarters of al-Ahsa voted, but when it became clear that Shia would be marginalised once more, they complained to the Amir and asked for a

[45] This council was headed by Muhammad 'Ali al-Jishi, while 'Ali bin Hasan Abu al-Su'ud was its secretary and Hasan al-Shammasi, Ahmad Hasan 'Ali al-Khunayzi and Mahdi Ahmad al-Jishi were amongst its leading members. *Sawt al-Tali'a* 1 (1973), 21; al-Hasan, *al-shi'a*, vol. 2, 259.

[46] It was composed of Ahmad al-Majid, 'Abdallah 'Ali Ikhwan, Hasan 'Ali al-Marzuq, Hasan b. Nasrallah, and was headed by Khalid al-Faraj. Al-Shurafa', *al-mintaqa*, 335.

[47] Mohammed A. al-Jarbou, *Regional and Municipal Administration in Saudi Arabia: Problems and Issues* (MSc, California State University, 1983), 59. The next laws to regulate the local administration were the System of Governors and Administrative Councils in 1940, the 1963 Ordinance of Regions, the 1976 Ordinance of Municipalities and the 1992 Law of the Provinces. Al-Saud, *Evolution*, appendix.

[48] Anderson, *Differential Urban Growth*, 112f. Qatif municipality included all the towns and oases of Qatif, except Saihat, which was an independent municipality. Hufuf municipality included all of al-Ahsa, while Khobar municipality included just its suburbs. Dammam municipality included Dhahran, Ras Tanura, Abqaiq and various other towns along the Tapline. Dhahran to State, 23 November 1960, *Municipality Elections in Qatif, Al-Khobar, Dammam and Hofuf: No election in Saihat*, 786A. 0/11–2360. For a more detailed account of the elections across the Eastern Province, including in Khobar, Dammam and Rahimah see Toby Matthiesen "Center-Periphery Relations and the Emergence of a Public Sphere in Saudi Arabia: The Municipal Elections in the Eastern Province, 1954–1960," *British Journal of Middle Eastern Studies* (forthcoming).

proportional confessional representation on the municipal council. This was not accepted by the Amir, and although new elections were held in November 1960, most Shia and a number of 'progressive Sunnis' boycotted them; the result was an all-Sunni municipal council.[49]

Shia in Qatif, on the other hand, used the municipality to gain a foothold in the local administration. 'Ali al-'Awwami became an employee in the municipality in 1954 but was also a leader of the labour movement at ARAMCO and later of the communists in Qatif. In his memoirs, the municipal council in Qatif is described as a corrupt and lethargic institution that was paralysed by the rapid development of the new oil towns. He blames the members of the municipal council in the 1940s and early 1950s and the then-director of the municipality, Muhammad Salih al-Faris, for not trying to develop Qatif. In 1951, a new municipal council was appointed in Qatif, including 'Abdallah al-Shammasi and Hasan al-Khunayzi,[50] and the two launched a commission of inquiry into the municipality's workings and finances that found pervasive misconduct.[51]

The activists behind *jami'iyyat al-'ilm li-l-nidal* formed an unofficial list for the 1954 and 1956 elections and some of their candidates won. In the wake of the 1956 strikes, widespread arrests occurred; also targeted were some of the campaigners in Qatif and even some of the elected members of the municipal council. In addition, differences amongst the members paralysed the 1956 council. The council was dissolved after a couple of months and new elections were called in 1957. The general enthusiasm about the vote had largely waned, participation was lower, and many of the campaigners were in prison. Still, the leftists gained a majority for the second time.[52] That council, too, was dissolved in 1959, and Hasan al-Khunayzi was replaced as director of Qatif municipality with Yusuf al-Mu'aybad. The members of this council were appointed by the government and were mainly notables.[53]

---

[49] Phebe Ann Marr, *Confidential Memorandum 'Municipal Election – Hofuf'*, 19 December 1960, Dhahran, Box 3, Folder 4, Mulligan Papers.

[50] Hasan al-Khunayzi was born in 1900 in Najaf, where his father, 'Ali Abu al-Hasan al-Khunayzi, studied. Hasan became director of the municipality from 1955 to 1959. Al-Sayyid 'Ali al-Sayyid Baqir al-'Awwami, *rijal 'asaratuhum* (The Men I Was a Contemporary of) (Beirut: Majallat al-Waha, 2002), 29–37.

[51] Al-'Awwami, *al-haraka al-wataniyya*, vol. 1, 133–8.

[52] Ibid., 148.

[53] This contradicts the account in the journal of the Saudi Baath Party, which argues that the council of 1960 consisted mainly of baathists, Nasserists and communists and they elected Hasan al-Jishi as the head of the municipal council. "Min qawafil al-shuhada': al-shahid Hasan Salih al-Jishi" (From the Convoys of Martyrs: The Martyr Hasan Salih al-Jishi), *Sawt al-Tali'a* 8, Kanun al-Awwal 1974, 52–62, 56–7.

In June 1960, new elections were held. The elections were announced two weeks before election day, all male residents older than 21 were allowed to vote and all literate residents older than 25 could stand in the elections. Each voter could vote for nine candidates, and the nine with the most votes were elected. An election committee appointed by the Amir of the Eastern Province counted the results in secret, and the committee was composed primarily of Sunnis from outside Qatif.[54] The elected members were all from Qatif and Safwa, as on previous councils, meaning that candidates from outside these two urban centres were not represented. Only one member of the old council was re-elected, and apart from two ARAMCO employees, most other elected members were merchants and notables. Crucially, unlike in other cities, the Council of Ministers had to approve the results in Qatif.[55] Locals claimed that around five thousand people voted in Qatif municipality, with two thousand from Safwa. The government, on the other hand, claimed that participation was much lower and that the most popular candidate only got 115 votes.[56] Hasan al-Jishi became director of the council while Yusuf al-Mu'aybad remained director of Qatif municipality. When a dispute occurred between some of the members, three elected members resigned and were replaced by three others, who had been on the election list.[57] But disagreements within the council did not ease and a majority led a no-confidence vote against Hasan al-Jishi as director of the council that

---

[54] Phebe Ann Marr, *Election in the Baladiyah of Qatif*, Dhahran, 23 August 1960, Mulligan Papers.

[55] Dhahran to State, *Municipality Elections*.

[56] Email correspondence with Phebe Marr, April 2014. This was the village headman (*'umda*) of Safwa, Hussayn ibn Salih. Population figures from a survey by the economics department in 1958 put Qatif's population at 10,000, Safwa's at 4,800 and Saihat's at 4,000 out of a population of about 40,000 for the whole of Qatif oasis. Marr, *Election in the Baladiyah of Qatif*.

[57] Hasan al-'Awwami, Ahmad Sunbal, 'Ali al-Shaykh Hussayn al-Qudayhi, Muhammad Hasan al-Faraj, 'Abd al-Rasul al-Bayyash, 'Abd al-Rasul al-Mustafa and Nasr al-Shaykh 'Ali were members on the council. Hasan al-'Awwami, 'Abd al-Rasul al-Mustafa and Nasr al-Shaykh 'Ali resigned and 'Abdallah Rida al-Shammasi, Muhammad Sa'id al-Shaykh Muhammad 'Ali al-Khunayzi and 'Abd al-Karim Mihna were appointed. In his memoirs of the municipal council elections, 'Abdallah Rida al-Shammasi does not remember the exact date of these elections. But it is likely that this is the June 1960 election the American diplomatic documents refer to. 'Abdallah Rida al-Shammasi, "ta'liq wa-idah" (Comment and Note), in al-'Awwami, *al-haraka al-wataniyya*, vol. 1, 152–8, 152. 'Abdallah al-Shammasi was originally called 'Abd al-Rasul, which was a distinctively Shia first name, but was then banned in Saudi Arabia. The ARAMCO report has a slightly different list of members from that mentioned earlier. Marr, *Election in the Baladiyah of Qatif*. This may be because Phebe Marr at times just wrote down first names.

was submitted to the governor. The latter tried to pressure the council members to revoke their statement, which they refused. Instead of dismissing just Hasan al-Jishi, the governor dissolved the whole council.[58]

Like many of the council members, the secretary of Qatif municipal council was often a leftist intellectual from a notable family. Hasan al-'Awwami, the brother of 'Ali al-'Awwami, was secretary of the council from 1954 until 1959. He participated in many of the activities of the young activists. After Hasan al-'Awwami resigned to become a lawyer and eventually went to study in Najaf, 'Abd al-Ra'uf Hasan al-Khunayzi took over the position. Al-Khunayzi had participated in the strikes of 1953 and 1956, had been imprisoned thereafter, and held the position after his release from prison in the late 1950s until his second arrest in 1964. He died in prison in 1971, according to oppositional accounts under torture.[59] In 1962, after the death of Yusuf al-Mu'aybad, Hasan al-Jishi succeeded him as director of Qatif municipality. He retained that post until he, too, was arrested for allegedly subversive activities in 1970 and died in jail in 1972.[60]

Sa'ud bin Jiluwi, the governor of the Eastern Province, opposed the strengthening of local councils that could challenge his authority.[61] As the American consul in Dhahran remarked in 1946, Sa'ud bin Jiluwi's 'position is unique in Saudi Arabia. His authority, unlike that of any other Amir, is next-to-absolute within his province … in no other province does an Amir possess such autonomous power.'[62] Like his father, Sa'ud was suspicious and dismissive of the Shia, and a British diplomat wrote in 1970 that 'it was old Saud bin Jiluwi's boast for many years that though he was Governor of the area he had never been near the place (Qatif) (he eventually had to go when the King expressed a wish to see it)'.[63] After the seat of the Amir had moved to Dammam in 1953, his brother, 'Abd al-Muhsin bin Jiluwi, acted as local governor in the oasis of al-Ahsa.[64]

[58] Al-Shammasi, "ta'liq wa-idah," 152–8.

[59] "Al-Shahid 'Abd al-Ra'uf al-Khunayzi," *Sawt al-Tali'a* 5, Adhar 1974, 66–70.

[60] Al-'Awwami, *al-haraka al-wataniyya*, vol. 1, 176–8, vol. 2, 198–201, 268f.; *Sawt al-Tali'a* 7 (1974), 52–62.

[61] A. L. P Burdett, ed., *Records of Saudi Arabia 1966–1971*, 6 vols. (Slough: Archive Editions, 2004), vol. 1: 1966, 100f.

[62] Ibrahim al-Rashid, *Saudi Arabia Enters the Modern World: Secret U.S. Documents on the Emergence of the Kingdom of Saudi Arabia as a World Power 1936–1949*, 2 vols., vol. 2 (Salisbury, NC: Documentary Publications, 1980), 40f.

[63] Burdett, *Records*, vol. 5: 1970, 511.

[64] Dhahran to State, *Municipality Elections*.

When Faysal had consolidated his power in the 1960s, these attempts to delegate some decision making to the municipalities were reversed and authority returned to the governor or became centralised in the expanding bureaucracy in the Ministry of Interior in Riyadh and, from 1975 onwards, in the Ministry of Municipal and Rural Affairs (MOMRA). This centralisation of the bureaucracy led to over-lapping interests and competing responsibilities of different ministries in the provinces.[65] The central government thought the experiment of municipal elections did more harm than good and some conservative Sunni clerics deemed elections per se unlawful.[66] Between the early 1960s and 2004, no more municipal elections were held in the Eastern Province. But the legacy of popular protest, of elections and of a public sphere of newspapers, libraries and discussion salons had changed the ways in which residents of the Eastern Province engaged in politics.

SEARCHING FOR THE ARAB NATION

After the repression of 1956, the remaining activists and some of those who were gradually released continued to be active clandestinely and in exile. Repression had been harsh, and there was little chance of quick success. In exile, they had to align themselves to the shifting foreign policy preferences of Arab nationalist, baathist and Marxist regimes. They also faced the problem that the Arab Left was highly divided, and these divisions fragmented the relatively few Saudi leftists even further. Some Saudi workers at ARAMCO became followers of the Baath Party, influenced by the ideas of Arab teachers and workers and by Saudi students returning from Baghdad, Damascus, Cairo and Beirut. They included Muhammad al-Rabi', an ARAMCO worker who was arrested in 1956 and died in prison;[67] Mirza al-Khunayzi, who was imprisoned in 1956 after participating in the demonstrations at ARAMCO; as well as 'Ali Ghannam from Jubail. They founded the Organisation of Free Men of the Arabian Peninsula *(munazzamat ahrar al-jazira al-'arabiyya)*, which

---

[65] Hertog, *Princes*, 82, 86f., 90, 97; Al-Jarbou, *Regional*, 48–50; al-Saud, *Evolution*; Fayhan Gweed, *Participation in Decision Making to Improve the Saudi Arabian Municipal System* (MA, Sangamon State University, 1987).

[66] Ja'far al-Shayib, "Saudi Municipal Councils and Political Reform," *Arab Reform Bulletin*, 20 November 2005.

[67] *Sawt al-Tali'a* 2 (1973), 63–5.

was the nucleus for the Saudi Baath Party, and participated in the labour mobilisation at ARAMCO in 1956.[68]

The actual Saudi branch of the Baath Party, the Arab Socialist Baath Party in Saudi *(hizb al-ba'th al-'arabi al-ishtiraki fi al-su'udiyya)*, published a secret journal – *Sawt al-Jamahir* (Voice of the Masses) – from 1961 onwards. 'Ali Ghannam, who had been working for ARAMCO since 1950, became the representative of the Baath Party branches in the 'Peninsula and the Arab Gulf' in the Baath Party National Command in Iraq from the early 1960s until at least the late 1970s.[69] Another Saudi member of the National Command was 'Abd al-Rahman Munif, who was born in Amman to a Saudi father and an Iraqi mother. An oil expert, he then left the Baath Party and published novels that were highly critical of Saudi Arabia. The first part of his famous pentalogy describes the impact of the oil industry on the Eastern Province and the labour movement at ARAMCO.[70]

Baathist and other left-wing students set up the Revolutionary Students Vanguard *(al-tali'a al-tullabiyya al-thawriyya)* in 1962; it spread to Dammam, Riyadh and Qasim, but its members were arrested in 1964.[71] The Saudi author Turki al-Hamad describes in an autobiographical novel how the protagonist, a Sunni from a Najdi family, gets recruited into a Baath party cell in a Dammam high-school. A key topic of the novel is the cross-sectarian nature of the party, and how coming into contact with Shia from Qatif and al-Ahsa through the party forces the protagonist to critically reflect his anti-Shia stereotypes. The novel further describes how young members read and discuss socialist and baathist literature in weekly meetings of their clandestine cells.[72]

'Abd al-Majid al-Shammasi from Qatif, who had studied in Iraq in the early 1950s, became a leading member of the Baath Party in 1962. His

---

[68] Najib al-Khunayzi claims the *Organisation of Free Men* was founded in 1958. Najib al-Khunayzi, "al-ihtifa' bi-l-shakhsiyya al-wataniyya al-bariza Mirza al-Khunayzi" (The Celebration of the Outstanding National Personality Mirza al-Khunayzi, *Rasid* (24 December 2009); Falah 'Abdallah al-Mudayris, *al-ba'thiyyun fi al-khalij wa-l-jazira al-'arabiyya* (The Baathists in the Gulf and the Arabian Peninsula) (Kuwait: Dar Qurtas li-l-Nashr, 2002), 52f.; Evans, *U.S. Records*, vol. 4, 661f.

[69] Hanna Batatu, *The Old Social Classes and the Revolutionary Movements of Iraq: A Study of Iraq's Old Landed and Commercial Classes and of its Communists, Ba'thists, and Free Officers* (Princeton, NJ: Princeton University Press, 1978), 1224–9.

[70] Abdelrahman Munif, *Cities of Salt* (London: Vintage, 1994).

[71] *Sawt al-Tali'a* 1 (1973), 25.

[72] Turki al-Hamad, *Adama* (London: Saqi, 2003).

family, too, was a prominent notable family and already as a child in the 1930s he accompanied his father to local gatherings, where state policies towards the Shia were denounced. More than a dozen members of the al-Shammasi family were imprisoned in the 1950s and 1960s for left-wing activism. In the 1960s he worked in a bank first in Dammam and then in Qatif and allegedly died under torture in 1969.[73] Yusuf Makki, a Shia from Saihat, became a supporter of the party in 1963 and co-organised the demonstrations in 1967, after which he was arrested.[74]

While the Baath Party was relatively strong amongst intellectuals and in Shia areas, it also sought to infiltrate the army, yet without much success.[75] The party was weakened by the split that emerged within the region-wide Baath Party over its ideological direction after 1963. The left wing of the Saudi Baath Party established the Popular Democratic Front in the Arabian Peninsula (*al-jabha al-dimuqratiyya al-sha'biyya fi al-jazira al-'arabiyya*) in 1965 with Anwar Thabit as one of its leaders and Mirza al-Khunayzi as its secretary. It was Marxist-Leninist, and although it believed in armed struggle, it did not succeed in carrying out any planned attacks.[76] It was initially related to the Bahraini branch of the Movement of Arab Nationalists (MAN) (*harakat al-qawmiyyin al-'arab*).[77]

The other Saudi baathists who were loyal to Saddam Hussein received support after the coup in Iraq in 1968 and its leaders such as 'Ali Ghannam moved to Baghdad, where Iraqi support gained them time on Radio Baghdad and enabled the production of its publication *Sawt al-Tali'a* (Voice of the Vanguard) from 1973 onwards. The journal was edited by exiled members of the Baath Party in Cairo and Baghdad and was printed in Iraq. After the 1975 amnesty it ceased to publish regularly; occasional issues appeared until the early 1980s.[78] When Saddam Hussein and Saudi Arabia allied themselves against Iran in the Iran-Iraq

---

[73] "Shahid 'Abd al-Majid al-Shammasi," *Sawt al-Tali'a* 3 (July 1973), 71–4.

[74] Interview with a former member of the Saudi Baath party, Beirut, 2013.

[75] See this detailed analysis of the different Army and National Guard branches and of dissident groups within the army. *Sawt al-Tali'a* 5 (1974), 8–39; 6 (1974), 10–27.

[76] Al-Khunayzi, "al-ihtifa';" al-Mudayris, *al-ba'thiyyun*, 57f.

[77] This was *al-jabha al-sha'biyya al-dimuqratiyya – al-Bahrayn*, which emerged in 1968 out of members of the MAN and later became *al-jabha al-sha'biyya fi al-Bahrayn*. Falah 'Abdallah al-Mudayris, *al-harakat wa-l-jama'at al-siyasiyya fi al-Bahrayn 1937–2002* (The Political Movements and Groups in Bahrain 1937–2002) (Beirut: Dar al-Kunuz al-Adabiyya, 2004), 26–32; al-'Akri, *al-tanzimat*, 151–74.

[78] Interview with a former member of the Saudi Baath party, Beirut, 2013.

War, the propaganda activities of the few remaining Saudi baathists were curbed.[79]

One of the main activities of the baathists was their involvement in the demonstrations and riots that occurred in 1967 as a response to the Six Day Arab-Israeli War. The demonstrations involved several thousand people in Dhahran, Ras Tanura, Qatif and Dammam, leading to attacks on the American Consulate in Dhahran as well as on ARAMCO infrastructure. Mirza al-Khunayzi, the secretary of the Popular Democratic Front in the Arabian Peninsula, was one of the leaders of these demonstrations.[80] The arrests of hundreds of left-wing activists in 1967 and 1969 after a foiled coup attempt dealt a blow to all Saudi opposition organisations, including the baathists. In 1969, several cells in the Air Force and amongst Hijazis were accused of planning coups. As the plots focussed on the army, where Shia were only marginally represented, few Shia were involved. Yet in 1970, many Shia, some accused of membership in the Baath Party, were arrested.[81]

One of the coup plots has been attributed to MAN.[82] Kuwaitis had traditionally led the Gulf wing of MAN but the non-Kuwaiti members from the Gulf decided during a secret conference in Dubai in 1968 to form national branches for each territory of the Gulf. The Saudis established

---

[79] Abir, *Saudi Arabia: Government*, 36; Hamza al-Hasan, "al-muʿarada fi al-suʿudiyya: al-taʾarjuh bayn al-hawa al-iqlimi wa-l-wataniyya al-jamaʿa" (The Opposition in Saudi: Oscillation between Regional Sentiment and Comprehensive Nationalism), *al-Jazira al-ʿArabiyya* 18 (July 1992), 40–7; al-Mudayris, *al-baʿthiyyun*, 56f.; Holden and Johns, *The House of Saud*, 532; Helen Lackner, *A House Built on Sand: A Political Economy of Saudi Arabia* (London: Ithaca Press, 1978), 105; Yusuf Makki, "hizb al-baʿth al-ʿarabi al-ishtiraki fi al-ʿarabiyya al-suʿudiyya" (The Arab Socialist Baath Party in Saudi Arabia), in *al-ahzab wa-l-harakat wa-l-tanzimat al-qawmiyya fi al-watan al-ʿarabi* (The Nationalist Parties, Movements and Organisations in the Arab Homeland), ed. Muhammad Jamal Barut (Beirut: Markaz Dirasat al-Wahda al-ʿArabiyya, 2012), 291–301; Peterson, *Historical Dictionary*, 120; Salameh and Steir, "Political Power," 22; *Sawt al-Taliʿa* 2 (1973), 27.

[80] Local Government Relations, *The June 1967 Riots*, 26 July 1967, Box 16, Folder 8, Mulligan Papers; al-Khunayzi, "al-ihtifaʾ;" Anthony Cave Brown, *Oil, God, and Gold: The Story of ARAMCO and the Saudi Kings* (Boston: Houghton Mifflin, 1999), 272–80; Ibrahim, *Shiʿis*, 115; Lackner, *House*, 101; Vassiliev, *The History*, 370. Abir argues that this was organised by Nasir al-Saʿid's group. Abir, *Saudi Arabia in the Oil Era*, 111f.

[81] Some of these arrests may have been related to the Ashura processions at the same time. The Saudi Baath Party probably exaggerates when it claims that 2,500 people were arrested after 1969, 400 of them in Qatif. But five Qatifis died in prison, some of them as a result of torture: the aforementioned Hasan al-Jishi, as well as ʿAbd al-Wahid ʿAbd al-Jabbar, Majid al-Shammasi, Hasan al-ʿUmran and Ahmad ʿAtuq. *Sawt al-Taliʿa* 1 (1973), 29.

[82] Lackner, *House*, 102f.

the National Revolution Organisation in Saudi (NROS) (*munazzamat al-thawra al-wataniyya fi al-su'udiyya*).[83] In 1969/70 the latter formed the Marxist-Leninist Popular Democratic Party in the Arabian Peninsula (PDPAP) (*al-hizb al-dimuqrati al-sha'bi fi al-jazira al-'arabiyya*) with the remaining cadres of the Popular Democratic Front in the Arabian Peninsula such as Anwar Thabit.[84] The idea of the party was to remain independent of foreign regimes and to spread across the whole of Saudi Arabia, and so a committee of four composed of Mirza and 'Abd al-Muhsin al-Khunayzi in the Eastern Province as well as one Najdi and one Hijazi was set up. It was common for members of a family to become politicised and join the same movements. 'Abd al-Muhsin worked together with Mirza until the latter's arrest in 1969. Contrary to other members of the al-Khunayzi family, who were based in the Old city of Qatif, 'Abd al-Muhsin had grown up in the village of Awwamiyya. This was one of the reasons why he did not join the communists or the Baath Party, who had their power base in the Old city of Qatif. The PDPAP, on the contrary, was popular in Shia villages such as Awwamiyya, Safwa and then in Saihat.[85]

It maintained limited links to MAN and its Palestinian branch, the Popular Front for the Liberation of Palestine (PFLP), and some Saudis fought with the PFLP against Israel. Together with Dhufari tribal groups, MAN led the Dhufar rebellion in Oman. The Kuwaiti and Bahraini MAN branches were heavily involved in Dhufar, and the Saudi branch of MAN also supported this rebellion and a couple of its members were active there. The first foreign fighter who died in Dhufar supporting the rebellion was a Saudi, and Saudi leftist movements expressed their support for the Dhufar rebellion.[86]

In 1971, PDPAP was weakened by the breakaway of two factions, the Popular Struggle Front (*jabhat al-nidal al-sha'bi*), which published the journal *al-Nidal* (The Struggle), and the National Liberation Front in Saudi (*jabhat al-taharrur al-watani fi al-su'udiyya*). By 1972 many PDPAP members were arrested in the Hijaz, Riyadh and the Eastern

---

[83] Al-'Akri, *al-tanzimat*, 72–80, 202f.

[84] Al-Mudayris, *al-ba'thiyyun*, 58f.; al-'Akri, *al-tanzimat*, 202–11; Lackner, *House*, 105.

[85] Interview with members of the al-Khunayzi family, London, June 2010.

[86] This was 'Ali Muhammad al-Muslim, whose nom de guerre was "Comrade Nayif." *Al-Jazira al-Jadida* 1 (March 1972); al-'Akri, *al-tanzimat*, 204f.; Abdel Razzaq Takriti, *Monsoon Revolution: Republicans, Sultans, and Empires in Oman 1965–1976* (Oxford: Oxford University Press, 2013), 126. See, for example, the supporting statements by the Saudi Communist Party and *hizb al-'amal* on the 20th anniversary of the start of the Dhufar Revolution: *Sawt al-Thawra* 460, July/August 1985, 20.

Province, reflecting the group's cross-regional and cross-sectarian membership. It had several hundred members, roughly half of them Shia.[87] It was also the probably first Saudi opposition group to have a female wing, four of whom were arrested in 1969. Although it hoped to liberate the country by armed struggle, the remaining cadres left Saudi Arabia after 1972 and used Damascus, Beirut and South Yemen to publish the journal *al-Jazira al-Jadida* (The New Peninsula) from 1972 to 1974. South Yemeni support also enabled the broadcast of its radio program *Sawt al-Jazira al-'Arabiyya* (Voice of the Arabian Peninsula) into the Kingdom until 1975.[88] Reflecting the strong membership of Shia, PDPAP not only used class analysis in its publications but also explicitly condemned sectarian discrimination in Saudi Arabia. The party denounced the prohibition of Shia rituals, Shia religious courses and the banning of Shia workers from some sectors and raised the issue of Shia courts.[89]

COMMUNISTS AND CO-OPTATION

After King Faysal was assassinated in 1975, Khalid succeeded him on the throne. Upon King Khalid's accession, a general amnesty was issued to release the remaining political prisoners from left-wing movements and allow those abroad to return. The returnees became integrated into the patronage networks of the Saudi rentier state that was expanding since the oil crisis in 1973. They established themselves as "liberals" in the Saudi intellectual field.[90] Some, such as 'Abd al-Karim al-Humud, became integrated into Shia notable politics.[91] Indeed, this amnesty was a

---

[87] Interview with members of the al-Khunayzi family, London, June 2010.

[88] Al-Hasan, "al-mu'arada"; al-Mudayris, *al-ba'thiyyun*, 58–60; al-'Akri, *al-tanzimat*, 202–13; Fred Halliday, *Arabia without Sultans*, 2nd ed. (London: Saqi Books, 2002), 69; Lackner, *House*, 105; Yusuf Makki, "harakat al-qawmiyyin al-'arab fi al-khalij wa-l-jazira al-'arabiyya" (The Movement of Arab Nationalists in the Gulf and the Arabian Peninsula), in *al-ahzab wa-l-harakat wa-l-tanzimat al-qawmiyya fi al-watan al-'arabi* (The Nationalist Parties, Movements and Organisations in the Arab Homeland), ed. Muhammad Jamal Barut (Beirut: Markaz Dirasat al-Wahda al-'Arabiyya, 2012), 467–86; Peterson, *Historical Dictionary*, 120; Ayman Yassini, *Religion and State in the Kingdom of Saudi Arabia* (Boulder, CO: Westview Press, 1985), 122.

[89] *Al-Jazira al-Jadida* 7 (December 1974), 12–22.

[90] Abir, *Saudi Arabia: Government*, 57; Hertog, *Princes*, 99; Najib al-Khunayzi, "al-nishat al-siyasi li-l-shi'a fi al-su'udiyya" (The Political Discourse of the Shia in Saudi), *Rasid* (25 October 2003); Krimly, *Political Economy*, 349; Stéphane Lacroix, *Awakening Islam: The Politics of Religious Dissent in Contemporary Saudi Arabia* (Cambridge, MA: Harvard University Press, 2011), 15–20.

[91] Throughout the 1980s and 1990s, al-Humud was an emissary in the negotiations between the Saudi Shia opposition and the ruling family. Ibrahim, *Shi'is*, 180.

precedent for the 1993 amnesty for Saudi Shia opposition activists. But in the 1980s Saudi Shia Islamists would ridicule the leftists for having been bought off in 1975 and for becoming capitalists and bureaucrats.[92] The amnesty also led to the dissolving of PDPAP, which ceased its propaganda activities and whose members returned.[93]

The Socialist Action Party in the Arabian Peninsula (*hizb al-ʿamal al-ishtiraki fi al-jazira al-ʿarabiyya*, hereafter *hizb al-ʿamal*), became the ideological successor to PDPAP. It was also Marxist-Leninist and aligned to MAN and PFLP. Saudi students in the United States, who had been under the influence of Arab nationalism, founded the party in 1972. The baathists (mainly the Iraqi wing), communists, Arab nationalists, and Libyans were all fighting for dominance in the *munazzamat al-talaba al-ʿarab* (Organisation of Arab Students) in the United States. The thousands of Saudi students were important in this organisation and the different currents tried to influence them and make them read their publications.[94] Eventually, many *hizb al-ʿamal* members, amongst them several Shia, returned to the Eastern Province to become bureaucrats and journalists. *Hizb al-ʿamal* made the end of discrimination against Shia one of its main demands. It also continued to advocate armed struggle, and was involved in the armed uprising in Qatif, the intifada of 1979/80. Therafter, it did not carry out any military operations.[95]

While a communist faction had existed within the NLF and the ANLF since 1961, the remaining communists only established the Communist Party in Saudi (*al-hizb al-shuyuʿi fi al-suʿudiyya*) in 1975.[96] The

---

[92] See *al-Thawra al-Islamiyya* 38 (June 1983), 7; ʿAbd al-Latif Muhammad al-ʿAmir, *al-haraka al-islamiyya fi al-jazira al-ʿarabiyya* (The Islamic Movement in the Arabian Peninsula) (n.p.: Munazzamat al-Thawra al-Islamiyya fi al-Jazira al-ʿArabiyya/al-Safa li-l-Nashr wa-l-Tawziʿ, 1408AH [1987/88]), 48. For a critique of the 1975 amnesty and attempts to win over former oppositionists through co-optation by the Baghdad-based 'Saudi Council for Solidarity and Peace' see *Middle East Contemporary Survey* (hereafter *MECS*), 1977–8, vol. 2, 679.

[93] Al-ʿAkri, *al-tanzimat*, 205–11.

[94] Interview with ʿAbd al-Nabi al-ʿAkri, London, July 2010.

[95] There were other *hizb al-ʿamal al-ishtiraki* branches in Palestine, Lebanon, Iraq and other countries, with which the Saudi *hizb al-ʿamal* maintained relations. Interview with a representative of *hizb al-ʿamal al-ishtiraki al-ʿarabi fi al-jazira al-ʿarabiyya* in February 1984, printed in *MERIP Reports* 130 (February 1985), 15–19. Al-Hasan, "al-muʿarada;" al-ʿAkri, *al-tanzimat*, 214–27.

[96] For more on the communists in Saudi Arabia see memoirs by two former communists from the Eastern Province, a Shia (ʿAli al-ʿAwwami) and a Sunni (Ishaq al-Shaykh Yaʿqub). ʿAli al-ʿAwwami was the first Saudi Shia leftist to write an autobiography, which was published posthumously in 2012 because of the sensitivity of the topic. Al-ʿAwwami, *al-haraka*. See Yaʿqub's four volume memoir, Ishaq al-Shaykh Yaʿqub, *wujuh fi masabih*

Communist Party held a founding congress in which it aligned itself staunchly to the Soviet Union and demanded a constitution, a parliament and the nationalisation of oil resources.[97] It received limited support from the Soviet Union and was mainly active in publishing statements and broadcasting on Radio Moscow.[98] Its regular publication was called *Tariq al-Kadihin* (Path of the Downtrodden). Some of its cadres such as Najib al-Khunayzi stemmed from the main Shia notable families and its main support base was amongst the Shia. Others were journalists such as the Sunni ʿAli al-Dumayni. Many of its followers were educated in the Soviet Union, East Germany or other countries of the Communist bloc.[99] Some were sons of strike leaders of the 1950s.[100] During its second congress in 1984 it adopted a general program, which called for the admission of Shia into the military and security services.[101] Several organisations for the youth, students, women and workers were attached to the party, all with their own internal publications and representatives outside Saudi Arabia. Again, descendants of Shia notable families were strongly represented in these organisations, especially the youth wing.[102]

al-dhakira (Faces of the Lamps of Memory), 4 vols., vol. 1 (Kuwait: Dar Qurtas li-l-Nashr, 2001), vol. 2 (Kuwait: Dar Qurtas li-l-Nashr, 2005), Vol. 3 (Kuwait: Dar Qurtas li-l-Nashr, 2007), vol. 4 (Beirut: Dar al-Farabi, 2011). For another part of his memoirs and his time in the German Democratic Republic see Ishaq al-Shaykh Yaʿqub, *inni ashummu raʾihat Mariyam* (I smell Mariam), vol. 2 (Beirut: Dar al-Farabi, 2010), and his account of his time as a political prisoner: Ishaq al-Shaykh Yaʿqub, *al-musaʾala* (The Interrogation) (Beirut: Dar al-Farabi, 2011).

97 Al-ʿAttar, *al-harakat*, 154, 176f.; Salameh and Steir, "Political Power," 20f.

98 Fahd al-Qahtani, *shuyuʿiyyun fi al-suʿudiyya: dirasa fi al-ʿalaqat al-sufitiyya al-suʿudiyya* (Communists in Saudi: A Study of Soviet-Saudi Relations) (n.p.: n.p., 1988); Mark N. Katz, *Russia and Arabia: Soviet Foreign Policy toward the Arabian Peninsula* (Baltimore: Johns Hopkins University Press, 1985), 142f.; Aryeh Y. Yodfat, *The Soviet Union and the Arabian Peninsula: Soviet Policy towards the Persian Gulf and Arabia* (London: Croom Helm, 1983), 133f.

99 See, for example, this magazine, which was directed at Saudi students in the Soviet Union and included articles on the intifada in 1979 as well as on Moscow's People's Friendship University. Rabitat al-Talaba al-Suʿudiyyin fi al-Ittihad al-Sufiti, *al-Ishʿaʿ* 3 (July 1980). Nachlass Prof. Dr. Gerhard Höpp, Signatur 10.15.087, Zentrum Moderner Orient, Berlin, Germany.

100 Louër, *Transnational*, 44.

101 Al-ʿAkri, *al-tanzimat*, 45; Vassiliev, *The History*, 464.

102 Interview with a former member of the Communist Party in Saudi, Riyadh, November 2008. Their names were *rabitat al-nisaʾ al-dimuqratiyya fi al-suʿudiyya* (Association of Democratic Women in Saudi) and *ittihad al-talaba fi al-suʿudiyya* (Students' Union in Saudi). Al-ʿAkri, *al-tanzimat*, 55f. For the youth wing see Ittihad al-Shabab al-Dimuqrati fi al-Suʿudiyya, *wathaʾiq al-muʾtamar al-thani li-ittihad al-shabab al-dimuqrati fi al-suʿudiyya 1986* (Documents of the Second Congress of the Union of Democratic Youth in Saudi) (n.p.: n.p., n.d.).

The branch for the workers, *ittihad al-'ummal fi al-su'udiyya* (Union of Workers in Saudi), was founded in 1984 and printed basic publications that adhered strictly to Soviet Communist Party lines.[103] The actual membership of the Communist Party, though, did not exceed one hundred.[104]

CONCLUSION

In many Arab countries as well as in Iran, religious minorities such as Jews, Christians and others sought refuge in non-sectarian, secular, leftist and nationalist movements, and so did Shia in Iraq, Lebanon and the Gulf.[105] The Shia in Saudi Arabia were subject to extraordinary surveillance and repression at the hands of the security forces, because the disregard that the security forces felt for the Shia was coupled with the Shia's potential involvement in subversive leftist movements and fears of links to Iraq.[106]

Many members of the educated Saudi Shia elite – the notable families and ARAMCO employees – were drawn into these movements. By the early 1970s, many notable families of Qatif and the surrounding areas had family members in jail or killed because of alleged involvement in oppositional activities. Many of those who were pardoned subsequently refrained from political activism. Two decades of secular oppositional activism had not yielded the desired change and the temptations of the emerging rentier economy and the oil boom were too great to be missed. As a result, the children of leftists saw the dangers and ineffectiveness of political opposition in Saudi Arabia. Therefore, they largely refrained from political activism, although some joined the Communist Party. Their fascination with secular ideologies and their partial integration into the Saudi political economy largely prevented them from undertaking religious studies. The importance of their families in the nineteenth and early twentieth centuries, however, had depended on a mix of clerical

---

[103] Its central publication, *Sawt al-'Ummal* (Voice of the Workers), at times only consisted of 8 pages, and in 1989 denounced the hiring of foreign workers at ARAMCO and the laying off of Saudi workers. *Sawt al-'Ummal* 10 (April 1989), 1f.

[104] Interview with a former member of the Communist Party in Saudi, Saudi Arabia, 2011. Some speak of only thirty members, most of them living in exile. Holden and Johns, *The House of Saud*, 532; Peterson, *Historical Dictionary*, 121.

[105] For the role of Shia in the Iraqi Communist Party see Johan Franzén, *Red Star over Iraq: Iraqi Communism before Saddam* (London: Hurst, 2011).

[106] U.S. Diplomatic Cable, *Shi'ah Community of Saudi Arabia*, From American Consul Dhahran to Department of State, January 20, 1974. National Archives at College Park, RG 59 General Records of the Department of State, Central Foreign Policy Files, Box 5D, P740005-2389.

authority and economic and political power. By slowly turning their back on religious studies, the notable families opened up the religious field to new forces. Their involvement in clandestine leftist movements in parts explains their absence in the new Shia Islamist movements that spread to Saudi Arabia in the 1970s.

The mobilisation of these leftist and nationalist movements had turned the Gulf region into a transnational field in which ideas, students, and revolutionaries travelled across national borders and increased political mobilisations in other countries.[107] In many respects, these transnational mobilisations set precedents for the ways in which the Islamist movements would spread. The failure of leftist and pan-Arab ideals at a regional level, and their difficulty in mobilising Saudi society more widely, left the field of oppositional politics in Saudi Arabia wide open for Islamist groups.

[107] John Chalcraft, *Monarchy, Migration and Hegemony in the Arabian Peninsula* (London: LSE Kuwait Programme on Development, Governance and Globalization in the Gulf States, 2010).

3

Shia Islamism

> A religious book had as much worth as a rifle. A cassette tape equaled the shot of a pistol. A mourning ceremony for Hussayn was tantamount to a whole opposition corps. Maybe it was then that Qatif learned how to be on permanent alert, always ready, always closed and incomprehensible to strangers. … I have searched, but I have not found anyone writing any histories of Qatif for that period. Perhaps it was all an affair about which we were better off keeping quiet.
>
> Seba al-Herz – *The Others*

In the 1950s and 1960s, while the oil workers at ARAMCO went on strike and the first leftist activists moved underground, Shia political and religious discourse in the Iraqi shrine cities was profoundly transformed. Some clerics of the Qatifi notable families such as 'Abdallah al-Khunayzi were studying in Najaf. They were following the line of the mainstream Najafi *maraji'* such as Muhsin al-Hakim and Abu al-Qasim al-Khu'i and advocated a religious role for the clergy rather than a political one. Other Saudi Shia clerics were at the forefront of the emerging Shia political parties in Iraq. Muhammad Baqir al-Shakhs (1315–81, 1897/8–1961/2) from al-Ahsa, for example, was a founder of the Society of 'Ulama' *(jama'at al-'ulama')* in Najaf in 1959/60. This was an early group of politically minded clerics who sought to counter secularism and constituted a nucleus for Iraqi Shia Islamist parties.[1] Another cleric, who was originally from al-Ahsa, 'Abd al-Hadi al-Fadli, was also active in the

---

[1] Al-Shakhs, *a'lam*, vol. 3, 294–6; T. M. Aziz, "The Role of Muhammad Baqir al-Sadr in Shii Political Activism in Iraq from 1958 to 1980," *International Journal of Middle East Studies* 25, no. 2 (1993), 207–22, 219; Faleh A. Jabar, *The Shi'ite Movement in Iraq* (London: Saqi Books, 2003), 111.

PICTURE 3.1. Muhammad al-Shirazi.
Source: Imam Shirazi World Foundation.

society, published and edited its main publication, and cofounded the Islamic al-Da'wa Party (*hizb al-da'wa al-islamiyya*: hereafter *al-da'wa*) in Iraq. Some Saudi students were drawn into *al-da'wa* and went back to Saudi Arabia.[2] Yet, unlike amongst other Gulf Shia in Kuwait and Bahrain, *al-da'wa* did not become very important in the Saudi context and membership remained limited to some prominent individuals.[3]

Islamist political activism amongst Saudi Shia followed a different trend, namely, the one espoused by the Karbala-based *ayatallah* Muhammad al-Shirazi (see Picture 3.1). Like *al-da'wa*, his group, too, tried to counter socialism and communism from the 1950s onwards. Yet, they were opposed to *al-da'wa* and denounced the adoption of the Western party model. Muhammad al-Shirazi's brother, Hasan, had formulated a theory of a political organisation of the *marji'iyya* with the *marji'* at the head, the *wukala'* in the middle and the *muqallidin* (followers) at the bottom.[4]

---

[2] 'Ali 'Isa Al Mahna, *mun'ataf al-qarar: al-Fadli bayn 'Iraqayn* (The Turn of Decisions: al-Fadli between Two Iraqs) (Beirut: Dar al-Mahajja al-Bayda', 2007); Jabar, *Shi'ite*, 96, 112f.; Joyce N. Wiley, *The Islamic Movement of Iraqi Shi'as* (Boulder, CO: Lynne Rienner, 1992), 157–9; Robin B. Wright, *Sacred Rage: The Crusade of Modern Islam* (London: Andre Deutsch, 1986), 157. Interview with Ghanim Jawad, London, July 2009. See also Fu'ad 'Abd al-Hadi al-Fadli, ed., *qira'at fi fikr al-'allama al-duktur al-Fadli* (Readings in the Thought of the Learned Doctor al-Fadli) (al-Ahsa: al-Lajna al-Diniyya bi-l-Qara, 2008); hizb al-da'wa al-islamiyya: al-maktab al-i'alami, "hizb al-da'wa al-islamiyya yuni'a al-faqid al-'allama samahat ayat allah al-shaykh 'Abd al-Hadi al-Fadli" (The Dawa Party Announces the Death of Ayatallah 'Abd al-Hadi al-Fadli), www.al-daawa. org, 8 April, 2013.

[3] Louër, *Transnational*, 104.

[4] Jabar, *Shi'ite*, 216–19.

In 1968, the group created a secret political organisation, *harakat al-risaliyyin al-tala*ʿ (Movement of Vanguards' Missionaries, MVM).[5] While Muhammad al-Shirazi was the spiritual head, day-to-day operations were masterminded by his nephew, Muhammad Taqi al-Mudarrisi.[6]

The struggle with *al-daʿwa* was also due to the rivalry between Najaf, where *al-daʿwa* originated, and Karbala, the base of the *shiraziyya*, as centres of Shia learning. The Najafi *maraji*ʿ had never accepted the *marjiʿiyya* of Muhammad al-Shirazi. After the death of al-Hakim in 1970, Muhammad al-Shirazi reasserted his claims to the *marjiʿiyya*, prompting al-Hakim's successor al-Khu'i to enact several rulings dismissing the scholarly credentials of al-Shirazi.[7] Another difference was the *shirazi* insistence on popular Shia religious practices such as self-flagellation (*tatbir*) during Muharram, which *al-daʿwa* opposed.[8] Despite these differences, however, the two groups had a lot in common.

These divisions between *maraji*ʿ and political networks were also fostered by competition over revenue from the *khums* tax. After the death of the last local *maraji*ʿ in the mid-twentieth century, Saudi Shia clerics became firmly integrated into the systems of the centralised *marjiʿiyya* in Najaf and Karbala. In the Eastern Province, neighbouring villages often follow different *maraji*ʿ, and different *wukala*ʾ represent a given *marji*ʿ in a village or city. The taxpayer chooses the one that he respects most. So rivalry between Shia clerics has also been driven by competition over resources, and if *wukala*ʾ are not trusted anymore, people may choose another *wakil* or even another *marji*ʿ.[9] Most *wukala*ʾ have permission to collect *khums* for more than one *marji*ʿ. The *wukala*ʾ should invest half of the *khums* locally in social and charitable services and send the other half to the *marji*ʿ. In the 1970s and 1980s the links of the Gulf Shia to the *maraji*ʿ in Najaf were strong. Pilgrims took their own *khums* – and often that of family and friends – and paid it directly to the *marji*ʿ or his associates. The embargo on Iraq after the first Gulf War, however, weakened

---

[5] Munazzamat al-ʿAmal al-Islami fi al-ʿIraq, *al-taʾsis al-sira wa-l-ahdaf* (The Foundation, the Path and the Goals), www.iao-iraq.org; Ibrahim, *Shiʿis*, 73. Interview with Ahmad al-Katib (pseudonym), London, September 2008. Some other names were also used for the group. Jabar calls it *al-haraka al-marjiʿiyya (al-diniyya)*. Jabar, *Shiʿite*, 221.

[6] Louër, *Transnational*, 98f.

[7] Interview with Ahmad al-Katib, London, September 2008. Ahmad al-Katib, *al-marjiʿiyya al-diniyya al-shiʿiyya ... wa-afaq al-tatawwur: al-imam Muhammad al-Shirazi namudhajan* (The Shia Religious Marjiʿiyya ... and the Horizons of Evolution: Imam Muhammad al-Shirazi as an Example) 2nd ed. (Beirut: Arab Scientific Publishers, 2007).

[8] Jabar, *Shiʿite*, 220.

[9] Interview with a Saudi Shia cleric, Beirut, August 2008.

these links because travel to Iraq became difficult. In the absence of pilgrimage, the financial representative of the senior Iraqi *marji'*, Abu al-Qasim al-Khu'i, would collect the money in Saudi Arabia and then hand it on to al-Khu'i or one of his aides.[10]

THE SHIRAZI MOVEMENT

MVM's expansion into the Gulf countries started when Muhammad al-Shirazi and several members of his family and entourage settled in Kuwait in 1971, escaping Iraqi repression. Some Shia notable and merchant families from Kuwait saw the presence of a *marji'* as an honour and facilitated his move. They were, apparently, not aware of the quarrels between al-Shirazi and the Najafi establishment and *al-da'wa*. And while the Shia notable families in Kuwait were confronted by *al-da'wa* activists, they did not initially feel challenged by the *shiraziyyun*. They introduced al-Shirazi to the Kuwaiti upper class and to the Amir. Al-Shirazi vowed to invest the *khums* locally in Kuwait, leading many Kuwaiti Shia merchants to start paying *khums* to al-Shirazi. With this *khums* money, al-Shirazi founded a mosque, a *hussainiyya*, a library, a charitable association and the *hawzat al-Rasul al-'Azam* in the largely Shia suburban neighbourhood of Bneid el-Gar in Kuwait city.[11] It was this *hawza* that would emerge as the breeding ground for the first generation of Saudi Shia Islamist activists, as well as many Bahrainis and Iraqis. The Baath regime's persecution of *hawza* students in Iraq was another reason to establish a *hawza* outside Iraq.

The Saudi students were recruited through personal contacts with Muhammad al-Shirazi and his close associates, as well as through family networks. One of the main former pearl trading families from the island of Tarut (see Picture 3.2), the al-Sayf family, was key in this respect. Muhammad Taqi al-Sayf was an early contractor to ARAMCO, providing food and other basic goods. He used the income from the family's *awqaf* to support young Shia religious students and to invite foreign preachers to the Eastern Province. He had close relations with *maraji'*

---

[10] Interview with Ghanim Jawad, London, September 2008. For a Saudi Shia discussion of *khums* and the system of *wukala'* see Salman bin Hussayn al-Hijji, *ru'ia muhasibiyya li-l-khums wa-l-fara'id al-maliyya* (An Accounting Perspective of the Khums and the Financial Duties) (Beirut: Mu'assasat Umm al-Qura li-l-Tahqiq wa-l-Nashr, n.d.).

[11] Interviews with *shirazi* activists, Kuwait, 2012. Azoulay, *Entre marchands*, 44–9. Interview with Muhammad Taqi al-Mudarrisi on the TV show *Fulan al-Fulani* on al-Sharqiyya TV, Iraq, 2005, http://bahrainonline.org/showthread.php?t=122908.

PICTURE 3.2. Aerial view of parts of Tarut Island.
Source: Tor Eigeland/Saudi Aramco World/SAWDIA.

such as Muhammad Baqir al-Sadr and Muhammad al-Shirazi, who from the mid-1960s onwards would send their associates on preaching tours to the Eastern Province. These preachers such as Murtada al-Qazwini, a cleric from a prominent family in Karbala that had intermarried with the al-Shirazi, stayed at al-Sayf's house and he organised lecture tours across the Qatif area. Amongst the young Saudi Shia who listened to these sermons were Muhammad Taqi al-Sayf's sons Tawfiq, Fawzi and Mahmud. He sent them to Najaf to study in the early 1970s in the hope that one of them would eventually become a *mujtahid*.[12]

In 1971, at the age of thirteen, Hasan al-Saffar, the later spiritual leader of the Organisation for the Islamic Revolution in the Arabian Peninsula, OIRAP (*munazzamat al-thawra al-islamiyya fi al-jazira al-'arabiyya*), went to Najaf as well. At that time, al-Saffar was already known in Qatif as an eloquent preacher and *khatib* and had become acquainted with Muhammad al-Shirazi through his father. Although his family was religious, it was not considered one of the notable families and his father was

---

[12] Interviews with Fawzi and Tawfiq al-Sayf, Eastern Province, Saudi Arabia, November 2008. 'Abd al-Jalil Al Sayf, "al-Hajj Muhammad Taqi Al Sayf," *al-Waha* 47 (2007), 73–7; 'Abd al-Jalil al-Sayf, *mishwar fi durub al-watan: tajriba haya* (Errands on the Path of the Homeland: Experience of a Life) (Riyadh: n.p., 2008), 18–26.

a small merchant.[13] Indeed, the background of the al-Sayfs was rather unusual as they were the only Islamist activists from notable families before the intifada.[14] Al-Saffar stayed in Najaf for two years, enrolling at the *hawza* of al-Khu'i and attending lectures by the most prominent *maraji'*. He also became acquainted with other Saudis in Najaf such as 'Abdallah al-Khunayzi, Ahmad bin Mansur al-Sayf, Mansur bin 'Abdallah al-Bayat and Hasan al-'Awwami. Hasan al-'Awwami had been the secretary of the Qatif municipal council in the 1950s and one of the young leftist activists. When the government tried to arrest him in 1970 he fled Saudi Arabia to undertake religious studies in Najaf, where he stayed until after a general amnesty for Saudi leftist dissidents in 1975. He became an important link between the older generations of Shia notables and leftists and the *shiraziyyun* and would later become one of the most important Shia political notables.[15] He encouraged the young students in Najaf to become active in politics.[16] But the Iraqi security services arrested many clerics, including some Qatifi students, and this led al-Saffar and around fifteen other Saudi students to leave for Qom, the center of Shia religious scholarship in Iran. They enrolled at the *hawza* of one of the leading *maraji'* of Iran, Muhammad Kazim Shariat-Madari.[17]

Around 1974 the al-Sayf brothers, Hasan al-Saffar and some others moved to Kuwait to study in the *hawzat al-Rasul al-'Azam*. The *hawza* was effectively used to build the MVM cadres and its regional branches.

[13] Interview with Hasan al-Saffar, Qatif, November 2008. The biographical material on al-Saffar is partially based on my interview with him and partially on a series of interviews with al-Saffar published in book form: Hasan Musa al-Saffar, *al-madhhab wa-l-watan: mukashafat wa-hiwarat sariha ma' samahat al-shaykh Hasan al-Saffar ajraha al-ustadh 'Abd al-'Aziz Qasim* (The Confession and the Homeland: Interviews and Open Discussions with Shaykh Hasan al-Saffar Conducted by 'Abd al-'Aziz Qasim) (Beirut: al-Mu'assassa al-'Arabiyya li-l-Dirasat wa-l-Nashr, 2008). See also Hasan Musa al-Saffar, *al-imam al-Shirazi: malamih al-shakhsiyya wa-samat al-fikr* (Imam al-Shirazi: Features of the Personality and Attributes of the Thought) (Beirut: al-Amin li-l-Tiba'a wa-l-Nashr wa-l-Tawzi', 2002), 44–8; Louër, *Transnational*, 144–6.

[14] Interview with Tawfiq al-Sayf, Saudi Arabia, November 2008.

[15] He was briefly detained after the intifada in the Eastern Province of 1979/80 and banned from travelling abroad from 1988 until 1994. Al-'Awwami, *al-haraka al-wataniyya*, vol. 1, 259f. See also al-Sayyid Hasan al-'Awwami, *min wahi al-qalam: rasa'il jari'a fi tafa'il al-mujtama' wa-ta'sil al-wahda: al-halaqa al-thalitha* (Of the Inspiration of the Pen: Daring Letters on the Activation of Society and the Rooting of Unity: Part Three) (Beirut: Dar al-Mahajja al-Bayda'/al-Waha li-l-Khadamat al-Thaqafiyya, 2005); al-Sayyid Hasan al-Sayyid Baqir al-'Awwami, *min thamarat 'amri: hasila qira'at 70 'aman* (Of the Fruits of My Life: Outcome of Readings of 70 Years), 2 vols. vol 1. (Beirut: Mu'assasat al-Intishar al-'Arabi, 2008).

[16] Al-Saffar, *al-madhhab*, 74.

[17] Ibid., 84–6.

As one of the leaders of the *shiraziyya* stated, 'Under the protection of the *hawza*, we started a secret political organisation and expanded into the Gulf countries'.[18] From around 1978 onwards Gulf security services became aware of teachings emerging from the *hawza* and spreading to Bahrain and the Eastern Province.[19] The first floor of the *hawza* was used for traditional religious lectures, while the second floor, under the guidance of Muhammad Taqi al-Mudarrisi, was dedicated to political education. It seems that the *hawza* was intended to do nothing less than revolutionise the whole *hawza* system of Shia learning. Al-Mudarrisi introduced disciplines such as literature, historical studies and politics, while trying to limit the impact of Greek-influenced philosophy.[20] The students read books by Muhammad al-Shirazi, Muhammad Taqi al-Mudarrisi, Hadi al-Mudarrisi, as well as movement-internal literature written by anonymous authors for indoctrination purposes and the classics of Sunni Islamism such as Hasan al-Banna, Sayyid Qutb or Abu al-A'la Mawdudi.[21] According to Ibrahim, the very name of the movement, the 'vanguards' missionaries', reflected Qutb's vision of the idea of the vanguard that would root out *jahili* society.[22] Ali Shariati's revolutionary re-reading of Shia history and his emphasis on activism and martyrdom also heavily influenced the MVM discourse.[23] The pamphlets by Hasan al-Saffar from the late 1970s and early 1980s show how he adapted this ideology and how he used Hussayn[24], Imam Mahdi[25] and other aspects of Islamic history.

Tawfiq al-Sayf recalls that going to Kuwait from the traditional *hawza* in Najaf felt like entering a different world. Here, they had tutors and were encouraged to read widely. One of the first books was an introduction to the movement, a book about the messages of Prophet Muhammad

[18] Interview with Ahmad al-Katib, London, September 2008.
[19] Wright, *Sacred Rage*, 126.
[20] Louër, *Transnational*, 124.
[21] Ibrahim, *al-faqih*, 357–69; Ibrahim, *Shi'is*, 73–104; Louër, *Transnational*, 124; 'Adil Ra'uf, *al-'amal al-islami fi al-'Iraq bayn al-marji'iyya wa-l-hizbiyya: qira'a naqdiyya li-masirat nisf qarn (1950–2000)* (The Islamic Action in Iraq between the Marji'iyya and the Party System: A Critical Reading of the Voyage of Half a Century 1950–2000) (Damascus: al-Markaz al-'Iraqi li-l-I'lam wa-l-Dirasat, 2000), 265–81.
[22] Ibrahim, *Shi'is*, 84.
[23] Ibid., 90–8.
[24] Hasan al-Saffar, *al-Hussayn wa-mas'uliyyat al-thawra* (Hussayn and the Responsibility of Revolution), 7th ed. (Beirut: Dar al-Bayan al-'Arabi, 1991).
[25] The lecture reprinted in this booklet was delivered by al-Saffar in Saihat on 21 July 1978 during the birthday of Imam Mahdi. Hasan al-Saffar, *al-imam al-mahdi: amal al-shu'ub* (Beirut: Mu'assasat al-A'lami li-l-Matbu'at, 1979).

stating that the Prophet had sided with the poor and tried to liberate them. He also read books by Nehru and Churchill as well as Hitler's *Mein Kampf*.[26] Hasan al-Saffar recounts that he initially attended the religious classes of Muhammad al-Shirazi, to whom he became very close, and that he only gradually became acquainted with the political side through Muhammad Taqi al-Mudarrisi.[27] It seems that the MVM leaders, mainly Muhammad Taqi and his brother, Hadi al-Mudarrisi, decided in 1975 to establish a Saudi and a Bahraini branch of the movement.[28]

The Saudi group was headed by Hasan al-Saffar and Tawfiq al-Sayf and after the intifada it adopted the name OIRAP. Others from the Qatif region who belonged to the first generation of the movement in Kuwait in the 1970s were Yusuf al-Mahdi, Hasan al-Khuwayldi and Fawzi, Mahmud, and Mansur al-Sayf.[29] Although MVM was initially a movement opposed to the Iraqi regime, it also conceived itself as a global movement with goals that went beyond Iraq. MVM did not want to endanger relations with the Kuwaiti authorities and therefore refrained from overt political activities in Kuwait itself. But Muhammad al-Shirazi gained many new followers from Bahrain and Saudi Arabia during his time in Kuwait, who also expected that some of their *khums* would benefit people in their countries.[30]

The young Saudi students were given propaganda materials to distribute on their trips back to Saudi Arabia, where they sought to recruit young students for the *hawza* in Kuwait. Notably Hasan al-Saffar and Tawfiq al-Sayf held discussion sessions and participants who were prepared to join were then sent to Kuwait. There, they attended a two-week course during the summer holidays in which they were indoctrinated and prepared for underground organisational activities. Some stayed on to become full-time students in Kuwait, while others returned and gathered in Qatif and al-Ahsa. The groups focussed on areas around Qatif, mainly Safwa, Tarut and villages like Awwamiyya, but a number of people from al-Ahsa were also recruited early on. A descendant of the prominent Abu Khamsin clerical family of Hufuf, Musa Abu Khamsin, became involved at the instigation of Hasan al-Saffar after having visited Muhammad

---

[26] Interview with Tawfiq al-Sayf, Eastern Province, November 2008.
[27] Al-Saffar, *al-madhhab*, 97.
[28] Al-Hasan, "al-muʿarada;" al-ʿAmir, *al-haraka*, 145; Fandy, *Saudi Arabia*, 198; Ibrahim, *Shiʿis*, 7.
[29] Ibid., 108.
[30] Interview with Ahmad al-Katib, London, September 2008; al-Katib, *al-marjiʿiyya*, 62–5.

al-Shirazi in Kuwait. His younger brother, Hussayn, also went to study in Kuwait in 1977.[31]

Discussion sessions held in private raised the importance of intellectual change in the Islamic *umma* and criticised the traditional Shia trends. The taped sermons and pamphlets of Muhammad al-Shirazi were widely circulated. Young clerics such as Hasan al-Saffar increasingly preached to larger audiences in *hussainiyyat* and at Shia religious festivities.[32] Recruitment focussed on high school and university students but some teachers and graduates were also brought into the Saudi movement soon after its inception. The presence of young preachers was a novelty and resonated well with the youth. One later member of the movement from Awwamiyya recalls that his father, who was an Akhbari, would not take him to the *hussainiyya* and if he went himself he would be sent home because of his age. In contrast, the teenagers felt taken more seriously by the young preachers such as the al-Sayf brothers and al-Saffar.[33]

While virtually all the clerical OIRAP leadership passed through the *hawza* in Kuwait, some of the later lay cadres, who were called the *effendiyya* within the movement, stayed in Saudi Arabia. Hamza al-Hasan, who became a key figure in the movement later on, was recruited in 1976/77. Until the intifada, however, he did not join the *hawza* in Kuwait and just met and discussed movement literature with his supervisor from his hometown, Safwa. Until 1979 al-Hasan did not know how many members the movement had and only during the intifada did he become aware of the full extent of mobilisation.[34]

Young unmarried women between fifteen and twenty were also recruited. One female activist recalls how her relative returned from Kuwait around 1977 and told her about the Islamic awakening. He said that time was ripe for change and gave her books and articles to distribute to her cousins and friends and she started to gather with them.[35] Apart from photocopied pamphlets the cells were distributing the magazine *al-Shahid* (The Martyr), which was the regular MVM publication. The first fifteen issues of this bi-monthly magazine were published from early 1978 in the United Kingdom and from 1979 to 2003 it was published in

---

[31] Al-Hijji, *hakatha*, 99, 321; al-Saffar, *al-madhhab*, 156.
[32] Interviews with Tawfiq al-Sayf and Hasan al-Saffar, November 2008, Eastern Province; Ibrahim, *Shi'is*, 106–8, 119.
[33] Interview with a Saudi Shia, Eastern Province, November 2008.
[34] Interview with Hamza al-Hasan, London, April 2008.
[35] Interview with a group of female OIRAP activists, Eastern Province, November 2008.

Iran.[36] Just as before the Iranian Revolution, in which cassette tapes of revolutionary clerics played a decisive role, taped sermons by al-Saffar and others started to circulate widely in the Eastern Province from the mid-1970s onwards and had a considerable impact.[37]

The Shia notables opposed this new movement for several reasons. Firstly, it was seen as a direct threat to their political, social and religious position. They knew that they would be held responsible if they could not control political dissent. Other reasons were their alliance with the Najafi establishment and their disapproval of the *marji'iyya* of Muhammad al-Shirazi. But maybe even more important was the fact that a youngster from a non-notable family such as Hasan al-Saffar started to denounce their relations with the state. They thus appealed to Abu al-Qasim al-Khu'i, the highest-ranking *marji'* in Najaf at the time, who issued several communiqués in the late 1970s discrediting Hasan al-Saffar as well as Muhammad al-Shirazi.

Similar developments took place in Oman, where Hasan al-Saffar mainly resided from 1974 until 1979. There are two main Twelver Shia groups in Oman, the Lawatiyya and the Baharina. The Lawatiyya are Shia of Indian origin and the Baharina stem originally from Bahrain. While al-Saffar was initially invited to Muscat by the Bahrani merchant 'Abd al-Rida al-'Asfur, he was mainly active amongst the Lawatiyya. Al-Saffar became Friday prayer leader in a mosque in Muscat and tried to spread Islamic awareness, recruited young men to send them to the *hawza* in Kuwait, opened libraries in Muscat and encouraged some Lawatiyya to hold Ashura processions with banners in public. This led to a conflict with the Luti merchant notables, who enjoyed very close relations with the Sultan.[38] It might have been that some Omani merchants asked al-Khu'i for a fatwa against al-Saffar as well. But at

---

[36] Interview with a former leading MVM member, August 2008, Syria. 'Abd al-Rahman al-Shaykh, Salih al-Dukhayyil, and 'Abdallah al-Zayir, *intifadat al-mintaqa al-sharqi-yya 1400AH-1979m* (The Uprising of the Eastern Province 1979) (n.p.: Munazzamat al-Thawra al-Islamiyya fi al-Jazira al-'Arabiyya, 1981), 77; Ibrahim, *Shi'is*, 10; Wiley, *Islamic*, 164.

[37] Mamoun Fandy, "Saudi Opposition between Globalization and Localization," *Comparative Studies in Society and History* 41, no. 1 (1999), 124–47, 131; Annabelle Sreberny and Ali Mohammadi, *Small Media, Big Revolution: Communication, Culture, and the Iranian Revolution* (Minneapolis: University of Minnesota Press, 1994), 119–21. In the 1980s, Sunni Islamists in Saudi Arabia also made use of Islamic cassettes to spread their message. Lacroix, *Awakening*, 140–4.

[38] Marc Valeri, "High Visibility, Low Profile: The Shi'a in Oman under Sultan Qaboos," *International Journal of Middle East Studies* 42, no. 2 (2010), 251–68, 259f., 263f.

least one communiqué was issued at the request of Qatifi scholars from notable families in September 1979.[39] But by that time the *shiraziyyun* had already decided to revolt against their own political elite as well as against the state.

THE UPRISING OF 1979

The first ten days of Muharram are especially important for Shia and culminate on the tenth of Muharram (Ashura), when they commemorate the martyrdom of Hussayn in 680. During these ten days public processions and passion plays re-enact Hussayn's life and death as a struggle against oppression in general. For Shia Muslims around the world these processions are probably the most important events in re-enacting Shia collective memories.[40] These general Shia narratives have been interwoven with particularly Saudi Shia narratives of oppression that have been spread by Shia Islamist activists. They have tried to create a distinctively Saudi Shia 'collective memory', to incorporate a term coined by Halbwachs.[41] This collective memory is evoked through a variety of rituals, re-enactments, and religious ceremonies and processions.[42]

In Saudi Arabia, however, Shia have been largely banned from observing these rituals in public since 1913 in order not to arouse the anger of Wahhabi *'ulama'*. Yet, they have held these and other rituals in private in their *hussainiyyat* or in confined spaces, and tensions with the religious police and the security forces increased every year during Muharram.[43]

---

[39] Al-Saffar, *al-madhhab*, 160–2; Ibrahim, *Shi'is*, 107; Louër, *Transnational*, 146–9.

[40] Ibrahim Haidari, *Zur Soziologie des schiitischen Chiliasmus* (Freiburg in Breisgau: Klaus Schwarz, 1975); Ibrahim Haydari, "The Rituals of Ashura: Genealogy, Functions, Actors and Structures," in *Ayatollahs, Sufis and Ideologues: State, Religion and Social Movements in Iraq*, ed. Faleh A. Jabar (London: Saqi Books, 2002), 101–13; Sabrina Mervin, "Ashura: Some Remarks on Ritual Practices in Different Shiite Communities (Lebanon and Syria)," in *The Other Shiites: From the Mediterranean to Central Asia*, ed. Alessandro Monsutti, Silvia Naef, and Farian Sabahi (New York: Peter Lang, 2008), 137–47; Yitzhak Nakash, *The Shi'is of Iraq*, 2nd ed. (Princeton, NJ: Princeton University Press, 2003).

[41] Maurice Halbwachs, *On Collective Memory* (Chicago: The University of Chicago Press, 1992).

[42] Maurice Halbwachs, *La topographie légendaire des Évangiles en Terre Sainte: Étude de memoire collective* (Paris: Presses Universitaires de France, 1941).

[43] Burdett, *Records of Saudi Arabia 1966–1971*, vol. 5: *1970*, 512f. When Major H. R. P. Dickson, the British political agent in Bahrain, undertook an expedition to al-Ahsa in 1920 he observed, 'In Hassa Shiahs [*sic*] are not allowed to celebrate Hussayn's death in the way they do in Basrah [*sic*] nor are they allowed to call to prayer. Both are also

In 1958, for example, sectarian clashes broke out during Muharram in Qatif, after Sunnis mocked Shia for their rituals. Some Shia reacted with violence and the police had to call in reinforcements to restore order. Saihat 'was ringed with police armed with tommy guns who put the disturbances down and arrested some of the leaders'.[44] Because of fears that renewed sectarian clashes 'would lead to further discrimination against Shia and oppression of their religious observances', the Shia confined their rituals to areas where they were a majority. In mixed areas such as Safwa and Anak, mourners would only move from *hussainiyya* to *hussainiyya* if these were nearby and in areas that are only inhabited by Shia, or at night to prevent confrontations with local Sunnis. During Ashura 1960, Shia from across the Eastern Province flocked to Saihat and Awwamiyya to hold the processions in public and engage in self-flagellation. The Muharram processions did not, however, include large re-enactments of the death of Hussayn or the 'self-mutilation with swords and knives'.[45] So by and large, Eastern Province Shia refrained from holding these processions in public or traveled to rather isolated villages such as Awwamiyya and majority Shia towns such as Saihat to perform the rituals in public. During Muharram many would also go on pilgrimage or travel to Bahrain, where the rituals could be held in public.

Given the huge emotional attachment of many religious Shia to these mourning processions, it was perhaps obvious that political dissent was articulated through these rituals and the legacy of political Shia Islam. The political discourse that the *shiraziyyun* had spread over the past years constituted a powerful ideology and served to frame the feelings of dissent. Hadi al-Mudarrisi, the MVM's deputy leader and the head of its Bahraini branch, Islamic Front for the Liberation of Bahrain (IFLB) (*al-jabha al-islamiyya li-tahrir al-Bahrayn*), had travelled to the Eastern Province in the late 1970s to organise new MVM cells. Other senior figures such as Sahib al-Sadiq, the headmaster of the *hawza* in Kuwait and Murtada al-Qazwini, a close associate of Muhammad al-Shirazi, also went to Qatif. The latter delivered fiery sermons during Ashura 1978 and a year later

forbidden to sell rifles or ammunition or to possess them.' Tuson and Burdett, *Records of Saudi Arabia*, vol. 3: 1918–1926, 260.

[44] Malcolm Quint, *Mourning Ceremonies during the First Ten Days of Muharram in Qatif Oasis*, Dhahran, 11 July 1960. Box 3, Folder 2, Mulligan Papers.

[45] Ibid.

in a *hussainiyya* in Qatif that became a rallying point for the protesters during the intifada.[46]

Ashura processions were held in public in Awwamiyya in 1978, leading to clashes with security forces.[47] But the decision to hold these processions in public across the region including in Qatif during Muharram 1979 was an open act of defiance of the government. Some Shia clerics had announced in the summer of 1979 that they wanted to hold Muharram processions in public.[48] This was even more significant because protests during Muharram a year earlier had been key in the Iranian Revolution, which had caused the Shah to flee Iran in January 1979. In addition, on 1 Muharram 1400 (20 November 1979), the first day of the new century according to the Islamic calendar, a group of Sunni rebels led by Juhayman al-'Utaybi occupied the Grand Mosque of Mecca. They held out for three weeks. This occupation at the heart of the Muslim world was a shock to the Saudi rulers, and the first demonstrations in Qatif only five days later must have alerted them to the possibility of a rebellion cutting across sectarian lines.[49] Initially, many observers thought the al-'Utaybi group was a Shia- or Iranian-backed rebel group, a false view that persists in some accounts.[50] Although the al-'Utaibi group was unrelated to the uprising in the Eastern Province and made up of dissatisfied tribal elements and former National Guard officials, the Saudi Shia opposition later published widely on the events and tried to link the two *intifadat* and portray them as two sides of the same coin, namely, an Islamist opposition cutting across sectarian lines.[51]

---

[46] Ibrahim, *Shi'is*, 108; Louër, *Transnational*, 165.

[47] *Ahdath november (muharram) 1979 fi al-su'udiyya* (Events of November (Muharram) 1979 in Saudi) (n.p.: Manshurat al-Hizb al-Shuyu'i fi al-Su'udiyya, n.d.), 26; al-Shaykh, et al., *intifadat*, 106.

[48] Buchan, "Opposition," 119

[49] Holden and Johns, *The House of Saud*, 511–26; Louër, *Transnational*, 162; Gary Samuel Samore, *Royal Family Politics in Saudi Arabia (1953–1982)* (PhD, Harvard University, 1983), 441; Yaroslav Trofimov, *The Siege of Mecca: The Forgotten Uprising* (London: Allen Lane, 2007).

[50] See, for example, Brown, *Oil*, 345.

[51] *Intifadat al-haram* (The Uprising of the Sanctuary) (London: Munazzamat al-Thawra al-Islamiyya fi al-Jazira al-Arabiyya, 1981); Fahd al-Qahtani, *zilzal Juhayman fi Makka* (Juhayman's Earthquake in Mecca) (London: Munazzamat al-Thawra al-Islamiyya fi al-Jazira al-Arabiyya, 1987). See also Thomas Hegghammer and Stéphane Lacroix, "Rejectionist Islamism in Saudi Arabia: The Story of Juhayman al-'Utaybi Revisited," *International Journal of Middle East Studies* 39, no. 1 (2007), 103–22, 112, 119.

PICTURE 3.3. Protest during the 1979 uprising.
Source: OIRAP.

On the same day as the seizure of the Grand Mosque, 1 Muharram, some Shia in Safwa took to the streets. The *shiraziyyun* later wrote that 'notables' and 'feudalists', whom the government told to keep the processions off the streets after the first night, impeded the 'revolutionary youth' in other areas.[52] The chief security officer in ARAMCO reported to the American Consulate in Dhahran that there had been agitation by ARAMCO's Shia 'work force in sensitive Ras Tanura area to "chase" Americans out of refinery' and that similar demands had been voiced during meetings in Qatif and Saihat. Quoting a 'reliable Shi'a source within the company', he stated that the 'emotions of the Shi'as here will likely peak on 7th, 8th and 9th of muharram (26, 27 and 28th of November) and warned that there could be disturbances during this period'.[53]

In a pamphlet published just days later, in December 1979, the newly founded 'Organisation for the Islamic Revolution in the "Saudi" Arabian Peninsula' (OIRAP) argued that a letter had been sent to American employees of ARAMCO warning them that they would be targeted,

---

[52] Al-Shaykh et al., *intifadat*, 97–9, 129, 172–5.
[53] U.S. Diplomatic Cable, American Consulate Dhahran, *Update on Mood of Saudi Shi'as and Current Security Situation*, Cable 1854, 21 November 1979.

especially if the United States attacked Iran from Saudi soil. The group later dropped "Saudi" from its name. The letter was signed by the Islamic Group of ARAMCO Workers *(al-tajammu' al-islami li-'ummal aramku)*, and the pamphlet claims that this letter caused a hundred Americans and their families to leave Saudi Arabia.[54] The CIA apparently gave Crown Prince Fahd an intelligence report suggesting that Shia revolutionaries intended to blow up a major refinery in the Eastern Province.[55] Indeed, the American government was deeply worried by the Shia unrest and asked its embassy to draw up evacuation plans after the first days of protests.[56] U.S. Ambassador John C. West replied to the State Department that Prince Bandar had promised to crush the Shia uprising 'as long as (Washington) didn't complain too much about human rights violations'.[57]

On 25 November 1979 thousands finally joined the demonstrations. After they had listened to revolutionary sermons in the Sinnan *hussainiyya* in Qatif, a group of mainly young Shia went out into the streets shouting, "God is Great". In the previous days, pamphlets had been widely circulated urging Shia to perform Muharram rituals in public.[58] People also took to the streets and clashed with security forces in Saihat and Awwamiyya.[59] The next day, 7 Muharram/27 November, the crowds grew even bigger. Some speak of seventy thousand protesters in the whole region on that day,[60] while others claim there were four thousand in Safwa alone.[61] Yet others mention four thousand, including many

---

[54] *Intifadat al-muharram fi al-mintaqa al-sharqiyya: al-halqa al-ula (watha'iq al-intifada)* (The Uprising of Muharram in the Eastern Province: The First Part [Documents of the Uprising]) (n.p.: Munazzamat al-Thawra al-Islamiyya fi al-Jazira al-'Arabiyya 'al-Su'udiyya', 1979), 15–18; Jones, "Rebellion," 225; U.S. Diplomatic Cable, American Consulate Dhahran, *Anti-American Letters Being Sent to ARAMCO Employees*, Telegram 1956, 9 December 1979; "Envoy Tells Uneasy Americans in Saudi Arabia They'll Be Safe; Troops Said to Fire on Shiites," *New York Times*, 6 December 1979. For OIRAP statements in 1979 and 1980 see Munazzamat al-Thawra al-Islamiyya fi al-Jazira al-'Arabiyya, *al-bayyanat al-lati sadarat khilal 'am 1400–1401 A.H.* (The Statements that were Published in the Year 1979/1980) (n.p.: n.p., n.d.).

[55] Trofimov quotes the diary of the U.S. ambassador to Saudi Arabia at the time, John C. West. Trofimov, *Siege*, 181f.

[56] U.S. Diplomatic Cable, from Secretary of State to Ambassador West, *Possible Evacuation of American Citizens from Saudi Arabia*, 29 November 1979.

[57] Ambassador John C. West's diary, quoted after Trofimov, *Siege*, 199.

[58] Al-Shaykh et al., *intifadat*, 100–10; Trofimov, *Siege*, 183f. See also U.S. Diplomatic Cable, American Consulate Dhahran, *Tensions Rise among Saudi Shi'as in Eastern Province*, Cable 1872, 26 November 1979.

[59] *Ahdath november*, 26; al-Shaykh, et al., *intifadat*, 106.

[60] Ibrahim, *Shi'is*, 119

[61] Jones, "Rebellion," 223.

PICTURE 3.4. Protest on 29 November 1979 (9 Muharram 1400), Safwa.
Source: OIRAP.

women, in Awwamiyya on 27 November[62] and tens of thousands on 28
November, with sixteen thousand to eighteen thousand in Qatif alone.[63]
On 28 November, the clashes turned violent in Saihat, Qatif, Safwa and
the surrounding villages, as the National Guard opened fire on protesters.
This led to the first deaths on both sides, as demonstrators assaulted soldiers and stole several guns. The demonstrators used Molotov cocktails,
burned government vehicles and hid in the narrow lanes of the Old Town
of Qatif, where they ambushed the National Guard. Some demonstrators carried pictures of Ruhollah Khomeini (see Picture 3.5), chanting
slogans popularised during the Iranian Revolution such as '*la sunniyya
la shi'iyya … thawra thawra islamiyya*' (Not Sunni, not Shia … Islamic
Revolution). Some even called for the death of the ruling family, chanting,
'*al-mawt li-Al Saud*'.[64]

In the following days, Qatif was effectively cut off from the outside
and protests resumed the next day in even higher numbers to commemorate the martyrs. Protesters looted offices of the Saudi British Bank and
of Saudia, the national airline. They also stormed the seat of the governor
of Qatif. The situation in the province calmed down after Ashura, 10
Muharram/30 November 1979, although protests erupted again on 12

[62] Al-Shaykh et al., *intifadat*, 128.
[63] *Ahdath november*, 23.
[64] Al-Labad, *al-inqilab*, 36; al-Shaykh et al., *intifadat*, 128–51.

PICTURE 3.5. Protesters carry a picture of Khomeini during the 1979 uprising.
Source: OIRAP.

January 1980, forty days after the death of the first 'martyr', and on 1
February, the first anniversary of Ruhollah Khomeini's return to Iran (see
Picture 3.6).[65] The newly formed OIRAP claimed responsibility for these
last demonstrations, which also turned violent.[66] The Iranian newspaper *Jomhuri-ye Eslami* (Islamic Republic) claimed that the protests on 1
February 1980 were in support of the Iranian Revolution and published
an OIRAP statement vowing that the protests would continue until an
Islamic republic was established in Saudi Arabia.[67] Overall, between seventeen and twenty-six Shia and up to ten soldiers were killed during the
clashes, and hundreds injured and even more arrested.[68]

Even though the intifada was mainly the work of the *shiraziyyun*,
some leftists also participated. They were unaware that the Islamists had

<hr>

[65] *Ahdath november*, 33f.; al-Rasheed, *A History*, 146–8; Ibrahim, *Shiʿis*, 117–23; Jones,
      "Rebellion;" Robert Lacey, *Inside the Kingdom: Kings, Clerics, Modernists, Terrorists
      and the Struggle for Saudi Arabia* (London: Penguin, 2009), 39–45; Louër, *Transnational*,
      161–7; Nakash, *Reaching*, 50–2; Ramazani, *Revolutionary*, 39–42; Trofimov, *Siege*,
      179–86, 198–201; Vassiliev, *The History*, 397.
[66] Al-Hasan, *al-shiʿa*, vol. 2, 388.
[67] Foreign Broadcast Information Service (*FBIS*), 6 February 1980.
[68] Kostiner, "Shiʿi Unrest," 179. OIRAP sources present a list of twenty-six 'martyrs of the
      intifada'; al-Hasan, *al-shiʿa*, vol. 2, 385; al-Labad, *al-inqilab*, 27f.

PICTURE 3.6. Protest in Qatif on 17 January 1980 (28 Safar 1400).
Source: OIRAP.

planned an escalation during Muharram. The religious leaders feared
that cooperation with leftists would undermine their status. As a result,
the leftists joined the demonstrations independently, carrying their own
banners and trying to urge the Islamists not to use sectarian slogans,
reminding them that 'Saudi Arabia was not Iran'. They argued that protesters should focus on wider issues and that the government would use a
sectarian discourse as a pretext for even harder repression.[69]

Especially younger leftists joined the demonstrations out of a feeling of
'communal solidarity' and a desire to revolt, over-coming the ideological
and organisational rivalries between leftists and Islamists after the first
waves of violence.[70] The communists even claimed that in the first days of
Muharram, the protests spilled over to Khobar and Dammam.[71] Mainly
communists and *hizb al-'amal* members joined the demonstrations[72] but
the baathists also published their own version of the events in a special
issue of their magazine. Like the Shia Islamists, the leftists tried to link the

---

[69] *Ahdath november*, 21f.; Jones, "Rebellion," 226f.
[70] Louër, *Transnational*, 163.
[71] *Ahdath november*, 24.
[72] Al-'Akri, *al-tanzimat*, 217f. For an account of the events in the *hizb al-'amal* journal see
al-Masira 10 (June 1980), 10f.

seizure of the Grand Mosque in Mecca with the uprising in the Eastern Province. They did not see it as an 'Islamic uprising', however, describing both uprisings as part of a people's revolution in Saudi Arabia.[73] Another peculiarity was the participation of hundreds of women, mostly from the *shirazi* movement but also some leftists, in the demonstrations. Some of them were injured and one woman was killed by shots fired from a helicopter.[74]

In the aftermath of the intifada, OIRAP considered the ideological differences too big to cooperate with the leftists.[75] The diverging interpretations of the intifada by OIRAP and the Communist Party even led to a sharp exchange of words in the mid-1980s, when members of both groups were in exile in Damascus and had contact with one another. In 1987, OIRAP attacked the Communist Party after one of its spokesmen – OIRAP calls him Abu ʿAjib (Father Strange) – had delivered a speech at a meeting of the Communist Party in Lebanon in December 1986, where he had attacked the Islamists, described them as backward, and emphasised the Communist Party's role in the *intifada November*, as the communists called the uprising in November 1979. OIRAP responded that the Communist Party had participated with 'ten youths' and asked whether the timing of the intifada was based on the religious importance of Muharram or it occurred on that date because 'the people celebrate in that month the birthday of the glorious Communist Party'? OIRAP argued that the communists had only left their 'closed rooms and ARAMCO offices' after the Islamists – the real vanguard (*al-taliʿa*) – and the masses had taken to the streets.[76]

OIRAP ensured that Saudi Shia did not forget about the intifada, using it as a main element to foster Saudi Shia collective identities.[77] It published several accounts of the intifada, which was a recurrent theme in its mouthpiece *al-Thawra al-Islamiyya* (The Islamic Revolution); every year a special issue focussed on the intifada.[78] OIRAP also held annual commemorations of the intifada in Tehran, where al-Saffar gave speeches.[79] Just after the intifada, OIRAP urged its supporters to donate 25 percent

---

[73] *Sawt al-Taliʿa* 22 (1980). A Saudi baathist also published a book on the Mecca events. See Hegghammer and Lacroix, "Rejectionist Islamism," 119.
[74] *Ahdath november*, 5, 21, 27; al-Labad, *al-inqilab*, 28. See the biography of *Shahida Fatima al-Gharib* in *al-Thawra al-Islamiyya* 9 (December 1980), 8.
[75] Al-ʿAmir, *al-haraka*, 171f.
[76] *Al-Thawra al-Islamiyya* 82 (January 1987), 21–3.
[77] Ibrahim, *Shiʿis*, 139.
[78] See for example *al-Thawra al-Islamiyya* 42 (October 1983).
[79] *Al-Thawra al-Islamiyya* 57 (January 1985), 40–2.

of their income in the month of Muharram to 'finance the revolution in its propaganda and political activities and to help the families of the martyrs and the prisoners'.[80]

THE LIMITS OF NOTABLE POLITICS

After the first protests, Prince Ahmad bin 'Abd al-'Aziz, the deputy minister of interior, went to the Eastern Province and met several times with local notables.[81] He told them that it was their duty to end the protests. According to the Communist Party, the state worked with the 'feudalists and the big bourgeoisie' but some of them argued that 'the situation had gotten out of their hands and that they could not stop' the protests. One of the main notables of Saihat, the businessman 'Abdallah al-Matrud, was very outspoken about Shia grievances. In return, Prince Ahmad acknowledged that Qatif 'had not received its fair share of central government funds and promised to rectify' the situation. He argued that if the Shia co-operated their situation would improve.[82] Although most notables were opposed to the uprising, it also emboldened them to voice Shia grievances. In a letter to King Khalid after the uprising, the notables of Qatif regretted the loss of dozens of lives and the atmosphere of fear in the months afterward. They argued, however, that the uprising was a result of discrimination against Shia on ideological, social and cultural levels, which had fostered a sense of exclusion.[83]

The state sought to address some of the economic causes of the uprising, while using repression against those deemed responsible.[84] In the weeks and months following Muharram, the government announced an electricity project, the building of new streets and schools, a new hospital, and projects for additional street lighting, communications and sewage and provided loans through the Real Estate Development Fund (REDF) to enable citizens to build homes. King Khalid also visited the area, including

---

[80] *Al-Thawra al-Islamiyya* 8 (1980).

[81] Samore, *Royal*, 441.

[82] The communists mention a Hasan al-Matrud: *Ahdath november*, 22. An American cable described details of this meeting and says that al-Matrud was an 'establishment type': U.S. Diplomatic Cable, American Consulate Dhahran, *SAG Attempts to Mollify Shi'as*, Telegram 1916, 2 December 1979; Holden and Johns, *The House of Saud*, 525. For more on al-Matrud see Field, *Merchants*, 82f., 241; *ARAMCO World* (January–February 1972), 2–5.

[83] Letter from notables of Qatif to King Khalid, 1980. From a private collection of letters and petitions by Shia notables, Saudi Arabia.

[84] U.S. Diplomatic Cable, American Consulate Dhahran, *SAG Attempts to Mollify Shi'as*.

PICTURE 3.7. Ruins of the Old City of Qatif.
Source: Photographer unkwnown/Saudi Aramco World/SAWDIA.

Qatif, accompanied by local notables.[85] Some Shia, however, distrusted the government and were reluctant to apply for these loans.[86] The notables continued to petition the government throughout 1980 to release the hundreds of prisoners arrested during the uprising.[87] The announcement of their release just days before Muharram 1980 and the permission to hold limited Ashura processions were seen as part of a slight shift in state policy.[88] But it was also harsh repression and the large-scale deployment of security forces that restored a sense of calm to the Eastern Province.

It is an irony of history that much of the fighting took place in the historical seat of the notable families, the Old Town of Qatif (*al-qal'a*). As a response to the intifada, the Saudi state destroyed the centre of the Old Town and the remnants of the Portuguese fort (See Picture 3.7). The narrow alleys were difficult to police and a perfect hideout. The state wanted to prevent this from happening again. But the destruction of the historical centre of Qatif was also a humiliation of the notable families

---

[85] Goldberg, "Shi'i Minority," 244; Ramazani, *Revolutionary*, 41; MECS, 1980–1, 733f.

[86] Jones, *Dogma*, 228f.; William B. Quandt, *Saudi Arabia in the 1980s: Foreign Policy, Security, and Oil* (Washington, DC: The Brookings Institution, 1981), 97.

[87] See several letters from notables of Qatif reprinted in al-Hasan, *al-shi'a*, vol. 2, 423–31.

[88] Abir, *Saudi Arabia: Government*, 86f.; Goldberg, "Shi'i Minority," 244; Ramazani, *Revolutionary*, 40–2.

and the Shia.[89] To symbolise its dominance physically, the state turned the centre of *al-qal'a* into a car park and built a large Sunni mosque adjacent to it.[90] The notable families used the traditional channels – meetings and petitions – in an attempt to prevent the razing, but without success. As many of the properties there were the old houses of the notable families, they tried to gain adequate compensation. But this, too, proved difficult. The state apparently agreed to pay homeowners 50 percent of the value of their homes. However, as some of the land and *awqaf* registries were issued by the Shia court or the previous Shia judges in Qatif, they were not recognised by the Sunni *katib 'adl*, reflecting some of the problems surrounding the Shia courts discussed in the first chapter.[91] The notables had effectively become an 'imagined community' to use a term coined by Benedict Anderson.[92] They still refer to themselves as being 'from al-qal'a (the castle)', although the castle is not there anymore.

CONCLUSION

After the intifada the state began to see the Shia in the Eastern Province as a serious security threat. This perception has dominated the state's view of the Shia ever since.[93] This also had an impact on the several thousand Shia who worked for ARAMCO. Towards the end of the 1970s, the number of new workers in ARAMCO increased. But the Iranian Revolution, the intifada and the seizure of the Grand Mosque in Mecca led to stronger measures to ensure security in the oilfields of the Eastern Province, where the Saudis further increased their military presence after the outbreak of the Iran-Iraq War in September 1980. The security of the oil and gas industry was the responsibility of the Ministry of Interior, which established a commission for industrial security. This commission decided who would get sensitive jobs. It worked together with the Saudi Arab Manpower Committee (SAMCOM), created in 1979, which carried out recruitment at ARAMCO.[94]

---

[89] Jones, *Dogma*, 266f.

[90] Interviews with Saudi Shia and personal observations, Qatif, Saudi Arabia, November 2008.

[91] Letters from notables of Qatif, 1980 to 1985. From a private collection of letters and petitions by Shia notables, Saudi Arabia. See also al-Hasan, *al-shi'a*, vol. 2, 465–8; Jones, *Dogma*, 267.

[92] Benedict Anderson, *Imagined Communities: Reflections on the Origin and Spread of Nationalism*, 2nd ed. (London: Verso, 1991).

[93] Long, "Impact," 105. Interview with a Shia notable, November 2008, Saudi Arabia.

[94] Other names are 'Supreme Commission for Industrial Security' and 'High Commission of Industrial Security'. Interview with former senior ARAMCO official, Eastern Province,

One of its unwritten policies was that Shia should not be hired in security or any other key sector of the oil industry. If Shia were hired at all, they were employed as drivers, clerks, gardeners, or in storehouses, food and community services. The recruiters would look at first or last names, locations of issuance of their national identification cards, or locations of high schools to find out who was Shia.[95] By 1980, the Saudi government had bought all shares in ARAMCO and gradually took over control of the company. 'Ali al-Na'imi was appointed the first Saudi president of ARAMCO in 1983 and Saudi ARAMCO was formally established in 1988.[96] This Saudisation of ARAMCO did not help Shia employees, however, since they had benefitted from American recruitment policies and the discriminatory policies operative across the Saudi government were also being implemented in the oil industry from the 1980s onwards.

The *intifadat al-Muharram* was thus a turning point for Saudi Shia and confirmed the mobilising power of Islamism. It was a community-building event par excellence as many Shia had briefly felt a sense of collective strength and then collective humiliation after the National Guard crushed the protests. While the Saudi government implemented some development projects after 1980, it also intensified institutional discrimination, which it justified on security grounds. So, instead of starting a revolution, the intifada soured relations with the Saudi state and spurred Shia infighting. The notable families were opposed to the intifada as they were frightened by this outburst of violence and the open challenge to their authority by a social movement with its power base in the hinterland of Qatif. But the political power of the notable families had begun to wane, and hundreds of Saudi Shia went into exile to escape the crackdown.

November 2008; Abir, *Saudi Arabia: Government*, 86. For more on SAMCOM see Steffen Hertog, "Petromin: The Slow Death of Statist Oil Development in Saudi Arabia," *Business History* 50, no. 5 (2008), 645–67, 655.

95 Interview with former senior ARAMCO official, Eastern Province, November 2008. See also al-Hasan, *al-shi'a*, vol. 2, 319–29; Anthony H. Cordesman, *Saudi Arabia Enters the Twenty-First Century: The Political, Foreign Policy, Economic, and Energy Dimensions* (Westport, CT: Praeger, 2003), 207–9; Ibrahim, *Shi'is*, 33f., 186; Louër, *Transnational*, 249.

96 Brown, *Oil*, 359, 364; Ismail I. Nawwab et al., eds., *Saudi ARAMCO and its World: Arabia and the Middle East* (Dhahran: The Saudi Arabian Oil Company (Saudi Aramco), 1995), 223–8.

4

A Decade of Confrontation

> Why did they have to go through fifteen years of siege and absence from
> the world and keeping people in the dark, only to reap such a paltry har-
> vest? What real gains did we glean from it?
>
> Seba al-Herz – *The Others*

REVOLUTIONARY IRAN AND THE GULF SHIA

Immediately after the Iranian Revolution the MVM and its leaders such as
Muhammad Taqi al-Mudarrisi became very close to some political factions
in Iran. The MVM cadres as well as Muhammad al-Shirazi moved to Iran.[1]
Given the harsh response of the security forces and the arrest of scores of
demonstrators, many OIRAP leaders and activists went into exile. After the
intifada several hundred young Saudi Shia went to the *hawzat al-Qaʾim*
of the MVM in Tehran.[2] MVM was provided with the grounds of the former women's association (*sazeman-e zanan*) in Mamazand outside Tehran
to establish a large educational centre. This *hawza* was modelled on the
hawza in Kuwait. Muhammad Taqi al-Mudarrisi was the main supervisor
and administered the *hawza* with the help of Hasan al-Saffar, Muhammad
Fawzi, Muhammad al-Sayf, Sahib al-Sadiq and some others.[3] The *hawza*
had several hundred students, most of whom were Saudis.[4]

---

[1] Louër, *Transnational*, 179. Interview with Muhammad Taqi al-Mudarrisi on the TV show
Fulan al-Fulani on al-Sharqiyya TV, Iraq, 2005.

[2] Interview with a former leading MVM member, Damascus, August 2008.

[3] Interview with a member of the clerical wing of MVM, Damascus, August 2008; al-
Mushaykhas, *al-Qatif*, vol. 1, 498f.

[4] Louër, *Transnational*, 167, 232; "lamaha ʿan al-marjiʿ al-Mudarrisi" (About the Marjiʿ
al-Mudarrisi), www.almodarresi.info/1430/modules/alseyra.

In post-revolutionary Iran MVM and its regional branches mainly dealt with Muhammad Montazeri, the son of Hossein 'Ali Montazeri, and after Muhammad's death with Mehdi Hashemi. Muhammad was the main interlocutor between the Iranians and the 'Liberation Movements', until he was killed in the bombing of the headquarters of the Islamic Republic Party in 1981.[5] After Muhammad's death, OIRAP printed condolence telegrams to Ruhollah Khomeini and Hossein 'Ali Montazeri and published a long article about Muhammad's achievements in which it praised his support of the foreign revolutionary movements in Iran and acknowledged that OIRAP had known him for years before the Iranian Revolution. Thereafter, Mehdi Hashemi, who was Hossein 'Ali Montazeri's son in law, was in charge of coordinating the activities of the liberation movements from 1981 until he was arrested in 1986 during the Iran-Contra affair.[6] It is still not clear who exactly in the Iranian government knew about assistance to Gulf Shia and some argue that the Iranian Foreign Ministry, for example, was opposed to many of the export operations.[7] The Montazeri/Hashemi group was one of several factions wrestling for influence in post-revolutionary Iran and its role largely ended with the arrest of Mehdi Hashemi in 1986.

Iranian propaganda efforts in support of the intifada, the fact that some of the protesters carried posters of Khomeini and the relocation of the Shia opposition to Iran after the intifada led many to portray it as a derivative of the Iranian Revolution.[8] Others emphasised that local Shia grievances led to the revolt and argued that the influence of the Iranian Revolution was above all symbolic.[9] Clearly, the success of the Iranian Revolution led some Saudi Shia to believe that revolution was a viable

---

[5] *Al-Thawra al-Islamiyya* 15 (July 1981), 2, 8–12, 16. See also *FBIS*, 6 November 1986.

[6] Louër, *Transnational*, 179–85. Muhammad Taqi al-Mudarrisi was sometimes described as chairing another body for the export of the revolution. *MECS*, 1983–4, 173. According to one account, a 'Gulf office' was attached to this assembly. Micheal Dunn, "Until the Imam Comes: Iran Exports its Revolution," *Defense & Foreign Affairs* (July/August 1987), 43–51, 45. But Louër and people who were close to al-Mudarrisi at the time argue that he never assumed a state position in Iran and doubt whether this assembly or the Gulf office ever existed. Email correspondence with Tawfiq al-Sayf, June 2012. See also Louër, *Transnational*, 180; Marschall, *Iran's*, 31.

[7] Marschall, *Iran's*, 27.

[8] Henner Fürtig, *Iran's Rivalry with Saudi Arabia between the Gulf Wars* (Reading, UK: Ithaca Press, 2002), 34–8; Goldberg, "Shi'i Minority," 239–46; Kostiner, "Shi'i Unrest;" Marschall, *Iran's*, 35; *MECS*, 1979–80, 688–70.

[9] Jones, "Rebellion."

option and that street protests could change their situation for the better. And the local Shia leaders could not have started the intifada without at least the approval of Muhammad Taqi al-Mudarrisi, who was then already in Iran.[10]

On 22 October 1979, Mohammad Reza Shah Pahlavi flew to New York City to undergo medical treatment, heightening anti-American feelings of Iranians and others, including some Saudi Shia.[11] Partly as a result, several hundred Iranian students stormed the American embassy in Tehran on 4 November 1979 and took hostage the Americans inside. A few days later Prime Minister Mehdi Bazargan and Foreign Minister Ebrahim Yazdi resigned.[12] With the fall of the Bazargan government in November 1979, Iranian foreign policy became influenced by those who wanted to export the revolution. This phase lasted until the outbreak of the Iran-Iraq War in September 1980.[13]

Iranian propaganda against Saudi Arabia had intensified by the beginning of Muharram 1979, particularly through Radio Tehran and Radio Ahwaz, but also through the TV stations of the Islamic Republic of Iran, which reached Qatif for the first time on the first day of Muharram.[14] Indeed, for General Maliki, the chief of the General Intelligence Directorate for the Eastern Province, it was clear that the 'Shiʿas have been exceptionally agitated by Khomeini and other outside influences'.[15] MVM members were in charge of the Arabic radio and some Arabic TV programmes broadcast out of Iran. The MVM cadre Ahmad al-Katib recalls that in spring 1979, 'we called our old friend Muhammad Montazeri ... and asked if he would allow us to open an Arabic branch of Iranian Radio, which had been closed during the revolution'. Montazeri, who was a main driver behind Iran's attempt to export its revolution, agreed. Al-Katib and other MVM members established a radio in Abadan on the Iranian coast of the Gulf, from which they broadcast first anti-Iraqi and then

---

[10] Interview with Fuʾad Ibrahim and Hamza al-Hasan, London, March 2010; Louër, *Transnational*, 165.

[11] U.S. Diplomatic Cable, American Consulate Dhahran, *Update on Mood of Saudi Shiʿas*.

[12] Michael M. J. Fischer, *Iran: From Religious Dispute to Revolution* (Cambridge, MA: Harvard University Press, 1980), 232–4.

[13] Fred Halliday, "Iranian Foreign Policy since 1979: Internationalism and Nationalism in the Islamic Revolution," in *Shiʿism and Social Protest*, ed. Juan R. I. Cole and Nikki R. Keddie (New Haven, CT: Yale University Press, 1986), 88–107, 95–7.

[14] U.S. Diplomatic Cable, American Consulate Dhahran, *Update on Mood of Saudi Shiʿas*.

[15] U.S. Diplomatic Cable, American Consulate Dhahran, *Tensions Rise among Saudi Shiʿas*.

anti-Bahraini and anti-Saudi programmes. This was an outcome of the close relations the MVM enjoyed with some factions in Iran.[16] Once the intifada started, the Arabic language Iranian radio stations devoted hours to the events in the Eastern Province, urging the 'revolutionary masses, heroic people in Qatif' to 'resist the government from the deserts'. From 1 February 1980 onwards there were daily broadcasts denouncing the corruption of the ruling family and specifically calling on the Shia to rise up.[17]

After the beginning of the Iran-Iraq War, Iran focussed its export of the revolution on Iraq and Lebanon but continued to support Shia groups in the Gulf. Khomeini's war of words against Saudi Arabia from 1979 onwards, the intifada, Iran's support for OIRAP, and demonstrations during the hajj all contributed to a severe worsening in Saudi-Iranian relations.[18]

After the Iranian Revolution, MVM officially announced the creation of three regional organisations. Apart from the Saudi OIRAP these were the Iraqi branch, Islamic Action Organisation in Iraq (IAO) (*munazzamat al-'amal al-islami fi al-'Iraq*), founded in 1979; and the Bahraini branch, IFLB, officially founded in 1980 and led by Hadi al-Mudarrisi.[19] Hadi al-Mudarrisi had since the early 1970s set up a Bahraini MVM branch and established links with some key Shia notables in Bahrain.[20] Young Saudi Shia activists constituted the bulk of lower-ranking MVM members and worked not only in the Saudi movement but also in its Iraqi and Bahraini branches. Indeed, Saudi Shia 'participated in nearly all activities of the MVM in various parts of the world', while OIRAP 'drew its membership from the Saudis alone'.[21] Inspired by the revolutionary mood in the

---

[16] Interview with Ahmad al-Katib, London, September 2008. See also his memoirs: Ahmad al-Katib, *mudhakkirat Ahmad al-Katib: sirati al-fikriyya wa-l-siyasiyya … min nazari-yyat al-imama … ila al-shura* (Memoirs of Ahmad al-Katib: My Intellectual and Political Biography … from the Theory of the Imamate … to the Shura), www.alkatib.net; munaz-zamat, *al-ta'sis*.

[17] Louër, *Transnational*, 181. OIRAP also started to broadcast its statements on Radio Tehran. *FBIS*, 8 January 1980.

[18] Fürtig, *Iran's Rivalry*, 34–8; Long, "Impact:" Marschall, *Iran's*, 26–45.

[19] Al-Mudayris, *al-harakat*, 101; Rashid Hammada, *'asifa fawq miyah al-khalij: qissa awwal inqilab 'askari fi al-Bahrayn 1981* (A Storm on the Waters of the Gulf: Story of the First Military Coup in Bahrain 1981) (London: al-Safa li-l-Nashr wa-l-Tawzi', 1990), 233f.; *FBIS*, 12 September 1979; *FBIS*, 6 May 1980.

[20] Louër, *Transnational*, 139–43.

[21] Ibrahim, *Shi'is*, 134. One Saudi member of the Bahraini branch (IFLB) has written a memoir about his time as an activist that includes details about the military training he received in Iran: al-Labad, *al-inqilab*.

region, some Saudi Shia received military training in Iran. Several of them joined the MVM's military branches in Bahrain and Iraq. Others fought on the Iranian side in the Iran-Iraq War and in South Lebanon.[22] Some of these militants later joined Hizbullah al-Hijaz, the Saudi branch of the transnational Hizbullah networks aligned with Iran.

MVM gave the Bahraini case, where Shia are a majority of the citizen population, a lot of attention. It thought that military operations could be fruitful there. Its boldest move in Bahrain was an attempted coup, which was uncovered in December 1981. IFLB militants had smuggled weapons into Bahrain and were planning to take over police stations, ministries and radio stations.[23] Iran is frequently accused of being behind the 1981 coup plot.[24] There was likely cooperation with elements of the IRGC, but people involved in the coup insist that they acted without the knowledge of the Iranian political establishment at the time.[25]

Several hundred IFLB members and sympathisers were arrested, and in 1982, seventy-three of them, mostly Bahrainis but also a dozen Saudis, were convicted. The Saudis were all in their twenties and mostly stemmed from Tarut, Qatif, Safwa and Saihat. Two members of the al-Sayf family, 'Ali Muhammad Taqi al-Sayf and Nadir Muhammad al-Sayf, were amongst those arrested. The Saudis were transferred to a Saudi prison, and most of them received a sentence of fifteen years, although three of them were released in autumn 1988.[26] This event and especially the involvement of Saudis worried the Saudi government. After the establishment of the Gulf Cooperation Council (GCC) in May 1981, which in itself was partly a reaction to the Iranian Revolution, Saudi Arabia saw the coup plot as an attack on all GCC states. In December 1981 Saudi Arabia signed a security agreement with Bahrain and increased security checks in the Eastern Province.[27] In early 1982, the Saudi authorities

---

[22] *Risalat al-Haramayn* 23 (1991); *Risalat al-Haramayn* 43/44 (August/September 1993); *al-Thawra al-Islamiyya* 85 (April 1987), 56.

[23] *MECS*, 1981–82, 490–2.

[24] Hasan Tariq Alhasan, "The Role of Iran in the Failed Coup of 1981: The IFLB in Bahrain," *The Middle East Journal* 65, no. 4 (2011), 603–17.

[25] Interview with a Bahraini activist involved in the 1981 coup attempt, London, 2010.

[26] Hammada, *'asifa*, 377–80. The coup attempt and the convictions were also covered by *al-Thawra al-Islamiyya*, and OIRAP published a statement condemning the trials. *Al-Thawra al-Islamiyya* 23 (March 1982), 1f.; 24 (April 1982), 9; 32 (December 1982), 10.

[27] *Al-Thawra al-Islamiyya* 20 (December 1981), 3; Frauke Heard-Bey, *Die arabischen Golfstaaten im Zeichen der islamischen Revolution* (Bonn: Europa Union Verlag, 1983), 21f.; Marschall, *Iran's*, 36; Wright, *Sacred Rage*, 160.

arrested fifty-eight OIRAP sympathisers,[28] and after the failed coup the majority of the remaining Bahraini and Saudi IFLB activists left Bahrain and joined the MVM cadres in Iran.[29]

Although there was no such military branch for Saudi Arabia, the Iranian authorities repeatedly pressured MVM and OIRAP to intensify military efforts in Saudi Arabia. But after the failure of the intifada in 1979/80, MVM thought that military action was of little use in the Saudi case, and it claims to have rejected bombings and assassinations there.[30] OIRAP then focussed more on publishing, the recruitment and education of new members, fundraising, and the building of a social movement inside Saudi Arabia. From March 1980 onwards, it published the monthly *al-Thawra al-Islamiyya* (The Islamic Revolution), which served as a platform for its revolutionary rhetoric and criticism of the Saudi government.[31]

LOST IN EXILE

Before the intifada there had been a number of *shiraziyyun* in the United States, who distributed books and tapes with sermons of *shirazi* preachers. After the intifada they formed what became known as the Islamic Union of Students of the Arabian Peninsula (*al-ittihad al-islami li-talabat al-jazira al-'arabiyya*), whose first political activity was a demonstration near the White House in Washington, D.C., on the first anniversary of the intifada in November 1980.[32] They started to publish a journal called *al-Hijaz*. Calling Saudi Arabia "al-Hijaz" reflected the Shia opposition's rejection of the Saudi ruling family. The *shiraziyyun* soon expanded their activities throughout the United States.[33]

---

[28] *Al-Thawra al-Islamiyya* 24 (April 1982). There were rumours that the authorities had also arrested several hundred mainly Sunni Muslims in early 1983 on suspicion of trying to organise an Iranian-backed coup. Marschall, *Iran's*, 36f.

[29] Al-Mudayris, *al-harakat*; International Crisis Group, *Bahrain's Sectarian Challenge* (2005), 11; Fuller and Francke, *Arab Shi'a*, 126, 134f.; Hammada, *'asifa*; Ibrahim, *Shi'is*, 134; Louër, *Transnational*, 160; Marschall, *Iran's*, 36; Falah al-Mdaires, "Shi'ism and Political Protest in Bahrain," *Domes* 11, no. 1, (Spring 2002); Ramazani, "Shi'ism in the Persian Gulf," 49–51; Ramazani, *Revolutionary*, 50–3.

[30] Interview with a former leading MVM member, Damascus, August 2008. Leftist groups are quoted as saying that OIRAP was involved in a number of explosions in Khobar and Dammam in 1980, although this is not confirmed from OIRAP's side. *MECS*, 1980–1, 737.

[31] Introduction to the bound volume of *al-Thawra al-Islamiyya*, issues 8 to 36 (1983).

[32] Ibrahim, *Shi'is*, 146–50; *al-Thawra al-Islamiyya* 9 (December 1980), 3–5.

[33] *Al-Thawra al-Islamiyya* 44 (December 1983), 11–13.

In March 1983, the OIRAP Central Committee held its annual meeting in Damascus and decided to gradually move some activities out of Iran so that OIRAP would not be at risk of changes in Iran's policies and Saudi-Iranian relations. The Central Committee also decided to move some of its journalistic and political activities to London and use Cyprus as a base for organisational communications with members inside Saudi Arabia.[34] The very fact that the meeting was held in Damascus was an example of the gradual shift of operations out of Iran and the emergence of the Damascus suburb Sayyida Zaynab as a transnational hub for Shia politics.

Sayyida Zaynab – located six miles to the southeast of central Damascus – is named after the tomb of the daughter of ʿAli Ibn Abi Talib, whom Shia Muslims consider the first Imam. Hasan al-Shirazi, Muhammad's brother, had established the first Shia learning institution in Sayyida Zaynab in 1975, when the area was still a small suburb of Damascus and the tomb of Zaynab was not refurbished yet. Hasan al-Shirazi promoted a rapprochement between Twelver Shia and Alawites, which was one of the reasons why the Syrian regime allowed the establishment of Shia institutions in Sayyida Zaynab. In 1973, Musa al-Sadr had certified that Alawites were indeed Shia, a move that pleased Hafiz al-Assad. Hasan al-Shirazi argued the same in a publication and it seems that he developed relatively close relations with Hafiz al-Assad. In addition, the rivalry between the two Baath regimes in Iraq and Syria favoured the activities of an Iraqi opposition figure such as Hasan al-Shirazi in Syria, although the latter was killed in Beirut in May 1980.[35]

For the MVM activists, Sayyida Zaynab was a convenient place because it was much easier to travel to than Iran. Saudi Arabia forbade travel to Iran for several years after the intifada.[36] Saudi Shia intending

[34] Ibrahim, *Shiʿis*, 145f.

[35] For more see Alessandro Cancian, *La Hawza ʿIlmiyya: E la formazione dell' elite religiosa nei collegi teologici nello sciismo duodecimano: elementi dottrinali e indagine di campo* (PhD, Universita degli Studi di Siena, 2005); Martin Kramer, "Syria's Alawis and Shiʿism," in *Shiʿism, Resistance, and Revolution*, ed. Martin Kramer (Boulder, CO: Westview Press, 1987), 237–54, 247–9; Louër, *Transnational*, 196–8; Sabrina Mervin, "Sayyida Zaynab, Banlieue de Damas ou nouvelle ville sainte chiite?" *Cahiers d'Études sur la Méditerranée Orientale et le Monde Turco-Iranien* 22 (1996), 149–62; Khalid Sindawi, "The Shiite Turn in Syria," *Current Trends in Islamist Ideology* 8 (June 23rd, 2009), 82–107; Yvette Talhamy, "The Fatwas and the Nusayri/Alawis of Syria," *Middle Eastern Studies* 46, no. 2 (2010), 175–94; Wiley, *Islamic*, 78. See also the Website of the *hawza Zaynabiyya*, http://alhawzaonline.com/neshatat/about.php.

[36] *Al-Thawra al-Islamiyya* 23 (March 1982), 10.

to travel to Iran had to go via a third country without having their passports stamped. Damascus still hosted parts of the Communist Party in Saudi, many of whose members were Shia. The Saudi opposition groups were also subject to changes in Saudi-Syrian relations. While from the mid-1970s onwards Saudi Arabia mirrored Syria's provision of a base for Saudi opposition activists with turning a blind eye to Saudi funding for the Syrian Muslim Brotherhood, relations became more stable after 1990.[37] The *shirazi hawza Zaynabiyya* remained the main religious institution in Sayyida Zaynab. Nevertheless, the political arm of the *shirazi* movement, MVM, opened its own *hawza* in Sayyida Zaynab in 1983, the *hawzat al-Sadiq*, and established several *hussainiyyat*. In 1989, the *hawzat al-Qa'im* in Tehran was closed and relocated to the *hawzat al-Sadiq* in Sayyida Zaynab, which was renamed *hawzat al-Qa'im* in 1995.[38] The *hawzat al-Sadiq* was mainly under the supervision of Saudi Shia clerics and therefore became a focal point for the Saudis within MVM, as well as for Saudi students, pilgrims and new recruits.[39]

While OIRAP was moving its operational base out of Iran, it also started to publish more in Beirut, Damascus and London. In the mid-1980s, OIRAP members founded a publishing house in London, Dar al-Safa, which published movement pamphlets as well as studies of Saudi politics and history.[40] Other MVM members, including from IFLB, also went to London.[41] Throughout the 1980s, OIRAP continued to publish short leaflets with transcripts of al-Saffar's sermons. The titles of a collection published under the heading *Culture for the Masses (al-thaqafa li-l-jamahir)* attempt a revolutionary re-interpretation of Shia history. One book, entitled *The Masses and the Revolution*, discusses the role of the masses in Hussayn's revolution and employs the discourse of the Iranian Revolution by emphasising the uprisings of the oppressed (*mustada 'fin*).[42] OIRAP published two party programmes, in

---

[37] Sonoko Sunayama, *Syria and Saudi Arabia: Collaboration and Conflicts in the Oil Era* (London: I. B. Tauris Academic Studies, 2007), 92f.

[38] Al-Mushaykhas, *al-Qatif*, vol. 1, 497–500.

[39] The supervisors of the *hawza* were Muhammad al-Habib, Muhammad al-'Alaywat, Mahmud al-Sayf, 'Abd al-Latif al-Shabib, Nimr al-Nimr and 'Ali Hilal al-Suyud. Ibid., 501f.

[40] Ibrahim, *Shi'is*, 144.

[41] In June 1985, eight members of IFLB, including one Saudi, were deported from the United Kingdom to Syria. *MECS* 1984–85, 154.

[42] Hasan al-Saffar, *al-jamahir wa-l-thawra* (The Masses and the Revolution) (Qatif: n.p., 1981).

which it declared the Saudi government illegitimate.[43] OIRAP also tried to discredit Saudi Arabia in the wider Arab world, for example, by highlighting the hypocritical nature of Saudi government policies regarding Palestine.[44] OIRAP discourse and publications remained uncompromising towards the Saudi state until the late 1980s. In theory, violence could have been one of its tools but it argued that Saudi Shia were not ready for this yet.[45]

A FEMALE VANGUARD

While women did not become leaders in the *shirazi* movement, they played a very important role at the grassroots level and in the literature of the movement. The ideal type of the woman was *al-mar'a al-risaliyya*,[46] or the 'vanguard woman', who should adhere to Islamic values but also actively take part in social life.[47] After some women had participated in the intifada several dozen Saudi women went to the *hawzat al-Qa'im* in Tehran. Most of them were unmarried teenagers and had a relative studying in the *hawza*. This development was unprecendented in Saudi Shia society, and many conservatives criticised it. But some female activists remember this as an era of empowerment.[48] Apart from the classical *hawza* subjects, female students were taught politics, social sciences and history. There were around one hundred single female students in the *hawza* in Tehran, most of them from Saudi Arabia and others from Bahrain, Iraq, Kuwait and Africa. Apart from making society more Islamic, they wanted to change the position of both women and Shia. Many of them married male movement members. There were also around twenty Saudi

---

[43] Al-'Amir, *al-haraka*; *kalimat al-haraka al-islamiyya fi al-jazira al-'arabiyya* (The Word of the Islamic Movement in the Arabian Peninsula) (n.p.: Munazzamat al-Thawra al-Islamiyya fi al-Jazira al-'Arabiyya, 1986).

[44] 'Abd al-Rahman al-Shaykh, *al-mas'ala al-filastiniyya fi al-manzar al-su'udi* (The Palestinian Question in the Saudi View) (n.p.: Munazzamat al-Thawra al-Islamiyya fi al-Jazira al-'Arabiyya, 1982).

[45] Interview with a former leading MVM member, Damascus, August 2008; Ibrahim, *Shi'is*, 129.

[46] *Al-Thawra al-Islamiyya* 28 (August 1982), 12.

[47] See, for example, the article 'Muslim Women in America' in *al-Thawra al-Islamiyya*, 28 (August 1982), 11f. See also Ibrahim, *Shi'is*, 131; Hadi al-Mudarrisi, *hiwar 'an al-mar'a* (Discussion of the Woman) (Beirut: Dar al-Ta'arruf, 1978); Hasan al-Saffar, *al-mar'a mas'uliyya wa-mawqif* (The Woman: Responsibility and Position) (Qatif: n.p., 1981); Hasan al-Saffar, *al-mar'a wa-l-thawra* (The Woman and the Revolution), 2nd printing (Beirut: Mu'assasat al-A'lami li-l-Matbu'at, 1981).

[48] Interview with OIRAP female activists, Eastern Province, November 2008.

women who accompanied their husbands to Qom, but the women were not allowed to study in the *hawza* there.

The cell structure of female activists inside Saudi Arabia set up in the late 1970s remained operational and activists educated other women, copied *shirazi* journals and leaflets and generally encouraged Islamic behaviour. In the early 1980s, it was also common that young male activists and clerics would meet with groups of women. And the women abroad would return to Saudi Arabia to preach amongst women.[49] Some, including ʿAliyya Makki al-Farid and Makkiyya ʿAbdallah Hamdan, were arrested in the mid-1980s, and the remaining women started to publish statements under the name Association of Muslim Women in the Arabian Peninsula (*rabitat al-muslima fi al-jazira al-ʿarabiyya*).[50] The Iraqi branch (IAO) also had a female wing called *rabitat al-mujahidat al-muslima fi al-ʿIraq* (Association of Female Muslim Mujahidin in Iraq).[51]

Women also suffered from repression. Al-Farid wrote a book about her time in prison and became perhaps the most outspoken female *shirazi* activist and writer from Saudi Arabia.[52] In Iran the activities of women were restricted. It was only after the move to Syria in the late 1980s that female activists started to publish two magazines. One was *al-Zahra*, which was published around 1990/1 for one year, and the other, *ʿAfaf* (Modesty), was published monthly for around five years until 1993/4. The journal did not deal with politics nor did it promote a sectarian discourse and generally focussed on the 'Islamic woman', the 'Islamic family', and the 'Islamic child'. It contained articles about health, maternity, marriage, and cultural and religious issues.[53]

A NEW GOVERNOR AND THE DECLINE OF THE LEFT

Meanwhile, developments within the ruling family slowly changed the situation in the Eastern Province. After the death of King Khalid in June 1982, Fahd became king and Abdullah crown prince. King Fahd wanted to reduce tensions in the Eastern Province. He had already after the intifada instructed Prince Ahmad bin ʿAbd al-ʿAziz to form a committee

---

[49] Interview with OIRAP female activists, Eastern Province, November 2008.
[50] *Al-Thawra al-Islamiyya* 78 (September 1986), 11.
[51] Wiley, *Islamic*, 164.
[52] For more on the role of women in OIRAP see Ibrahim, *Shiʿis*, 131, 139; ʿAliyya Makki, *yawmiyyat imraʾ fi al-sujun al-suʿudiyya* (Diary of a Woman in Saudi Prisons) (London: al-Safa, 1989), 9–19.
[53] Interview with OIRAP female activists, Saudi Arabia, November 2008.

PICTURE 4.1. Street scene in Qatif.
Source: Tor Eigeland/Saudi Aramco World/SAWDIA.

to supervise the development of Shia areas (see Picture 4.1). Fahd became the head of this committee, while Ahmad became its director, a step that was seen as a prelude towards the appointment of Ahmad as governor of the Eastern Province. But Fahd eventually appointed his son Muhammad as governor of the Eastern Province in 1984/5, replacing ʿAbd al-Muhsin bin Jiluwi.[54] The latter had been governing the Eastern Province since the death of Saʿud bin Jiluwi in 1967.[55] Muhammad bin Fahd introduced various development programmes for Shia areas and all Saudi Shia arrested since 1979 were released upon his accession.[56] He also met more regularly with Shia notables than his predecessor and sought to win over some of the new Shia elites and students.[57]

Partly as a response to these developments, Hasan al-Saffar proposed at the 1985 OIRAP Central Committee meeting in Damascus to give the organisation a more moderate name (their name still called for an Islamic Revolution). Many committee members agreed, but no decision was taken

[54] *MECS*, 1976–7, 565–7; *MECS*, 1979–80, 697; Samore, *Royal*, 465f.
[55] Abir, *Saudi Arabia in the Oil Era*, 187, 190f.; Al Suʿud, *al-amir ʿAbdallah*, 79–83; al-Rasheed, *A History*, 73; Cordesman, *Saudi Arabia*, 207f.; Kechichian, *Succession*, 4, 8, 29, 34; www.easternemara.gov.sa/start.asp.
[56] Ibrahim, *Shiʿis*, 135; Lacey, *Inside*, 99.
[57] Abir, *Saudi Arabia in the Oil Era*, 190f.

out of fear that this would enrage the MVM leadership and the cells in the country.[58] Nonetheless, it would be an overstatement to argue that tensions between the Shia and the state significantly eased in the second half of the 1980s. The project of transforming OIRAP into a more moderate force was only the idea of some of its leaders and not yet reflected in its publications, and the state continued to police Shia areas. In the mid-1980s, the religious police's persecution of Shia religious practices in the Eastern Province increased.[59] Between 1982 and mid-1984, hundreds of OIRAP sympathisers were arrested. Their main activities inside Saudi Arabia had been the distribution of movement literature, the writing of graffiti and fundraising.[60] In fact, any attempts at large-scale mobilisations, such as public demonstrations in Qatif, Safwa and Saihat during Ashura 1985 were quickly repressed by the security services, who arrested scores.[61]

In 1982 and early 1983, several *hizb al-'amal* and Communist Party members were also arrested; both groups had increased their activities since the intifada.[62] Some *hizb al-'amal* cadres left Saudi Arabia after the intifada and in 1981 established relations with the Communist Party and the quasi-communist Popular Front in Bahrain (*al-jabha al-sha'biyya fi al-Bahrayn*) in exile.[63] *Hizb al-'amal* continued to produce its journal *al-Masira* between 1975 and 1984 and published books on the working class and on oil politics. It also criticised the difficult position of women in the country.[64] Some *hizb al-'amal* and Communist Party leaders worked at the newspaper *al-Yawm* (Today) published in Dammam. Its weekly literary supplement had become a focal point for young leftist writers, as had cultural supplements of other Saudi newspapers.[65] But in May 1982 *al-Yawm* was suspended and its editors Muhammad al-'Ali and 'Ali al-Dumayni arrested. At the same time, Salih al-Azzaz, a former

---

[58] Ibrahim, *Shi'is*, 141.

[59] Abir, *Saudi Arabia in the Oil Era*, 192.

[60] Ibrahim, *Shi'is*, 135f.

[61] See the condemnation by Muhammad Taqi al-Mudarrisi of these arrests in *al-Thawra al-Islamiyya* 67 (November 1985).

[62] Hamza al-Hasan, *The Role of Religion in Building National Identity: Case Study: Saudi Arabia* (PhD, University of Westminster, 2006), 311; Ibrahim, *Shi'is*, 136; MECS, 1982–83, 746f.

[63] "Saudi Opposition: 'We Are Rebuilding Our Organization,'" *MERIP Reports* 130 (February 1985), 15–18.

[64] *Al-Masira* 10 (June 1980); Hizb al-'Amal al-Ishtiraki al-'Arabi fi al-Jazira al-'Arabiyya, *al-naft wa-l-mujtama' fi al-jazira al-'arabiyya "al-su'udiyya"* (Oil and Society in the "Saudi" Arabian Peninsula) (n.p.: al-Dar al-Lubnaniyya, 1984); al-'Akri, *al-tanzimat*, 216–26; al-Hasan, "al-mu'arada."

[65] Lacroix, *Awakening*, 15–20.

managing editor of the newspaper, and dozens of others were arrested for *hizb al-'amal* membership. Most were released in 1983 under a general amnesty after vowing to abstain from politics, but some remained banned from writing, travelling and taking up government jobs.[66] In 1989, six *hizb al-'amal* members were arrested. They were technocrats from Safwa, four of them working for ARAMCO.[67]

The 1980s saw a declining appeal of leftist parties. Whereas previously, many intellectuals had been drawn to leftist ideals, OIRAP reached out towards university graduates and the petty bourgeoisie, especially as its publications grew more substantial. Throughout the 1980s, the Communist Party, *hizb al-'amal* and OIRAP had chances to get to know each other better, as members of the organisations were imprisoned together in Saudi Arabia and others shared Damascus as place of exile. Despite the occasional confrontation, this experience led both the Communist Party and *hizb al-'amal* to call for a nationwide democratic front.[68] In 1985, another wave of arrests dismantled almost the whole internal organisation of OIRAP. As a consequence, its members decided to rethink their political strategy and some withdrew completely from political activity. OIRAP was further weakened by the emergence of a group of Saudi MVM members who called for the adoption of Khomeini's theory of *wilayat al-faqih* and his *marji'iyya* (see Picture 4.2). This group split away from MVM and in 1987 became the nucleus of Hizbullah al-Hijaz. One of the main reasons for the creation of Hizbullah al-Hijaz was the clash between Saudi Arabia and Iran over the 'hajj incident' of 1987.[69]

THE HAJJ AND SAUDI-IRANIAN TENSIONS

Ideologues and leaders of the Iranian Revolution such as 'Ali Shariati and Ruhollah Khomeini had sought to re-interpret pilgrimage in a political

---

[66] Article 19, *Silent Kingdom: Freedom of Expression in Saudi Arabia*, London, October 1991, 23f.

[67] Amnesty International, *Saudi Arabia: Detention without Trial of Suspected Political Opponents* (London: 1990); Human Rights Watch, *Empty Reforms: Saudi Arabia's New Basic Laws* (New York: 1992).

[68] *Tariq al-Kadihin* 36 (May 1987), quoted in *al-Thawra al-Islamiyya* 92 (November 1987), 40f.; *al-Masira* 11 (November 1980), quoted in al-'Akri, *al-tanzimat*, 218. See also a joint interview with representatives from the Communist Party and *hizb al-'amal* in an East German publication. "Die Königsmacht mit dem Schwert erhalten: Gespräch mit Führern des saudischen Widerstands," *AIB 10/1984*; *AIB 11/12 1984*, Nachlass Prof. Dr. Gerhard Höpp, Signatur 10.15.085, Zentrum Moderner Orient, Berlin, Germany.

[69] Ibrahim, *Shi'is*, 137f.; Matthiesen, "Hizbullah," 183–5.

PICTURE 4.2. Picture of Khomeini on a door in Awwamiyya, 2008.
Source: Toby Matthiesen.

way. Since around 1971 followers of Khomeini had started to distribute anti-Shah, anti-Israeli and anti-American propaganda during the hajj.[70] After the revolution Iran used the hajj to present itself as the defender of the Muslim cause, to assert its claim that the hajj and the Holy Places should be placed under international oversight as opposed to being managed by the Saudis alone. Therefore, the hajj became a focal point of Saudi-Iranian tensions in the 1980s and also had an impact on the Saudi Shia opposition.[71]

The hajj is an important legitimising factor for the Saudi ruling family – symbolised by King Fahd's adoption of the title 'Custodian of the Two Holy Places' (Khadim al-Haramayn) in 1986 – and so the Saudi government reacted to these disturbances with anger.[72] The first large-scale protests and clashes between Shia pilgrims and Saudi police erupted in 1981 and would intensify until the deadly events of the hajj in 1987. These protests, however, usually involved Iranians and there is little evidence of a Saudi Shia role.[73] But OIRAP issued annual messages to hajj pilgrims throughout the 1980s denouncing the Saudi government as un-Islamic

---

[70] Martin Kramer, *Arab Awakening and Islamic Revival: The Politics of Ideas in the Middle East* (New Brunswick, NJ: Transaction, 1996), 166f.; Ali Shariati, *Hajj* (Bedford, OH: Free Islamic Literature, 1977).

[71] Saleh al-Mani', "The Ideological Dimension in Saudi-Iranian Relations," in *Iran and the Gulf: A Search for Stability*, ed. Jamal S. al-Suwaida (Abu Dhabi: Emirates Center for Strategic Studies and Research, 1996), 158–74, 166–8; Hooshang Amirahmadi, "Iranian-Saudi Arabian Relations since the Revolution," in *Iran and the Arab World*, ed. Hooshang Amirahmadi and Nader Entessar (London: Macmillan, 1993), 139–60, 146–8; Shahram Chubin and Charles Tripp, *Iran–Saudi Arabia Relations and Regional Order: Iran and Saudi Arabia in the Balance of Power in the Gulf* (London: Oxford University Press/International Institute for Strategic Studies, 1996), 54–7; Mohammad-Reza Djalili, *Diplomatie Islamique: Stratégie Internationale du Khomeynisme* (Paris: Presses Universitaires de France, 1989), 158–67; Graham E Fuller, *The "Center of the Universe": The Geopolitics of Iran* (Boulder, CO: Westview Press, 1991); Fürtig, *Iran's Rivalry*, 42–55; Jacob Goldberg, "Saudi Arabia and the Iranian Revolution: The Religious Dimension," in *The Iranian Revolution and the Muslim World*, ed. David Menashri (Boulder, CO: Westview Press, 1990), 155–70; Ignace Leverrier, "L'Arabie Saoudite, le pèlerinage et l'Iran," *Cahiers d'Études sur la Méditerranée Orientale et le Monde Turco-Iranien* 22 (1996), 111–47; Chang-Cheng Liu, *Saudi-Iranian Relations, 1977–1997* (PhD, University of Durham, 2003), 145–56; Ramazani, *Revolutionary*, 93–100.

[72] J. Piscatori, "Managing God's Guests: The Pilgrimage, Saudi Arabia and the Politics of Legitimacy," in *Monarchies and Nations: Globalisation and Identity in the Arab States of the Gulf*, ed. P. Dresch and J. Piscatori (London: I. B. Tauris, 2005), 222–45.

[73] The OIRAP publication reported the arrest of several Iranians and unspecified IAO members in 1980 in Mecca: *Al-Thawra al-Islamiyya* 8 (1980). For more details on the hajj disturbances see Kramer, *Arab Awakening*, 161–87; Leverrier, "L'Arabie Saoudite."

and urging pilgrims to speak out against it.[74] Khomeini then appointed Mohammad Mousavi Khoeiniha, the mentor of the students who had seized the U.S. embassy in Tehran, as his pilgrimage representative.[75]

With the outbreak of the Iran-Iraq War in 1980, pilgrimage to Shia shrines in Iraq became almost impossible for Iranian and other Shia, and so the importance of the pilgrimage to Mecca and the visitation of al-Baqi' cemetery in Medina and shrines such as Sayyida Zaynab in Syria became more important. In 1982, Khoeiniha chose al-Baqi' as the site for a series of demonstrations. The al-Baqi' cemetery is the final resting ground of many important Islamic historical figures. Shia Muslims in particular value the cemetery because they believe four men that they see as Imams or successors to the Prophet Muhammad are buried there. In 1926, however, the Saudi government demolished the tombs over the Imams' graves and the cemetery ceased to be a place of organised Shia visitation until the 1980s.[76]

Al-Baqi' and the two holy places Mecca and Medina were very important in OIRAP discourse: Its Persian-language magazine, nominally published by the Group of Fighting 'Ulama' in the Arabian Peninsula (*jama'at al-'ulama' al-mujahidin fi al-jazira al-'arabiyya*) in Tehran, was called *al-Baqi'*,[77] while others of its publications were called *al-Haramayn* (The Two Holy Places) and *Mecca Calling*. Its cultural production wing, which was founded in 1987 to gather documents and manuscripts about Saudi Shia, was called al-Baqi' Foundation for the Revival of Heritage (*mu'assasat al-baqi' li-ihya' al-turath*). The destruction of the tombs over the graves of the Imams in Medina was the subject of articles[78] and books published by the foundation.[79] The foundation had an office above the *hussainiyyat al-Zahra* in Sayyida Zaynab, where it collected documents

---

[74] *Al-Thawra al-Islamiyya* 16 (August 1981), 2–5; *al-Thawra al-Islamiyya* 41 (September 1983), 21–3; *FBIS*, 9 September 1982; Ibrahim, *Shi'is*, 111.

[75] Dunn, "Until the Imam," 47; Kramer, *Arab Awakening*, 167f.

[76] Ibid., 169f.; Werner Ende, "Steine des Anstoßes: Das Mausoleum der Ahl al-bayt in Medina," in *Differenz und Dynamik im Islam: Festschrift für Heinz Halm zum 70. Geburtstag*, ed. H. Biesterfeldt and V. Klemm (Würzburg: Ergon Verlag, 2012), 181–200.

[77] See *al-Thawra al-Islamiyya* 96 (February 1988), 30, for a list of contents. Al-Baqi' mainly translated articles from other MVM publications, was edited by Saudi Shia and published from around 1987 to 1992/3.

[78] *Al-Thawra al-Islamiyya* 100 (July 1988), 15–22.

[79] Yusuf al-Hajiri, *al-baqi': qissa tadmir Al Su'ud li-l-athar al-islamiyya fi al-Hijaz* (The Story of the Destruction of Islamic Archaeological Sites in the Hijaz by the Al Saud) (Beirut: Mu'assasat al-Baqi' li-Ihya' al-Turath, 1990).

on Shia history. The entrance to the *hussainiyya* was adorned with images of deceased Shia scholars from al-Ahsa and Qatif.[80]

From 1983 to 1986, tensions during the hajj eased slightly. Khoeiniha was replaced as pilgrimage representative with Mehdi Karroubi in 1985 and appointed prosecutor general in Iran, but continued to denounce Saudi hajj policies in an interview with the OIRAP publication *al-Thawra al-Islamiyya*.[81] In May 1985, Foreign Minister Saud al-Faysal visited Tehran and at the end of the year the Iranian Foreign Minister ʿAli Akbar Velayati made a return visit to Riyadh.[82] In addition, the first attempts towards a dialogue between OIRAP and the Saudi government occurred in late 1983/early 1984. After the relocation of the Saudi Shia opposition to Sayyida Zaynab, Tawfiq al-Sayf and other leaders met in Damascus with Ahmad al-Kuhaymi, the ambassador of Saudi Arabia to Syria.[83] Al-Sayf recalls that both sides were positively surprised about this encounter and the activists refrained from using the confrontational discourse of their publications. Although al-Kuhaymi apparently recommended to the government to find a solution, the talks did not lead to any concrete results.[84]

Another dialogue was held in August 1986 in Damascus between Tawfiq al-Sayf and three Shia notables, ʿAbd al-Hamid al-Mutawwaʿ, Salman al-Nasir and ʿAbd al-Karim al-Humud. They presented an offer by Muhammad bin Fahd involving a general amnesty for OIRAP members if they ceased all oppositional activities. OIRAP rejected this offer because it did not include the religious and socio-economic demands of the Shia.[85] Publicly, however, OIRAP condemned every possibility of a dialogue with the government, arguing that the people should be able to choose their own government.[86] Its publications remained so pro-Iranian that OIRAP even issued a condemning statement when Saudi Arabia raised its oil output in early 1986, an action that led to a fall in oil prices and therefore in revenues for Iran.[87]

---

[80] Al-Labad, *al-inqilab*, 350f.

[81] *Al-Thawra al-Islamiyya* 65 (September 1985), 40–4.

[82] Fürtig, *Iran's Rivalry*, 47.

[83] Riyyad Najib al-Rayyis, *riyyah al-sumum: al-suʿudiyya wa-duʾul al-jazira baʿd harb al-khalij 1991–1994* (Poisonous Winds: Saudi Arabia and the States of the Peninsula after the Gulf War 1991–1994) (Beirut: Riyyad al-Rayyis li-l-Kutub wa-l-Nashr, 1994), 209.

[84] Interview with Tawfiq al-Sayf, Eastern Province, November 2008.

[85] *FBIS*, 4 November 1993; Ibrahim, *Shiʿis*, 180.

[86] Al-ʿAmir, *al-haraka*, 175; Ibrahim, *Shiʿis*, 179f.

[87] *Al-Thawra al-Islamiyya* 72 (March 1986), 40, 46f.

Throughout the 1980s, the Saudis financed the Iraqi side in the Iran-Iraq War.[88] There were even minor direct military confrontations. When the Iran-Iraq War entered the phase known as the 'Tanker War' after March 1984, several Saudi and Kuwaiti tankers were hit by Iran and some even by Iraq.[89] On 5 June 1984 the Saudis shot down an Iranian Phantom Jet but a standoff between aircraft from both countries ended without fighting.[90] On 31 July 1987 several hundred people, most of them Iranian pilgrims but also some Saudi policemen, were killed and many more injured at a demonstration and a stampede during the hajj outside the Grand Mosque in Mecca. Iran and Saudi Arabia blamed each other for the deaths and the episode led to a severe worsening of Saudi-Iranian relations.[91] Although the clashes mainly involved Iranians, some have alleged links to Saudi Shia organisations.[92] As a result, both countries increased their efforts to influence Muslim public opinion and to discredit the other side. This included the publication of propaganda materials about the Mecca event.[93]

THE LINE OF THE IMAM

The factions in Iran that had supported the *shirazi* movement since 1979 were severely weakened by the Iran-Contra affair in late 1986.[94] At the centre of the affair was a plan by Reagan administration officials to sell arms to Iran via Israel in order to secure the release of American hostages held by Shia groups in Lebanon. The money for the weapons was then diverted to the 'Contras' in Nicaragua. While secrecy still surrounds the deal, the affair was uncovered after the Lebanese journal *al-Shira‘*

[88] Shahram Chubin and Charles Tripp, *Iran and Iraq at War* (London: I. B. Tauris, 1988), 158–79.

[89] Nadia El-Sayed El-Shazly, *The Gulf Tanker War: Iran and Iraq's Maritime Swordplay* (Houndmills, UK: Macmillan, 1998), 27f., 208–10; Martin S. Navias and E. R. Hooton, *Tanker Wars: The Assault on Merchant Shipping during the Iran-Iraq Conflict 1980–1988* (London: I. B. Tauris, 1996), 77–85.

[90] Fürtig, *Iran's Rivalry*, 67; Gerd Nonneman, *Iraq, the Gulf States and the War* (London: Ithaca Press, 1986), 71.

[91] *MECS*, 1987, 172–76, 589–91, 601–5; Marschall, *Iran's*, 52f.; Kramer, *Arab Awakening*, 170–8.

[92] *FBIS*, 19 November 1987; Peterson, *Historical Dictionary*, 122. Others have argued that earlier protests during the hajj involved Saudi Shia. Cordesman, *Saudi Arabia*, 209.

[93] See Werner Ende, "Sunni Polemical Writings on the Shi'a and the Iranian Revolution," in *The Iranian Revolution and the Muslim World*, ed. David Menashri (Boulder, CO: Westview Press, 1990), 219–32.

[94] Louër, *Transnational*, 183–6; Ibrahim, *Shi'is*, 145.

published details of a secret trip of U.S. National Security Adviser Robert McFarlane to Tehran. Mehdi Hashemi, who was the MVM's main interlocutor in Iran, and some of his supporters were arrested on 12 October 1986. In response to these arrests, supporters of Mehdi Hashemi leaked the story.[95]

The *al-Shira'* article refers to the informants as 'Hashemi's supporters' and indicates that they leaked the story of McFarlane's visit in order to retaliate against Akbar Hashemi Rafsanjani and 'Ali Khamenei, who were allegedly behind Mehdi Hashemi's arrest. The article laments that Iran is torn between the logic of the state and the logic of the revolution and glorifies the export of the revolution by Muhammad Montazeri and Mehdi Hashemi. It states that Hashemi was arrested for two reasons: The kidnapping of the Syrian chargé d'affaires in Tehran and the organisation of an arms transport during the hajj 1986, which was uncovered. Hashemi's supporters argue that the arms were smuggled by the IRGC. Concerning McFarlane, the article goes on to say that in return for arms he also wanted Tehran to stop its support for liberation movements and to guarantee the security of the Arab Gulf States.[96] One report indicated that the Saudis had specifically demanded that Iran stop its support for Shia opposition activists in Saudi Arabia and the Gulf.[97] The episode ended badly for those that wanted to export the revolution: Mehdi Hashemi was executed in 1987, the Office of the Liberation Movements closed and Hossein 'Ali Montazeri deposed in 1989 as the successor of Khomeini.[98]

[95] Ayatollah Hossein 'Ali Montazeri, *khaterat* (Memoirs) 2 vols. (2000), vol. 1, 607, www.amontazeri.com/Farsi/khaterat/html/0543.htm; for more on Mehdi Hashemi see vol. 1, 608–16. Ibrahim claims that Mehdi Hashemi and an MVM leader decided to leak the information. Ibrahim, *Shi'is*, 145.

[96] *Al-Shira'*, 3 November 1986; *FBIS*, 6 November 1986.

[97] *MECS*, 1986, 106. Other theories argue that a Syrian diplomat or undercover intelligence officer in Tehran, Iyad al-Mahmud, heard of the story, wired it back to Damascus, was then kidnapped by Mehdi Hashemi's faction on 2 October 1986 and it was Hafiz al-Assad who leaked the story. Patrick Seale, *Asad of Syria: The Struggle for the Middle East* (London: I. B. Tauris, 1988), 489f. Yet another theory states that it was published in a "Hizbullah" journal in Baalbek a week before it was published in *al-Shira'* and the latter merely picked up the story. John Bulloch and Harvey Morris, *The Gulf War: Its Origins, History and Consequences* (London: Methuen London, 1989), 96f.

[98] *MECS*, 1986, 136–9, 329–35; Kenneth Katzman, *The Warriors of Islam: Iran's Revolutionary Guard* (Boulder, CO: Westview Press, 1993), 150f.; Nikki R. Keddie, *Modern Iran: Roots and Results of Revolution* (New Haven, CT: Yale University Press, 2006), 260; Louër, *Transnational*, 184f.; Baqer Moin, *Khomeini: Life of the Ayatollah* (London: I. B. Tauris, 1999), 263f.

MVM and OIRAP chose to gradually leave Iran and the OIRAP Central Committee made a decision in 1987 to soften its stance towards the Saudi government after an amnesty led to the release of many of its imprisoned members.[99] But according to former Saudi Shia opposition activists, Iran wanted to retaliate militarily against Saudi Arabia after the hajj incident. The IRGC allegedly urged OIRAP to create a military wing and carry out attacks inside Saudi Arabia but OIRAP refused.[100] In response, Iran worked with another group of Saudi Shia who had become followers of the *marji'iyya* of Khomeini.[101]

This group was loosely known as Khat al-Imam (The Line of the Imam), referring to followers of the line of Imam Khomeini. The origins of this political trend go back to the early 1980s, when a number of Saudi students from the *hawza* in Najaf moved to Qom. They had been studying with Muhammad Baqir al-Sadr in Najaf, where they had also had contact with Khomeini, who was teaching there until 1978. When Saddam Hussein cracked down on Shia activism in 1980 and had al-Sadr killed, these Saudi Shia left Najaf for Qom. Amongst this group of students were Hussayn al-Radi, Hashim al-Shakhs and Hasan al-Nimr from al-Ahsa, as well as 'Abd al-Karim al-Hubayl and Sa'id al-Bahar from Tarut.[102] In Qom they established the Hijaz 'Ulama' Group *(tajammu' 'ulama' al-Hijaz)*, which was based in the *hawzat al-Hijaziyya*, the hawza for the Saudi students. *Tajammu' 'ulama' al-Hijaz* initially focussed on religious activities and the spreading of the idea of *wilayat al-faqih* and the *marji'iyya* of Khomeini in the Eastern Province and amongst Saudi pilgrims in Sayyida Zaynab. The clerics became politicised only gradually, and most of them had been considered apolitical in the late 1970s and early 1980s. They also had not taken part in the intifada that was *the* key founding event of the *shirazi* movement.

According to its own account, Hizbullah al-Hijaz was founded in May 1987.[103] One week after the hajj incident it vowed to fight the Saudi

---

[99] Ibrahim, *Shi'is*, 143.

[100] Interview with a former leading MVM member, August 2008; al-Ibrahim and al-Sadiq, *al-hirak al-shi'i fi al-su'udiyya*, 146.

[101] Louër, *Transnational*, 211; Matthiesen, "Hizbullah," 182–6.

[102] Interview with a former member of *tajammu' 'ulama' al-Hijaz*, Eastern Province, November 2008; al-Ibrahim and al-Sadiq, *al-hirak al-shi'i fi al-su'udiyya*, 142f.; Matthiesen, "Hizbullah," 180f.

[103] Hizb Allah al-Hijaz, *tasrih sahafi li-hizb Allah al-Hijaz raddan 'ala tasrihat al-Saffar li-qanat al-'arabiyya* (Presse Communiqué by Hizbullah al-Hijaz Refuting Statements Made by al-Saffar to al-Arabiyya TV Channel), 9 March 2005, www.alhramain.com. Its probably first statement was issued on 10 July 1987 denouncing the closure of a

ruling family.[104] The relationship between the broader social, cultural and religious movement that is referred to as Khat al-Imam, its clerical wing *tajammuʿ ʿulamaʾ al-Hijaz* and its military wing, Hizbullah al-Hijaz, still remains somewhat unclear. Former members insist, probably also for security reasons, that while these wings shared a common ideology, there was very limited integration on the operational level. The military wing operated through a cell structure, and information about specific operations was often limited to the handful of members of that cell.[105]

The military wing was initially made up mainly of MVM members who wanted to use violence against the Saudi state but could not do so within the framework of the MVM and who preferred the *marjiʿiyya* of Khomeini.[106] Ahmad Ibrahim al-Mughassil, who became the general secretary of Hizbullah al-Hijaz, was born in 1967 in Qatif. After the intifada he left to Iran, where he studied in the *hawzat al-Qaʾim* of the MVM and had military training in a MVM military camp. He gained military experience fighting alongside Lebanese Hizbullah in South Lebanon against Israeli forces.[107] Some Saudi Shia students from the United States who had only recently joined MVM also joined Hizbullah al-Hijaz.[108] Hizbullah al-Hijaz's long-term political goal was the establishment of an Islamic republic in the Arabian Peninsula after the Iranian model, and it advocated the overthrow of the Saudi government through violence.[109] Even if not explicitly stated, the secession of the Eastern Province was an implied goal, since the rest of the country could not be expected to support an Iranian-style political system.

The fragmentation of the Saudi Shia Islamist opposition had a profound impact on the opposition and on society in the Eastern Province. Hizbullah al-Hijaz and *tajammuʿ ʿulamaʾ al-Hijaz* were initially rather hostile towards OIRAP. The emergence of Hizbullah al-Hijaz contributed

Shia mosque in Dammam. https://web.archive.org/web/20071224113032/http://www.alhramain.com/text/payan/alhejaz/1.htm

[104] This statement, which was published on 7 August 1987 in the Lebanese newspaper *al-Safir* is reproduced in a book on the hajj published by an OIRAP publishing house, Fahd al-Qahtani, *majzarat Makka: qissat al-madhbaha al-suʿudiyya li-l-hujjaj* (Mecca Massacre: The Story of the Saudi Bloodbath of the Pilgrims) (London: al-Safa li-l-Nashr wa-l-Tawziʿ, 1988).

[105] Al-Ibrahim and al-Sadiq, *al-hirak al-shiʿi fi al-suʿudiyya*, 156f.

[106] Interview with a former leading MVM member, August 2008.

[107] Al-Ibrahim and al-Sadiq, *al-hirak al-shiʿi fi al-suʿudiyya*, 158f.

[108] Interview with a former leading OIRAP member, Damascus, August 2008.

[109] Al-Hasan, "al-muʿarada;" Hussayn Musa, *al-ahzab wa-l-harakat al-islamiyya fi al-khalij wa-l-jazira al-ʿarabiyya* (The Islamic Parties and Movements in the Gulf and the Arabian Peninsula) (Manama: n.p., 2004), 68.

to the change of OIRAP's ideology and tactics, as the uncompromising spectrum of the Saudi Shia political field was now occupied by Hizbullah al-Hijaz. Khat al-Imam took over OIRAP's role in the Iranian propaganda effort against Saudi Arabia, first through the journal *al-Fath* (The Opening) in late 1987 and then through the journal *Risalat al-Haramayn* (Message of the Two Holy Places).[110]

Hizbullah al-Hijaz quickly started to carry out attacks against Saudi interests. Its first military attack occurred on 16 August 1987: an explosion at a liquid petroleum plant in Ras al-Juaima. Although the government claimed that it was an accident, it was later ascribed to Hizbullah al-Hijaz.[111] In March 1988, the Sadaf (Saudi Arabia Petrochemical Company) petrochemical plant in Jubail was set on fire through several explosions, for which Hizbullah al-Hijaz claimed responsibility.[112] A Hizbullah al-Hijaz cell with four members from Tarut had carried out the attack. One of them had been an employee of Sadaf, while another had fought with Hizbullah in Lebanon and had received military training.[113] Widespread arrests occurred and when the security forces confronted three members of the Hizbullah al-Hijaz cell, several Saudi policemen were killed and injured before the militants could be captured. These three and the fourth member of the cell were later publicly executed (see Picture 4.3).[114] Several bombs also detonated at the Ras Tanura refinery and one allegedly failed to explode in Ras al-Juaima.[115] These attacks on

[110] For a summary of the contents of the second issue of *al-Fath* see *al-Thawra al-Islamiyya* 96 (February 1988), 31.

[111] Marschall, *Iran's*, 38; Peterson, *Historical Dictionary*, 122; "Mine Sinks Vessel in a Staging Area for Gulf Shipping," *New York Times*, 16 August 1987; "8 U.S. Helicopters Arrive for Mission to Sweep the Gulf," *New York Times*, 17 August 1987; "Saudi Group Tied to Other Attacks," *New York Times*, 29 March 1997. The OIRAP publication argued that the arrests after the attacks proved that it was not an accident. See *al-Thawra al-Islamiyya* 98 (May 1988), 8–13.

[112] *Al-Thawra al-Islamiyya* 98 (May 1988), 8–13; "Saudis and Iran: New Assertiveness," *New York Times*, 4 May 1988; "Saudi Arabia Beheads 16 Kuwaitis Linked to Pro-Iranian Terrorism," *New York Times*, 22 September 1989; Ibrahim, *Shi'is*, 142.

[113] First four issues of *Risalat al-Haramayn* (1989–90). See *al-Thawra al-Islamiyya* 105 (December 1988); al-'Ali, *sha'b al-Qatif*, 77f.

[114] They were Azhar 'Ali al-Hijjaj, 'Ali 'Abdallah al-Khatim, Muhammad 'Ali al-Qarus, Khalid 'Abd al-Hamid al-'Alq. Abir, *Saudi Arabia: Government*, 158; Ibrahim, *Shi'is*, 142; Krimly, *Political Economy*, 301f.; MECS, 1988, 687f.; "The Gulf: Shi'ites: Poorer Cousins," *Time Magazine*, 24 September 1990. See also statement by Hizbullah al-Hijaz, 5 August 1988, www.alhramain.com. See the portraits of the 'martyrs' in *Risalat al-Haramayn* 43/44 (August/September 1993); *al-Thawra al-Islamiyya* 103 (October 1988), 18–32.

[115] Al-Ibrahim and al-Sadiq, *al-hirak al-shi'i fi al-su'udiyya*, 159; Peterson, *Historical Dictionary*, 122.

PICTURE 4.3. Picture of the four Hizbullah al-Hijaz members executed in
1988, Azhar ʿAli al-Hijjaj (bottom left), ʿAli ʿAbdallah al-Khatim (center),
Muhammad ʿAli al-Qarus (top right), Khalid ʿAbd al-Hamid al-ʿAlq (bottom
right); as well as Muhammad Hasan al-Hayik (top left), who was arrested in
1996 and subsequently died in prison.
Source: alwelayah.net.

the oil industry by Saudi Shia further cemented a policy by ARAMCO
not to employ Shia in sensitive areas.[116]

Hizbullah al-Hijaz and its backers wanted to avenge the executions
and assassinated several Saudi diplomats and agents abroad. A Hizbullah
al-Hijaz cell from al-Ahsa also allegedly attempted to attack the American-
manufactured AWACS planes stationed at Dhahran Airbase towards
the end of the Iran-Iraq War in mid-1988. But a bomb detonated in the
hands of one of the militants during the preparation for the attack. The
members of the cell were arrested at a local hospital, but released after
a few months, possibly upon lobbying by notables from al-Ahsa.[117] As
a response to the hajj incident, the bombings by Hizbullah al-Hijaz, an

---

[116] Fuller and Francke, *Arab Shiʿa*, 183–5; Matthiesen, "Hizbullah," 185–8; Woodward,
Oil and Labor in the Middle East, 93. In 1983, Shia activists apparently stole security
passes at the Ras Tanura refinery. Wright, *Sacred Rage*, 171. OIRAP claimed that it had
followers inside ARAMCO and published interviews with 'sources inside ARAMCO'.
Al-Thawra al-Islamiyya 61 (May 1985), 6f.

[117] Interview with a former member of Hizbullah al-Hijaz, Beirut, August 2008; al-Ibrahim
and al-Sadiq, *al-hirak al-shiʿi fi al-suʿudiyya*, 160.

attack on the Saudi embassy in Tehran, and Iranian raids on ships leaving or heading for Saudi Arabia, Saudi Arabia severed diplomatic relations with Iran on 26 April 1988.[118]

The Soldiers of Justice *(Jund al-Haqq)* and the Islamic Jihad Organisation in the Hijaz *(Munazzamat al-Jihad al-Islami fi al-Hijaz)*, probably related to the military wing of Hizbullah al-Hijaz, claimed responsibility – or were blamed – for assassinations of Saudi diplomats in Ankara in October 1988 and in 1989 and the wounding of a Saudi diplomat in Karachi in December 1988 in addition to bomb attacks in Riyadh in 1985 and 1989.[119] Some assert that the Islamic Jihad Organisation in the Hijaz was a new front organisation made up of Lebanese and Saudi Shia with links to Palestinian groups and factions inside Iran that were opposed to an Iranian rapprochement with Saudi Arabia.[120] The Islamic Jihad Organisation in the Hijaz claimed that the assassination of a Saudi diplomat in Bangkok in January 1989 was in revenge for the execution of four of its members in Saudi Arabia[121], as was the October 1988 killing of a Saudi diplomat in Ankara.[122]

The Saudi branch of the transnational Hizbullah networks had ideological and organisational relations with similar organisations amongst other Gulf Shia, most notably in Kuwait and Bahrain. In September 1989, sixteen Kuwaiti Shia were beheaded for smuggling explosives and placing them in the vicinity of Mecca's Grand Mosque in July 1989. They were members of Hizbullah al-Kuwayt, and all of them were Kuwaiti Shia of Iranian and Saudi origin.[123] Some Shia from al-Ahsa were also arrested[124]

---

[118] John Calabrese, *Revolutionary Horizons: Regional Foreign Policy in Post-Khomeini Iran* (New York: St. Martin's Press, 1994), 51; Fürtig, *Iran's Rivalry*, 49, 260.

[119] Joshua Teitelbaum, "Saudi Arabia's Shi'i Opposition: Background and Analysis," *Policy Watch* 225 (Washington, DC: Washington Institute for Near East Policy, 14 November 1996), 1; "Saudi Group Tied to Other Attacks," *New York Times*, 29 March 1997; Abir, *Saudi Arabia*, 158f.; Centre de Recherche sur les Menaces Criminelles Contemporaines, *Atlas Mondial de l'Activisme* (Paris, 1990), 35; *Risalat al-Haramayn* 0 (1989); *Risalat al-Haramayn* 5 (1990); Peterson, *Historical Dictionary of Saudi Arabia*, 122.

[120] "Pro-Iranian Terror Groups Targeting Saudi Envoys," *New York Times*, 8 January 1989; "Saudis Overhaul Secret Service after Terrorist Killings," *The Independent*, 14 January 1989.

[121] "Pro-Iranian Terror Groups Targeting Saudi Envoys."

[122] *Risalat al-Haramayn* 0 (1989).

[123] "Saudi Arabia Beheads 16 Kuwaitis Linked to Pro-Iranian Terrorism," *New York Times*, 22 September 1989.

[124] See statement by Hizbullah al-Hijaz, "*Bi munasibat al-i'tiqalat fi al-mintaqa al-sharqiyya*" (On the Occasion of the Arrests in the Eastern Province), 10 July 1989, www.alhramain.com.

and members of Hizbullah al-Kuwayt and Hizbullah al-Hijaz jointly announced vengeance at a press conference in Beirut.[125] In November 1989, the Islamic Jihad Organisation claimed responsibility for the assassination of a Saudi diplomat in Beirut in revenge for the beheading of the sixteen Kuwaitis and the four Saudis (in 1988).[126]

CONCLUSION

Since the 1970s, two communal Islamist movements, the *shiraziyyun* and Khat al-Imam, became the strongest political forces amongst Saudi Shia. Communal militancy as practised by Khat al-Imam and to a lesser extent the *shiraziyyun* is 'a responsive, segmentary movement caused by political, economic or cultural group-discrimination, and opts to remedy these and other grievances in multi-communal societies'.[127] Communal Islamist movements want to Islamise society and at the same time address communal grievances. The *shiraziyyun* and Khat al-Imam sought to enforce public morality and counter secular tendencies in society. Groups of Khat al-Imam youth, for example, started to act as local vigilante forces enforcing public morality in the villages around Qatif.[128]

Throughout the 1980s, relations between the Shia and the state remained very tense. Hundreds of activists lived abroad, and had to adjust to the downsides of Middle Eastern exile politics. Eventually, the *shiraziyyun* fell out with the Iranians. Relations deteriorated so much that the Saudis gradually left Iran and the spiritual leader of the *shirazi* movement, Muhammad al-Shirazi, would spend the last decade of his life until his death in 2002 under house arrest in Iran. A new group that propagated the *marji'iyya* of Khomeini started to challenge the monopoly the *shiraziyyun* had on Shia Islamist activism in the Eastern Province and amongst Saudi Shia abroad. With assistance from Iran and Lebanese Hizbullah, they quickly established a new political organisation in 1987 and took the confrontation with the state to a new, more violent level. But this violence also gave the state a justification, not least in the eyes of its Western allies, to crack down on all Shia opposition movements.

---

[125] Centre de Recherche sur les Menaces Criminelles Contemporaines, *Atlas Mondial de l'Activisme*, 36. See also the press communiqués by Hizbullah al-Kuwayt and Hizbullah al-Hijaz in *Risalat al-Haramayn* o (1989).
[126] *Risalat al-Haramayn* 1 (1989); "U.S. Links Teheran to Terror Squads," *New York Times*, 12 November 1989.
[127] Jabar, *Shi'ite*, 41.
[128] Al-Ibrahim and al-Sadiq, *al-hirak al-shi'i fi al-su'udiyya*, 155f.

After 1989 the networks of Hizbullah al-Hijaz and Khat al-Imam inside Saudi Arabia were severely weakened through the arrests of many of its leaders.[129] And because of its pro-Iranian outlook and its dependence on Iranian support, Hizbullah al-Hijaz was susceptible to changes in Saudi-Iranian relations.

At the same time, Khat al-Imam posed a real challenge to the *shiraziyyun* on religious grounds, since several Khat al-Imam clerics were the heavyweights on the Saudi Shia religious scene, whose knowledge and publications on Islamic jurisprudence were widely seen to be superior to those of the *shirazi* clerics. In addition, they were plugged into the mainstream networks of the Shia *hawzat* in Najaf and Qom, while the *shiraziyyun* were regarded with suspicion in these centres of learning and had originated in Karbala. Khat al-Imam emphasised the need to defend the Shia of Qatif and al-Ahsa against the "Wahhabis", in their view a derogatory term for the followers of Muhammad Ibn ʿAbd al-Wahhab, through violence and the establishment of local militant cells. Young recruits would be indoctrinated with ideas about jihad as formulated by Khomeini. While the general discourse of Khat al-Imam and Hizbullah al-Hijaz was pan-Islamic, in their indoctrination and study circles they insisted on the strengthening of a distinct sectarian identity.[130] One of the main legacies of Saudi Shia communal Islamist movements then was this insistence on sectarian identities.

---

[129] Ibrahim, *Shiʿis*, 142; *al-Thawra al-Islamiyya* 103, October 1988, 18–32. Four members of Hizbullah al-Hijaz were released in 1990 but at least four other leaders remained in prison until 1993: ʿAbd al-Karim al-Hubayl, Jaʿfar al-Mubarak, ʿAbd al-Latif al-Nasir and ʿAbdallah al-Nimr. See *Risalat al-Haramayn* 32, 1992; *Arabia Monitor*, 9 October 1992, 8.

[130] Interview with a former member of Hizbullah al-Hijaz, Beirut, August 2008; al-Ibrahim and al-Sadiq, *al-hirak al-shiʿi fi al-suʿudiyya*, 161.

5

No More Revolution

When Iran accepted the ceasefire with Iraq on 18 July 1988, the Iraqi opposition activists in Iran saw their hopes disappointed.[1] An era of war and confrontation was coming to an end, and together with the death of Khomeini on 3 June 1989 paved the way for improved Saudi-Iranian relations. Khomeini, who saw the Saudi ruling family as one of the arch enemies of Islam and in his last will denounced the Saudi king as a 'traitor to God', had been a major obstacle to such a rapprochement.[2] His death led to small demonstrations in the Eastern Province, after which some Shia were arrested.[3] Hizbullah al-Hijaz announced that it would now follow the *marji'iyya* of 'Ali Khamenei,[4] but some of Khomeini's admirers from the Eastern Province continued to follow him as a *marji'* even after his death.

The MVM, which had hoped for a victory of Iran over Iraq, was riven by internal disagreements and splinter movements. Many of the remaining *shirazi* activists left Iran; some of the Iraqis went to Northern Iraq, while others went to Sayyida Zaynab, Western Europe, the United States, India, Malaysia and other places. The MVM had had links to India and dozens of young MVM members, including some Saudis who worked

---

[1] Henner Fürtig, *Der irakisch-iranische Krieg, 1980–1988: Ursachen, Verlauf, Folgen* (Berlin: Akademie, 1992), 177–9.

[2] *MECS*, 1988, 189f., 689–92; Moin, *Khomeini*, 305.

[3] "The Gulf: Shi'ites: Poorer Cousins," *Time Magazine*, 24 September 1990; *FBIS*, 14 July 1989.

[4] Interview with an unnamed cleric of Hizbullah al-Hijaz in *Risalat al-Haramayn* o 1989.

in the Bahraini branch (IFLB), went to India.[5] These developments led the Saudi Shia in MVM to think more about their own political goals. Although the Saudis made up a large part of MVM members they had little say in decision making. While there were some Saudis in the MVM Central Committee, the two al-Mudarrisi brothers and the Iraqis were dominant.[6] Since the late 1980s most *khums* and funding for MVM came from Saudi Arabia and the Saudis wanted to have more say over its distribution and invest more locally in Saudi Arabia. The Saudis, led by al-Saffar, pressed for the adoption of a clear programme that would limit the authority of al-Mudarrisi, including movement-internal elections, but to no avail. Saudi funding became so important that even IFLB opened a *hussainiyya* in Damascus specifically to receive Saudi alms givers and created a secret fundraising branch inside Saudi Arabia.[7]

OIRAP reorganised and distanced itself from MVM in 1989. The OIRAP Central Committee (*al-lajna al-markaziyya*), which hitherto had consisted of eight members, was enlarged and complemented by a Majlis al-Shura of forty members.[8] Damascus became the centre for religious and organisational activities, while many political and journalistic activities moved to London and Washington, D.C.[9] The general shift towards an insistence on human rights was symbolised by the establishment of the International Committee for Human Rights in the Gulf and Arabian Peninsula by a group led by Ja'far al-Shayib in Tennessee, which moved to Washington, D.C., in 1990. It denounced human rights violations and the arrests of opposition activists and lobbied the media, NGOs and the U.S. government; it also issued the newsletter *Arabia Monitor*.[10] But tensions also moved to the fore within OIRAP. A group led by Salih al-Taruti criticised Hasan al-Saffar for his leadership style. Al-Taruti used to be in charge of the Damascus office and the office in Cyprus where operations inside the Kingdom were planned. People close to him had published the journal *Ahl al-Bayt* (The People of the House (of the Prophet)), which specifically dealt with sectarian discrimination in Saudi Arabia.[11]

---

[5] Jabar, *Shi'ite*, 259; al-Labad, *al-inqilab*, 257–77, 283–6, 305–8; Ru'uf, *al-'amal*, 292–7. Interview with a former MVM member, who was in India, Eastern Province, November 2008.

[6] Louër, *Transnational*, 232.

[7] Al-Labad, *al-inqilab*, 355f.

[8] Ibrahim, *Shi'is*, 155–7.

[9] Ibid., 145f.

[10] Ibid., 149–51.

[11] Interview with former OIRAP member, Damascus, August 2008.

In 1990, al-Taruti and al-Saffar fell out personally and both were weakened inside the movement. Thereafter, al-Taruti went to Beirut and he and a number of other members left the movement and formed their own group.[12] Al-Taruti was no longer convinced of the value of the propaganda work abroad and was ready to return to Saudi Arabia.[13] This was one of the factors that led the OIRAP Majlis al-Shura to elect a compromise candidate, Tawfiq al-Sayf, as secretary general in 1991.[14] After these events, OIRAP sought to reformulate its ideology. An early public step in this direction was a seminal work published by Hasan al-Saffar in 1990 entitled *Pluralism and Freedom in Islam*. In this book he addresses the possibility for Islamic pluralism and argues that different Islamic sects should be open-minded towards each other.[15]

THE GULF CRISIS AND CALLS FOR REFORM

Iraq's invasion of Kuwait in August 1990 and the ensuing First Gulf War accelerated OIRAP's reorientation. It profoundly changed the political balance in the Gulf, affected the relations between the Shia opposition and the Saudi government, and led to the emergence of a lively debate over politics and society and the rise of a broad Islamist opposition. The main event that triggered these developments was the decision that the expulsion of Iraqi troops from Kuwait was to take place from Saudi soil. In the following months up to 500,000 American troops were deployed to Saudi Arabia.[16] This was criticised both regionally[17] and within Saudi Arabia by a wide range of religious figures and other social forces, who thought that it was improper to invite the U.S. military to Saudi Arabia and did not understand why Saudi Arabia could not defend

---

[12] Interview with former OIRAP member, Damascus, August 2008.

[13] Interview with Muhammad Mahfuz, Damascus, August 2008; but al-Taruti continued to publish in a Saudi *shirazi* publication. See *al-Jazira al-ʿArabiyya* 8 (September 1991), 24–8.

[14] Al-Rayyis, *riyyah al-sumum*, 203; Ibrahim, *Shiʿis*, 155.

[15] Hasan al-Saffar, *al-taʿaddudiyya wa-l-hurriyya fi al-Islam: bahth hawla hurriyyat al-muʿtaqad wa-taʿaddud al-madhahib* (Pluralism and Freedom in Islam: A Study on the Freedom of Belief and the Plurality of Confessions) (Beirut: Dar al-Manhal/Dar al-Bayan al-ʿArabi, 1990). This book has been discussed widely in the academic literature: Fandy, "From Confrontation;" Fandy, *Saudi Arabia*, 199; Ibrahim, *Shiʿis*, 160f.; Louër, *Transnational*, 233; Meijer and Wagemakers, "The Struggle." Parts of it were reprinted in *al-Jazira al-ʿArabiyya* 1 (January 1991), 45–7.

[16] Al-Rasheed, *A History*, 163f.

[17] See, for example, James P. Piscatori, ed., *Islamic Fundamentalisms and the Gulf Crisis* (Chicago: The American Academy of Arts and Sciences, 1991).

itself. Foremost amongst them were the Sunni clerics Salman al-ʿAwda and Safar al-Hawali. Another line of conflict was between these Islamists and the liberals. The liberals supported a women's "drive-in", whereby women drove around major urban centres.[18] The liberals also presented a petition to King Fahd urging social and political reforms such as the establishment of a Majlis al-Shura in 1990/1. This petition was signed by forty-three intellectuals, predominantly from the Hijaz, but also by a number of liberal Shia.[19] Some signatories were remnants of the earlier clandestine left-wing organisations, and it was a novelty that these letters were published with the names of the signatories. The Islamists, however, were angered by the elections of the liberals and branded them secularists (*ʿilmaniyyun*).[20] This petition was followed in November 1990 by a letter from Shia notables to King Fahd in which they asked for the inclusion of Shia in a future Majlis al-Shura.[21]

During the Gulf crisis, publicly voiced dissent and demands for political reform reached a level that had not been seen in Saudi Arabia since the 1950s and 1960s.[22] While in the 1980s the Shia opposition and the leftists had been almost the only public opponents of the Saudi ruling family, the Gulf War catalysed widespread political activism across the country. In this context OIRAP changed its name to Reformist Movement in Saudi (RMS) (*al-haraka al-islahiyya fi al-suʿudiyya*) in early 1991.[23] This coincided with an important public step by the Saudi *shiraziyyun*.

During the Gulf War, Saddam Hussein had called for jihad against the U.S. forces.[24] Some of his emissaries apparently traveled to Sayyida Zaynab and promised OIRAP a base in Iraq including its own radio

---

[18] *Al-Jazira al-ʿArabiyya* 1 (January 1991), 31–3. For a list of fatwas denouncing the drive-in see *al-Jazira al-ʿArabiyya* 2 (February 1991), 31–4.

[19] For example, ʿAbd al-Khaliq Al ʿAbd al-Hayy, Ahmad al-Shuwaykhat, Muhammad al-ʿAli, and ʿAli Jawad al-Khars. *Al-Jazira al-ʿArabiyya* 1 (January 1991), 4–6; *rabiʿ al-suʿudiyya wa-mukhrijat al-qamaʿ: duʿat al-islah al-siyasi* (The Saudi Spring and the Outcomes of Repression: A Call for Political Reform) (Beirut: Dar al-Kunuz al-Adabiyya, 2004), 187–9.

[20] Richard Dekmejian, "The Liberal Impulse in Saudi Arabia," *The Middle East Journal* 57, no. 3 (2003), 400–13, 401–4.

[21] Article 19, *Silent Kingdom*, 50.

[22] *MECS*, 1993, vol. 2, 575–81; Stéphane Lacroix, "Islamo-Liberal Politics in Saudi Arabia," in *Saudi Arabia in the Balance: Political Economy, Society, Foreign Affairs*, ed. Paul Aarts and Gerd Nonneman (New York: New York University Press, 2005), 35–56, 41; Teitelbaum, *Holier*, 25–47.

[23] Al-Rayyis, *riyyah al-sumum*, 203; Ibrahim, *Shiʿis*, 155. In February 1991, al-Saffar still gave an interview to the Iranian daily *Keyhan* as the leader of OIRAP. It was reprinted in *al-Jazira al-ʿArabiyya* 2 (February 1991).

[24] *FBIS*, 13 August 1990.

station if it supported Saddam Hussein.[25] But OIRAP refused and Hasan al-Saffar urged Saudi Shia to defend Saudi Arabia against Iraq in the Gulf crisis of 1990/1. Although the Shia could not contribute very much, as they were largely barred from entering the military, several hundred Shia enrolled in a training program.[26] This pleased the Saudi ruling family but the security forces were quick to suppress demonstrations in Qatif between 21 and 24 March 1991 in support of the Iraqi Shia uprising against Saddam Hussein, and follow-up demonstrations after the *marji'* of many Saudi Shia, Abu al-Qasim al-Khu'i, was arrested as part of Saddam's crackdown on the Shia in Iraq.[27] Yet, since 1990, Muharram processions had been allowed in some majority Shia areas, as long as mourners did not engage in self-flagellation or display banners.[28]

The new discourse of RMS was mainly propagated through the journal *al-Jazira al-'Arabiyya* (The Arabian Peninsula), published in London from January 1991 until September 1993 as the successor of *al-Thawra al-Islamiyya*.[29] It sought to capitalise on the changes at the international and local levels such as the fall of the Soviet Union and the rise of religious forces in the Gulf.[30] Many of the articles in the journal were written by its editors Hamza al-Hasan, Fu'ad Ibrahim and 'Abd al-Amir Musa, and other leading RMS members such as Hasan al-Saffar, Tawfiq al-Sayf and Muhammad al-Marzuq. The journal called for cooperation among opposition groups in the Gulf through a Cooperation Council for the Gulf Opposition, playing on the name of the GCC.[31] Therefore, political activists and members of other Gulf opposition groups from Qatar, the UAE, Kuwait and Bahrain, both leftists and Islamists, wrote in the journal.[32] It emphasised the national stance of the RMS, moving away from the Islamic and Shia discourse and imagery of *al-Thawra al-Islamiyya*.[33]

[25] Lacey, *Inside*, 167–9.

[26] *MECS*, 1990, 619; Ibrahim, *Shi'is*, 156f., 184. Interestingly, this editorial calls upon the Saudi government to let the people defend their country themselves without the help of the Americans (it does, however, not make special reference to the Shia). *Al-Jazira al-'Arabiyya* 1 (January 1991), 1–3.

[27] Press Release by International Committee for Human Rights in the Gulf and Arabian Peninsula, Demonstrations in Saudi Arabia, n.d., Nashville.

[28] Cordesman, *Saudi Arabia*, 209.

[29] Available online at www.saudiaffairs.net/webpage/aljazeera/aljazeera.htm.

[30] *Al-Jazira al-'Arabiyya* 1 (January 1991), editorial.

[31] *Al-Jazira al-'Arabiyya* 5 (June 1991), 22–4.

[32] See, for example, *al-Jazira al-'Arabiyya* 8 (September 1991); 25 (February 1993), 26–31; 26 (March 1993), 38–42.

[33] See, for example, Hasan al-Saffar's article on 'national unity' in *al-Jazira al-'Arabiyya* 12 (January 1992), 3–7.

PICTURE 5.1. Logo of the Organisation for the Islamic Revolution in the Arabian Peninsula.
Source: OIRAP.

The cover pages of *al-Thawra al-Islamiyya* often carried the OIRAP logo, featuring the Kaaba, from which a globe and a rifle in a clenched fist arise (see Picture 5.1).[34] By contrast, *al-Jazira al-ʿArabiyya* made fewer references to religion and was called a 'Political Monthly that Deals with the Affairs of the Saudi Arabian Peninsula'. It even gave a platform to *salafis*[35] and communists.

After the fall of the Soviet Union, the Saudi communists were in a crisis.[36] The Communist Party changed its discourse and during its third congress in 1989 advocated democracy, human rights and a parliament. In March 1991 it announced the formation of the National Democratic Group in Saudi (*al-tajammuʿ al-watani al-dimuqrati fi al-suʿudiyya*),[37] and some of its members moved to London while others remained in Damascus.[38] It also started to denounce human rights abuses through the

---

34 Above the rifle is a famous Quranic phrase praising jihad. The Prophet urged his followers to proceed against Tabuk: 'Go forth lightly and heavily (equipped) and strive with your wealth and persons in the cause of God' (9:41). The OIRAP logo is discussed in Dale F. Eickelman and James P. Piscatori, *Muslim Politics*, 2nd ed. (Princeton, NJ: Princeton University Press, 2004), 65f.

35 See, for example, the article by ʿUbayd bin Faraj al-ʿUtaybi in *al-Jazira al-ʿArabiyya* 6 (July 1991), 30f.

36 Vassiliev, *The History*, 464.

37 Al-ʿAkri, *al-tanzimat*, 52–5.

38 Sunayama, *Syria*, 93.

Committee for the Defense of Human Rights in Saudi (*lajnat al-difa ' 'an huquq al-insan fi al-su'udiyya*). *Hizb al-'amal*, on the other hand, which had been severely weakened by the 1982 arrests, promised to cease its activities and in return several of its members were released in 1991.[39] A member of the executive committee of the National Democratic Group in Saudi stated in an interview with *al-Jazira al-'Arabiyya* that the change in discourse came in response to a general turn towards calls for democracy amongst political opposition groups in the region and the wave of petitions inside Saudi Arabia. He argued that the opposition would have to abandon its radical discourse and instead focus on democracy and human rights. According to him, revolutionary ideology was one of the reasons for the failure of the opposition in Saudi Arabia, and socialism and the establishment of an Islamic system after the Iranian model were simply not possible. He also argued that the opposition, both Islamist and secular, had mainly been active in al-Ahsa and Qatif and that it was time to establish a broad national coalition.[40]

From the beginning, *al-Jazira al-'Arabiyya* gave wide coverage to petitions by different political groups[41], advocated an elected Majlis al-Shura with real powers[42] and reproduced the statements by the International Committee for Human Rights in the Gulf and Arabian Peninsula and international human rights organisations on Saudi Arabia, which were largely based on information provided by Shia activists.[43] Different writers also pointed to the *badu-hadar* (nomad/settled) dichotomy and the prominence of regional identities, not only in the Eastern Province but also in the Hijaz and Najd, which – if not replaced by an all-encompassing national identity – could lead to the fragmentation of the country.[44] With its broad contributor base from across Saudi Arabia and the wider Gulf, the magazine annoyed the Saudi government so much that it was a key factor that led to the 1993 deal (and its closure became a precondition of the government for the deal).[45]

The number of actual RMS members, however, was small, as two factions (those who joined Hizbullah al-Hijaz and Salih al-Taruti's group)

---

[39] Human Rights Watch, *World Report 1992: Saudi Arabia*.

[40] *Al-Jazira al-'Arabiyya* 6 (July 1991), 19–21.

[41] See *al-Jazira al-'Arabiyya* 1 (January 1991), 4–6.

[42] *Al-Jazira al-'Arabiyya* 1 (January 1991), 9–11, 23–5, 40–2.

[43] See *al-Jazira al-'Arabiyya* 1 (January 1991), 22, 37–9; 10 (November 1991), 6f.

[44] *Al-Jazira al-'Arabiyya* 16 (May 1992), 12–18, 24f; 18 (July 1992), 24–30; al-Rasheed, "The Shia," 125–30. Hamza al-Hasan later wrote a PhD dissertation about the lack of coherent national identities in Saudi Arabia: al-Hasan, *Role*.

[45] Al-Rayyis, *riyyah al-sumum*, 197–214.

had broken away and the clerical wing continued its religious activities mainly in Sayyida Zaynab under the auspices of MVM. In addition, a number of Saudi Shia remained within MVM or ceased their oppositional activities. Throughout the 1980s some had received a passport from Saudi embassies and returned to Saudi Arabia.[46]

In the late 1980s exploratory meetings between representatives of the Saudi government and the Shia opposition became more frequent. Tawfiq al-Sayf met with a delegate of Prince Turki al-Faysal, the head of the Saudi General Intelligence Directorate, in London in the late 1980s. During this meeting al-Sayf was offered a safe return for the movement to Saudi Arabia if it disbanded all its activities but was not offered any further concessions. In 1990, al-Sayf met with 'Abd al-'Aziz al-Tuwayjri, a former deputy of the National Guard and close advisor of Crown Prince Abdullah, to exchange views. It was only in 1991 that al-Tuwayjri asked the group about their specific demands and conditions for a return.[47] Al-Sayf wrote a number of letters to al-Tuwayjri outlining religious, socio-economic and political demands, emphasising that the Shia had hopes that their situation could improve under Crown Prince Abdullah.[48]

The International Committee for Human Rights in the Gulf and Arabian Peninsula was in contact with the Saudi embassy in Washington, D.C., and Prince Bandar, the Saudi ambassador to the United States, met with some RMS leaders including Ja'far al-Shayib, 'Isa al-Miza'il and 'Ali al-Shuwaykhat in October 1990. Prince Bandar apparently told them that in the wake of the Gulf crisis some political reforms such as an elected Majlis al-Shura should be introduced. The two sides exchanged letters and the Shia held meetings with other important Saudi officials in Washington, D.C., between 1991 and 1993.[49]

The improvement in Saudi-Iranian relations was another factor that facilitated the 1993 agreement. Iran was firmly opposed to Iraq's invasion of Kuwait and a certain tactical alliance was formed by all of Iraq's neighbours. This led to a rapprochement between Saudi Arabia and Iran and the restoration of diplomatic ties on 26 March 1991. In an act of

[46] Ibrahim, *Shi'is*, 159. Interviews with former OIRAP members, Damascus, 2008.

[47] Interview with Tawfiq al-Sayf, November 2008, Eastern Province. Lacey writes that the first meeting between 'Abd al-'Aziz al-Tuwayjri, Tawfiq al-Sayf and Hamza al-Hasan took place in 1992 at the Knightsbridge Holiday Inn. Lacey, *Inside*, 170f. My research shows that this was not the first meeting. An *al-Quds al-'Arabi* article also refers to a meeting with a high-ranking National Guard official in London at the time of the former Saudi ambassador Nasir al-Manqur. See *al-Quds al-'Arabi*, 1 November 1993.

[48] For a transcript of the letters see: Ibrahim, *Shi'is*, 187–9.

[49] Ibid., 152, 183f. Interview with 'Isa al-Miza'il, Eastern Province, November 2008.

trust, the Saudis agreed to raise the quota of 45,000 Iranian pilgrims that was in place since the 1987 clashes to 115,000 in 1991, although they reduced it again in 1994. In return, President Rafsanjani promised that Iranian pilgrims would not chant anti-Saudi slogans during the hajj.[50] Yet, this rapprochement remained fragile and various factions in Iran frequently accused President Rafsanjani and his entourage of departing from Khomeini's line, often pointing to the mistreatment of Saudi Shia.[51] This and a similar rapprochement between Saudi Arabia and Syria as a result of the Gulf crisis made the prospects of Saudi Shia exiles more precarious. They, for example, did not know how long they could safely stay in their places of exile such as Sayyida Zaynab.

It is noteworthy that while Hizbullah al-Hijaz carried out several attacks against Saudi targets between 1987 and 1989, there are no such reports between late 1989 and 1996. The religious wing of Khat al-Imam remained active and Hizbullah al-Hijaz continued to recruit young Saudis. Several of these were sent for military training, initially in Lebanon. But some of these youth claim that their military training was very short, ranging from a few days to a few weeks. The most serious recruits were then sent to Iran for further training. But Hizbullah al-Hijaz did not carry out or claim responsibility for any other military attack until it was blamed for the Khobar Towers bombings in 1996.[52]

THE PETITIONS MOVEMENT

These meetings with representatives of the Saudi state led to heated discussions amongst Saudi Shia opposition activists. The Pan-Shia Association in Saudi (*rabitat 'umum al-shi'a fi al-su'udiyya*), which was founded in 1989 by Hasan al-Saffar and headed by Musa Abu Khamsin, published the Shia demands in a booklet. Shia leaders in other countries such as India and Lebanon had advocated the creation of such an association, possibly across national boundaries, but this had proven difficult to realise.[53] Their demands included the recognition of Shia Islam as an Islamic sect; the granting of religious freedoms that would include the permission to construct mosques, *hussainiyyat* and *hawzat*; a revision of

---

[50] Al-Mani', "Ideological," 170–2; Liu, *Saudi*, 231–5.

[51] Chubin and Tripp, *Iran-Saudi*, 52–7.

[52] Interview with a former member of Hizbullah al-Hijaz, Beirut, August 2008; al-Ibrahim and al-Sadiq, *al-hirak al-shi'i fi al-su'udiyya*, 157, 162f.

[53] Interview with a former member of the Pan-Shia Association in Saudi Arabia, Damascus, August 2008. See also al-Hasan, *al-'amal al-matlabi*, 211f.

the education system so that religious education in Shia areas could be according to Shia beliefs; the allowing of Shia magazines and books; an end to anti-Shia propaganda campaigns and sectarian discrimination in education, government employment, the military, and the security establishment; and the strengthening of Shia courts.[54]

From 1991 onwards, the movement discussed the negotiations with Middle Eastern politicians, clerical figures and political groups. Most said that engagement was necessary but that the Shia should beware of being used in a political game. The notables in the Eastern Province, especially in Qatif, were sceptical whether the government would keep its promises and stated that the Shia would lose their voice abroad.[55] Al-Saffar sent a letter to the Shia *qadi* of Qatif, 'Abd al-Hamid al-Khatti, with whom al-Saffar and OIRAP had repeatedly clashed and whom they had described as 'traditionalist' in the past. Even al-Khatti apparently said that the movement should not return and that they should beware of the government (see Picture 5.2).[56] Notables sympathetic to OIRAP suggested that a part of the movement should return but another part should stay abroad since the cooperation with human rights organisations and news outlets as well as the Shia heritage programme would not be possible after a return. These demands of notables and members inside Saudi Arabia were also presented at the 1993 general meeting in Ghuta, a suburb on the outskirts of Damascus that includes Sayyida Zaynab.[57]

At the same time, the Sunni Islamist social movement that came to be known as the Sahwa openly criticised the American presence in Saudi Arabia. In 1991, a group of fifty-two religious figures, most of whom belonged to the Sahwa, presented King Fahd with a reformist petition. In 1992, they followed up the petition with the 'Memorandum of Advice' (*mudhakkirat al-nasiha*), which demanded the creation of a Majlis al-Shura, respect for human rights, as well as the strengthening of religious institutions.[58] In addition, RMS leaders such as Tawfiq al-Sayf

[54] *Al-shi'a fi al-su'udiyya: al-waqi'a al-sa'b wa-tatalla'at al-mashru'a* (The Shia in Saudi: Difficult Reality and Legitimate Aspirations) (n.p.: Rabitat 'Umum al-Shi'a fi al-Su'udiyya, 1991), 125f.; Ibrahim, *Shi'is*, 174; Muhammad 'Abd al-Majid, *al-tamayyiz al-ta'ifi fi al-su'udiyya* (Sectarian Discrimination in Saudi) (n.p.: Rabitat 'Umum al-Shi'a fi al-Su'udiyya, n.d.), 125–31. The journal of Hizbullah al-Hijaz also reported on their activities: *Risalat al-Haramayn* 30/31 (1992).

[55] Interview with Tawfiq al-Sayf, November 2008, Eastern Province.

[56] Al-Labad, *al-inqilab*, 372. Interviews with Saudi Shia, Eastern Province, November 2008.

[57] Interview with former OIRAP member, Eastern Province, November 2008.

[58] For more on the Sahwa see *MECS*, 1993, vol. 2, 575–81; *al-Jazira al-'Arabiyya* 21 (October 1992), 35–48; 22 (November 1992), 30–8; 23 (December 1992), 2f.; Champion,

PICTURE 5.2. From left to right: ʿAbd al-Hamid al-Khatti, ʿAbdallah al-Khunayzi, Hasan al-Saffar, ʿAbd al-Rasul al-Basara, in Qatif.
Source: Archive of Hasan al-Saffar.

started to present national demands in the Arab press, for example, that the Majlis al-Shura should be elected and that the new district system should transfer power from the central government to the provinces and that provincial councils should be elected.[59]

King Fahd responded in March 1992 by introducing three statutes: the Basic Law of Government, which is sometimes referred to as the constitution; the Law of the Provinces and the Law of the Majlis al-Shura. The Law of the Provinces turned the country's regions into administrative units and called for some consultation with the local population. This was to be achieved through the newly introduced local councils.[60] But a close

---

Paradoxical, 217–20; R. Hrair Dekmejian, "The Rise of Political Islamism in Saudi Arabia," *The Middle East Journal* 48, no. 4 (1994), 627–43, 629–35; Fandy, *Saudi Arabia*; Lacroix, "Islamo-Liberal," 41f.; Lacroix, *Awakening*; Teitelbaum, *Holier*, 25–47.

[59] *FBIS*, 21 February 1992.

[60] They consist of the governor, who is the president of the council, the vice governor, other government officials, and at least ten appointed residents of the respective province. See Rashed Aba-Namay, *The Constitution of Saudi Arabia: Evolution, Reform and Future Prospects* (PhD, University of Wales-Aberystwyth, 1992); Abdulaziz H. al-Fahad, "Ornamental Constitutionalism: The Saudi Basic Law of Governance," *Yale Journal of International Law* 30 (2005), 375–96; Joseph J. Nevo, "Religion and National Identity in Saudi Arabia," *Middle Eastern Studies* 34, no. 3 (1998), 34–53, 47f.; Madawi al-Rasheed, "God, the King and the Nation: Political Rhetoric in Saudi Arabia in the 1990s," *The Middle East Journal* 59, no. 3 (1996), 359–71, 363–5; Faisal Bin Mishal

look at the appointees reveals that the provincial councils were used to institutionalise neo-patrimonial ties of patronage. On the 1994 Eastern Province Provincial Council only two out of fifteen representatives were Shia. One of them was 'Abd al-Hamid al-Mutawwa', a friend of the governor Muhammad bin Fahd and an envoy used to convey messages to the Shia opposition. A government document classifies him as 'from amongst the important men (*a'yan*) of the region of Saihat from the group of the Shia'.[61] The other was Hussayn bin 'Ali al-'Ali, from a prominent family in Hufuf. In addition, the government appointed technocrats from Sunni notable families such as 'Abd al-Hamid al-Mubarak and powerful tribes such as a 'notable from al-Ahsa from the al-Murra tribe'.[62] Hasan al-Saffar publicly denounced the reforms as superficial,[63] while Tawfiq al-Sayf said that they were a step in the right direction.[64] In June 1992 *al-Jazira al-'Arabiyya* carried an interview with Hasan al-Saffar in which he declared that the opposition would be open to a dialogue with the government but affirmed that they would continue to work with other political groups, including the *salafis,* and strive for political reforms.[65]

Meanwhile, the government was under pressure to take a tough anti-Shia stance. In 1992 Sunni *'ulama'* asked the Grand Mufti Ibn Baz in a letter to curtail Shia activities and to close the Shia al-'Anud mosque in Dammam.[66] Later the same year, the Shia Sadiq 'Abd al-Karim Mal Allah was beheaded in Qatif on charges of apostasy after questioning the flawlessness of the Quran and the Prophet.[67] Some allege that he had converted to Christianity, but the Shia opposition publications sought to portray this as an attack on Shia Muslims.[68] In addition, the authorities

al-Saud, *Political Development in the Kingdom of Saudi Arabia: An Assessment of the Majlis Ash-Shura* (PhD, University of Durham, 2000); al-Saud, *Evolution.*

[61] A list of council members is reproduced in appendix 5 of al-Saud, *Evolution.*

[62] Both al-'Ali and al-Mutawwa' retained their seats until June 2001, when 'Ali al-Mulla became the Shia representative in the council. This information stems from appendix 5 of al-Saud, *Evolution.* In the late 2000s the wealthy Shia businessman Ghassan bin 'Abdallah al-Nimr was the only Shia member on the council. He stems from the al-Nimr family, who are originally from al-Ahsa and then moved to Dammam. He is not directly related to the politically active al-Nimr families from Awwamiyya. Previously available on the Internet, www.easternemara.gov.sa/Council.asp.

[63] *FBIS,* 26 March 1992.

[64] *The Independent,* March 3, 1992; letter from al-Sayf to al-Tuwayjri: quoted in Ibrahim, *Shi'is,* 188.

[65] *Al-Jazira al-'Arabiyya* 17 (June 1992), 18–21.

[66] *FBIS,* 27 January 1993.

[67] Dekmejian, "Political Islamism," 638.

[68] *Risalat al-Haramayn* 32 and 33 (1992); *Arabia Monitor,* September 1992, 8; *al-Jazira al-'Arabiyya* 21 (October 1992), 14f.; al-'Ali, *sha'b al-Qatif,* 79.

suppressed the activities of the informal *hawza* in Mubarraz in 1991, and the teaching circles of Shia clerics such as 'Abdallah al-Dandan were prohibited.[69]

SECRET NEGOTIATIONS

When Ghazi al-Qusaybi became Saudi ambassador to the United Kingdom in spring 1992, he started meeting with members of the Shia opposition on public occasions at the Saudi Embassy. Al-Qusaybi was born in Hufuf. His family was one of the most important allies of Ibn Saud in the Eastern Province and became powerful in business and politics. While he played a role in facilitating a better atmosphere between the two sides,[70] it was 'Uthman al-'Umayr, the editor of the Saudi-sponsored pan-Arab daily *al-Sharq al-Awsat* and personal advisor to King Fahd,[71] who was the key negotiator on the Saudi side. The negotiations would only gain pace after pressure on the ruling family by Sunni Islamists increased.

On 3 May 1993, the foundation of the Committee for the Defence of Legitimate Rights (CDLR) (*lajnat al-difa' 'an al-huquq al-shari'iyya*) was announced in a communiqué signed by five prominent Sunni Saudi Islamists: Hamad al-Sulayfih, 'Abdallah al-Mas'ari, 'Abdallah bin Jibrin, 'Abdallah al-Hamid and 'Abdallah al-Tuwayjri. CDLR 'was the first Saudi opposition group that, unlike earlier Shi'a groups, appealed to the mainstream Saudi culture'.[72] To increase pressure on the government, the June 1993 issue of *al-Jazira al-'Arabiyya* focussed on the creation of CDLR.[73]

RMS seriously thought about working together with CDLR. In an internal report distributed to RMS Central Committee members, Hamza al-Hasan argued that they should contact CDLR. He proposed that Hasan al-Saffar write to bin Jibrin and 'Abdallah al-Mas'ari to inform them of RMS's support. The report also acknowledged CDLR's widely known anti-Shia stance – bin Jibrin had once issued a fatwa denouncing Shia

---

[69] Al-Majid, *al-tamayyiz*, 149–51; *Risalat al-Haramayn* 29 (1992); *Risalat al-Haramayn* 32 (1992).

[70] *FBIS*, 4 November 1993; Madawi al-Rasheed and Loulouwa al-Rasheed, "The Politics of Encapsulation: Saudi Policy towards Tribal and Religious Opposition," *Middle Eastern Studies* 32, no. 1 (1996), 96–119, 113.

[71] Al-'Umayr later founded *Elaph*, the first Saudi online newspaper, which gives relatively wide coverage to Saudi Shia issues, www.elaph.com/editorial.htm.

[72] Fandy, *Saudi Arabia*, 117.

[73] *Al-Jazira al-'Arabiyya* 29, (June 1993).

as infidels who deserved to be killed. Safar al-Hawali, for example, had distributed cassette tapes in the 1980s in which he declared Shia Islam as contradicting Sunni Islam.[74] Citing this anti-Shia rhetoric, which had spread throughout the Eastern Province via cassettes, Hizbullah al-Hijaz warned against an alliance with Sunni Islamists.[75] But al-Hasan argued that in direct contact and negotiations, the RMS could encourage the members of the CDLR to overcome their anti-Shiism. Hamad al-Sulayfih was identified as a good person to approach. After the intifada he had been sent to the Eastern Province as a special governmental envoy to reorganise educational institutions in Shia areas and was therefore familiar with Shia issues.[76] It is questionable, however, whether a Sunni-Shia opposition alliance could ever have worked, given the distrust between the two factions of the opposition. The rise of the Sunni Islamists may have convinced many Shia that they would fare even worse under their rule than they do under the ruling family and may have contributed to their decision to reach an accommodation with the state.[77]

Two weeks after CDLR's foundation, Muhammad al-Mas'ari was arrested with other CDLR members, and Ja'far al-Shayib called al-Mas'ari's father, 'Abdallah, and offered to try to pressure the Saudi government to release the detainees.[78] The RMS London office forwarded a copy of a letter of support to 'Abdallah al-Mas'ari to the Saudi Embassy in London.[79] Some Shia activists still believe that fears of a possible alliance between them and CDLR were the main reason for the timing of the 1993 negotiations. Others argue that Ja'far al-Shayib bluffed when he called al-Mas'ari to offer his and RMS's support to CDLR.[80] But it seems

[74] See Mansoor Jassem Alshamsi, *Islam and Political Reform in Saudi Arabia: The Quest for Political Change and Reform* (New York: Routledge, 2011), 74f.

[75] *Risalat al-Haramayn* 29 (1992).

[76] Internal report to the members of the Central Committee, 10 May 1993. If not otherwise stated, the following information is from a series of interviews conducted with Hamza al-Hasan in 2008 and 2009 in London. Al-Hasan also gave me access to his unpublished memoirs surrounding the negotiations and to his personal archive, from which the following documents on the negotiations originate. For more details on the negotiations and the movement-internal discussions see al-Hasan, *al-'amal al-matlabi*, 209–28; Ibrahim, *Shi'is*, 178–208; Matthiesen, *The Shia of Saudi Arabia*, 248–62; Tawfiq al-Sayf, *an takun shi'iyan fi al-su'udiyya: ishkalat al-muwatana wa-l-hawiyya fi mujtama' taqlidi* (To Be a Shia in Saudi: Questions of Citizenship and Identity in a Traditional Society), http://talsaif.blogspot.co.uk, 119–24.

[77] Fandy, *Saudi Arabia*, 146, 173, 227f.

[78] Ibrahim, *Shi'is*, 152.

[79] Al-Labad, *al-inqilab*, 350.

[80] Various interviews with Saudi Shia, 2007–10.

clear that the Saudi ruling family mainly wanted to contain the emerging Sunni Islamist opposition.[81]

On 11 May 1993, 'Uthman al-'Umayr called the RMS office in North London. Hamza al-Hasan received the call at the RMS office and he and al-'Umayr met that day to discuss a possible deal.[82] During their next meeting on 12 May, al-'Umayr said that the king himself was behind this initiative and that he wanted to be accepted by all groups in Saudi society as the religious leader of the country. When al-Hasan spoke to Tawfiq al-Sayf and other members of the RMS Central Committee in Damascus, they were astonished and did not believe this. The king had been contacted before through a different channel, his Ismaili advisor 'Ali bin Musallam.[83] During the following weeks al-'Umayr, al-Hasan and al-Sayf, who returned to London, met repeatedly and drafted a letter that should be sent to the king in order to ask for a dialogue.[84]

Simultaneously, a second channel of communication was opened with the movement by the governor of the Eastern Province, Muhammad bin Fahd, through 'Abd al-Hamid al-Mutawwa', a Shia notable from the Eastern Province. In mid-May, al-Mutawwa' contacted Salih al-Taruti, who used to be the number three in RMS. Al-Taruti had, however, split away from RMS and did not have a strong position within the *shirazi* movement anymore. Al-Mutawwa' proposed a deal similar to the one offered by the king himself. Al-Taruti reported that he urged al-Mutawwa' to accept a number of conditions, such as the freeing of prisoners and that wives of movement members, many of whom were Iraqi Shia, could also move to Saudi Arabia.[85] By the end of May, it was up to RMS to decide on a common strategy and whether to accept the proposals or not, and so the London office corresponded with the other offices. Several key leaders agreed that it would make sense to go back if the movement could work inside Saudi Arabia. However, there was no overall agreement on the demands of the movement and most realised that it was difficult to go back without concessions.[86]

---

[81] Michael C. Hudson, "Arab Regimes and Democratization: Responses to the Challenge of Political Islam," in *The Islamist Dilemma: The Political Role of Islamist Movements in the Contemporary Arab World*, ed. Laura Guazzone (Reading: Ithaca, 1995), 217–45, 231.

[82] Internal report from Abu Hani (Hamza al-Hasan) to the members of the Central Committee, 11 May 1993.

[83] For 'Ali bin Musallam see Bradley, *Saudi Arabia Exposed*, 75.

[84] Interview with Hamza al-Hasan, London, April 2008.

[85] Letter from Salih al-Taruti to Hamza al-Hasan, 22 May 1993.

[86] Internal memorandum, issued in London, end of June 1993; internal memorandum, issued in London, 10 July 1993.

Many Saudi *shiraziyyun* did not hear about the negotiations until the general meeting in Ghuta. The leadership around al-Saffar called the conference, which lasted for several days, to inform members of the negotiations and hear their views. Around one hundred Saudi Shia from the United States, Iran, Beirut, from inside Saudi Arabia and most Saudi Shia in Damascus as well as Tawfiq al-Sayf from London attended. The attendees were informed that negotiations with the government had started and a number of internal memorandums were circulated. It was, however, not stated explicitly under which circumstances the movement would return.[87] RMS leaders also attempted to win over Saudi MVM members who had not joined RMS and had continued to work within MVM. Especially in the *hawza* wing there were many who had remained loyal to al-Mudarrisi and in the MVM *hawza*. Some of those attended the conference on the first day. But a group including Nimr al-Nimr, a cleric from Awwamiyya, successfully urged the *hawza* wing not to attend the second day of the meeting.[88]

The *hawza* wing was particularly furious that it had not been informed at an earlier stage about the negotiations. Out of about one hundred Saudi students in the *hawza* only around seventeen attended the meeting and the *hawza* wing circulated a petition in which it outlined the limits of negotiations. It made clear that the *hawza* was a part that could not be separated from MVM and they would therefore have to seek the approval of Muhammad Taqi al-Mudarrisi and Muhammad al-Shirazi. The *hawza* wing was not ready to return without the realisation of religious demands such as an end to sectarian discrimination and the permission to build *hawzat*. They also requested that a leader from the *hawza* wing be present in the negotiations with the government and that there be wider consultations with those inside Saudi Arabia who were opposed to the negotiations. In addition, they wanted the deal to include an amnesty for all Shia opposition groups, including Hizbullah al-Hijaz.[89]

Others argue that 85 percent of the attendants were in favour of the agreement if there was an amnesty and a release of prisoners. The remainder was split between those who wanted more concessions and a number of MVM members, who were against it altogether.[90] Eventually,

---

[87] Interviews with former OIRAP members, Eastern Province, November 2008.
[88] Interview with Hamza al-Hasan, London, November 2009.
[89] The petition, which was signed by the three clerics 'Ali al-Hussayn al-Hadad, 'Abd al-Hadi Salman and Hussayn Salih al-Shaykh, is reprinted in al-Labad, *al-inqilab*, 372–82.
[90] Interview with Muhammad Mahfuz, Damascus, August 2008.

the people who attended the conference agreed that the negotiations should go on with the ten-point program of Shia demands previously published by the Pan-Shia Association in Saudi Arabia and with the aim to end sectarian discrimination. However, it was agreed that outlining the exact definition of sectarian discrimination would be the task of the RMS Central Committee and the delegation.[91]

After this conference the other opposition groups as well as MVM and the Iranians were officially informed. Al-Saffar sat down with the *hawza* wing and promised to include them in future negotiations, and thereafter al-Saffar went to Tehran to discuss it with some Iranian officials and *ayatallahs*.[92] RMS had one more crucial obstacle to address, the attitudes of Muhammad Taqi al-Mudarrisi and Muhammad al-Shirazi. There is considerable debate as to what exactly their position was. A close aide of al-Mudarrisi argues that al-Mudarrisi was not opposed to the negotiations as such but warned RMS that the government would trick them.[93] But others claim that the MVM leaders were firmly against the accord and that al-Shirazi had reservations as well, although he said that if the majority of Saudis within the movement were in favour, then the negotiations were legitimate.[94]

THE DEAL WITH KING FAHD

After the Ghuta conference, the RMS Central Committee took the decision that the movement should return. Hasan al-Saffar thought that they could do religious works such as the opening of *hawzat* inside Saudi Arabia. The concrete demands during the negotiations were limited: the release of about four hundred Shia political prisoners, the return of twelve hundred to fifteen hundred Shia outside and the lifting of travel bans on around 2000–2500 Shia inside Saudi Arabia. The other political, religious and social demands that were raised in the negotiations were to be implemented at a later stage and were not part of the agreement.[95]

In July 1993, 'Isa al-Miza'il was the first of the leaders to return. He was arrested at the airport, an unusual action because when other

---

[91] Al-Labad, *al-inqilab*, 384.

[92] Al-Labad does not specify which officials and *ayatallahs* Hasan al-Saffar met in Iran. Al-Labad, *al-inqilab*, 382f.

[93] Interview with a former leading MVM member, Damascus, August 2008.

[94] Ibrahim, *Shi'is*. Al-Labad argues that only a minority of Saudi Shia abroad were in favour of it and it was hence not legal. Al-Labad, *al-inqilab*, 383f.

[95] Interview with Hasan al-Saffar, Eastern Province, November 2008.

movement members returned they were usually given a few days to visit their families before they would be questioned. He thinks that he was arrested because none of the officials in the Eastern Province knew about the negotiations between the king and the movement. When he said he was here to meet the king they would not believe him.[96] When the RMS London office heard of his arrest, it called the mediator, al-ʿUmayr, who in turn had al-Mizaʿil released.[97] The government took a first trust-building measure on 28 July 1993, when it released forty Shia political prisoners after a royal decree to that effect. Most of those were members and leaders of Hizbullah al-Hijaz, such as Jaʿfar al-Mubarak, who had been arrested after the 1988 explosions and the shoot-out between members of the group and the security forces in Qatif.[98] This seemed to prove that the government was serious about the general amnesty.

In further negotiations with al-ʿUmayr it was decided that an RMS delegation should meet the king. The RMS Central Committee selected four delegates from its ranks: Tawfiq al-Sayf, Jaʿfar al-Shayib, Sadiq al-Jubran and ʿIsa al-Mizaʿil. Hasan al-Saffar was not an option, because the movement feared for his security and wanted him to stay abroad as long as possible. The delegates were chosen from different areas of the movement. Sadiq al-Jubran, for example, was active in human rights, represented the activists in Syria and was originally from al-Ahsa. As most movement members and cadres were from Qatif, it was important to include someone from al-Ahsa in the delegation.[99] ʿIsa al-Mizaʿil became the interlocutor between the activists inside and outside Saudi Arabia. He travelled to Damascus in September to prepare for the return of the other leaders, some of whom did not even have a passport.[100] The government fulfilled another promise in mid-August with a directive to different Saudi embassies stating that a royal decree pardoned Shia who had been engaged in oppositional activities and allowed their return.[101]

The Shia delegation met King Fahd and Muhammad bin Fahd in late September 1993 at the king's palace in Jeddah. The meeting was held in a friendly atmosphere and the Shia delegates recall that the king was not wearing the *mislah*, the cloak that Saudi ruling family members only put

---

[96] Interview with ʿIsa al-Mizaʿil, Eastern Province, November 2008.

[97] Interview with Hamza al-Hasan, London, April 2008.

[98] Press Release by International Committee for Human Rights in the Gulf and Arabian Peninsula, Washington, D.C., 29 July 1993; Ibrahim, *Shiʿis*, 193.

[99] Interview with Sadiq al-Jubran, Eastern Province, November 2008.

[100] Interview with ʿIsa al-Mizaʿil, Eastern Province, November 2008.

[101] Ibrahim, *Shiʿis*, 190.

PICTURE 5.3. From left to right: Tawfiq al-Sayf, Hasan al-Saffar, Crown Prince Sultan bin ʿAbd al-ʿAziz, Sadiq al-Jubran, Muhammad Baqir al-Nimr, in Jeddah in 2008.
Source: Archive of Hasan al-Saffar.

aside if in the company of their family or close friends.[102] The delegation thanked the king for the release of prisoners and addressed the issue of passports for those abroad, the lifting of travel bans, the employment of Shia in local companies, and the issue of foreign wives of opposition activists. The king agreed that these issues could be resolved and that wider religious and political issues would have to be discussed with the relevant ministries. But the delegation did not present the more specific demands that were discussed within the movement beforehand relating to Shia religious practices. The delegation then met with a number of other high-ranking officials, including Minister of Interior Prince Nayef and Crown Prince Abdullah.[103] Subsequently, they flew to the Eastern Province, where relatives and supporters greeted them.[104]

As a response, the editor of *al-Jazira al-ʿArabiyya* sent a letter to its subscribers informing them that it was suspended, after the August issue

---

[102] Some details of the meeting are outlined in Lacey, *Inside*, 172f.

[103] Interviews with ʿIsa al-Mizaʿil, Tawfiq al-Sayf, and Sadiq al-Jubran, Eastern Province, November 2008, and with Jaʿfar al-Shayib, London, December 2010. See also al-Rayyis, *riyyah al-sumum*, 211f.; Ibrahim, *Shiʿis*, 190f.

[104] *FBIS*, 20 October 1993.

had called for negotiations between the government and the different opposition groups.[105] The RMS Central Committee decided that some movement members should return to Saudi Arabia and that the rest, including Hasan al-Saffar, should stay outside the country and await the outcomes of the dialogue. Members of the first group were issued passports and returned. People in the Eastern Province hoped that the sectarian problems could be resolved once and for all, especially as details of the dialogue remained scarce.[106] In October, RMS leaked the story to the international media, although domestic Saudi media remained silent.[107] The RMS also did this to counter reports that the release of prisoners in summer 1993 was a result of improved Saudi-Iranian relations.[108] While the Shia were waiting for the implementation of further measures, Saudi officials argued that 'the agreement had settled all outstanding issues with the minority' and that 'there are no deals as such, but those who issued these publications will stop them, and they can come back home where they are welcome'.[109]

The returnees were interrogated about their time abroad, especially about relations with Iran. They had to prove that the movements were actually dissolved and that there were no attempts at regrouping. In addition, they were compelled to sort out their legal and financial affairs and find jobs.[110] The appointment of the Shia Jamil al-Jishi to the newly created Majlis al-Shura was seen as a step in the right direction.[111] In the short term, Saudi-Iranian relations improved, and a couple of days after the Saudi Shia delegation had met the king, President Rafsanjani called King Fahd. The latter agreed to cut Saudi oil production in order to raise prices, thereby benefitting Iran.[112] In the coming months, the group

---

[105] Letter from Fu'ad Ibrahim to subscribers, 27 September 1993, and *al-Jazira al-'Arabiyya* 31 (August 1993).

[106] Ibrahim, *Shi'is*, 191–208.

[107] Caryle Murphy, "Saudi King Reconciles with Shiite Opposition," *Washington Post*, 16 October 1993; *FBIS*, 20 October 1993 and 4 November 1993.

[108] Interview with Hamza al-Hasan, London, April 2008.

[109] "Saudi Officials Reporting Accord with Shiite Foes," *New York Times*, 29 October 1993.

[110] Interviews with former OIRAP and MVM members, Damascus, August 2008. See also Ibrahim, *Shi'is*, 207, 210.

[111] Jamil al-Jishi stems from a prominent Qatifi notable family. In 1975, he became director general of the Royal Commission for Jubail, an industrial city to the north of Qatif, where many Shia found work. Buchan, "Opposition," 119; Fuller and Francke, *Arab Shi'a*, 186; Kostiner, "Shi'i Unrest," 175; Andrea H. Pampanini, *Cities from the Arabian Desert: The Building of Jubail and Yanbu in Saudi Arabia* (Westport, CT: Praeger, 1997), 25; International Crisis Group, *The Shiite Question in Saudi Arabia* (2005), 9.

[112] *FBIS*, 28 September 1993; Chubin and Tripp, *Iran-Saudi*, 68f.

abroad and the returnees corresponded with each other and when the RMS Central Committee met in Damascus on 8 April 1994 many were already dissatisfied. Some argued that the security services and the local government in the Eastern Province were harassing the returnees and hindering the implementation of the terms of the agreement. Despite this, it was agreed that the rest of the movement members should return to Saudi Arabia and by July 1994, all RMS members had returned.[113]

DIVIDED OPPOSITION AND THE KHOBAR BOMBINGS

Apart from the *shiraziyyun* most members of Hizbullah al-Hijaz and *tajammu' 'ulama' al-Hijaz* as well as the Shia leftists returned to Saudi Arabia. RMS had negotiated in the name of all Saudi Shia opposition groups, including Hizbullah al-Hijaz and the leftists who were active in Syria and beyond. Some Saudi Shia abroad were members of the Communist Party, *hizb al-'amal* and the Baath Party.[114] Several signatories of the liberal petition in 1990/1 were former leftist activists, and the remaining Communist Party cadres thought that they could now return and openly demand reforms from within Saudi Arabia. These developments led the remaining communists outside the country to agree with the negotiations between RMS and the government. The Communist Party members inside Saudi Arabia held a meeting with Crown Prince Abdullah in Riyadh, where they were assured of their safety and told that they would be allowed to travel and find easier employment if they stopped their political activities. The Communist Party members abroad had to wait for the deal between RMS and the government to be sealed.[115]

Although Hizbullah al-Hijaz and *tajammu' 'ulama' al-Hijaz* formally opposed the agreement, they wanted to profit from its outcomes. Most Shia political prisoners were members of these groups, and those abroad faced difficult personal situations, often without passports.[116] Hizbullah al-Hijaz was informed in mid-1993 about the negotiations but argued that it would only support the negotiations if an end to sectarian discrimination and real gains for the Shia were achievable. The group warned

---

[113] Ibrahim, *Shi'is*, 203–8.

[114] The few remaining baathists, however, did not profit from the 1993 deal and some such as 'Ali Ghannam remained in Iraq until the invasion of 2003. Interview with 'Abd al-Nabi al-'Akri, July 2010, London.

[115] Al-'Akri, *al-tanzimat*, 238.

[116] Interview with a former member of *tajammu' 'ulama' al-Hijaz*, Eastern Province, November 2008.

that the opposition would lose its strength if it ceased its publications and returned to Saudi Arabia, where it would be under tight supervision by the security services. Hizbullah al-Hijaz also stated that the negotiations were intended to pit the Shia opposition against the *salafis*.[117]

Indeed, according to Muhammad al-Mas'ari, a Sunni Islamist opposition leader, the 1993 deal was a 'masterly stroke' by King Fahd.[118] When al-Mas'ari and Sa'd al-Faqih went into exile in London in 1994, they had to start their information activities from scratch. They would have been stronger if they could have built on the experiences, networks and resources of the Shia opposition, and they only reached the level of reporting and political analysis of *al-Jazira al-'Arabiyya* by the late 1990s.[119] They would later comment that the Shia 'have been misled and pacified ... by fake "settlements" and promises of reform and justice'.[120]

Divisions amongst the different Shia opposition groups over the 1993 agreement are key to understanding the Saudi Shia issue post 1993. Those who became dissatisfied with the outcome of the agreement – supporters of Hizbullah al-Hijaz and members of the *hawza* wing such as Nimr al-Nimr – maintained their oppositional stance after 1993. A number of members of the military wing of Hizbullah al-Hijaz stayed abroad and others continued to be active clandestinely inside Saudi Arabia. In 1994, two Saudi Shia delegates took part in an annual conference of revolutionary organisations in Tehran.[121] *Tajammu' 'ulama' al-Hijaz* was given time on Radio Tehran urging Iranian clerics to work for the sake of Islamist detainees in Saudi Arabia in 1995.[122] The suspension of its main publication *Risalat al-Haramayn* was not a condition of the 1993 agreement, and so the magazine was only stopped in 1995.[123] From the end of 1996 onwards a number of less comprehensive publications were published on a new website set up after 1996 by supporters of Hizbullah al-Hijaz abroad.[124] While Sayyida Zaynab continued to be an important Shia transnational hub, Lebanon and particularly the Shia dominated

---

[117] Several interviews with former members of Hizbullah al-Hijaz and *tajammu' 'ulama' al-Hijaz*, Saudi Arabia and Lebanon, 2008 to 2009. *Risalat al-Haramayn* 45, (October 1993). For their stance towards the 1993 agreement see Matthiesen, "Hizbullah," 190f.

[118] Quoted in Champion, *Paradoxical*, 255.

[119] Fandy, *Saudi Arabia*, 174.

[120] Committee for the Defence of Legitimate Rights Communiqué no. 47, *Oppression and Persecution of the Shi'a*, London, 3 October 1996.

[121] *MECS*, 1994, 113, quoting *Mideast Mirror*, 18 February 1994.

[122] *MECS*, 1995, 550.

[123] Interview with Muhammad Mahfuz, Damascus, August 2008.

[124] Joshua Teitelbaum, "Dueling for Da'wa: State vs. Society on the Saudi Internet," *The Middle East Journal* 56, no. 2 (2002), 222–39, 227. The al-Haramain Islamic

southern suburbs of Beirut became more important. Ahmad al-Mughassil, allegedly the secretary general of Hizbullah al-Hijaz, resided in Beirut's southern suburbs from where he recruited young Saudis in the city and in Sayyida Zaynab and coordinated their activities.[125]

An American indictment claims that surveillance of possible American targets inside Saudi Arabia by members of Hizbullah al-Hijaz started in 1993 and intensified in 1994.[126] On 25 June 1996, a tanker truck filled with several tons of TNT exploded near the Khobar Towers housing compound for the U.S. Air Force in Dhahran, killing nineteen American soldiers and injuring hundreds of others. Shortly afterwards, the Saudi government started to blame Hizbullah al-Hijaz for the attack and arrested up to two thousand people, most of them Shia but also some Sunni Islamists.[127] The widespread arrest campaign targeted not only members of Hizbullah al-Hijaz but also clerics associated with Khat al-Imam and general supporters of the movement. The prisoners included its main religious leaders such as Hashim al-Shakhs, Ja'far al-Mubarak, 'Abd al-Karim al-Hubayl, and Hussayn al-Radi.[128]

Alleged Hizbullah al-Hijaz members were indicted in the United States in 2001 for the bombings and nine Saudi Shia remain in jail in Saudi Arabia after being convicted of involvement in the plot in a closed trial.[129] Four of those in jail were arrested before the attack took place, in March and April 1996, on the suspicion of planning an attack in Saudi Arabia. Fadil al-'Alawi was arrested in March 1996 at the Saudi-Jordanian border with explosives in his car, and 'Ali al-Marhun, Mustafa al-Mu'allim, and Salih al-Ramadan were arrested in April 1996. Mustafa al-Qasab, 'Abdallah al-Jarash, and Hussayn al-Mughis were arrested after the

---

Information Center (*markaz al-haramayn li-l-i'lam al-islami*) published statements by Hizbullah al-Hijaz and *tajammu' 'ulama' al-Hijaz* and publications such as *al-Rasid al-Sahafi* (The Journalistic Observer), *'Uyun al-Jazira* (Eyes of the Peninsula), or *al-Haramayn* (The Two Holy Places) and was available on the Internet, www.alhramain.com until May 2013. The first entry for its website in the web archive stems from 28 June 2002 and includes back issues of these publications, http://web.archive.org/web/20020628064848/http://www.alhramain.com.

[125] Al-Ibrahim and al-Sadiq, *al-hirak al-shi'i fi al-su'udiyya*, 157.

[126] United States District Court Eastern District of Virginia Alexandria Division, *Indictment against Saudi Hizbullah Members/Khobar Bombings* (June 2001), 7f.

[127] Thomas Hegghammer, *Jihad in Saudi Arabia: Violence and Pan-Islamism since 1979* (Cambridge: Cambridge University Press, 2010), 74.

[128] Statement by Tajammu' 'Ulama' al-Hijaz, "*I'tiqalat rijal al-din fi al-Hijaz*" (Arrests of Men of Religion in the Hijaz), 2 September 1996, http://www.alhramain.com.

[129] "Saudi Militants Are Sentenced in '96 Bombing," *New York Times*, 2 June 2002; "Convicted Khobar Bombers Are All Saudis," *Arab News*, 14 June 2002.

bombings. Hani al-Sayigh was arrested in Canada in 1997, then extradited to the United States and from there to Saudi Arabia in 1999. 'Abd al-Karim al-Nimr was arrested in 1999.[130] Several of those considered leaders of Hizbullah al-Hijaz in the 2001 indictment such as Ahmad al-Mughassil, the alleged head of the military wing of Hizbullah al-Hijaz, and 'Abd al-Karim al-Nasir, the alleged leader of Hizbullah al-Hijaz, as well as 'Ali al-Huri and Ibrahim al-Ya'qub, could not be arrested. The only one in the indictment who was arrested and later released is the cleric Sa'id al-Bahar, who joined Hizbullah al-Hijaz in 1988 and studied in the *hawza* in Qom. He stayed there until 1990 and also received military training in southern Iran. He was arrested after the bombings in July 1996 but released later that same year.[131]

The allegations made in the indictment were particularly sensitive since they claimed that Hizbullah al-Hijaz was aided by a Lebanese Hizbullah member in the making of the tanker truck bomb used in the attack and repeatedly hinted at Iranian involvement.[132] Since no evidence has been made public by either Saudi or American authorities, it is impossible to ascertain the ultimate responsibility of Hizbullah al-Hijaz for the bombings. Most Saudi Shia do not think that Hizbullah al-Hijaz was behind the attack. They point the finger towards al-Qaeda and highlight that Osama bin Laden repeatedly lauded the attack, without, however, taking responsibility for it. On an ideological level, both Hizbullah al-Hijaz and al-Qaeda were firmly opposed to the presence of American troops on Saudi soil and were willing to use violence to achieve the withdrawal of these troops.[133] Nevertheless, most analysts agree that a Saudi Shia group carried out the attack with foreign help.[134]

---

[130] Human Rights Watch, "Precarious Justice: Arbitrary Detention and Unfair Trials in the Deficient Criminal Justice System of Saudi Arabia," (2008), 125–8.

[131] *Indictment against Saudi Hizbullah Members*, 5–8. He was banned from travelling until 2010 and was then briefly arrested in October 2010 after he organised a mourning ceremony commemorating Khomeini's death in Sanabis on Tarut Island. Committee for the Defense of Human Rights in the Arabian Peninsula (lajnat al-difa' 'an huquq al-insan fi shibh al-jazira al-'arabiyya) "sulutat al-kiyyan al-su'udi tu'taqil 'alim din al-shi'i al-shaykh Sa'id al-Bahar" (The Forces of the Saudi Entity Arrest the Shia Cleric Shaykh Sa'id al-Bahar), 30 October 2010.

[132] *Indictment against Saudi Hizbullah Members*.

[133] Al-Ibrahim and al-Sadiq, *al-hirak al-shi'i fi al-su'udiyya*, 195. See statement of Hizbullah al-Hijaz: *"Bayan i'lami raddan 'ala al-itihamat al-amrikiyya bi-khusus infijar al-khubar"* (Press Statement Refuting the American Accusations with Regards to the Khobar Bombing), 23 June 2001, http://www.alhramain.com.

[134] F. Gregory Gause III, *The International Relations of the Persian Gulf* (Cambridge: Cambridge University Press, 2010), 128–32; Thomas Hegghammer, "Deconstructing the

Hizbullah al-Hijaz itself denied involvement in the Khobar Towers bombings of 1996 on several occasions.[135] But shortly after the attack it vowed to continue its fight against the Saudi government, denounced the outcome of the 1993 deal and in several statements invoked the example of the intifada martyrs, the four 1988 martyrs, as well as the sixteen beheaded Kuwaiti Hizbullah members and the victims of the 1987 hajj incident.[136] But apart from these online activities, not much was heard of Hizbullah al-Hijaz after most of its members were arrested.

CONCLUSION

In 1993 almost two decades of grass-roots activism and exile politics ended with the integration of *shirazi* leaders into Saudi networks of patronage. By directly negotiating with the *shiraziyyun* and granting them as well as Hizbullah al-Hijaz an amnesty, the state accepted the *shiraziyyun* as the main representatives of the Saudi Shia. Many of the returning Khat al-Imam leaders such as Hashim al-Shakhs were from al-Ahsa, where they became preachers and established social initiatives after 1993. They briefly gained prominence when people became disillusioned with the outcomes of the 1993 accord until the tough crackdown on supporters of Khat al-Imam after the Khobar Towers bombings in 1996. While Iran could not stop RMS from going back to Saudi Arabia, it maintained an influence over Hizbullah al-Hijaz and it seems that at least the military wing of Hizbullah al-Hijaz continued to be active after 1993.

But for the mainstream of Saudi Shia, represented in RMS, cultivating relations with Iran was no longer desirable once the Saudi government

Myth about Al-Qaʿida and Khobar," *CTC Sentinel* 1, no. 3 (2008), 22; Hegghammer, *Jihad*, 73f. An exception to this narrative is the investigative journalist Gareth Porter, who claims that senior American officials, who wanted to implicate Iran, diverted the American investigation away from leads of al-Qaeda involvement. *Inter Press Service*, 22–6 June 2009, www.ipsnews.net.

[135] For a refutation of the indictment by Hizbullah al-Hijaz see *Infijar al-Khubar: dirasa tawthiqiyya mufasala li-tafjir mabnat sakan al-quwwat al-jawiyya al-amrikiyya fi madinat al-Khubar wa-l-ladhi waqaʿa bi-tarikh 25/6/1996* (The Khobar Bombing: A Detailed Documentary Study of the Explosion of the Residence Building of the American Air Forces in Khobar City that Took Place on 25/6/1996) (n.p.: Markaz al-Haramayn li-l-Iʿalam al-Islami, 2002), previously available on www.alhramain.com.

[136] See *al-Haramayn* 1, 22–9 December 1996, as well as numerous statements by Hizbullah al-Hijaz, http://web.archive.org/web/20021029231547/www.alhramain.com/text/nshrah/0/no.htm.

began to take it seriously.[137] Because of the crackdown, Khat al-Imam ceased to be a serious challenge to the *shiraziyyun* on the local political scene. By targetting the other Saudi Shia Islamist movement, the crackdown also helped the *shiraziyyun* to become the key interlocutors with the state.[138] So the 1993 deal changed the local political landscape in the Eastern Province profoundly.

From the state's perspective, the deal was a success. It silenced the most outspoken media outlets abroad, co-opted many opposition activists and placed them under the surveillance of the security services. In 1993 almost two decades of grass-roots activism and exile politics ended with the integration of *shirazi* leaders into Saudi networks of patronage. By not fundamentally altering the situation of the Shia it also put the *shirazi* leaders in an awkward position.

The lack of tangible improvements for Shia after 1993, and the lack of political and religious reforms, meant that those involved in the negotiations were soon criticised for having been bought. In essence, the stance of Shia political actors post 1993 was determined by their views regarding the agreement. Those who were against the terms of the deal, including Nimr al-Nimr, the *hawza* wing, and some supporters of Khat al-Imam, remained critical of the Saudi government, and of the mainstream *shiraziyyun* around Hasan al-Saffar, and in 2011 pushed for popular protests. Others who were initially in favour, such as Hamza al-Hasan, then became disillusioned with the implementation of the 1993 deal and resumed opposition activities abroad.

While the international dimension was key for the Saudi Shia opposition after the intifada, it was not just Iran after the revolution that was relevant as a place of exile, but also Syria, Lebanon, Cyprus, India, London and the United States. Exile had a deterritorialising effect on the activists. In the absence of any other large opposition movements in the country that could undermine the Saudi ruling family's grip on power, the Shia opposition had to come to terms with the logic of the state and accepted the offer to negotiate their return with King Fahd. Their integration into local politics was not going to be straightforward and neither was fundamental change of the status of Saudi Shia going to come about quickly. Nevertheless, the period after 1993 was characterised by a marginal recognition of the Shia by the Saudi state.

---

[137] Chubin and Tripp, *Iran-Saudi*, 63.
[138] See Matthiesen, "Hizbullah," 191–194.

6

Marginal Recognition

After 1993 the returning Shia activists were integrated into an established network of supporters in their places of origin and allowed to give a public face to their social and religious institutions. The clerics started to preach in mosques, established informal study circles and became representatives of a *marji'*. The political cadres became active in the intellectual field and wrote in Saudi newspapers. Saudi media were slowly opening up and together with the Internet led to a lively public sphere. The Saudi state created new institutions as part of a superficial reform process, which was not intended to democratise the country or redistribute power but rather to reconfigure authoritarianism. At the same time, however, these processes also opened up new discursive fields.[1]

In the Eastern Province these changes created new opportunities for the returnees and local activists. The former opposition activists also focussed on establishing civil society organisations. If one sees civil society as an arena where hegemonic power struggles between different social and political forces are played out, one can discern civil society organisations in Saudi Arabia, particularly in Shia areas. This chapter will look at various intermediary organisations such as Shia religious schools, sport clubs, charities, courts, the Majlis al-Shura, municipal councils and human rights organisations, as well as a public sphere of newspapers, TV channels, websites, historical debates, and social media.

---

[1] Andrzej Kapiszewski, "Saudi Arabia: Steps toward Democratization or Reconfiguration of Authoritarianism?" *Journal of Asian and African Studies* 41, no. 5/6 (2006), 459–82.

THE INTEGRATION OF THE OPPOSITION

The clerical wing of the Shia opposition wanted to re-establish local religious schools, so-called *hawzat mahalliyya,* that prepare religious students for further studies in the centres of Shia learning, mainly in Iraq, Iran and Syria. This was partly a response to the difficulty of studying in Najaf since Saddam Hussein's crackdown on Shia clerics in the late 1970s. Saudi students also faced problems in Qom. After the fallout of OIRAP with the Iranians it was difficult for *shiraziyyun* to study in Qom, while those Saudis that remained there became suspected of being members in Hizbullah al-Hijaz.

The issue of a Saudi Shia *hawza,* however, is anathema for many Sunni clerics, and Shia were not issued licences for the building of *hawzat,* an obstacle that did not stop the clerics from opening several *hawzat* without a licence. The new *hawza* in Qatif, which was established after 1993, was neither 'legal nor illegal', a characterisation that applies to many Shia issues in the country. In 2003 it moved to a new purpose-built house on the outskirts of Qatif, with a library, study rooms and a large basement *majlis.* Most of its teachers were previously at the *hawzat al-Sadiq* in Sayyida Zaynab or the *hawzat al-Qaʾim* in Tehran, and it therefore largely followed the *marjiʿiyya* of Muhammad al-Shirazi and Sadiq al-Shirazi.[2] But Khat al-Imam clerics such as ʿAbd al-Karim al-Hubayl and Hasan al-Nimr are also on its governing board.[3] Since the government does not recognise these *hawzat,* it also does not recognise certificates of local *hawza* graduates or provide them with employment.[4]

The Saudi Shia *hawzat* cannot teach up to the highest level, the *bahth al-kharij,* which is required to be taught by a *mujtahid* and ideally a *marjiʿ.* Before 1979 it was common that *maraji* and other high-ranking Shia clerics visited the Eastern Province while on hajj or for special occasions, but after some foreign clerics incited the crowds during the intifada in 1979/80 this was forbidden.[5] Two other major *hawzat* as well as the *hawza Sayyida Khadija* for women were opened in Qatif and another one in al-Ahsa. The *hawzat* in al-Ahsa, particularly the one in Mubarraz

---

[2] Interview with a director of the *hawza ʿilmiyya* in Qatif, Eastern Province, November 2008; al-Mushaykhas, *al-Qatif,* vol. 1, 497–500.

[3] The other directors are Fawzi al-Sayf, Hussayn al-Mustafa, Jaʿfar al-Ribh and Yusuf al-Mahdi: "al-hawza al-ʿilmiyya fi al-Qatif" (The Community of Learning in Qatif), *Sanabes Cultural Forum,* www.sanabes.com.

[4] U.S. Department of State, Bureau of Democracy, Human Rights, and Labor, *International Religious Freedom Report: Saudi Arabia* (2007).

[5] Interviews with Saudi Shia clerics, Eastern Province, November 2008.

operated by the Al al-Sayyid Salman family, maintained more continuity throughout the twentieth century, although some were repeatedly closed and only opened semi-officially in 1993, when the main *hawza* moved to a new building.[6] In addition, there are dozens of unlicensed private religious schools in the Eastern Province, which are at times closed by the state.[7]

Associated with this restoration of Shia religious learning are religious journals such as *al-Faqaha* (Knowledge of Jurisprudence), which was started in Awwamiyya in 2006 by a *shirazi* cleric. It publishes articles by senior Saudi Shia clerics while engaging with the legacy of scholars from the region.[8] Saudi Shia also publish the Quranic studies journal *al-Quran Nur* (The Quran is Light) in Qatif since 2003[9] and *Nusus Mu'asira* (Contemporary Texts) in Beirut. The latter translates articles by leading Iranian reformist intellectuals and clerics into Arabic.[10]

The *hawzat*, journals and many of the civil society projects, are financed by the *khums* tax. The networks of *khums* and the *marji'iyya*, which became more visible since 1993, allow for a certain independence from the state and strengthen communal boundaries. As local representatives of a *marji'*, the clerics can use half of the *khums* for local projects, sometimes without consulting the *marji'*. This is especially so in Saudi Arabia, where unlike in other countries, no Shia *marji'* is allowed to have an office and the *maraji'* therefore have to rely on their *wukala'*. 'Ali al-Sistani became the most popular *marji'* for Saudi Shia after the death of Muhsin al-Hakim and Abu al-Qasim al-Khu'i.[11] The *khums* al-Sistani

---

6 Hussayn al-'Ayyash, "al-hawza al-'ilmiyya bi-l-Ahsa' wa-tatalla'atuha al-mustaqbali-yya" (The Community of Learning and Its Future Aspirations), in *al-mashad al-thaqafi fi al-Ahsa': muntada al-mu'ayli unmudhajan* (The Cultural Scene in al-Ahsa: The al-Mu'ayli Forum as an Example) ed. Salman bin Hussayn al-Hijji, vol. 1, (Beirut: Dar al-'Ulum li-l-Tahqiq wa-l-Tiba'a wa-l-Nashr wa-l-Tawzi', 2007), 215–74.

7 "Religious Freedom Conditions in Saudi Arabia: Restriction on Freedom of Worship," www.saudishia.com, 21 June 2009.

8 Interview with editor of *al-Faqaha*, Eastern Province, November 2008. It mainly publishes the writings of *shirazi* clerics and others such as 'Abd al-Hadi al-Fadli. See, for example, *al-Faqaha* 5 (Autumn 2007), and www.alfaqaha.net.

9 "Mu'assasat al-Quran Nur bi-l-Qatif" (The Quran Is Light Foundation in Qatif), *al-Sahil* 4 (2007), 182–6.

10 It was initiated by 'Abd al-Hadi al-Fadli, although an editorial board from various countries later published it. www.nosos.net; *al-Thulatha Cultural Forum Newsletter* 11 (27 January 2009).

11 Some put his following at 70–85 percent of Saudi Shia. John Solomon, "Saudi Arabia's Shiites and Their Effect on the Kingdom's Stability," *Terrorism Monitor* 4, no. 15 (2006).

receives from Saudi Arabia increased exponentially after 2003.[12] The Lebanese cleric Muhammad Hussayn Fadlallah also had followers in the Eastern Province until his death in 2010.[13] Because these money flows are difficult to control, allegations of corruption are widespread.[14] As a result, some Saudi Shia demanded an institutionalisation of this system and argued that less money should be sent to the *marji'* and more should be invested locally so that it would be visible if a cleric kept funds for himself.[15]

After the death of Muhammad al-Shirazi in 2001 his followers split between those following his younger brother and designated successor from within the *shirazi* movement, Sadiq al-Shirazi, and those favouring his nephew, Muhammad Taqi al-Mudarrisi. The former Movement of Vanguards' Missionaries (MVM) leader, who moved to Karbala after 2003, announced his own *marji'iyya* and his followers came to be known as the *mudarrisiyya*. While al-Mudarrisi has fewer followers in Saudi Arabia than the mainstream *shiraziyya*, he positioned himself as a revolutionary *marji'*, and supported the protests in the Eastern Province and Bahrain from 2011 onwards.[16] Muhammad al-Habib from Qatif and Nimr al-Nimr from Awwamiyya became leading *wukala'* for al-Mudarrisi in Saudi Arabia.[17] The *shiraziyya* and the *mudarrisiyya* now constitute two distinct religious and political networks with different political strategies in the Gulf.[18]

After the death of the eminent *shaykhi marji'* Mirza Hasan al-Ha'iri al-Ihqaqi al-Usku'i (1900/1901–2003), whom most Shaykhis in Saudi Arabia followed, a crisis of leadership also weakened the *shaykhiyya*. His son, Mirza 'Abdallah al-Ha'iri al-Ihqaqi al-Usku'i (b. 1963), officially became the new *marji'* but was challenged by another contender

<hr>

[12] Some of his most important *wukala'* in the Eastern Province are 'Ali al-Sayyid Nasir, Hasan al-Saffar, Hussayn Faraj al-'Umran and 'Ali al-Dihnin. Interview with Hamid al-Khaffaf, spokesman for 'Ali al-Sistani and head of his Beirut office, Beirut, August 2008.

[13] Interview with a Saudi Shia cleric who taught in one of Fadlallah's *hawzat* in Beirut and dealt with his representatives in Saudi Arabia. Beirut, August 2008.

[14] Al-'Ali, *sha'b al-Qatif*, 315.

[15] "Ittihamat fasad wukala' 'al-khums' bi-l-Qatif wa-wakil Fadlallah yaruddu" (Charges of Corruption of the "Khums" Representatives in Qatif; and the Representative of Fadlallah Replies), www.alarabiya.net, 23 October 2013.

[16] Matthiesen, *Sectarian Gulf*, 39–42.

[17] U.S. Diplomatic Cable, from Embassy Riyadh to Secretary of State, *Shi'a Political Movements in Saudi Arabia's Eastern Province*, 27 August 2008, http://wikileaks.org/cable/2008/08/08RIYADH1321.html. Nimr al-Nimr published a collection of al-Mudarrisi's fatwas in 2003: See Al Jumay', *mu'jam al-mu'allafat* (Dar al-Mahajja al-Bayda'/Mu'assasat al-Baqi' li-Ihya' al-Turath, vol. 2, 2006), 521.

[18] Interview with Ahmad al-Shirazi, Kuwait, February 2012.

from a different branch of the family, Mirza Kamal al-Din al-Sulaymi al-Ha'iri al-Ihqaqi al-Usku'i (b. 1964).[19] As a result, some *shaykhis* in al-Ahsa became followers of Sadiq al-Shirazi or of other *maraji'* such as 'Ali al-Sistani.[20]

'Ali Khamenei, the supreme leader of Iran, who also acts as a *marji'*, is followed by supporters and clerics of Khat al-Imam, who believe that the line of Imam Khomeini is being continued by Khamenei. The main *wakil* of Khamenei in Saudi Arabia was 'Abd al-Hadi al-Fadli.[21] After the latter's death in 2013, 'Abd al-Karim al-Hubayl, a Khat al-Imam cleric from Tarut, became his successor as main *wakil* of Khamenei in Qatif.[22] In addition to *khums*, many clerics gain income from organising hajj and *umra* tours.[23]

CIVIL SOCIETY

Some of the lay Shia activists had spent decades petitioning the government on Shia matters such as the building of mosques and *hussainiyyat* and had focussed on education and social affairs. This was particularly true for the small number of Saudis associated with *al-da'wa*. They had refrained from direct political or military operations in Saudi Arabia and rather focussed on social and religious issues.[24] The other groups emulated this approach, especially after 1993 and all worked towards the establishment of private schools, youth centres and sport clubs. Football clubs were founded in the Eastern Province in the early 1950s. Men who had picked up the sport from the British in Bahrain played the first football matches in the late 1920s. With the development of the oil economy in the late 1930s the sport grew rapidly and a local legend has it that the first foreign workers at ARAMCO, some of whom were Italians, Sudanese and Somalis, started playing with the Saudis in the labour camps.[25]

[19] Interview with Mirza Kamal al-Din al-Sulaymi al-Ha'iri al-Ihqaqi, Kuwait, 2012.

[20] Interview with Shaykhis from al-Ahsa, Kuwait, 2012.

[21] He became very ill in 2008. Interview with Iraqi and Saudi Shia, London and Saudi Arabia, 2008.

[22] Interview with Saudi Shia, London, 2013. See also U.S. Diplomatic Cable, from Embassy Riyadh to Secretary of State, *Shi'a Political Movements in Saudi Arabia's Eastern Province*, 27 August 2008.

[23] See also Salman bin Hussayn al-Hijji, *dirasa fi al-nizam al-mali wa-l-khadmati li-ba'd jama'iyyat al-hajj fi al-Ahsa'* (A Study of the Financial and Service System of some Hajj Societies in al-Ahsa) (al-Ahsa: Matba'a al-Ahsa' al-Haditha, 2006).

[24] Interviews with Ja'far al-Shayib, London, December 2010, and an *al-da'wa* activist, Eastern Province, November 2008. See also al-Hatlani, *al-shi'a*, 180.

[25] Al-Salih, *al-'Awwamiyya*, 97–107; ARAMCO World (October 1963), 2–7; (Summer 1972), 12–13.

Both leftists and Islamists used local football clubs for recruitment, and Hasan al-Saffar sees sport clubs as important institutions through which 'consciousness' can be built amongst the youth and where those who cannot be reached in mosques can be introduced to religion.[26] Sport clubs therefore are also cultural and social clubs and in some cases have libraries and prayer rooms and host Quran lessons and other events.[27] Al-Saffar calls upon wealthy citizens to sponsor sport clubs and argues that doing so is as worthy in religious terms as supporting mosques and charitable work. According to al-Saffar, this is specially so as the government does not pay as much attention to the sport clubs in 'our region',[28] a complaint echoed by a number of interviewees.[29] In November 2008, al-Saffar took the author to a football tournament in Qatif, where al-Saffar was received as a prominent politician would be. The organisers announced his arrival via loudspeakers and had comfortable sofas reserved for him besides the pitch. Before he left, al-Saffar gave the organisers *khums* money, re-distributing some of the funds he had received as *wakil* of major *maraji*'.[30]

While a widespread network of local and national charitable organisations exists in Saudi Arabia, they are usually chaired, initiated or funded by a member of the ruling family. Therefore, the charitable associations in Saudi Arabia are also legitimising tools for the ruling family and serve as 'an alternative channel of communication and influence'.[31] The state has also called institutions such as the official human rights associations and the National Dialogue forums 'civil society'.[32] Shia charities in villages and towns across the Eastern Province, on the other hand, strengthen Shia collective identities vis-à-vis the state. They maintain relations with the state and have to be registered with the Ministry of Social Affairs but are not chaired by members of the ruling family and receive only limited government funding.[33]

---

[26] Hasan al-Saffar, *al-nadi al-riyadi wa-l-mujtama'* (The Sport Club and Society) (Khobar: Matabi' al-Raja', 2004), 41.

[27] Ibid., 14f.

[28] Ibid., 37–40.

[29] Interviews with members of sport clubs in the Eastern Province, November 2008.

[30] Personal observation and interview with Hasan al-Saffar, Eastern Province, November 2008.

[31] Caroline Montagu, "Civil Society and the Voluntary Sector in Saudi Arabia," *The Middle East Journal* 64, no. 1 (2010), 67–83, 83.

[32] Stéphane Lacroix and Steffen Hertog, "Dissidenz und Institutionalisierung: Die zweischneidige Debatte der Modernisierung," *inamo* 42 (2005).

[33] The Saihat Society for Social Services and the Qatif Charitable Society for Social Services, for example, receive government funding. Montagu, "Civil", 76, 79.

Some nationwide societies such as al-Birr, which receives funding from the Department of Zakat and Income Tax, are active in al-Ahsa[34] and Sanabis on Tarut Island.[35] The Saihat Society for Social Services, which was founded in the 1930s, was initially the local branch of al-Birr. In 1962 it was registered under the patronage of the Shia businessman 'Abdallah al-Matrud, and it might have been its origins that ensured it donations from Sunni business families such as the al-Qusaybi.[36] The old Shia charities are often run by notables.[37] While these older charities co-operate with the *shiraziyyun* to a certain extent, they are also used by the notables in local power struggles. Therefore, the *shiraziyyun* founded their own charities in areas where they have strong support.[38] Women often participate in these charities. 'Aliyya Makki al-Farid, the most prominent *shirazi* female activist, worked in the al-Safa Charitable Society throughout the 1980s and 1990s and then founded the Ilaf Centre for Disabled Child Care.[39] Apart from social services, some charities focus on Quranic and religious education and facilitate marriages.[40]

Cultural festivals are other arenas where collective identities are re-enacted and hegemonic struggles become visible. The folkloristic *dukhala* festival, for example, is held since 2005 in the Sanabis quarter of Tarut. The festival provides demonstrations of traditional crafts and the fishing and pearl diving history of the coastal region; volunteers also participate to strengthen the Shia of Tarut. They argue that 'we need more initiatives and investments from inside the community. Too many of us think that because we are a minority we can't succeed and that everything we do will be blocked by some authorities. But we want to show that it is possible to organise such an event, also if the organisers are Shia.'[41] The festival revives the folkloric aspect of Gulf history. This follows patterns established by other Gulf states, which have tried to foster a sense of national heritage and historical identity by inventing

[34] www.ahsaber.org.

[35] www.sanabis.org.sa; Montagu, "Civil," 75f.

[36] See the history section of its website, previously available on the Internet, www.saihatss.org; Field, *Merchants*, 82f., 241.

[37] 'Abbas bin Rida al-Shammasi, for example, headed the Qatif Charity until he was elected chairman of the Municipal Council of Qatif in 2011. "Nahwa 'alaqa mujtama'iyya fa'ila" (Towards a Real Social Relationship), *Khayriyyat al-Qatif*, www.qateef.org.

[38] For example, the al-Awjam Charitable Society, www.aujamcs.org, and the al-Safa Charitable Society in Safwa.

[39] "Alya Farid," www.saudishia.com, 21 November 2009.

[40] Interview with an activist of the Tarut charitable society, Eastern Province, November 2008, www.taroot.org.sa.

[41] Interview with an organiser, Eastern Province, November 2008, www.sanabis.org.sa.

a folkloric popular culture for the seafaring peoples of the Gulf.[42] The Saudi government, however, was rather slow to expand funding for the popular festival, which draws tens of thousands of visitors each year.[43] As a result of local power struggles, other areas of Qatif and charities associated with notable families have since started their own festivities such as the Qatif Festival.[44] These examples show how social services, education and sport clubs become arenas for political struggles, particularly if the state provides these services only to a limited extent.

SHIA COURTS BETWEEN NOTABLES AND ISLAMISTS

The Shia courts, which were discussed extensively in chapter one, also play a key intermediary role between the state and society in the Eastern Province. They remained a major topic in petitions by Shia notables and in meetings with officials. A letter to King Fahd from 1992 outlines problems with the Shia courts and opposes the ban on building *hussaini-yyat* and mosques.[45] When King Fahd suffered a stroke in 1995, Crown Prince Abdullah became the de facto ruler, and Abdullah became king after Fahd's death in 2005. Abdullah seemed to look more favourably on the courts, but the fundamental issues that limit their jurisdiction persisted. A letter by Shia notables to Abdullah from 1997 complains that the competencies of the court are constantly infringed upon and that its rulings and certificates are not recognised: 'The works of the court can not be seen as really official if any of the judges at the *mahkamat al-kubra* can annul its judgments.' Furthermore, the letter claims that the municipality does not accept *awqaf* certificates and other documents issued by the court and that people are abandoning the Shia court as a result.[46]

---

[42] Muhammad Rajab al-Najjar, "Contemporary Trends in the Study of Folklore in the Arab Gulf States," in *Statecraft in the Middle East: Oil, Historical Memory, and Popular Culture*, ed. Eric Davis and Nicolas E. Gavrielides (Miami: Florida International University Press, 1991), 176–201; John W. Fox, Nada Mourtada-Sabbah, and Mohammed al-Mutawa, "Heritage Revivalism in Sharjah," in *Globalization and the Gulf*, ed. John W. Fox, Nada Mourtada-Sabbah, and Mohammed al-Mutawa (London: Routledge, 2006), 266–87; Sulayman Khalaf, "The Nationalisation of Culture: Kuwait's Invention of a Pearl-Diving Heritage," in *Popular Culture and Political Identity in the Arab Gulf States*, ed. Alanoud Alsharekh and Robert Springborg (London: Saqi, 2008), 40–70.

[43] Interview with an organiser, Eastern Province, November 2008.

[44] Interview with Ja'far al-Shayib, London, December 2010.

[45] Letter by Shia notables to King Fahd, 5 January 1992. Private collection of letters and petitions concerning Shia notables, Saudi Arabia.

[46] Letter by Shia notables to Crown Prince Abdullah, 6 August 1997. Private collection of letters and petitions concerning Shia notables, Saudi Arabia.

Two years later a similar letter even speaks of an 'effective suspension of the Court for Endowments and Inheritance in Qatif because of interference by the *mahkamat al-kubra*'. These letters, signed by 'your sons the families of Qatif', are an early sign that some Shia pinned their hopes on Abdullah.[47]

As the only government-sponsored institution providing jobs for Shia clerics in Saudi Arabia, the Shia courts carry enormous symbolic importance, and have also become an arena for power struggles amongst Shia. By and large, however, the courts have remained a stronghold of the notable families.

'Abd al-Hamid al-Khatti was *qadi* of Qatif until he died in 2000/1 and became one of the main interlocutors between the Shia and the state during his time in office. The *shiraziyyun* had since 1993 tried to put forward their own candidates for the position. After al-Khatti's death, they campaigned for Hasan al-Saffar, the former OIRAP leader, to become the next *qadi*. But the Ministry of Interior refused and so al-Khatti was succeeded by his half-brother, 'Abdallah al-Khunayzi.[48] In the early 1960s, he had been sentenced to death for arguing in a book that the Prophet's uncle, Abu Talib, became a sincere Muslim, an argument opposed to Sunni beliefs that had provoked the Wahhabi *ulama*'.[49] Upon pressure from some Najafi *maraji* such as al-Khu'i, the Shah of Iran intervened on behalf of al-Khunayzi and his death sentence was revoked.[50] This event toughened al-Khunayzi's stance towards the government and the Wahhabi *ulama*'. As judge he did not manage to establish himself in the same way as al-Khatti. Although the official reason given for his dismissal in 2005 was his bad health, some suggest that he was dismissed after an argument with the Minister of Justice.[51]

After their preferred candidate, al-Saffar, was not accepted, the *shiraziyyun* led a movement to oust 'Abdallah al-Khunayzi. Ja'far al-Shayib argued that the notables should not hold the position of judge anymore and that al-Khunayzi was not an effective representative of Qatif Shia. Instead, he endorsed the candidacy of the Khat al-Imam cleric Ghalib

---

47 Letter by Shia notables to Crown Prince Abdullah, 7 July 1999. Private collection of letters and petitions concerning Shia notables, Saudi Arabia.
48 Interview with Ja'far al-Shayib, London, December 2010.
49 'Abdallah al-Khunayzi, *Abu Talib mu'min Quraysh: dirasa wa-tahlil* (Abu Talib Believer of Quraysh: Study and Analysis) 6th ed. (Beirut: Mu'assasat al-Balagh li-l-Tiba'a wa-l-Nashr wa-l-Tawzi', 2005 [1st ed. 1961]).
50 Ibrahim, *Shi'is*, 39f.
51 Interviews with Saudi Shia, London, 2009.

al-Hammad, who had studied in Qom and was in Iran at the time, as a compromise candidate.[52] Al-Hammad initially became deputy of al-Khunayzi, and in December 2005 his appointment as judge was officially announced in the local daily, *al-Yawm*.[53] On 20 August 2005 the Ministry of Justice issued new regulations for the functioning of the Shia courts in Qatif and al-Ahsa. Initially, it seemed that the new king, Abdullah, was making concessions towards the Shia. Three Shia judges were appointed to a newly created Appeals Committee *(hay'at al-tadqiq)* in Qatif, increasing the number of Shia judges in Saudi Arabia to seven.

But just seven months after his appointment, al-Hammad was replaced by his assistant judge, Sulayman Abu al-Makarim, who had been in this position since 2005 and was seen as pro-government. A U.S. diplomatic cable argues that the Saudi government 'used the appointment in Qatif to assert more control over the court. We interpret the episode of Al-Hammad's replacement as a setback to Shi'a efforts to gain more autonomy over their own affairs.'[54] The father of Sulayman Abu al-Makarim was an important Akhbari scholar and many Usuli scholars saw the appointment of an Akhbari as an affront. When Sulayman Abu al-Makarim died in October 2007 at the age of forty-eight, he was initially replaced by Muhammad al-Jirani.[55] Soon after, Muhammad al-'Ubaydan took over as *qadi* of Qatif, while al-Hammad moved to the appeals court. Notables and activists from Qatif and al-Ahsa drafted an outline for new regulations that would prevent the other courts from overruling the Shia *qadi*. These proposals were discussed in meetings with King Abdullah and other high-ranking officials and sent to them thereafter.[56]

[52] U.S. Diplomatic Cable, from Embassy Riyadh to Secretary of State, *Shi'ite Council Member Predicts Sacking of Saudi Arabia's Leading Shi'a Judge*, 13 December 2005, http://wikileaks.org/cable/2005/12/05RIYADH9142.html; Louër, *Transnational*, 249. Al-Hammad has become Friday prayer leader in the Hussayn Mosque in the al-Manakh quarter of Tarut. He also attended the *hawza* of al-Hajari in al-Ahsa. See al-Hijji, *sirat ayatallah*, 32f.

[53] "Al-Qatif: Shaykh al-Hammad qadiyyan li-mahkamat al-awqaf wa-l-mawarith bi-l-niyyaba" (Qatif: Shaykh al-Hammad Is Deputy Judge of the Court of Awqaf and Inheritance), *Rasid*, 8 February 2005; U.S. Diplomatic Cable, from Embassy Riyadh to Secretary of State, *SAG Replaces Shi'ite Judge in Qatif*, 20 December 2005, http://wikileaks.org/cable/2005/12/05RIYADH9396.html.

[54] U.S. Diplomatic Cable, from Embassy Riyadh to Secretary of State, *SAG Removes Shi'a Judge in Qatif*, 26 July 2006, http://wikileaks.org/cable/2006/07/06RIYADH5949.html.

[55] "Ta'yyin al-Awjami qadiyyan bi-l-mahkama al-ja'fariyya fi al-Qatif khalfan li-l-Madluh" (Appointment of al-Awjami as Judge in the Ja'fari Court in Qatif as Successor of al-Madluh), *Rasid*, 8 April 2009.

[56] Collection of letters sent by notables from al-Ahsa and Qatif to high-ranking government officials since 2006. Interview with a Shia notable, Eastern Province, November 2008.

Yet, in 2008 Muhammad al-'Ubaydan was suspended from his post as judge and his successor, Sa'id al-Madluh, was dismissed within a year and replaced with Wajih al-Awjami.[57] Al-'Ubaydan related that this was a deliberate strategy to keep the Shia court weak, and he even called the Shia *qadi* of Qatif 'the weakest employee in the whole chain of government.'[58] Muhammad al-Jirani replaced al-Awjami in this post until 2012, when al-Awjami again became the main judge.[59]

In al-Ahsa, the *qadi* Muhammad al-Hajari died in 2004/5 and was succeeded by his assistant, Muhammad bin 'Abdallah al-Luwaymi.[60] In 2005, Hasan bin Muhammad Baqir Abu Khamsin was appointed assistant judge to the Shia court in al-Ahsa.[61] Al-Luwaymi tried unsuccessfully to get more resources for the court in al-Ahsa, which faced problems similar to those in Qatif.[62] He was succeeded in September 2008 by Muhammad Hasan al-Jaziri.[63] These frequent changes indicated that all was not well with the Shia courts, and that the government wanted to keep them in a situation where they would have only very limited jurisdiction.

A SAUDI PUBLIC SPHERE

After 1993 the lay activists, too, needed to find jobs and a place in society. Following a tradition in Gulf societies, where a salon culture for males has for decades played an important role in social life, prominent former Shia dissidents such as the communist Najib al-Khunayzi and the *shirazi* Ja'far al-Shayib established major discussion forums (*diwaniyya/muntada*). As a result, most villages and cities in the Eastern Province have at least one *diwaniyya*, many of which put discussion transcripts online or publish them in book form to reach wider audiences.[64] Najib al-Khunayzi

---

[57] "Ta'yyin al-Awjami."

[58] Interview with Muhammad al-'Ubaydan, Eastern Province, November 2008.

[59] "Al-sayyid al-Awjami ra'isan li-da'irat mahkama al-awqaf wa-l-mawarith bi-l-Qatif" (Sayyid al-Awjami Is President of the Department of the Court for Endowments and Inheritance in Qatif), *Qatif News*, 7 October 2012.

[60] Al-Hijji, *sirat ayatallah*, 55; al-Hijji, *hakatha*, 296–307; al-Shakhs, *a'lam*, vol. 4, 368f.

[61] "Ta'yyin al-Awjami."

[62] U.S. Diplomatic Cable, from Embassy Riyadh to Secretary of State, *Shi'a Judge in al-Hasa Seeks Greater Resources from SAG*, 2 January 2006, http://wikileaks.org/cable/2006/01/06RIYADH8.html.

[63] "Ta'yyin al-shaykh al-Jaziri qadiyyan bi-l-mahkama al-ja'fariyya bi-l-Ahsa' khalfan li-l-shaykh al-Luwaym" (Appointment of Shaykh al-Jaziri as Judge in the Ja'fari Court in al-Ahsa as Successor of Shaykh al-Luwaym), *Rasid*, 11 November 2008.

[64] Toby Matthiesen, "Diwaniyyas, Intellectual Salons and the Limits of Civil Society in Saudi Arabia," in *Viewpoints: Saudi Arabia 1979–2009: Evolution of a Pivotal State*

and prominent *shiraziyyun* such as Tawfiq al-Sayf also found a place as intellectuals in the Saudi public sphere and became columnists in Saudi newspapers. The *shirazi* cleric Muhammad Mahfuz founded the 'Islamic Intellectual-Cultural Journal' *al-Kalima* (The Word) in 1994. It soon became an intellectual mouthpiece of the *shiraziyyun* in Saudi Arabia but also gained prominence amongst intellectuals in other Arab countries due to its emphasis on political and religious reform (*tajdid*).[65] The OIRAP cadres Hasan al-Saffar, Tawfiq al-Sayf, Zaki al-Milad as well as left-wing Shia such as Muhammad al-ʿAli publish in the journal.

These Shia intellectuals also became champions of a new Saudi nationalism associated with the discourse of the National Dialogue. Muhammad Mahfuz, for example, has authored countless books and articles to this end.[66] Tawfiq al-Sayf emphasised the importance of citizenship and constitutionalism in Shia thought.[67] In another book, he also argued that democracy can be grounded in an Islamic context, without secularisation as a prerequisite.[68]

Many writings by Saudi Shia also concern Islamic ecumenism, the attempts at rapprochement (*taqrib*) between Shia and Sunni schools of Islam. Clerics such as Hasan al-Saffar have tried to counter suspicions of Shia amongst Sunni *ʿulamaʾ* and intellectuals in Saudi Arabia since 1993. Many of these Sunni-Shia dialogue meetings took place at reformist

(Washington, DC: Middle East Institute, 2009), 13–15. See for example: Salman bin Hussayn al-Hijji, ed., *al-mashad al-thaqafi fi al-Ahsaʾ: muntada al-muʿayli unmudhajan* (The Cultural Scene in al-Ahsa: The al-Muʿayli Forum as an Example), vol. 1 (Beirut: Dar al-ʿUlum li-l-Tahqiq wa-l-Tibaʿa wa-l-Nashr wa-l-Tawziʿ, 2007); *al-taqrir al-sanawi li-muntada al-ʿAwwamiyya: al-dawra al-ula* 1.7.1426–30.6.1427A.H. (The Annual Report for the Awwamiyya Forum: The First Round 2005–2006) (n.p.: n.p., n.d.). See the website of Jaʿfar al-Shayib's *diwaniyya*, www.thulatha.com.

[65] Interview with a Syrian intellectual, Damascus, 2008; http://kalema.net. For an example of this discourse see Zaki al-Milad, *min al-turath ila al-ijtihad: al-fikr al-islami wa-qadaya al-islah wa-l-tajdid* (From Heritage to Independent Reasoning: Islamic Thought and the Issues of Reform and Renewal) (Beirut: al-Markaz al-Thaqafi al-ʿArabi, 2004).

[66] For example, Muhammad Mahfuz, *al-hiwar wa-l-wahda al-wataniyya fi al-mamlaka al-ʿarabiyya al-suʿudiyya* (Dialogue and National Unity in the Kingdom of Saudi Arabia) (Beirut: Dar al-Saqi, 2004); Muhammad Mahfuz, *al-islah al-siyasi wa-l-wahda al-wataniyya: kayfa nabni watanan li-l-ʿaysh al-mushtarak* (Political Reform and National Unity: How We Build a Homeland to Live Together) (Beirut: al-Markaz al-Thaqafi al-ʿArabi, 2004). For an analysis of these writings see Meijer and Wagemakers, "The Struggle."

[67] Tawfiq al-Sayf, *nazariyyat al-sulta fi al-fiqh al-shiʿi* (The View of Political Power in Shia Jurisprudence) (Beirut: al-Markaz al-Thaqafi al-ʿArabi, 2002). For a discussion of this see Wehrey, *Sectarian Politics in the Gulf*, 116.

[68] Tawfiq al-Sayf, *Islamic Democracy and its Limits: The Iranian Experience since 1979* (London: Saqi, 2007). See also al-Sayf, *an takun shiʿiyan*.

diwaniyyat across the country.[69] Al-Saffar tried to place himself in a line of Saudi Shia scholars who promoted Sunni-Shia dialogue. During a meeting in 1996 with the Grand Mufti Ibn Baz, al-Saffar referred to previous scholars from Qatif who had written about *taqrib*.[70] Al-Saffar also denounced anti-Shia treatises and polemics, sometimes in Saudi-sponsored news outlets.[71] In 2010 he even met with the *salafi* cleric Sa'd al-Burrayk, who is well known for his anti-Shia views. Al-Saffar was in return criticised by another prominent Shia cleric from Qatif, Munir al-Khabbaz, who thought that Sunni-Shia dialogue should not include those who hold the most negative views of Shia Muslims.[72]

Returning *shirazi* activists also focussed on the writing of local historiography, something they had already started to do in exile. Since the late 1980s, but particularly since 1993, Saudi Shia local historians have profoundly rewritten the history of the Eastern Province. They have published hundreds of books on local history and founded two local history journals – *al-Waha* (the Oasis) and *al-Sahil* (the Coast). Some of those behind *al-Waha* are part of a group of *shiraziyyun* who became so disappointed with the slow change in the situation of Saudi Shia after 1993 that they started to leave Saudi Arabia again.[73] Hamza al-Hasan, Fu'ad Ibrahim

[69] See, for example, Maytham al-Fardan, ed., *al-hiwar al-madhhabi wa-l-masar al-sahih: muhadarat al-shaykh Hasan al-Saffar wa-hafl takrimihi fi ithnayniyya al-shaykh ʿAbd al-Maqsud Khuja* (Confessional Dialogue and the Right Path: Lecture of Shaykh Hasan al-Saffar and a Celebration for Him in the Monday Diwaniyya of Shaykh ʿAbd al-Maqsud Khuja) (Beirut: al-Intishar al-ʿArabi, 2008). For more on Sunni-Shia polemics and dialogue in Saudi Arabia see: Ibrahim, *Shiʿis*, 225–37; Raihan Ismail, "The Saudi Ulema and the Shiʿa of Saudi Arabia," *Journal of Shiʿa Islamic Studies* 5, no. 4 (2012), 403–22; Wehrey, *Sectarian Politics in the Gulf*, 109–12.

[70] Al-Saffar, *al-madhhab*, 151–3. See, for example, ʿAli Abu al-Hasan ibn Hasan bin Mahdi al-Khunayzi, *al-daʿwa al-islamiyya ila wahdat ahl al-sunna wa-l-imamiyya* (The Islamic Call for Unity of the People of the Sunna and the Imamiyya), 2 vols. (Beirut: Dar al-Fikr, 1956). See also Zaki al-Milad, "al-shaykh ʿAli Abu al-Hasan al-Khunayzi: manhajiyyat al-hiwar al-islami" (Shaykh ʿAli Abu al-Hasan al-Khunayzi: A Methodology for Islamic Dialogue), *al-Waha* 3 (1995), 129–31.

[71] See Hasan al-Saffar, *al-salafiyyun wa-l-shiʿa: nahwa ʿalaqa afdal* (Salafis and Shia: Towards a Better Relationship), 2nd printing (Qatif: Atyaf li-l-Nashr wa-l-Tawziʿ/Beirut: al-Intishar al-ʿArabi, 2007).

[72] "Al-Sayyid al-Khabbaz yarfudu 'takrim al-zulma' wa-yuʿtabiru al-taʿayush al-silmi qadiyya thanawiyya" (Sayyid al-Khabbaz Refuses the "Celebration of Darkness" and Argues that Peaceful Coexistence Is a Bilateral Issue), *Rasid*, 20 June 2010. Al-Khabbaz is a *mujtahid* teaching in the *hawza* in Qom, who at the same time has good relations with ʿAli al-Sistani. He regularly delivers sermons at al-Sistani's office in London during Ramadan and for the Shia in Oman during Muharram. See www.almoneer.org and Valeri, "High Visibility," 258.

[73] ʿAli al-Ahmad, a former *shirazi*, for example founded the Saudi Institute and later the Institute for Gulf Affairs in Washington, D.C. Interview with ʿAli al-Ahmad, Washington, D.C., November 2009, www.gulfinstitute.org.

and later Tawfiq al-Sayf returned to North London. Apart from writing for *al-Waha*, they also worked on their doctoral degrees.[74] *Al-Waha* was founded in London in 1995 by Hamza al-Hasan and Fu'ad Ibrahim with the help of 'Ali al-Shuwaykhat and Muhammad al-Nimr. They wanted to strengthen the identity of the people in the Eastern Province not based solely on religion but also on a shared history, which should be viable for the indigenous Sunni Muslims as well. After a few years, Muhammad al-Nimr took over the editorship of the journal, and it started to be produced inside Saudi Arabia.[75] *Al-Sahil* was founded in 2007 by Habib Al Jumay', a *shirazi* cleric, who returned to Saudi Arabia after the 1993 agreement and has been gathering sources on Shia history.[76]

From February 2003 to April 2005, Hamza al-Hasan, Fu'ad Ibrahim and Tawfiq al-Sayf also published a journal called *Shu'un Su'udiyya* (Saudi Affairs), which gave broad coverage to the petitions and was similar to their earlier journal *al-Jazira al-'Arabiyya*. *Shu'un Su'udiyya* had a national and reformist outlook and argued that only fundamental political changes could alter the situation of Saudi Shia.[77]

Another way in which Shia have become more visible is through Shia mourning rituals. Public Ashura ceremonies have been allowed in majority Shia areas like Qatif and the surrounding villages since 2004 (see Picture 6.1 and cover picture). Nevertheless, public processions remain forbidden in mixed Sunni-Shia areas such as Dammam, Khobar and al-Ahsa, which leads to annual tensions.[78]

---

[74] Al-Hasan, *Role*; Tawfiq AlSayf, *Religion and the Legitimation of the State: The Development of Political Thought in Contemporary Shi'ism (Case Study: Iran 1979–2004)* (PhD, University of Westminster, 2005); Fuad Ibrahim, *The Shiite Opposition in the Eastern Province from Revolution to Accomodation (Case Study: The Reform Movement in Saudi Arabia)* (PhD, SOAS, 2004). The latter two have formed the basis for these two books: al-Sayf, *Islamic*; Ibrahim, *Shi'is*. Tawfiq al-Sayf left Saudi Arabia for London in 2001 and returned to Saudi Arabia in 2006, while al-Hasan and Ibrahim remained in London.

[75] Interview with Hamza al-Hasan, London, July 2008; "Althulatha Forum Reviews Cultural Journals in the Region," in *al-Thulatha Cultural Forum Newsletter* 11 (27 January 2009), www.alwahamag.com.

[76] While *al-Sahil* discusses similar topics as *al-Waha*, it features more articles by non-Shia academics, as well as translations of articles and sources in Western languages and Ottoman Turkish on the Eastern Province. *Al-Sahil* is published by the Foundation for the Revival of Shia Heritage in the Arabian Peninsula (*mu'assasat li-ihya' al-turath al-shi'i fi al-jazira al-'arabiyya*), which was also founded by Al Jumay'. Interview with Habib Al Jumay', Damascus, August 2008. He has also compiled a bibliography of writings by Saudi Shia authors: Al Jumay', *mu'jam al-mu'allafat*.

[77] See, for example, *Shu'un Su'udiyya* 6 (July 2003), 27–31, www.saudiaffairs.net.

[78] Interview with Hasan al-Saffar, Eastern Province, November 2008; "In Legacy of a Revered Martyr, Saudi Shiites Find Sustenance," *Washington Post*, 31 January 2007.

PICTURE 6.1. Mulla Hussayn al-Hammadi during Ashura, Imam Hussayn Mosque in the Old Town of Qatif, 24 November 2012.
Source: Hussain Alrebeh.

ABDULLAH AND THE 2003 PETITIONS

After 9/11 the image of Saudi Arabia abroad reached a nadir. External pressure on the government was heightened by the build-up to the invasion of Iraq and rumours that policy makers in Washington, D.C., were playing mind games with the aim of uniting Bahrain and the Eastern Province to a 'Greater Bahrain'. The U.S. press in general became very critical of Saudi Arabia and some even suggested that the Shia in the Eastern Province would be willing to secede.[79] As in 1979 and 1991, a regional crisis led to an opening of the Saudi political field. Shia played an important role in the renewed petitions movement that emerged as a response to these regional developments.

A petition delivered to Crown Prince Abdullah in January 2003 entitled *Vision for the Present and the Future of the Homeland* was one of the first products of an 'Islamo-Liberal' alliance of Sunnis and Shia.[80] This petition drew on the networks of earlier clandestine leftists and the 1990/1 petitions movement[81] and moved to the fore a tactical Shia alliance between leftist members of notable families,[82] notables with a more Islamic outlook[83] and reformist *shiraziyyun*.[84] This alliance can be traced back to the journal *al-Jazira al-ʿArabiyya* and the 1993 accord. The petition asked for significant reforms such as elected national and regional parliaments, anti-corruption measures and an end to sectarian and regional discrimination. Crown Prince Abdullah received a group of signatories of the petition and invited them to a National Dialogue forum in mid-June 2003 that would form the basis for the National Dialogue sessions (see Picture 6.2).[85]

[79] "'Liberating' Saudi's Shiʿites (and Their Oil)," *Asia Times Online*, 18 March 2004; Jones, "Social Contract," 45; Louër, *Transnational*, 246.

[80] Stéphane Lacroix, "Between Islamists and Liberals: Saudi Arabia's New Islamo-Liberal Reformist Trend," *The Middle East Journal* 58, no. 3 (2004), 345–65. For the texts of the different petitions see *rabiʿ al-suʿudiyya*.

[81] Interview with Muhammad Saʿid Tayyib, Jeddah, November 2008; Dekmejian, "Liberal," 404–8. See also ʿAdnan, *al-sajin*, 32.

[82] For example, Najib al-Khunayzi, Taysir Baqir al-Khunayzi, ʿAbd al-Khaliq Al ʿAbd al-Hayy, ʿAbd al-Muhsin al-Khunayzi, ʿAdnan al-ʿAwwami, Kamil ʿAli al-ʿAwwami, Muhammad al-ʿAli, Yusuf Makki.

[83] Hasan al-ʿAwwami, ʿAdnan al-Shukhs.

[84] Jaʿfar al-Shayib, Zaki al-Milad, Muhammad Mahfuz, Muhammad al-Nimr.

[85] "Scholars Urge Moderation and Dialogue," *Arab News*, 21 June 2003; Nimrod Raphaeli, "Demands for Reforms in Saudi Arabia," *Middle Eastern Studies* 41, no. 4 (2005), 517–32, 522.

PICTURE 6.2. King Abdullah and Hasan al-Saffar at the first National Dialogue meeting, June 2003, Riyadh.
Source: Archive of Hasan al-Saffar.

This emboldened the Shia to follow up with their own petition in April 2003, which took up the political demands of the January 2003 petition while including Shia demands that had been part of previous Shia petitions and the 1993 negotiations. Entitled *Partners in the Nation (shuraka' fi al-watan)* it was printed in Lebanese and other Arab newspapers and circulated online. Never before had a Shia petition been published, let alone with the names of its signatories. After pledging allegiance to king and nation, the petition mentioned that the Shia of Qatif and al-Ahsa had peacefully accepted Ibn Saud in 1913 and supported the state-building endeavour financially. The petition demanded that the Saudi state recognise Shia *fiqh* as a school of Islamic jurisprudence, stop the incitement against Shia by Sunni clerics in the country, treat them as equal citizens, include Shia in Saudi-sponsored Islamic institutions such as the Muslim World League and the World Association for Muslim Youth, and admit Shia to higher positions within the bureaucracy, the security services and the diplomatic corps, while ensuring equal representation in the Majlis al-Shura, the strengthening of Shia courts, the legalisation of *hawzat* and private religious schools and the establishment of an official body within the Ministry of Endowments and Islamic Affairs staffed with Shia clerics.

The 450 signatories represented all major Shia political trends and regions. Foremost amongst the signatories were *shiraziyyun*, not only leading clerics such as Hasan al-Saffar but also local activists. In addition, notables, leftists and Khat al-Imam clerics such as 'Abd al-Karim al-Hubayl signed the petition, although some well-known Shia activists and clerics who take a more confrontational stance towards the Saudi state were absent, including those still in exile. Unlike the Shia signatories of the January 2003 petition, who were mainly from the Qatif area, these were from all the major Shia population areas such as Qatif, Dammam, and al-Ahsa and a small number from Medina.[86]

Abdullah was welcoming to the Shia delegation who delivered the petition and promised that some of the grievances would be addressed. But this reception was over-shadowed by reports of sectarian violence. Three Shia mosques and *hussainiyyat* in Tarut were torched in May 2003, skirmishes between Sunni and Shia youth occurred and a Shia cemetery in the mainly Sunni village of Anak between Qatif and Saihat was desecrated.[87] In addition, there were reports that Sunni militants plotted to kill Hasan al-Saffar in 2004 and attack the Ashura ceremonies in 2005.[88] While no major jihadi attack on Saudi Shia took place, al-Qaeda turned against the Saudi state.

The events of 9/11 and the U.S.-led invasion of Afghanistan had drastic repercussions for Saudi national security as Osama bin Laden and the al-Qaeda leadership decided to take jihad to Saudi Arabia. The overthrow of the Saudi government had been their goal for a long time, but they had vowed to fight the jihad abroad against the 'Far Enemy' and not in Saudi Arabia, which was home to many of al-Qaeda's leaders, followers and financiers.[89] Several factors that had stopped them so far – donations by wealthy Saudis and the reluctance of Saudi recruits to strike at home – were altered by the new post-9/11 security order, and mid-level Saudi jihadi veterans in Afghanistan wanted to capitalise on widespread

---

[86] *Rabi' al-su'udiyya*, 203–13. For translations of the petition see Werner Ende, "'Teilhaber an dem einen Vaterland': Die Petition saudischer Schiiten vom 30. April 2003," in *Iran und iranisch geprägte Kulturen: Studien zum 65. Geburtstag von Bert G. Fragner*, ed. Markus Ritter, Ralph Kauz, and Birgitt Hoffmann (Wiesbaden: Ludwig Reichert, 2008), 336–44, 340–4; Ibrahim, *Shi'is*, 257–62.

[87] "Emboldened Shi'ites," *Al-Ahram Weekly Online*, 15 May 2003; Jones, "Social Contract," 46.

[88] International Crisis Group, *Shiite Question*, 11.

[89] Fawaz A. Gerges, *The Far Enemy: Why Jihad Went Global* (Cambridge: Cambridge University Press, 2005).

anti-Americanism in Saudi Arabia after 2001. Although there had been several attacks against Western and government-related targets before, the attacks that started in mid-2002 and the devastating suicide-bombing campaign from May 2003 onwards were on a different scale.[90] This jihadi violence was a key factor for the increase in political activity in 2003 as well as for the initially benevolent ear of parts of the government, which was in need of new supporters.[91]

On the other hand, this reminded the Shia that al-Qaeda's activities in Saudi Arabia could be very dangerous for them, as could an erosion of state power. The Shia demands drew heavy criticism both from the official religious establishment and from *salafi* clerics. Safar al-Hawali, a popular cleric of the Sahwa, wrote an angry refutation of Shia demands, accusing them of trying to impose a Shia or secular state and emphasising that the bad economic situation in Shia areas was the result of the *khums*.[92] Confronted with violent challenges from Sunni Islamists, parts of the ruling family became more sceptical about making overtures to the Shia that could be seen as damaging to the legitimacy of the ruling family amongst its key constituencies.[93] The permission of anti-Shia fatwas, sermons, websites and books is evidence that the Saudi government does not want to be seen as appeasing the Shia at home too much, as anti-Shia discourse remains a legitimising tool and an instrument of foreign policy. The Sunni-Shia dialogue in Saudi Arabia did not manage to curb this sectarian incitement.[94]

Disappointed by the lack of reforms, several dozen Shia leftists, notables and *shiraziyyun* signed two further petitions together with liberals and Sunni Islamists in September and December 2003.[95] In spring 2004, the state used repression against jihadis and also briefly arrested about a dozen 'Islamo-liberals', amongst them some Shia as well as 'Ali al-Dumayni, a Sunni Communist, who remained in jail until Abdullah

---

[90] Hegghammer, *Jihad*, 143–85.

[91] Madawi al-Rasheed, *Contesting the Saudi State: Islamic Voices from a New Generation* (Cambridge: Cambridge University Press, 2007), 230–7.

[92] Ibid., 90f. For the text see: *Shu'un Su'udiyya* 6 (July 2003), 19–21.

[93] Joshua Teitelbaum, "The Shiites of Saudi Arabia," *Current Trends in Islamist Ideology* 10 (2010).

[94] Jones, "Anti-Shi'ism;" Ismail, "The Saudi Ulema;" Wehrey, *Sectarian Politics in the Gulf*, 126.

[95] Jones, "Violence." However, a number of Shia and Sunni liberals disagreed with the Islamic overtones of the December declaration and asked for their names to be removed, while the Shia Islamists stayed on. See Lacroix, "Islamo-Liberal," 53; *rabi' al-su'udiyya*, 163–78.

pardoned him upon his accession to the throne in 2005.[96] The timing of their arrest was related to rumours that they were about to establish an independent human rights organisation.[97] An April 2003 petition to the Minister of Labour and Social Affairs asking for the permission to establish a Saudi Civil Committee for Human Rights *(al-lajna al-ahliyya al-su'udiyya li-huquq al-insan)* had been initiated by liberals from all over Saudi Arabia, including some Shia.[98]

POLITICS OF REPRESENTATION

In response to these calls for political reform, Crown Prince Abdullah announced the opening of the King Abdul Aziz Centre for National Dialogue in August 2003, the expansion of the Majlis al-Shura and the holding of municipal elections. This led to a certain institutionalisation of politics and the co-optation of representatives of different constituencies that became a kind of 'political personnel'.[99] While these "reforms" were intended to strengthen the state rather than expand popular participation, a taboo was broken and conversation on the Islamic nature of the state, minority rights and popular participation became possible.[100] When Abdullah ascended to the throne in 2005, many Shia were optimistic that their demands would finally be met. Factional struggles within the Saudi ruling family characterised much of the 2000s. The main division was between supporters of Abdullah and the Sudayri faction, composed of seven sons of Ibn Saud and Hassa bint Ahmad al-Sudayri. Both the Sudayris and King Abdullah were looking for supporters from outside

[96] 'Ali al-Dumayni, *zaman li-l-sijn: azmina li-l-hurriyya* (Time for Prison, Times for Freedom) (Beirut: Dar al-Kunuz al-Adabiyya, 2005); Alain Gresh, "Between Tradition and Demands for Change: Saudi Arabia: Reality Check," *Le Monde Diplomatique*, February 2006; Lacroix, "Islamo-Liberal," 55.

[97] Lacroix and Hertog, "Dissidenz."

[98] Amongst the Shia signatories were Muhammad al-'Ali, Najib al-Khunayzi, Yusuf Makki, Wajiha Huwaydar, Ja'far al-Shayib, Zaki Abu al-Su'ud, Jawad bu Hulayqa, Ghassan al-Khunayzi and Sadiq al-Jubran. *Rabi' al-su'udiyya*, 179–83; *Shu'un Su'udiyya* 1 (February 2003), 16–18.

[99] Camille Ammoun, "The Institutionalization of the Saudi Political System and the Birth of 'Political Personnel,'" in *Constitutional Reform and Political Participation in the Gulf*, ed. Abdulhadi Khalaf and Giacomo Luciani (Dubai: Gulf Research Center, 2006), 213–40.

[100] Gwenn Okruhlik, "Making Conversation Permissible: Islamism and Reform in Saudi Arabia," in *Islamic Activism: A Social Movement Theory Approach*, ed. Quintan Wiktorowicz (Bloomington: Indiana University Press, 2004), 250–69; Gwenn Okruhlik, "The Irony of Islah (Reform)," *Washington Quarterly* 28, no. 4 (2005), 153–70.

the ruling family, and the Shia were seen as 'one of the king's constituencies, becoming in return the favorite target of the upsurge of religious orthodoxy from the Sudayri leaders and their allies in the Wahhabi religious establishment'.[101]

The invasion of Iraq and the ascent of Iraqi Shia to political power had raised the expectations of Saudi Shia. At the same time, increasing sectarian violence in Iraq rekindled Saudi fears over Iran's expanding sphere of influence.[102] The 2006 war in Lebanon, and signs of sympathy amongst Saudi Shia (but also some Sunnis) with Hizbullah's battlefield performance, again led to a more permissive atmosphere for anti-Shia discourse in Saudi Arabia.[103]

Although many participants and observers are somewhat dissatisfied with the actual outcomes of the national dialogue, it was quite important for the Shia.[104] Shia from all major political groups participated in the dialogue: *shiraziyyun*, Khat al-Imam, as well as liberals and notables. Hasan al-Saffar was invited to the first session together with Sufis, Ismailis and prominent Sunni Islamists such as Salman al-'Awda, although another Sunni Islamist, Safar al-Hawali, refused to attend alongside Shia.[105] Hasan al-Nimr, a former leader of Hizbullah al-Hijaz, argued at the fifth session entitled 'Us and the Others' in the presence of King Abdullah that 'national unity could only be achieved after a realisation of the diversity within the country'.[106]

The sessions also gave a platform to *nakhawila* as well as Ismailis from Najran.[107] This was symbolically important, since a few years earlier, in 2000, relations between the Ismailis and the state had deteriorated significantly. After the government closed several Ismaili mosques, severe clashes with Saudi security forces occurred and protesters surrounded a

[101] Laurence Louër, "The State and Sectarian Identities in the Persian Gulf Monarchies: Bahrain, Saudi Arabia, and Kuwait in Comparative Perspective," in *Sectarian Politics in the Persian Gulf*, ed. Lawrence G. Potter (London: Hurst, 2013), 117–42, 133.

[102] Jones, "Iraq Effect."

[103] Wehrey, *Sectarian Politics in the Gulf*, 116f., 122–30.

[104] Interviews with participants in the National Dialogue, Riyadh, Eastern Province, Jeddah, November 2008. For a detailed analysis of the meetings see Frauke Drewes, "Das Nationale Dialogforum in Saudi-Arabien – Ausdruck politischer Reformen oder Stagnation?" in *Saudi-Arabien: ein Königreich im Wandel?*, ed. Ulrike Freitag (Paderborn: Schöningh, 2009), 29–60.

[105] International Crisis Group, *Can Saudi Arabia Reform Itself?* (2004), 16; Lacroix and Hertog, "Dissidenz."

[106] "Dialogue Participants Meet King, Review Results," *Arab News*, 18 December 2005.

[107] The information stems from the official website of the National Dialogue, www.kacnd.org.

hotel that was the seat of the local governor. Mish'al bin Su'ud bin 'Abd al-'Aziz had been governor of Najran since 1996/7 and was disliked by many Ismailis. The security forces managed to gain the upper hand, but this episode brought the underlying tensions between the Ismailis and the state to the fore.[108] Thereafter, the Ismailis submitted their own petition asking for an end to sectarian discrimination against them.[109] Mish'al was removed as governor in 2008 in a move that a U.S. Diplomatic Cable described as intended to appease the Ismailis.[110] The king replaced him with one of his sons, Mish'al bin 'Abdallah, who remained in the post until 2013.[111]

The second official arena where Shia were included is the Majlis al-Shura that was established in 1993. Appointed by the Royal Cabinet, the Majlis al-Shura debates certain government policies and proposes draft regulations to the king. But it cannot legislate, decide about government and ministries' budgets or overrule decisions made by the king or the Council of Ministers.[112] Indeed, members lament their lack of legislative and executive powers and their inability to discuss political or religious issues freely.[113]

The first Majlis of 1993 saw the inclusion of one Shia (Jamil al-Jishi). In the second Majlis of 1997 the number of appointees increased from 60 to 90 with two Shia members, while in the third term there were 120 and then 150 representatives in the fourth Majlis, of whom three to four were Shia.[114] Shia members for the 2005 Majlis included Ihsan Bu Hulayqa, an economist in Riyadh originally from al-Ahsa,[115] as well as Muhammad Rida Nasrallah, a journalist and former official in the Ministry of Culture and Information. Nasrallah is a member of a prominent notable family

---

[108] Human Rights Watch, *The Ismailis of Najran: Second-Class Saudi Citizens* (2008).

[109] See *rabi' al-su'udiyya*, 215–21.

[110] U.S. Diplomatic Cable, from Embassy Riyadh to Secretary of State, *Najran Looks Forward to New Governor*, 24 November 2008, http://www.wikileaks.org/plusd/cables/08RIYADH1748_a.html.

[111] "Prince Mishaal Named New Makkah Governor," *Arab News*, 22 December 2013.

[112] Rashed Aba-Namay, "The New Saudi Representative Assembly," *Islamic Law and Society* 5, no. 2 (1998), 235–65: 241–4; International Crisis Group, *Can Saudi*, 12.

[113] Interview with members of the Majlis al-Shura, Riyadh, Eastern Province, Jeddah, Saudi Arabia, November 2008.

[114] "Shura in the Kingdom of Saudi Arabia: A Historical Background," www.shura.gov.sa; R. Hrair Dekmejian, "Saudi Arabia's Consultative Council," *The Middle East Journal* 52, no. 2 (1998), 204–18: 216.

[115] While he is outspoken on economic reforms and the integration of women into the work force, he does not see himself as representing particular Shia interests. Interview

from Qatif and one of the key Shia interlocutors for the ruling family. The third participant was ʿAbd al-Jalil al-Sayf. The al-Sayf family from Tarut claims to have had good relations with Ibn Saud but, as mentioned before, was also heavily involved in the *shirazi* movement. ʿAbd al-Jalil al-Sayf was long considered the highest-ranking Shia bureaucrat, working in the Ministry of Interior and the Public Traffic Department. ʿAbd al-Jalil is the uncle of the *shirazi* cadre Tawfiq al-Sayf, and he apparently encouraged Tawfiq and the Saudi Shia opposition to return from exile.[116] In 2009, the number of Shia in the Majlis al-Shura was raised to five.[117]

The official human rights organisations also have some Shia members. ʿAbd al-Jalil al-Sayf and ʿAbd al-Khaliq al-ʿAbd al-Hayy, for example, are founding members of the National Society for Human Rights (*al-jamaʿiyya al-wataniyya li-huquq al-insan*).[118] It was established in March 2004 and although it claims to be financially and administratively independent, King Fahd endowed the organisation with 100 million Saudi Riyal. It monitored the municipal elections and issued several annual reports on topics such as women's rights and prison conditions, without, however, mentioning the specific grievances of Shia Muslims.[119] In 2006, an Eastern Province branch was established in Dammam, and some Shia such as Jaʿfar al-Shayib were enlisted as collaborating members.[120] A Shia notable, Muhammad al-Khunayzi, was appointed to the Human Rights Commission.[121] These state-led initiatives were partly a response to the adoption of human rights discourse by Saudi dissidents, including by the Shia opposition, since the late 1980s and increasingly harsh reports by international human rights organisations concerning the situation of political prisoners and women in Saudi Arabia. Shia have also long pushed to establish official human rights organisations inside

with Ihsan Bu Hulayqa, Riyadh, November 2008. A member of the Ibrahim family from Safwa was also one of the Shia members of the council, but he died of natural causes during his time in office. Interview with Fuʾad Ibrahim, London, 2009.

[116] Interview with ʿAbd al-Jalil al-Sayf, Riyadh, October 2008. See also his autobiography al-Sayf, *mishwar*.

[117] They included Muhammad al-Khunayzi, an education official; Jamil al-Khayri, a biologist specialising in date palms from Tarut; and Saʿid b. ʿAbdallah al-Shaykh, the chief economist at the National Commercial Bank. "Members CV's," www.shura.gov.sa.

[118] Al-Sayf, *mishwar*, 223–32.

[119] Steffen Hertog, "The New Corporatism in Saudi Arabia: Limits of Formal Politics," in *Constitutional Reform and Political Participation in the Gulf*, ed. Abdulhadi Khalaf and Giacomo Luciani (Dubai: Gulf Research Center, 2006), 241–75, 253–5.

[120] Reports available on the Internet, http://nshr.org.sa.

[121] Ana Echagüe and Edward Burke, "'Strong Foundations'? The Imperative for Reform in Saudi Arabia," *FRIDE Working Paper* 84 (2009), 13f.

Saudi Arabia. In December 2011 a group of human rights activists from the Eastern Province unsuccessfully applied for a licence from the Saudi authorities and then started working without a licence under the name Adala Center for Human Rights.[122]

Shia members of the Majlis al-Shura were mainly technocrats from notable families. But Shia from all different political groupings were invited to the national dialogue and former Shia opposition activists won in the municipal elections in 2004/5. The elections were the first opportunity for male Saudis to vote since the municipal elections in the 1950s and 1960s. Overall turnout was low, but it was high amongst Shia, who were enthusiastic about the possibility of gaining at least a little power in local decision making. The example of Iraqi Shia voting in elections had set a precedent that other Arab Shia sought to emulate.[123] Initially, Qatif residents were supposed to participate in the Dammam municipal elections. Qatif municipality had its own municipal council in the 1950s but was in the 1970s integrated into the Eastern Province municipality. Only after petitions by Qatif residents did the government allow Qatif municipality to have its own municipal council, with separate elections.[124]

The voting system allowed residents to vote in all constituencies that make up a municipality. This worked in favour of the organised Shia campaign in Qatif and al-Ahsa, while it harmed independents and Shia candidates in majority Sunni municipalities.[125] Although lists were officially banned, Islamists across the country formed unofficial campaign lists. Candidates associated with the *shiraziyyun* won most of the seats. In Qatif, they campaigned as *qaʾimat al-shamʿa* (The Candle List). This list was endorsed by Hasan al-Saffar, who spoke at electoral campaigns of its candidates. Given their long history of political activism, the *shiraziyyun* knew how to deliver speeches, print leaflets and organise rallies and could rely on a network of mosques and *hussainiyyat*.[126] Initially, women's activists across Saudi Arabia started campaigning too, and two women from Qatif decided to stand in the elections. When it was announced that women would be barred from the elections, some female activists in the

---

[122] http://adalacenter.net.
[123] "Shiites See an Opening in Saudi Arabia: Municipal Vote in East Could Give Suppressed Minority Small Measure of Power," *Washington Post*, 28 February 2005.
[124] Interview with Jaʿfar al-Shayib, London, December 2010.
[125] Interview with a candidate in the municipal elections, Eastern Province, November 2008.
[126] Interview with a campaigner, Eastern Province, November 2008. See also International Crisis Group, *Shiite Question*, 7f.

PICTURE 6.3. From left to right: Hasan al-Saffar, Hussayn al-ʿAyash, ʿAli
al-Sayyid Nasir, Muhammad al-Jaziri, Hussayn al-Radi, Muhammad Rida
al-Sayyid Tahir al-Salman, ʿAdil Abu Khamsin, in al-Ahsa in 2013.
Source: Archive of Hasan al-Saffar.

Eastern Province reached an agreement with Jaʿfar al-Shayib that if he
was elected he would take up women's issues.[127]

Apart from al-Shayib (Tarut), the *shiraziyyun* ʿIsa al-Mizaʿil (Saihat),
Nabih al-Brahim (Awwamiyya) and ʿAli al-Hayy (Safwa) were elected.
As the *shirazi* movement was never strong in Qatif City, the old centre of
Qatif and the stronghold of the notable families, they had no suitable candidate there and so supported a leftist candidate from a notable family,
Zaki Abu al-Suʿud. This, in turn, facilitated the election of a traditionalist
candidate, Riyyad al-Mustafa. An engineer and academic, who directs a
school in Qatif, he became the second chairman of the council. But his
representation of the interests of the Qatifi notable families led to tensions with the *shirazi* members on the council.[128] Only half the seats were
elected, and after all the seats up for election in Qatif had gone to Shia
candidates, the government appointed four Sunnis[129] and one Shia. The
council was thus made up of four Sunni and six Shia representatives.

---

[127] Interview with Hatun al-Fassi, Riyadh, October 2008.

[128] Interview with Jaʿfar al-Shayib, London, December 2010. See the website of the Qatif
Municipal Council, www.qatifmb.org.

[129] Two of them, Falah al-Mulayhi and Khalid al-Khalidi, were from Anak, and another
Sunni was ʿAli al-Dusari, who was the head of the municipality of Dammam, www.
qatifmb.org.

Before the elections, *qa'imat al-sham'a* leaders asked Hasawi Shia to join the list. But the Hasawi activists refused because they wanted to demonstrate the size of the Shia population in al-Ahsa rather than to assert the strength of one particular political trend. Therefore, they incorporated all the different political and religious groups, although the 'Shia list' campaign was led by *shiraziyyun*. Hasawi Shia, too, used a network of mosques, *hussainiyyat*, and campaign centres, and around fifteen hundred volunteers helped to mobilise voters. The campaign team organised a meeting, in which clerics and intellectuals chose six out of twenty-one possible candidates. Of these six, five were elected and the sixth, Hussayn 'Abd al-Rahman al-Khamis, was disqualified, possibly because he could have won in a majority Sunni district.[130] Two elected candidates, 'Abd al-Rahim Abu Khamsin, a human rights lawyer and businessman, and 'Abdallah al-Hulaymi were from the *shirazi* movement, while Salman al-Hijji, a teacher, scholar and social activist, represented the Shaykhis in al-Ahsa.[131] According to a campaigner the elections strengthened the collective identities amongst Shia in al-Ahsa and confirmed their mobilisation capacity. As in Qatif, the government then appointed five Sunnis and one Shia.[132]

The most important municipal council in the Eastern Province is the council of Dammam, which also includes Khobar and Dhahran. Shia Muslims constitute a significant minority in these three cities. The prominent Shia clerics there, the Khat al-Imam cleric Hasan al-Nimr and 'Ali al-Sayyid Nasir, who is associated with *al-da'wa*, were initially sceptical of the elections but finally encouraged Shia to register for the elections and supported an unofficial list of Shia candidates. No Shia was elected, however, as the voting system in this case worked to the disadvantage of the Shia. Under the current voting system, Shia can succeed in Shia-majority municipalities. But they are at a disadvantage in districts that have a Shia majority but are part of municipalities that have a Sunni majority. In Dammam, some Sunnis also distinctively campaigned on an anti-Shia platform. Some Sunni candidates urged Sunnis to vote in order to keep Shia out of the municipal council

---

[130] Interview with campaigners, al-Ahsa, November 2008; "Saudi's Shi'ites walk tightrope," *Asia Times Online*, 17 March 2005.

[131] Interview with Salman al-Hijji, Eastern Province, November 2008. The other two were Hijji al-Nujayda, a retired Saudi Airlines employee, and 'Abd al-Munim al-Khalifa, who was elected even though he was only second choice on the 'Shia list'.

[132] Interview with campaigners, al-Ahsa, November 2008. See also the website of al-Ahsa Municipal Council, http://hasamc.gov.sa.

and anonymous leaflets were distributed across the city with similar slogans.[133]

Many municipal councils soon faced problems and it was more than half a year before they started their work. They had to assert their authority vis-à-vis the established bureaucracy, and tensions between appointed and elected council members surfaced.[134] These were issues that had already bedevilled the municipal councils of the 1950s. The members themselves and their close associates, however, argue that councils are more transparent and more in touch with the population than the normal bureaucracy.[135] But in general, the municipal councils were not able to satisfy the high expectations that some citizens had.[136]

As a result, participation was low in the next municipal elections in September 2011.[137] The second round of municipal elections had originally been scheduled for 2009 but was delayed and only held in 2011. Again, women were not allowed to vote and elections were for only half the seats.[138] Participation this time was also low in Shia areas. In Qatif, for example, only around 5,500 votes were cast and the fifth candidate was elected with only 581 votes, while in other districts representatives were elected with less than a hundred votes.[139] Candidates used social media and personal websites, as well as gatherings and talks to promote their campaigns. But those activists who mobilised the last time around, the *shiraziyyun*, were no longer so successful. While several clerics and

---

[133] "Marginalized Shiites Stand Up to Be Counted in Saudi Local Elections," *AFP/The Daily Star*, 28 February 2005; "Sectarian Lists Circulate for Second Round of Saudi Polls," *AFP/The Daily Star*, 3 March 2005; "Shiites Turn out in Large Numbers for Saudi Arabia's Local Polls," *AFP/The Daily Star*, 4 March 2005; Leo Kwarten, *Why the Saudi Shiites Won't Rise Up Easily* (Conflicts Forum, 2009), 10; Gengler, "Understanding Sectarianism in the Persian Gulf," 46f. See also the website of Dammam Municipal Council, www.dmc.gov.sa.

[134] Ja'far al-Shayib, "Saudi Local Councils Struggling to Produce Results," *Arab Reform Bulletin*, 18 October 2006.

[135] Interview with 'Isa al-Miza'il, Eastern Province, November 2008. See also Christoph Dinkelaker, "Im Osten nichts Neues? – Zur Situation der Schia in Saudi-Arabien," in *Saudi-Arabien: ein Königreich im Wandel?*, ed. Ulrike Freitag (Paderborn: Schöningh, 2009), 189–220, 205.

[136] "Kingdom Holds Free, Fair and Peaceful Civic Elections," *Arab News*, 29 September 2011.

[137] "Empty Voting Booths Signal Little Enthusiasm at Rare Saudi Polls," *The Daily Star*, 30 September 2011.

[138] King Abdullah promised in September 2011 to give women the right to stand for office and vote in municipal elections in 2015. "Saudi Women to Be Given Right to Vote and Stand for Election in Four Years," *The Guardian*, 25 September 2011.

[139] "Al-nata'ij al-awwaliyya li-l-intikhabat fi al-mintaqa al-sharqiyya" (The First Results for the Municipal Elections in the Eastern Province), *al-Yawm*, 7 October 2011.

websites such as *Rasid* called on people to vote, *shirazi* candidates were less prominent than during the 2004 elections.[140] This resulted in the election of several candidates from the notable families.[141] The government appointed four Sunnis and one Shia to the council.[142] While a number of Shia were elected in al-Ahsa, they were again underrepresented amongst the appointed members, resulting in a Shia minority on the council.[143]

AN IMAGINED COMMUNITY ONLINE

A final and key aspect of the new public sphere was the Internet. Public Internet access was only allowed in January 1999 after an Internet Services Unit was set up, through which all Internet traffic in Saudi Arabia would pass to monitor and filter pornographic, political and other undesired websites.[144] The number of Saudi Internet users increased from around 1 million in 2001 to more than 16 million in 2013, while almost half of all households in Saudi Arabia are said to have a broadband connection and most citizens have more than one mobile phone.[145]

Saudi Shia set up hundreds of news websites; websites of villages, social or religious personalities as well as discussion boards. They also became active on social media. Local news with a sensitive political or religious angle is not reported objectively. Even though many prominent Shia have been able to express their views in its opinion pages, the main Eastern Province newspaper *al-Yawm* is tightly regulated. In December 2011, another newspaper based in Dammam, *al-Sharq* (The East), was launched. Its founders had high ambitions of improving journalistic

[140] Interview with a Shia activist, Saudi Arabia, December 2011. *Rasid* carried banners for Muhammad al-Shuyukh throughout September, and he had an online campaign platform but was not elected.

[141] 'Abbas al-Shammasi, Najib 'Abdallah 'Ali al-Sayhati. The other three elected were Kamal al-Miza'il, 'Abd al-'Azim al-Khatir and Sharaf Hasan al-Sa'idi. "Al-nata'ij al-awwaliyya."

[142] The appointed members were Khalid al-Dusari, a Sunni from Dammam who also served as chairman of Qatif municipality; 'Ali al-Khalidi, a Sunni from Anak; the Sunni 'Abdallah al-Qahtani; Majid al-Hajari, as well as the *shirazi* Ja'far al-Shayib, who had been on the previous council. Al-Shayib had not participated in the elections, www.qatifmb.org.

[143] A Shayhki candidate, Ahmad al-Bu 'Ali, was elected, as were Khalid al-Jiriyan, Sami al-Huwayl, 'Abd al-Rahman al-Subay'i, 'Ali al-Sultan and Nahid al-Jabar. Appointed were Sa'd al-Barrak, Salman al-Hijji, 'Abdallah al-Hulaymi, Muhammad al-Mulham and Muhammad al-'Afaliq, http://hasamc.gov.sa.

[144] Teitelbaum, "Dueling," 223–5.

[145] Communications and Information Technology Commission, *ICT Indicators Report (Q1-2013)*, May 2013, www.citc.gov.sa.

standards in the country, and some prominent bloggers and liberals were involved with this project. But the tightening of the Saudi media landscape since the start of the Arab uprisings undermined the project. And yet, the ability to write and read local news online has profoundly eroded government censorship. While websites with a political angle are frequently blocked inside Saudi Arabia, people have become adept at bypassing online censorship. In other words and to paraphrase James Scott, the hidden symbols of resistance amongst Shia Muslims that have previously only been articulated privately, anonymously and by exiled activists, have simply been uploaded to the Internet.[146]

In the novel *The Others*, the protagonist and her group of friends frequently use the Internet and especially discussion boards, including some with sexual and political contents. One day, for example, she goes home and types 'Qatif 1400' into a search engine to read about the intifada of 1400A.H./1979 but finds most sites 'unavailable'.[147] Published in Beirut in 2006 under the pseudonym Siba al-Hirz, the novel features discourses that are usually confined to the Shia, such as the political history of Qatif and the internal organisation of OIRAP in the 1980s.[148] What has really shocked the Saudi public and led to the success of the novel, however, is that apart from criticising sectarian discrimination and patriarchy, the novel describes the lesbian sexual life of a young Shia girl, who is an activist in a local *hussainiyya*. It exposes practices of oppression even amongst members of a minority that are themselves often discriminated against, while making hidden Shia narratives available to the Arabic (and English) reader.[149] *The Others* then exemplifies the ways in which the Internet has opened up new spaces for Saudis, even though the story is told in prose form, which for decades has served as another way for Saudis to tell subversive stories.

The main Shia online portal – *Rasid* (Observer) – was set up in mid-2003 by *shiraziyyun* at the height of the petitions campaign. *Rasid* had contributors from most Shia villages, who wrote anonymously about local news, religious and cultural issues, and the activities of mainly *shirazi* clerics and politicians.[150] In addition, every village and city with

---

[146] Scott, *Domination*.

[147] Seba al-Herz, *The Others* (New York: Seven Stories, 2009), 124f., 205f.

[148] Siba al-Hirz, *al-akharun* (The Others) (Beirut: Dar al-Saqi, 2006).

[149] Madawi al-Rasheed, *A Most Masculine State: Gender, Politics, and Religion in Saudi Arabia* (Cambridge: Cambridge University Press, 2013), 236–9.

[150] This analysis is based on a reading of the website's entries between 2006 and 2014. See also Toby Matthiesen, "A 'Saudi Spring?' The Shi'a Protest Movement in the Eastern

a significant Shia population has its own information portal, with news about its religious and social leaders as well as its history and cultural traditions. Online discussion forums have also become very popular, not just amongst Shia but also amongst tribes.[151] The Ismailis in Najran and the *nakhawila* in Medina have also established news websites. Particularly the Ismailis write extensively about local politics and their religious history.[152] While social media started to become popular in the late 2000s, their usage in Saudi Arabia has increased exponentially since the start of the Arab uprisings. All these online activities help foster a sense of imagined common identities in the Andersonian sense amongst Shia Muslims in Saudi Arabia.[153]

CONCLUSION

This chapter has shown how civil society and representative institutions of the Saudi state have become arenas for hegemonic struggles between the state and the Shia on the one hand, and between different social and political forces amongst the Shia on the other. These spaces have also created various forms of interactions with the state, with at times very different outcomes. Social and discursive spaces that the state has left open by not focussing on the development of Shia areas, have been filled by charities operated by Shia identity entrepreneurs. Since 1993 Shia have established many independent institutions in the social and religious field that are often funded by *khums*. The spaces, activities and discourses described in this chapter operate in the grey area between legality and illegality. A Shia mosque may exist for decades without a licence until it is closed one day in the name of the rule of law, as has happened with several mosques in Khobar since 2008.[154]

Province 2011–2012," *The Middle East Journal* 66, no. 4, (Autumn 2012), 628–59, 631. The editors of Rasid announced on 6 June 2014 that they would stop their publication and erased the archive of the website. Parts of the archive can still be accessed at https://web.archive.org/web/*/rasid.com.

[151] Nadav Samin, "Dynamics of Internet Use: Saudi Youth, Religious Minorities and Tribal Communities," *Middle East Journal of Culture and Communication* 1, no. 2 (2008), 197–215.

[152] The name of the main Ismaili website, *Sawt al-Ukhdud*, invokes local historical narratives, as *al-Ukhdud* was the ancient name of Najran. See www.okhdood.com. The Medina Shia website is available at www.esharh.net.

[153] Anderson, *Imagined Communities*.

[154] See wide coverage of these events on *Rasid*, from 2008 until 2011, as well as U.S. Diplomatic Cable, from Consulate Dhahran to Secretary of State, *Saudi Provincial Authorities Close Shia Mosques in al-Khobar, Leaders Meet with King*, 15 August 2008, http://wikileaks.org/cable/2009/08/09DHAHRAN217.html.

At the same time, however, Shia elites have been co-opted by the state. But this has not fundamentally changed their subaltern status; nor has it succeeded in establishing long-term trust between the Shia and the state. Many had high hopes in the municipal elections of 2004/5 but these faded when it became clear that the councils' powers were limited, and elections planned for 2009 were delayed. The 2003 "reforms" created discursive arenas for Shia and other intellectuals and identity entrepreneurs. But the promises of political reform and of full rather than marginal recognition of Shia as Saudi citizens and their integration into the Saudi state remained largely unfulfilled. When Arabs revolted against ageing dictators, it was hence not surprising that some Saudi Shia once again took to the streets.

7

A New Intifada

Saudi Shia had occasionally held demonstrations since 1979. Yet, these were usually tied to a wider regional issue and only implicitly touched upon domestic Saudi matters. After anti-Israeli protests in 2002, Saudi Shia went out again in 2006 to voice their opposition to the Israeli attacks on Lebanon.[1] In December 2008, anti-Israeli protesters displayed Hizbullah flags and pictures of Hasan Nasrallah, and the security forces arrested thirty.[2] But in February 2009 sectarian clashes between Sunni and Shia pilgrims, the latter mainly from the Eastern Province, broke out at the al-Baqi' cemetery in Medina, leading to injuries and arrests. Follow-up demonstrations in Safwa, Awwamiyya and Qatif were the first large demonstrations on a domestic Saudi Shia matter since 1980.[3]

Some Shia arrested in February 2009 in the wake of the clashes and demonstrations were released after a Shia delegation met King Abdullah in Riyadh on 3 March 2009. After the clashes in Medina, security forces in the Eastern Province told religious leaders to refrain from communal prayers in order not to heighten tensions.[4] The cleric Nimr al-Nimr,

---

[1] "Tafriq thalith muzahara li-shi'at al-su'udiyya da'man li-hizb Allah" (Breakup of the Third Protest of Saudi Shia in Support of Hizbullah), *al-jazeera.net*, 5 August 2006.

[2] "Taking to Streets in Saudi Arabia," *Saudi Jeans Blog*, 31 December 2008; "Saudi Police Break Up Pro-Gaza Protest: Residents," Reuters, 29 December 2008; U.S. Diplomatic Cable, from Embassy Riyadh to Secretary of State, *The Thirteen Days of Ashura in Qatif*, 27 January 2009, http://www.wikileaks.org/plusd/cables/09RIYADH173_a.html.

[3] For more on the 2009 incidents see Toby Matthiesen, "The Shi'a of Saudi Arabia at a Crossroads," *Middle East Report Online* (May 6, 2009).

[4] Human Rights Watch, *Denied Dignity: Systematic Discrimination and Hostility toward Saudi Shia Citizens* (2009), 15–21.

however, did not obey this order. Opposed to the 1993 agreement, al-Nimr disavowed any engagement with the state, had called for a boycott of the municipal elections and had at one point demanded a share of the oil income for the Shia.[5] On 13 March he delivered an angry sermon in his small mosque on the outskirts of Awwamiyya that was widely disseminated on the web. In it, he blamed the Saudi leadership for the events in Medina and for the situation of the Shia in Saudi Arabia and reserved the right of the Eastern Province Shia to secede one day.[6] After the sermon, al-Nimr went into hiding to evade arrest. Small demonstrations were held in his support in Awwamiyya. The ruling family saw this as a confirmation of Shia disloyalty, while the remnants of the Shia opposition abroad tried to capitalise on these new developments.[7]

Increased sectarian tensions crystallised on religious occasions. In al-Ahsa, Ashura in late December 2009/January 2010 was overshadowed by the arrest of dozens for displaying Shia banners or participating in Shia religious festivals.[8] In July, the religious police closed down a Shia religious ceremony in Medina organised by a hajj tour operator from al-Ahsa.[9] Muhammad ʿAli al-ʿAmri, the son of the spiritual leader of the *nakhawila* Shia in Medina, was briefly arrested in August 2010. The simultaneous raid on a ranch belonging to his father outraged many Shia, as it housed a mosque and had been the main centre of religious practice for the *nakhawila*.[10] During Ashura 2010, which that year was in

---

5 International Crisis Group, *Shiite Question*, 7. For more on al-Nimr see al-Ibrahim and al-Sadiq, *al-hirak al-shiʿi fi al-suʿudiyya*, 268–76; Matthiesen, "A 'Saudi Spring,'" 631f., 635; al-Mushaykhas, *al-ʿAwwamiyya*, 209f.

6 "Al-Shaykh al-Nimr: imma karamatuna aw al-infisal ya Al Suʿud – al-Baqiʿ" (Shaykh al-Nimr: Either Our Dignity or the Secession oh Al Saud – al-Baqiʿ), www.youtube.com/watch?v=vSO_2LphRn4&feature=related, minute 9.

7 Statement by *Hizbullah al-Hijaz*, 25 February 2009. Previously available on the Internet, www.alhramain.com. The statement is discussed and partly reproduced in "hizb Allah al-Hijaz: al-sultat laysat bi-maʿzil ʿamma yahduth fi al-Madina" (Hizbullah al-Hijaz: The Authorities Are Not Isolated from What Happens in Medina), *Middle East Online*, 25 February 2009, http://middle-east-online.com.

8 See the coverage on www.rasid.com, for example, "Unprecedented Arrests Campaign in Al-Hassa," *Rasid English*, 24 February 2010. For a timeline of anti-Shia incidents see U.S. Department of State, *International Religious Freedom Report: Saudi Arabia* (July–December 2010).

9 "The Religious Police Attack a Religious Ceremony on the Anniversary of the Birth of Imam Mahdi in Medina," *Rasid English*, 14 August 2010.

10 "Crackdown on Shiites Steps Up: A Shiite Preacher Detained for Ten Days in Madina without Charge or Trial," *Rasid English*, 12 August 2010. ʿAli al-ʿAmri, who had been the leader of the *nakhawila* for decades, died in January 2011 at the age of 100. Al-Jadʿan, *Ayatallah*.

PICTURE 7.1. Ashura in Qatif, 24 November 2012.
Source: Hussain Alrebeh.

December, sectarian tensions resurfaced in Medina. According to Shia sources, Sunnis attacked Shia who wanted to perform Ashura, leading to clashes involving hundreds of men.[11] In the aftermath, the governor of Medina invited leaders of both sects for reconciliation talks and a Sunni-Shia declaration was signed.[12]

Shia voices from across the country, including *shirazi* leaders, condemned these incidents and as a result the government became more distrustful of the *shiraziyyun,* who had been the main interlocutors with the state since 1993.[13] In addition, some Shia became dissatisfied with the accommodationist stance that their political and clerical elite had pursued since 1993. A controversial new zoning law for the Municipality of Qatif also angered many. Critics argued that the new law restricts the city of Qatif and therefore the land on which Shia can build.[14] So tensions in the Eastern Province had been building up for years when the Tunisian street vendor Muhammad Bouazizi set himself on fire on 17 December 2010 and Saudis were watching the Arab uprisings spreading from country to country. Protests in the Gulf started in Oman in January 2011, but it was the mass uprising in Bahrain from 14 February 2011 onwards that encouraged Saudi Shia activists to organise their own protest movement.[15]

A RENEWED SHIA PROTEST MOVEMENT

The emergence of a new Saudi Shia protest movement reconfigured the local political field and marked a clear break with the post-1993 era. In this reconstituted political environment three loosely organised political groups again started to push for public protests.

The first were the Saudi followers of the *mudarrisiyya,* the group that split away from the mainstream *shirazi* movement and decided to follow

---

[11] Joshua Teitelbaum, "Sunni vs. Shiite in Saudi Arabia," *Jerusalem Issue Briefs* 10, no. 23, 16 January 2011.

[12] "Amir al-Madina yu'aqad ijtima' tasaluhi bayn al-sunna wa-l-shi'a tarafi ahdath al-shaghab al-madiyya bi-hayy quba'" (The Governor of Medina Holds a Reconciliatory Meeting between Sunnis and Shia regarding the Recent Fights in the Quba Quarter), www.esharh.net, 21 December 2010; "tawqi' wathiqa musaliha bayn al-sunna wa-l-shi'a fi al-Madina ba'd ahdath 'ashura'" (Signing of a Reconciliatory Document between Sunnis and Shia in Medina after the Ashura Events), *Rasid,* 25 December 2010.

[13] Interview with Ja'far al-Shayib, London, December 2010.

[14] Email correspondence with Ja'far al-Shayib, February 2012.

[15] For an account of the protests in Oman and of the Bahrain uprising see Matthiesen, *Sectarian Gulf,* chapters 1, 3, 4 and 7.

the *marji'iyya* of Muhammad Taqi al-Mudarrisi. One of its key Saudi figures, Nimr al-Nimr, became a figurehead of the protest movement.

The second group who protested were supporters of Khat al-Imam and family members of the nine prisoners jailed for their alleged membership in Hizbullah al-Hijaz and involvement in the Khobar Towers bombings of 1996.

The third strand of activists represents those *shiraziyyun* who became dissatisfied with the accommodationst stance of the *shirazi* leadership in Saudi Arabia around Hasan al-Saffar. This strand includes the London-based activists Hamza al-Hasan and Fu'ad Ibrahim. The split with their old colleagues became evident when from 2008 onwards al-Hasan started to describe his former fellow revolutionaries as the 'new notables of the Shia', a charge they vehemently reject.[16] Already after the Medina clashes in 2009, Fu'ad Ibrahim and Hamza al-Hasan had increased their online activities and demanded secession of the Eastern Province.[17] Since 2011, this trend operated the main social network accounts that were driving and covering protests under the name *Thawrat al-Mintaqa al-Sharqiyya* (Eastern Province Revolution).[18] It was also the key driver behind the establishment of i'tilaf al-hurriyya wa-l-'adala (Coalition for Freedom and Justice), a loose coalition of Saudi Shia opposition and youth groups that was announced on 25 March 2012.[19] In spring 2013, this trend even established the first satellite TV station of the Saudi Shia opposition, *Naba'*, with offices in Beirut and London.[20]

People first took to the streets in Awwamiyya on 17 February 2011 to demand the release of local political prisoners, initially of three political prisoners arrested for the protests in spring 2009. Three days later, the three were released,[21] together with six other Shia prisoners from al-Ahsa

---

[16] Al-Hasan, *al-'amal.*

[17] Their website was at www.moltaqaa.com (now defunct); Hamza al-Hasan, *al-wataniyya: hawajis al-wahda wa-l-infisal fi al-su'udiyya* (Nationality: Thoughts about Unity and Separatism in Saudi) (n.p.: Dar al-Multaqa, 2009).

[18] www.facebook.com/rev.east and @Sharqiyah on Twitter.

[19] Interview with Hamza al-Hasan, London, 2013.

[20] http://nabaa.tv.

[21] "Three Saudi Shi'ites Released after Rare Protest," *Reuters*, 20 February 2011. The rest of this chapter is based on a reading of thousands of articles on Shia news websites, on videos and on observations on social media. For more sources and details on the protest movement see Matthiesen, "A 'Saudi Spring?';" Toby Matthiesen, "The Local and the Transnational in the Arab Uprisings: The Protests in Saudi Arabia's Eastern Province," in *The Silent Revolution: The Arab Spring and the Gulf States*, ed. May Seikaly and Khawla Matar (Berlin: Gerlach Press, 2014). See also Frederic Wehrey, *The Forgotten Uprising in Eastern Saudi Arabia* (Carnegie Endowment for International Peace, 14 June 2013);

arrested a year earlier for performing Shia rituals.[22] On 24 February, 2011, more protesters in Awwamiyya demanded the release of other prisoners from the village. That same day, dozens of protesters in Qatif and Safwa called for the release of the nine Khobar Towers prisoners.[23] No one in Saudi Arabia had hitherto dared to call openly for the release of these prisoners. Soon a similar protest campaign was under way in Riyadh, where family members of political prisoners arrested on suspicion of membership in al-Qaeda protested in front of the Ministry of Interior in March 2011, and nationwide petitions for a constitutional monarchy emerged.[24]

While the first low-key demonstrations focused on Qatif, the 26 February arrest of the Hasawi cleric Tawfiq al-'Amir, who had demanded the introduction of a constitutional monarchy, galvanised feelings in al-Ahsa.[25] The largest protests yet were held on 4 March, both in Qatif, and for the first time also in al-Ahsa. This was just one week ahead of 11 March, the day social media sites had termed a "Day of Rage" in Saudi Arabia. Protesters in al-Ahsa called for the release of al-'Amir,[26] and more than one hundred Shia clerics signed a petition for his release.[27] Security forces arrested around twenty people during these protests.[28] In anticipation of the demonstrations planned for 11 March, the authorities in the Eastern Province urged Shia leaders to tell the people to stay at home on 11 March, and released al-'Amir.[29] Muhammad bin Fahd, the governor of the Eastern Province, met with youth representatives from Qatif.[30]

<hr>

'Abd al-Rahman Muhammad 'Umar al-'Uqayl, *ahdath al-'Awwamiyya wa-l-Qatif* (The Events of Awwamiyya and Qatif: From 10 February 2011 to 10 February 2012) (Riyadh: [leaked through www.awamia.net], 2012).

[22] "'Ulama' al-Ahsa' yazurun 'sujana' al-sha'a'ir' bi-l-Rumayla" (Clerics of al-Ahsa Visit the "Prisoners of the Religious Chants" in Rumaila), *Rasid*, 27 February 2011.

[23] "Masiratan fi al-Qatif wa-Safwa li-mutaliba bi-itlaq al-sujana' 'al-mansiyyun'" (Two Demonstrations in Qatif and Safwa Demanding the Release of the "Forgotten" Prisoners), *Rasid*, 25 February 2011.

[24] Stéphane Lacroix, "Is Saudi Arabia Immune?" *Journal of Democracy* 22, no. 4 (October 2011), 48–59, 56.

[25] Human Rights Watch, "Saudi Arabia: Free Cleric Who Backs Change," 28 February 2011.

[26] "More Shi'ite Protests in Saudi Oil Region," Reuters, 5 March 2011.

[27] "Mi'at 'alim din yatadamanun ma' al-shaykh al-'Amir" (Hundred Clerics Support Shaykh al-'Amir), *Rasid*, 4 March 2011.

[28] "Die arabische Revolte erreicht Saudiarabien," *Neue Zürcher Zeitung*, 8 March 2011; Human Rights Watch, "Saudi Arabia: Stop Stifling Peaceful Dissent," 8 March 2011.

[29] Interview with a Shia activist, December 2011, Saudi Arabia; "Saudi Arabia Frees Shia Cleric Ahead of 'Day of Rage,'" BBC, 7 March 2011.

[30] "Wafd shababi min al-Qatif yaltaqi amir al-mintaqa al-sharqiyya wa-yuwassil 'nabd al-shari'" (A Youth Delegation from Qatif Meets the Governor of the Eastern Province and Delivers the "Pulse of the Street"), *Rasid*, 9 March 2011.

A Shia delegation visited the king after he returned from medical treatment abroad in February.[31] On 23 February and again in mid-March, the king announced massive government spending programs largely intended to tackle youth unemployment and a housing crisis. While this additional spending would benefit all Saudis, large sums were distributed to government institutions from which Shia are largely banned, such as religious institutions and the Ministry of Interior.[32] In Qatif on 9–10 March protesters carried pictures of the nine prisoners and shouted slogans such as "Freedom," "Not Sunni, not Shia, Islamic Unity" and "Our protest is peaceful, our demands are just."[33] On the evening of 10 March, several hundred people protested in Qatif and security forces apparently fired into the air to scare them.[34] There were no protests in other parts of the country on 11 March, but in al-Ahsa, Safwa, Awwamiyya and Qatif, hundreds of people took to the streets.[35]

On 14 March, Saudi Arabia sent troops to Bahrain as Bahraini security forces cracked down on the protest movement there. This re-energised the Saudi Shia protests, and on 16, 17 and 18 March, thousands protested in most towns and villages surrounding Qatif. Security forces arrested dozens and on 17 March injured two protesters in Qatif.[36] *Shirazi* and Khat al-Imam clerics from Qatif and al-Ahsa denounced the crackdown in Bahrain publicly with varying degrees of criticism of the Saudi rulers,[37] and four hundred Saudi Shia affirmed their support for the 'Bahraini people' in a petition.[38]

ARRESTS AND THE POLITICS OF NOTABLES

The former Shia judge of Qatif 'Abdallah al-Khunayzi called for the cessation of protests on 23 March 2011 and argued that, in return, the authorities should release those arrested during the previous weeks. In

[31] F. Gregory Gause III., "Rageless in Riyadh," *Foreign Affairs*, 16 March 2011.

[32] "Royal Decrees: King Abdullah Ibn Abdulaziz Issues a Number of Royal Decrees," *Saudi Press Agency* (English), 23 February 2011, www.spa.gov.sa/english/awamer.php.

[33] For links to footage on YouTube see: "mushahid al-ihtijajat fi al-Qatif wa-l-Ahsa'" (Scenes of Protest in Qatif and al-Ahsa), *Rasid*, 5 March 2011.

[34] "Schüsse gegen Schiiten in Saudiarabien," *Neue Zürcher Zeitung*, 12 March 2011.

[35] "Mushahid," *Rasid*.

[36] Human Rights Watch, "Saudi Arabia: Arrests for Peaceful Protest on the Rise," 27 March 2011.

[37] "Saudi Shiites Call for Withdrawal and Shiite Religious Leaders Incriminate Massacres in Bahrain," *Saudishia.com*, 20 March 2011.

[38] "Arba' mi'a shakhsiyya su'udiyya shi'iyya tatadamun ma' al-sha'b al-bahrayni" (400 Saudi Shia Personalities support the Bahraini People), *Rasid*, 20 March 2011.

the same vein, younger notables asked the protesters not to return to the streets, arguing that their voices had been heard and that continued protests would just create more problems.[39] Munir al-Khabbaz, a leading Qatifi cleric, on 25 March also called for a halt of protests. From 2011, he repeatedly tried to mediate between the protesters and the government. He and a number of other clerics and notables tried to broker an agreement between Muhammad bin Fahd and the youth groups of Qatif.[40] Despite these calls, two small protests were held the same day in Awwamiyya and Rabia'iyya, where four were arrested.[41] Pressure by the government on the notables also bore fruit in al-Ahsa. A statement signed by seventy-five clerics from all strands of Hasawi Shia society, including *shirazi*, Khat al-Imam, Shaykhi and traditionalist clerics as well as supervisors of the *hawza* in al-Ahsa, reminded the youth that al-Ahsa was a mixed Sunni-Shia area and that the protests endangered sectarian relations. It urged the youth to voice their grievances in dialogue with clerics, notables and the rulers.[42]

On 30 March, a delegation of clerics who included 'Abdallah al-Khunayzi, Munir al-Khabbaz and 'Abd al-Karim al-Hubayl (but crucially, not Hasan al-Saffar) met with Muhammad bin Fahd. The governor apparently insisted that the clerics should use their position to stop the protests.[43] A youth delegation presented its demands to the vice governor of the Eastern Province, Jalawi bin 'Abd al-'Aziz bin Mus'ad, and asked for the release of all political prisoners, but he told them this could only be negotiated once protests stopped.[44] Thereafter, protests became smaller but did not end completely. On Friday, 1 April,

[39] They included Maytham al-Jishi, Hussayn al-Sannan, Muhammad al-Ghanim, and Sadiq al-'Ali. "Al-shaykh al-Khunayzi yada'u ila waqf al-tazahurat fi al-Qatif" (Shaykh al-Khunayzi Calls for an End to Demonstrations in Qatif), *Rasid*, 23 March 2011.

[40] "Al-Sayyid al-Khabbaz yada'u ila waqf al-masirat al-ihtijajiyya fi al-Qatif" (Sayyid al-Khabbaz Calls for an End to the Protests in Qatif), *Rasid*, 25 March 2011.

[41] Human Rights Watch, "Saudi Arabia: Arrests for Peaceful Protest on the Rise," 27 March 2011.

[42] Signatories included Nasir al-Salman, Hussayn al-Radi, Hasan al-Radi, 'Ali al-Dandan, Hashim al-Shakhs, Hashim al-Salman, 'Adil Bu Khamsin, Tawfiq al-'Amir and Tawfiq al-Bu 'Ali. "'Ulama' al-Ahsa' yasdurun bayanan bi-sha'an al-ahdath al-akhira" (The Clerics of al-Ahsa Issue a Statement regarding the Recent Events), *Rasid*, 24 March 2011.

[43] "Wafd rijal al-din al-shi'a yaltaqi amir al-sharqiyya" (A Delegation of Shia Clerics Meets Governor of the Eastern Province), *Rasid*, 30 March 2011.

[44] "Wafd shabab al-Qatif yaltaqi na'ib amir al-mintaqa al-sharqiyya" (A Youth Delegation of Qatif Meets the Deputy Governor of the Eastern Province), *Rasid*, 31 March 2011.

hundreds marched in Awwamiyya, again calling for the release of the Khobar Towers prisoners.[45]

Only one senior cleric publicly endorsed the demonstrations and argued that they were not contrary to religious law: Nimr al-Nimr. Al-Nimr, who had been in hiding since 2009, gave a Friday sermon on 25 February 2011 in which he called for political and religious reforms. He denounced the ongoing repression against Shia and other Saudis and argued that political power is only legitimate if it gives its citizens freedoms.[46] With this speech, and his participation in protests, al-Nimr positioned himself at the forefront of the protest movement, a position he had hinted at earlier. A leaked U.S. diplomatic cable quoted him as saying that in any future uprising, he would side with the people, not with the government, and he allegedly reserved the right of the Saudi Shia to seek external assistance if it came to a conflict.[47] While he mainly sought to oppose those Shia clerics who had called for a halt to the protests, this was also a rebuttal of the official Saudi clergy, who had deemed protests in Saudi Arabia illegal per se.[48]

Protests in support of Bahrain continued in the coming weeks. Hasan al-Saffar was intriguingly silent on the demonstrations in Qatif until he signed a crucial clerical declaration published on 21 April that called for a halt to the demonstrations. This statement came after some of the pro-government Shia clerics had unsuccessfully tried to obtain a fatwa from a *marji'* living in Iraq or Iran prohibiting protests in Saudi Arabia.[49] The landmark declaration was signed by thirty-five clerics who represented all the strands amongst the clerics of Qatif, including the notable families and the traditionalist camp ('Abdallah al-Khunayzi and Munir al-Khabbaz), the *shiraziyyun* (Hasan al-Saffar), Khat al-Imam ('Abd al-Karim al-Hubayl) and former Shia judges of Qatif (namely, Ghalib al-Hammad). The declaration argued that the demands of the youth had been submitted to Muhammad bin Fahd and that it was now time to stop

[45] "Saudi Shi'ites Protest Peacefully in East," Reuters, 1 April 2011.

[46] "Al-shaykh al-Nimr yada'u li-islahat siyasiyya tastajib li-tatalla'at al-shu'ub" (Shaykh al-Nimr Calls for Political Reforms that Answer the Aspirations of the Peoples), *Rasid*, 26 February 2011.

[47] U.S. Diplomatic Cable, from Embassy Riyadh to Secretary of State, *Meeting with Controversial Shi'a Sheikh Nimr Al-Nimr*, 23 August 2008, http://wikileaks.org/cable/2008/08/08RIYADH1283.html. See also U.S. Diplomatic Cable, from Embassy Riyadh to Secretary of State, *Radical Shi'a Cleric Supports Iran, Warns of Clashes*, 5 August 2008, http://wikileaks.org/cable/2008/08/08RIYADH1197.html.

[48] "Saudi Clerics Slam Protest Calls," AFP, 6 March 2011.

[49] Rosie Bsheer, "Saudi Revolutionaries: An Interview," *Jadaliyya*, 21 June 2012.

the protests.[50] In defiance of the declaration, small protests continued, including by women, and one protest specifically called for the release of a Sunni human rights activist, Mikhlif al-Shammari, who had been arrested after he spoke out against sectarian discrimination. Women actually participated in most protests held in the Eastern Province from 2011 onwards.[51]

But the declaration, continued arrests – including of online activists – and a heavy security presence with checkpoints eroded the will of the protesters.[52] In the following weeks, the focus of the notables was on the release of the most recent prisoners. After some notables met in Riyadh with Ministry of Interior officials, prisoners were gradually released.[53] But sporadic protests and arrests continued over the next weeks.[54] Muhammad bin Fahd promised a delegation of Qatifi notables that more protesters would be released if the province remained calm,[55] and a statement signed by sixty-five people imprisoned for their role in the protests at the Central Prison of Dammam endorsed this call, urging the 'youth and the street' to remain calm so that they could be released.[56] Several dozen were released throughout July and August, and three Shia mosques in Khobar that had been closed since 2008 were allowed to re-open.[57] But others were arrested, including on 3 August, Tawfiq al-'Amir, the cleric from al-Ahsa whose earlier arrest in the spring had sparked protests.[58]

[50] "Rijal al-din fi al-Qatif yada'un li-waqf al-tazaharut al-ihtijajiyya" (Religious Scholars in Qatif call for an End to the Protests), *Rasid*, 21 April 2011.

[51] "Saudis Rally in Support of Bahrain Shi'ites," Reuters, 29 April 2011; "Khuruj masiratayn silmiyyatayn wasat al-Qatif wa-l-'Awwamiyya tadamunan ma' al-sujana'" (Two Protests Erupt in the Middle of Qatif and Awwamiyya in Support of the Prisoners), *Rasid*, 7 May 2011.

[52] Human Rights Watch, "Saudi Arabia: Rights Activists, Bloggers Arrested," 2 May 2011.

[53] "Wafd ahali al-mu'taqalin altaqi wakil wizarat al-dakhiliyya al-su'udiyya" (A Delegation of Prisoners' Families Met an Under-Secretary of the Saudi Interior Ministry), *Rasid*, 18 May 2011.

[54] "Khamsun sayyida min ahali mu'taqali al-masirat al-silmiyya bi-imarat al-sharqiyya" (Fifty Women of the Families of the Prisoners (Hold) Peaceful Protest in Front of the Governorate of the Eastern Province), *Rasid*, 14 June 2011.

[55] "Amir al-mintaqa al-sharqiyya yu'idd bi-itlaq jami' al-mawqufiyyin wa-talbiyyat al-matalib "al-ma'qula" (The Governor of the Eastern Province Is Willing to Release All the Arrested and to Realise the "Reasonable" Demands), *Rasid*, 21 June 2011.

[56] "Sujana' yada'un li-waqf al-masirat al-silmiyya fi al-Qatif wa-yunashidun amir al-mintaqa itlaqhum" (Prisoners Call for a Stop of Peaceful Protests in Qatif and Plead to the Governor of the Province for their Release), *Rasid*, 30 June 2011.

[57] See "Saudi Authorities Reopen Khobar Sealed Shiite Mosques," *Jafariya News*, 19 July 2011.

[58] Amnesty International, *Saudi Arabia: Repression in the Name of Security* (2011), 48.

THE FIRST DEATHS

There was no real rapprochement over the summer and a confrontation in October in Awwamiyya was an indication of the tense atmosphere. Shia activists and human rights organisations relate that authorities arrested the fathers of two young activists who had been sought for protests earlier in 2011, in order to force the youths to hand themselves over. As news of the arrests of the two elderly men, Hasan Al Zayid and Sa'id 'Abd al-Al, on 2 October 2011, spread throughout the village of Awwamiyya, villagers started to gather in front of the police station. The situation became increasingly tense as Al Zayid collapsed inside the police station and had to be taken by ambulance to a nearby hospital. One human rights activist, Fadil al-Manasif, followed the ambulance and was arrested at the next checkpoint.[59] After these events, firefights ensued between armed residents and security forces. Unlike their more muted response after previous incidents and demonstrations, the Ministry of Interior was very quick to release a chilling statement that blamed them on "foreign entities".[60] Most Shia leaders felt threatened by the statement and the shootings and quickly denounced the use of violence.[61]

After these events, the security forces set up checkpoints in Qatif and surrounding villages. This prevented mass demonstrations over the succeeding weeks but made locals feel "under siege" and led to small confrontations at checkpoints. The situation escalated on 19 November when a young man was injured by police in Awwamiyya, and then again a day later, after a Shia teenager, Nasir al-Muhayshi, was shot dead in Qatif.[62] Shia activists claim that he was walking in the streets when he was shot and that his body was not released, leading to a protest the following evening. During this protest, another young Shia, twenty-year-old 'Ali al-Filfil from Shuwaykha, was killed.[63] On 23 November, more than

[59] Human Rights Watch, "Saudi Arabia: Stop Arbitrary Arrests of Shia," 11 October 2011; Front Line Defenders, *Saudi Arabia: Arrest and Incommunicado Detention of Human Rights Defender Mr Fadel Mekki Al-Manasef as Part of Ongoing Government Crackdown*, 11 October 2011; Amnesty International, *Saudi Arabia: Repression in the Name of Security* (2011), 48f.

[60] Saudi Press Agency (English website), 4 October 2011, www.spa.gov.sa/English/details. php?id=931281.

[61] See, for example, "Saudis Pledge Loyalty to Kingdom Following Riots," *Gulf News*, 5 October 2011.

[62] "Saudi Security Forces Kill 19-Year Old Qatif Native," *Rasid English*, 21 November 2011.

[63] "Saudi Forces Crackdown Protests in Qatif and Kill a Protester," *Rasid English*, 23 November 2011.

ten thousand took to the streets for the burial of Nasir al-Muhayshi and 'Ali al-Filfil. Two more protesters were killed on that day and at least three injured, putting the death toll at four in one week.[64]

As the start of Muharram fell on 26 November, both the state and Shia leaders were wary of a full-fledged uprising with more bloodshed. So five of the most important Saudi Shia clerics, representing the notable families and the traditionalist camp ('Abdallah al-Khunayzi, Munir al-Khabbaz and Mansur al-Jishi), the *shiraziyyun* (Hasan al-Saffar) and Khat al-Imam ('Abd al-Karim al-Hubayl), signed a statement that called for a halt of protests during Muharram.[65] Muhammad bin Fahd promised an investigation into the deaths and met with the families of the deceased.[66] He also held a meeting with a delegation of Qatifi notables, where the current Shia judge of Qatif, Muhammad al-Jirani, proclaimed, 'We are working hand-in-hand with the state.'[67] This was a continuation of the notable politics described in the first chapter of this book. Indeed, the authorities in the Eastern Province reaffirmed their alliances with the Shia judges since 2011.[68] On the evening of the meeting, however, al-Jirani's car and parts of his house were set on fire, injuring two of his sons. This was widely reported as an attack on the 'moderate Shia' by 'radical Shia' groups.[69] After Ashura passed quietly, small Friday protests started again in remembrance of the four recent martyrs and the nine prisoners.[70] But as 2011 came to a close, the protests remained confined to Qatif. The Shia of al-Ahsa realised that if they protested, they would face even worse repression than in Qatif, as the government wanted to prevent protests from spilling over into Sunni areas.

[64] "Saudi Security Forces Killed Two People in Qatif," *Rasid English*, 24 November 2011.

[65] "Abraz al-'ulama' al-shi'a fi al-Qatif yarfudun istikhdam al-'unf" (The Most Prominent Shia Clerics in Qatif Reject the Use of Violence), *Rasid*, 24 November 2011.

[66] "Al-sultat al-su'udiyya tushakkil lajna li-l-tahqiq fi ahdath al-Qatif" (The Saudi Authorities Form a Committee for the Investigation of the Qatif Events) *Rasid*, 24 November 2011; "Governor of Eastern Region Receives Families of the Dead in Qatif Incidents," *Saudi Press Agency*, 3 December 2011.

[67] "Qatif Ulema Pledge Loyalty to Leadership," *Saudi Gazette*, 30 November 2011.

[68] See, for example, "al-Amir Muhammad bin Fahd yazur al-shaykh al-Jaziri fi al-Ahsa'" (Prince Muhammad bin Fahd Visits Shaykh al-Jaziri in al-Ahsa), *al-Riyyad*, 13 December 2011.

[69] One article even claimed that Hizbullah al-Hijaz was responsible, *"Hizb Allah al-Hijaz yaftah al-nar 'ala al-qiyyadat al-shi'iyya al-mu'tadila"* (Hizbullah al-Hijaz Opens Fire on the Moderate Shia Leadership), *Middle East Online*, 30 November 2011.

[70] For example, on 9 December 2011 in Awwamiyya: "Masira hashida fi al-'Awwamiyya wafa' li-shuhada' al-Qatif" (A Dense Protest in Awwamiyya in Honour of the Martyrs of Qatif), *Rasid*, 10 December 2011.

A MANHUNT AND SIMMERING TENSIONS

In January 2012 the Ministry of Interior published a wanted list of twenty-three Shia "rioters". The Ministry urged the twenty-three to hand themselves in and promised rewards for information on their whereabouts, starting an actual manhunt in the Eastern Province.[71] A group of pro-government interlocutors in Qatif who had been given ample coverage in Saudi media since the start of the protests in 2011, including the current Shia judge Muhammad al-Jirani, asked the wanted men to surrender.[72] While some did,[73] others remained in hiding and were hunted by the security forces. Another young Shia, twenty-two-year-old 'Issam Muhammad Abu 'Abdallah, was shot in Awwamiyya by security forces on the night of 12 January 2012, leading to large protests during his funeral.[74] A few days later, a police patrol came under fire in Qatif. On 22 January, there were massive protests in Qatif for the martyrs and a day later police raided a house in Qatif where nine people allegedly involved in shooting at police on 14 and 18 January were hiding and arrested them all.[75] On Thursday, 9 February, a celebration of the birthday of the Prophet Muhammad in Qatif turned into a demonstration calling for political reform and the release of prisoners. At the protest, Munir al-Maydani was shot and died of his wounds. Several others were also injured and further protests flared up outside al-Maydani's home.[76] A day later, another protester, Zuhayr Al Sa'id, was killed.[77] The funeral turned into huge demonstrations on 13 February, both in Qatif and in Awwamiyya.[78]

This time even Hasan al-Saffar spoke out. He had previously urged protesters to remain at home, but now criticised the security forces for

[71] "Arrest Warrants Issued for 23 Qatif Rioters," *Arab News*, 2 January 2012; Toby Matthiesen, "Saudi Arabia: the Middle East's Most Under-Reported Conflict," *The Guardian*, 23 January 2012.

[72] "Al-hurub la yakhdim maslahat al-matlubiyyin" (Flight Does Not Help the Interest of the Wanted), *al-Sharq*, 3 January 2012.

[73] Ministry of Interior, *Additional Statement about the 23-List*, 4 January 2012, www.moi.gov.sa.

[74] "Shia Protester 'Shot Dead' in Saudi Arabia," BBC, 13 January 2012.

[75] "Nine Held in Qatif as Police Raid Hide-Out," *Arab News*, 24 January 2012.

[76] "Police Kill Protester in Eastern Saudi Arabia-Activists," Reuters, 10 February 2012.

[77] "Activists Report Death of Second Protester in Saudi Arabia," *New York Times*, 10 February 2012.

[78] "Intilaq ziffat al-shahid Munir al-Maydani – al-Qatif 13 February 2012" (Unleashing of the Funeral Procession of the Martyr Munir al-Maydani), www.youtube.com/watch?v=6hqMhdGe5kY.

killing young Shia.[79] The response was swift: The Ministry of Interior attacked him harshly in a statement that denounced the protests in Qatif as 'new terrorism', which would be met 'with an iron fist'.[80] The intention was to intimidate him so that he would refrain from making similar remarks in the future. Smaller protests continued until late April. But the arrest campaign and the lack of more support by senior clerics ensured that protests eventually stopped.[81]

The Eastern Province was relatively calm throughout the spring until the 8 July arrest of Nimr al-Nimr, during which he was shot in the leg. Immediately, new protests demanded his release (see Picture 7.2). Al-Nimr had become a symbol of the protest movement and emotions ran high.[82] At a protest in Qatif, two demonstrators were shot, Akbar al-Shakhuri, from Awwamiyya and Muhammad al-Filfil from Shuwaykha.[83] As a result of this escalation, some young activists started to adopt more violent tactics, including throwing Molotov cocktails at government buildings[84] and at police patrols and the nightly burning of tires on busy roads. On 13 July security forces shot dead the eighteen-year-old ʿAbdallah al-Awjami.[85] The Ministry of Interior claimed he had hurled a fire-bomb at the police station in Awwamiyya and was then shot.[86]

Protests demanding al-Nimr's release continued, but pro-government Shia as well as Salafi clerics such as Muhammad al-ʿUrayfi and Nasir al-ʿUmar welcomed his arrest.[87] The situation remained extremely tense, and on 3 August, a Saudi soldier, Hussayn Zabani, and another young Shia, Hussayn al-Qallaf, were shot dead, allegedly in an exchange of fire.[88] Thousands again took to the streets for al-Qallaf's funeral, while the

[79] "Al-shaykh al-Saffar yastankir istikhdam al-quwwa ithra maqtal mutazahir fi al-Qatif" (Shaykh al-Saffar Condemns the Use of Force after the Killing of a Protester in Qatif), *Rasid*, 11 February 2012.

[80] "Masdar amni: khutbat ahad mashaʾikh al-Qatif musayyisa wa-tahtawi ʿala mughalatat ʿidda" (Security Source: A Speech of a Shaykh from Qatif Is Politicised and Contains Several Fallacies), *al-Riyyad*, 20 February 2012.

[81] For details see Amnesty International, *Saudi Arabia: Dissident Voices Stifled in the Eastern Province*, 28 May 2012.

[82] Toby Matthiesen, "Sable Rattling in the Gulf," *Foreign Policy*, 10 July 2012.

[83] "Two Die during Saudi Arabia Protest at Shia Cleric Arrest," BBC, 9 July 2012.

[84] The court in Qatif was attacked on 15 July 2012. "Saudi Court Hit by Petrol Bombs in Shiite-Populated East," AFP, 15 July 2012.

[85] "Saudi Security Forces Hurt by Gunmen in Oil-Rich Province," *Bloomberg*, 16 July 2012.

[86] "Saudi Protester Shot Dead," *al-Akhbar English*, 14 July 2012.

[87] "National Unity Is Red Line, Say Residents of Al-Qatif," *Saudi Gazette*, 11 July 2012.

[88] "Saudi Arabia: Soldier Shot Dead in Eastern Province," BBC, 4 August 2012. In mid-September Hussayn al-Muslim, a man suspected by the Ministry of Interior of killing

PICTURE 7.2. Protests in Qatif after the arrest of Nimr al-Nimr, 8 July 2012. Source: Anonymous Photographer.

circumstances of his death remain unclear.[89] On 19 August, seven prominent Shia clerics from all the major political strands, many of whom had signed the two earlier petitions calling for a stop of protests, issued yet another statement in order to placate tensions. The statement condemned any use of violence and affirmed the unquestionable loyalty of the Shia to Saudi Arabia.[90] It endorsed a call made the previous week by King Abdullah at the Organisation of Islamic Cooperation meeting in Mecca, to establish a Riyadh-based center for dialogue among Islamic schools of thought.[91] The statement was a way for *shirazi* leaders to approach the

the soldier, was arrested in Qatif. However, local activists claimed that the soldier died in an accidental shooting between security forces. "Saudi Says Arrests Man over Killing of Policeman in Shi'ite Area," *Reuters*, 16 September 2012.

[89] "Qatif's Eleventh Martyr: Hussain Al-Qallaf," *Qatif Observer*, 8 August 2012, http://qatifobserver.blogspot.co.uk.

[90] It was signed by 'Abdallah al-Khunayzi, 'Ali al-Sayyid Nasir, Hasan al-Saffar, 'Abd al-Karim al-Hubayl, 'Ali al-Muhsin, Yusuf al-Mahdi, and Ja'far al-Ribh. "'Ulama' al-Qatif yada'un li-wahdat al-mujtama' wa-yastankirun al-'unf wa-yu'ayyidun da'wat al-khadim al-haramayn li-insha' markaz li-l-hiwar bayn al-madhahib al-islamiyya" (Clerics of Qatif Call for the Unity of Society, Denounce Violence and Support a Call by the Guardian of the Two Holy Places for the Establishment of a Center for Dialogue between Islamic Confessions), *Qatif News*, 19 August 2012.

[91] "Dialogue Center to Help Ummah Narrow Its Gaps: Intellectuals and Scholars Applaud King's Initiative," *Saudi Gazette*, 16 August 2012.

government, after they had been sidelined in negotiations with the government for the previous months.[92]

The security forces, meanwhile, continued to hunt those on the list of twenty-three wanted for their role in the protests and frequently raided Shia towns such as Awwamiyya looking for suspects. Several on the list were severely injured or killed during these raids. Hussayn al-Rabi', for example, was shot and injured in Awwamiyya before he was arrested on 2 September 2012.[93] On 10 September, a Bangladeshi worker was shot in Awwamiyya, according to Shia activists while police were searching for one of the twenty-three.[94] On 26 September 2012, Saudi security forces went to arrest one of the twenty-three, Khalid al-Labad, and in the operation killed three locals, including al-Labad.[95] Funerals turned into large demonstrations, and on 27 December 2012, the eighteen-year-old Ahmad Al Matar was shot dead by the security forces.[96]

Protests continued sporadically on Thursdays and Fridays, with numbers usually in the hundreds and protests centered on Qatif and Awwamiyya. On 22 June 2013, security forces killed Ahmad al-Ribh, who had been one of the leaders of the protest movement in Awwamiyya and was on the list of twenty-three. In early September, another young Shia was shot dead in Awwamiyya and several on the list of twenty-three turned themselves in.[97] In February 2014, security forces stormed the house of the brother of one of the twenty-three. The wanted man was not there but two other young Shia and two policemen were killed in an exchange of fire.[98] Particularly in Awwamiyya, attacks on security forces became more frequent.[99] In response to this escalation of violence, ten

[92] Interview with Saudi Shia, London, 2013.

[93] "Saudi Authorities Arrest Qatif Activist," *al-Akhbar English*, 3 September 2012. Saudi media claim several policemen were injured during his arrest. "Prince Jelawi Visits Injured Policemen," *Arab News*, 5 September 2012.

[94] "Bangladeshi Man Shot Dead in Shi'ite Area of Saudi Arabia," Reuters, 11 September 2012.

[95] "Two Killed as Saudi Security Forces Try to Arrest Shi'ite Man," Reuters, 27 September 2012; "Shiite Dies of Wounds after Saudi Police Raid: Family," AFP, 29 September 2012.

[96] "Man Shot Dead as Police Clash with Shi'ites in Saudi Arabia," Reuters, 28 December 2012.

[97] "Saudi Police Deny Report of Young Man Killed in Security Raid," Reuters, 6 September 2013.

[98] One of them, Hussayn al-Faraj, was a photojournalist, who had covered protests in Awwamiyya. The other was 'Ali al-Faraj, who was the son of the owner of the house. "Call for Independent Probe into Journalist's Death in Police Raid," *Reporters without Borders*, 27 February 2014.

[99] "Saudi Police Hurt by Gunfire in Shi'ite Village," Reuters, 25 February 2014.

senior Shia clerics from all different political groups issued a statement denouncing the use of weapons against security forces.[100]

More than twenty Saudi Shia had been killed by the security forces by 2014, and several policemen had died as well. The government moved ahead with trials against those arrested for political subversion, both Sunni and Shia. In March 2013, the public prosecutor demanded the death penalty for the cleric Nimr al-Nimr.[101] In early 2014, seven men were convicted to between six and twenty years in prison for taking part in the Qatif protests.[102] Several others were also jailed for participation in protests and for online activism.[103] Several young Shia have even received the death sentence for allegedly attacking police.[104] The harsh crackdown meant that protests in the Eastern Province became more sporadic, although after each killing funeral processions turned into anti-government rallies.

CONCLUSION

Given a long history of political mobilisation in the Eastern Province, and failed promises of political and religious reform in the kingdom, it was no surprise that mainly young Saudi Shia found hope in the promises of the Arab uprisings. Linking the general demands of the Arab uprisings with the fate of their co-religionists in Bahrain, and with the disenfranchisement they feel as Shia in Saudi Arabia, activists found effective frames of reference for many. Demanding the release of prisoners emerged as a main theme for protests. When the first youth were shot dead, thousands mourned them in the streets of Qatif. Funeral processions were key in spreading protests beyond a narrow base of political activists and mobilising entire villages and urban quarters.

The protest movement in the Eastern Province did not spill over to the rest of the country. In December 2011 a group of mainly Sunni liberals signed a statement condemning the security crackdown in Qatif. In return they were criticised heavily in Saudi media and some received a travel ban.[105] The state succeeded in preventing Sunnis from solidarising

---

[100] "Shiite Saudi Clerics Warn against Violence: Statement," AFP, 9 March 2014.

[101] "Saudi: Sheikh Nimr's Crucified Fate," *al-Akhbar English*, 30 March 2013.

[102] "Saudi Arabia Jails Seven Men for up to 20 Years for Demonstrating," Reuters, 19 February 2014.

[103] "Saudi Protester Jailed for 10 Years over Twitter Messages," Reuters, 10 March 2014.

[104] "Saudi Court Sentences Shi'ite to Death for Sedition", Reuters, 28 May 2014.

[105] "Saudi Arabia's Press: The New McCarthyism," *al-Akhbar English*, 27 December 27, 2011.

themselves with the protests by denouncing the Shia as an Iranian fifth column.[106]

The protests also shared similarities with the intifada. In 1979, as in 2011, a young generation was dissatisfied with the status quo and disillusioned with its political leadership. International events – then the Iranian Revolution, now the Arab uprisings – galvanised public opinion and gave young activists hope that their grievances could be addressed. Unlike in 1979, activists have at their disposal the Internet, social media and smart phones, which are useful for organising protests but at the same time are easy for the state to monitor. The *shirazi* interlocutors found themselves in a similar position to that of the notables in 1979. They tried to work within the system but could not deliver the changes they had hoped for; a basic feeling of disenchantment amongst Saudi Shia persisted. The politics of Shia notables have entered a new phase since 2011 but their basic limitations remain. The state tried to work with the Shia judges and notables to quell protests. Apart from current and former Shia judges, Muhammad Rida Nasrallah, a journalist and member of the Majlis al-Shura, has become the most prominent pro-government Shia. Trusted by the ruling family, he spearheaded efforts to stop the protest movement.[107] This has led to a slight marginalisation of the *shirazi* movement as interlocutors with the state.

In January 2013, King Abdullah replaced Muhammad bin Fahd as governor of the Eastern Province with Saʿud bin Nayef, giving residents of the Eastern Province – both Sunni and Shia – some hope of a fresh start.[108] Nevertheless, the root causes of the protests in the Eastern Province were not addressed, and the state reacted with repression and an increased sectarian rhetoric in the country and beyond. Such entrenchment is key to the political logic of the Saudi state, which seeks to make Sunnis fear the Shia protesters in order to prevent a common Sunni and Shia opposition front. While the increased sectarianism in the country worked as a legitimising tool for the Saudi ruling family, it deepened mistrust between Sunni and Shia, and between the Shia and the state. And it reversed King Abdullah's policy of tentatively reaching out to all sections of Saudi society through a marginal recognition of religious difference.

---

[106] Madawi al-Rasheed, "Sectarianism as Counter-Revolution: Saudi Responses to the Arab Spring," *Studies in Ethnicity and Nationalism* 11, no. 3, (December 2011), 513–26.

[107] Interviews with Saudi Shia, 2011–13.

[108] Toby Matthiesen, "Saudi Royal Family Politics and the Arab Spring," *Foreign Policy*, 14 January 2013.

Conclusion

The Politics of Sectarianism

The Other Saudis has shown that the study of communal politics and
sectarianism needs to take a historical approach that gives people involved
in communal politics agency. The prominence of sectarian identities in
the Middle East is related to the nature of modern state building in the
region, which often relied on cultural groups as key constituencies – be
they ethnic, tribal or religious – and which is characterised by a strong
centralisation of power. In addition, many of these states, and particularly
those in the Gulf, did not have a strong sense of unity. They did not try to
foster such a sense of belonging amongst their citizens, at least not in earnest, until the late twentieth century. This is not to say that nationalism is
a particularly desirable phenomenon, or that it needs to be at odds with
strong sectarian identities.[1] But the absence of a strong inclusive nationalism, and in the Saudi case the emphasis on a religious nationalism that
per se excludes the Shia, helps to explain the prominence of other collective identities.[2] Until the mid-twentieth century, it would be difficult to
speak of Saudi national identities, and those who were advocating Arab
nationalism, including some of the leftist activists in the Eastern Province,
were punished severely. While the leftists sought to overcome sectarian
and religious identities, their defeat facilitated the emergence of Islamism.
At the periphery of the country and as the preferred Other of Saudi religious nationalism, Shia then sought refuge in their sectarian identities.

---

[1] See, for example, Max Weiss, "The Historiography of Sectarianism in Lebanon," *History
Compass* 7, no. 1 (2009), 141–54, 148f.
[2] For the notion of Saudi religious nationalism see al-Rasheed, *A Most Masculine State.*

The alliance of local elites with a state that is fundamentally suspicious of Shia Muslims set the stage for competition amongst local elites and political groups, a condition that played into the hands of those who divide and rule. Essentially, Shia elites have tried for a century to deliver to their constituencies what the state never wanted to give them. And the state has been quite skilful at fostering infighting amongst various political strands – notables, leftists, Islamists. The development of strong Islamist movements – both Shia and Sunni – since the 1970s made sectarianism more salient. If Islam becomes the main reference point for political activism, then the question of which sect one belongs to inevitably becomes more salient. While Islamist movements often have particular local agendas, they are also concerned with the affairs of the Islamic *umma* as a whole. And so Sunni and Shia Islamisms are related to the international context, and that relation is key for the escalation of communal conflict.

Without the rise of transnational Islamist movements and the success of the Iranian Revolution in 1979 Saudi Shia politics would have played out differently (but that does not mean that sectarian discrimination against them would have stopped). While the Iranian Revolution gave hope to Gulf Shia and spurred them to become more politically active, it soured relations between Gulf Shia and their Sunni co-nationals for a generation. The history of Iranian assistance to Gulf Shia opposition groups continues to be used by Gulf regimes to discredit domestic political claims by Shia groups. But the experiences of secular opposition groups in the mid-twentieth century showed that Iran was not the only country providing assistance to Saudi opposition activists. The politics of the Eastern Province and the Saudi Shia were at times related to the foreign policies of Iraq, Syria, South Yemen, Egypt, Kuwait, the United Kingdom and the United States, amongst others. The realities of Middle Eastern exile and opposition politics have at times pushed Shia opposition activists into temporary alliances with external actors, even though the goals of these activists were largely local.

Still, it is difficult to detach the post-1979 history of the Gulf Shia from Saudi-Iranian relations, especially as long as both countries continue to portray themselves as leaders of the Islamic world and of Sunni and Shia, respectively. After 2011 Saudi-Iranian relations reached yet another low point, and the escalating rhetoric and the extent of Saudi efforts to block democratisation across the Gulf and prevent the empowerment of Shia in Bahrain set very clear limits to the improvement of the situation of Saudi Shia. Sectarian relations in Saudi Arabia worsened after the riots in

Medina in 2009, the war against the Yemeni Houthi rebels in 2009/2010 and the Saudi intervention in Bahrain. Increasingly, Saudi Arabia used sectarianism as a tool for regime survival and power projection abroad.[3]

The political history of Shia in Saudi Arabia allows us to draw a number of conclusions about the factors that lead to the political importance of sectarian identities. They include a somewhat shared history, rituals where this history and other identity markers are enacted, elites that strengthen communal boundaries, institutions such as the Shia court and public spaces such as mosques, *hussainiyyat* and *diwaniyyat*, as well as someone who recognises (or despises) a community as such. Because Shia were left out of state-sponsored grand narratives, local memories and histories became key features of how Shia in Saudi Arabia define themselves and against whom and against what this definition occurs. The articulation of a certain personal identity and its transformation into a collective identity, that is, the feeling of being part of a larger group, is crucial. Rituals and daily practices are key in this respect, and Shia religious rituals are powerful enactors of religious identities. These rituals largely had to be practised in private throughout the twentieth century but since the 1990s have been allowed more openly.

Activists who try to foster Shia identities, I call them identity entrepreneurs, have been key in transforming relatively autonomous village- and quarter-based identities. The legacy of the Shia Islamist movements then is that something like a Saudi Shia collective identity exists in the first place. These identity entrepreneurs sought to create a unified historical narrative and through civil society organisations, publishing houses, online journals, discussion forums, sport clubs, private schools and public festivities tried to strengthen the boundaries of the community. But they clashed with the traditional Shia elites, the notable families, leading to factionalism amongst the Shia.

Structural resources have also been key for community building amongst Saudi Shia. In Saudi Arabia, Shia courts have historically been limited to legislating some aspects of personal status law. But their very weakness and the idea that they should have more authority, have been persistent topics in Shia notables' petitions since the mid-twentieth century. As such, the issue of Shia courts has been a constant reminder of the inferior status of Saudi Shia. The courts have, however, also helped to strengthen a notable class of Shia clerics and their families who served as intermediaries with the state. Another key structural resource largely

---

[3] Matthiesen, *Sectarian Gulf.*

beyond state interference is the network of mosques and *hussainiyyat* in the Eastern Province. Despite the fact that most *hussainiyyat* are illegal, they constituted the backbone of many political movements in the Eastern Province.

State policies have strengthened Shia communal boundaries. While the Ottomans regarded Shia subjects with suspicion, they also respected and used religious and sectarian differences, especially so at the frontiers of their empire. Since 1913, however, the Shia in the Eastern Province have been framed as Saudi Arabia's internal Other, both by the state and by Wahhabi clerics. According to the strict Wahhabi interpretation of Islam that dominates parts of the public and political spheres in Saudi Arabia they are heretics. A long history of sectarian discrimination has reinforced religious identities amongst Shia and has given rise to grievances that both leftists and Islamists have tried to exploit. While leftists occasionally complained about discrimination against Shia, Shia Islamists specifically sought to address sectarian discrimination. The rise of Shia Islamism is also related to the adoption of an Islamic discourse by the state and the rise of political Islam at a regional level.

State policies can have unintended consequences. After the limited political reforms and the opening up of the media in the 1990s, which led to the strengthening of the public sphere, previously marginalised groups were better able to articulate their demands on a national level. This, in turn, strengthened their sense of entitlement to the benefits of citizenship in a resource-rich country. The advent of new technologies such as the Internet and smart phones has accelerated this process and allowed for an unprecedented level of contact amongst Saudis, and the voicing of hitherto semi-secret narratives and practices online. But increasing repression, and the Saudi state's sectarian response to the Arab uprisings, may lead to a strengthening of pan-Shia bonds within Saudi Arabia, as well as with Shia in Bahrain, Kuwait and elsewhere.[4]

The ways in which a state treats cultural and religious difference is a touchstone of socio-political and religious reform. The political situation of Shia Muslims in Saudi Arabia ameliorated after 1993, when King Fahd reached an agreement with Saudi Shia opposition groups, who returned

---

[4] In April 2011, for example, a Shia dialogue forum held in Qatif called for a "Higher Shia Council" that would include Shia figures from Medina, Jeddah, Dammam, Khobar as well as Qatif and al-Ahsa. "Bi-l-suwwar: al-hiwar al-shi'i yu'akkid 'ala ahammiyyat ta'sis majlis a'la wa-wahdat al-watan" (With Pictures: The Shia Dialogue Affirms the Importance of Founding a Higher Shia Council and of National Unity), *Rasid*, 24 April 2011.

from exile to focus on Shia identity politics. Shia Muslims were probably the main beneficiaries of reforms introduced by Crown Prince Abdullah after 9/11 and the U.S.-led invasion of Iraq in 2003: they won in municipal elections, participated in the National Dialogue, were given space in national media and were appointed to newly created representative institutions.

But these changes did not address the inferior political, social and judicial status of Shia Muslims in Saudi Arabia; nor did they alter the political system of the country. They also did not lead to an acceptance of Shia Islam as a valid branch of Islamic law. While non-Wahhabi and non-Hanbali Sunni schools of Islam have gradually become more accepted by the official Saudi religious establishment, Shia Islam has not. The state has since 1913 reluctantly accepted the presence of Shia judges but has sought to keep their authority limited to matters of personal status law.

Moreover, Abdullah's marginal recognition of religious difference in the Kingdom was gradually reversed after 2005. The civil war in Iraq, the rise of hardliners in Iran combined with a waning of U.S. pressure for internal reform meant that the slow progress on the Saudi Shia dossier was all but halted. And some of the improvements that occurred under Abdullah's earlier reign were reversed as a response to the Shia protests since 2011. In the Eastern Province the history of political protest, organisational resources, feelings of oppression and discrimination, unfulfilled promises of integration, and solidarity with the protesters in Bahrain led to mass demonstrations from 2011 onwards. The protests in the Eastern Province and the state's response increased sectarianism in the country and beyond. While Shia intellectuals tried to reaffirm their allegiance to a 'Saudi nation', and called for inclusive citizenship and political reforms, Saudi ruling family members, Wahhabi clerics and pro-government intellectuals once again denounced *the Other Saudis* and the alleged international dimension of Shia political activism. As long as the state legitimises itself through a religious nationalism based on the Wahhabiyya the situation of Shia Muslims in Saudi Arabia will remain precarious.

Bibliography

Primary Sources

Personal Archives

Private archive of letters and petitions by Shia notables, Saudi Arabia. Identity of the owner in possession of the author.

Private archive of Hamza al-Hasan, including his memoirs surrounding the 1993 negotiations and some internal communications of the Reformist Movement in Saudi (*al-haraka al-islahiyya fi al-suʿudiyya*), London, UK.

Private archive of Fuʾad Ibrahim, London, UK.

Private archive of ʿAli al-Ahmad on the activities of the *shiraziyyun* in the U.S., Washington, D.C.

Archive on the history of left-wing movements in the Gulf, Bahrain. Identity of the owner in possession of the author.

William E. Mulligan Papers, Lauinger Library, Special Collections, Georgetown University, Washington, D.C.

Nachlass Prof. Dr. Gerhard Höpp, Zentrum Moderner Orient, Berlin, Germany.

Government Sources

A. Unpublished Government Sources

1. Great Britain

India Office Records (IOR), British Library, London
R/15/1 *Bushire Political Residency*
R/15/2 *Bahrain Political Agency*
R/15/5 *Kuwait Political Agency*
L/PS/11 Political and Secret Annual Files

2. United States of America

Diplomatic Correspondence
National Archives at College Park, Maryland
  RG 59 General Records of the Department of State, Central Foreign Policy
    Files
  786A.oo Department of State, Decimal Files, 1950–1963
American Consulate Dhahran, Saudi Arabia, correspondence, 1979[1]
U.S. Diplomatic Cables released by Wikileaks[2]
  Embassy Riyadh, selected cables 1985–2010
  Consulate Dhahran, selected cables 2009–10

B. Published and Edited Government Sources

1. Great Britain

Burdett, Anita L. P., ed., *Saudi Arabia: Secret Intelligence Records 1926–1939*, 8
    vols. (Slough: Archive Editions, 2003).
  Records of Saudi Arabia, 1961–1965, 6 vols. (Slough: Archive Editions,
    1997).
  Records of Saudi Arabia 1966–1971, 6 vols. (Slough: Archive Editions, 2004).
Jarman, Robert L., ed., *Political Diaries of the Arab World: Saudi Arabia 1919–
    1965*, 6 vols. (Slough: Archive Editions, 1998).
Lorimer, John Gordon, *Gazetteer of the Persian Gulf, 'Oman, and Central Arabia*,
    2 vols. (Calcutta: Superintendent Government Printing, 1908–15).
Saldanha, Jerome Anthony, and C. H. Gabriel, *The Persian Gulf Précis*, 8 vols.
    (Gerrards Cross: Archive Editions, 1986).
Tuson, Penelope, and Anita Burdett, eds., *Records of Saudi Arabia: Primary
    Documents 1902–1960*, 10 vols. (Slough: Archive Editions, 1992).

2. United States of America

al-Rashid, Ibrahim, ed., *Saudi Arabia Enters the Modern World: Secret U.S.
    Documents on the Emergence of the Kingdom of Saudi Arabia as a World
    Power 1936–1949*, 2 vols. (Salisbury, NC: Documentary, 1980).
Evans, K. E., ed., *U.S. Records on Saudi Affairs 1945–1959*, 8 vols. (Slough:
    Archive Editions, 1997).

Court Records

United States District Court Eastern District of Virginia Alexandria Division,
    Indictment against Saudi Hizbullah Members / Khobar Bombings (June
    2001).

---

[1] These 1979 American diplomatic cables, which were originally classified 'secret', have
been obtained under the Freedom of Information Act and made available online, www.
randomhouse.com/doubleday/siegeofmecca/declassifiedDocuments.php.
[2] Available on the Internet, http://wikileaks.ch/cablegate.html.

Journals and News Media (and years used)

Opposition Journals

al-Jazira al-Jadida, 1972–4
Sawt al-Tali'a, 1973–80
al-Masira, 1980
Sawt al-'Ummal, 1989
al-Ish'a', 1980[3]
al-Thawra al-Islamiyya, 1980–8
al-Jazira al-'Arabiyya, 1991–3
Arabia Monitor, 1992
Risalat al-Haramayn, 1989–93
al-Haramayn, 1996
al-Rasid al-Sahafi, 2007–11
Shu'un Su'udiyya, 2003–5
al-Hijaz, 2002–10

Cultural Journals

Sawt al-Bahrayn, 1950–4[4]
al-Ish'a', 1955–7[5]
Aramco World, 1960–2000[6]
al-Waha, 1995 to 2011
al-Mawsim, 1989–99
al-Sahil, 2007–10
Al-Thulatha Cultural Forum Electronic Newsletter, 2009–10

Religious Journals

al-Kalima, 1994–2008
al-Faqaha, 2007–8
Nusus Mu'asira, 2010

News Media

AFP
Al-Ahram Weekly
al-Akhbar English

---

[3] This small magazine was published by the Association of Saudi Students in the Soviet Union (Rabitat al-Talaba al-Su'udiyyin fi al-Ittihad al-Sufiti).

[4] *Sawt al-Bahrayn: majalla adabiyya ijtima'iyya* (The Voice of Bahrain: A Social and Literary Magazine), 4 vols. (Muharraq: Bayt 'Abdallah al-Zayid li-Turath al-Bahrayn al-Sahafi/Markaz al-Shaykh Ibrahim bin Muhammad Al Khalifa li-l-Turath wa-l-Buhuth, 2003).

[5] *Al-ish'a': majalla shahriyya adabiyya ijtima'iyya* (The Shining Light: A Social and Literary Monthly Magazine) (Riyadh: Dar al-Mufradat li-l-Nashr wa-l-Tawzi', 2010).

[6] *Saudi ARAMCO World,* 1950–2007, PDF Archive, DVD (2008).

Arab News
BBC
Bloomberg
The Daily Star
The Guardian
Gulf News
The Independent
Le Monde Diplomatique
Neue Zürcher Zeitung
The New York Times
al-Quds al-ʿArabi
Reuters
al-Riyyad
Saudi Gazette
al-Sharq
al-Sharq al-Awsat
Time Magazine
ʿUkaz
The Washington Post
al-Yawm

News Digests

Foreign Broadcast Information Service (*FBIS*)
Middle East Contemporary Survey (*MECS*)

Websites

www.ahsaber.org
www.alarabiya.net
www.aujamcs.org
www.awamia.net
www.cdhrap.net
www.citc.gov.sa
www.al-daawa.org
www.dmc.gov.sa
www.easternemara.gov.sa
www.elaph.com
www.facebook.com/rev.east
www.alfaqaha.net
www.esharh.net
www.gulfinstitute.org
http://hasamc.gov.sa
http://alhawzaonline.com
www.alhramain.com
www.iao-iraq.org
www.jadaliyya.com

www.jafariyanews.com
www.aljazeera.net
www.kacnd.org
http://kalema.net
www.alkatib.net
http://middle-east-online.com
www.almodarresi.info
www.moltaqaa.com
www.almoneer.org
www.amontazeri.com
http://nabaa.tv
http://nshr.org.sa
www.nosos.net
www.okhdood.com
www.qateef.org
www.qatifnews.com
www.qatifmb.org
www.rasid.com
www.sanabes.com
www.sanabis.org.sa
www.saudiaffairs.net
www.saudishia.com
www.saihatss.org
www.shura.gov.sa
www.spa.gov.sa
www.taroot.org.sa
www.thulatha.com
www.alwahamag.com
www.alwelayah.net
www.wikileaks.org

Videos

"al-Shaykh al-Nimr: imma karamatuna aw al-infisal ya Al Suʿud – al-Baqiʿ"
(Shaykh al-Nimr: Either our Dignity or the Secession oh Al Saud – al-Baqia),
available on the Internet, www.youtube.com/watch?v=vSO_2LphRn4&feat
ure=related, minute nine.

Interviews[7]

Damascus, August 2008

Interviews with Muhammad Mahfuz.
Interview with Habib Al Jumayʿ.

---

[7] Identities of interviewees in possession of the author.

Interview with a former member of the clerical wing of MVM.
Interview with a former leading MVM member.
Interview with a former leading OIRAP member.
Interviews with former OIRAP members.
Interview with a former member of the Pan-Shia Association in Saudi Arabia.
Interview with a Syrian intellectual.

Beirut, August 2008

Interview with Hamid al-Khaffaf, spokesman for ʿAli al-Sistani and head of his
    Beirut office.
Interview with a former member of Hizbullah al-Hijaz.
Interview with a Saudi Shia cleric.

Eastern Province, Saudi Arabia, November 2008

Interview with Hasan al-Saffar.
Interview with ʿIsa al-Mizaʿil.
Interview with Tawfiq al-Sayf.
Interview with Fawzi al-Sayf.
Interview with Zaki ʿAli al-Salih.
Interview with Muhammad Saʿid al-Shaykh ʿAli al-Khunayzi.
Interview with Sadiq al-Jubran.
Interview with Salman al-Hijji.
Interview with Muhammad al-ʿUbaydan.
Interview with a director of the *hawza ʿilmiyya* in Qatif.
Interview with a former member of *tajammuʿ ʿulamaʾ al-Hijaz*.
Interview with an organiser of the *dukhala* festival.
Interview with an activist of the Tarut charitable society.
Interviews with members of sport clubs in the Eastern Province.
Interview with a notable from Qatif.
Interview with former senior ARAMCO official.
Interview with campaigners in the municipal elections, Qatif.
Interview with campaigners in the municipal elections, al-Ahsa.
Interview with a candidate in the municipal elections.
Interview with *al-daʿwa* activist.
Interview with editor of *al-Faqaha*.
Interview with editor of *al-Waha*.
Interview with a former MVM member, who was in India.
Interview with OIRAP female activists.
Interviews with Saudi Shia clerics.

Riyadh, October and November 2008

Interview with ʿAbd al-Jalil al-Sayf.
Interview with Ihsan Bu Hulayqa.
Interview with Hatun al-Fassi.
Interview with a former member of the Communist Party in Saudi.

Interviews with Saudi officials.
Interviews with participants in the National Dialogue.
Interviews with members of Majlis al-Shura.
Interview with Shia from Medina.

Jeddah, November 2008

Interview with Muhammad Sa'id Tayyib.
Interviews with participants in the National Dialogue.

Riyadh and al-Ahsa, Eastern Province, December 2011

Interview with a Shia activist.
Interview with a former member of the Communist Party in Saudi.

Kuwait, February/March 2012

Interview with Ahmad al-Shirazi.
Interview with Mirza Kamal al-Din al-Sulaymi al-Ha'iri al-Ihqaqi.
Interview with Tawfiq al-Bu 'Ali.
Interview with Shaykhis from al-Ahsa.
Interviews with *shirazi* activists.

Cairo, 2013

Interview with a Sufi leader from the Hijaz, Cairo, 2013.

Beirut, 2013

Interview with a former member of the Saudi Baath party, Beirut, 2013.

London, UK

Interviews with Hamza al-Hasan, April 2008, July 2008, November 2009, March
    2010, 2013.
Interview with Ahmad al-Katib (pseudonym), September 2008.
Interview with a Saudi Shia cleric, September 2008.
Interview with Ghanim Jawad, September 2008.
Interview with a member of the Abu Khamsin family, September 2008.
Interview with Fu'ad Ibrahim, January 2009, March 2010.
Interview with a member of the al-Khunayzi family, July 2009.
Interview with a member of the al-Khunayzi family, June 2010.
Interview with 'Abd al-Nabi al-'Akri, July 2010.
Interview with Ja'far al-Shayib, December 2010.
Interview with a Bahraini activist involved in the 1981 coup attempt,
    London, 2010.
Interview with Saudi Shia, 2013.

United States of America

Interview with ʿAli al-Ahmad, Washington, D.C., November 2009.
Interview with a senior member of the Saudi royal family, November 2009.
Interview with ʿAli al-Yami, Washington, D.C., October 2013.

Online Correspondence

Email correspondence with Kamil al-Khatti al-Khunayzi, June 2009.
Email correspondence with a member of the al-Khunayzi family, July 2009.
Email correspondence with Suʿud al-Sarhan, July 2009.
Email correspondence with Nawaf Obaid, May 2010.
Email correspondence with Jaʿfar al-Shayib, February 2012.
Email correspondence with Tawfiq al-Sayf, June 2012.
Email correspondence with Phebe Marr, April 2014.

Published Interviews

Interview with Muhammad Taqi al-Mudarrisi on the TV show *Fulan al-Fulani* on
   al-Sharqiyya TV, Iraq, 2005, available on the Internet, http://bahrainonline.
   org/showthread.php?t=122908.
Interview with a representative of *hizb al-ʿamal al-ishtiraki al-ʿarabi fi al-jazira
   al-ʿarabiyya* in February 1984, printed in *MERIP Reports* 130 (February
   1985), 15–19.

Unpublished PhD Dissertations

Aba-Namay, Rashed, *The Constitution of Saudi Arabia: Evolution, Reform and
   Future Prospects* (PhD, University of Wales-Aberystwyth, 1992).
al-Awaji, Ibrahim Mohamed, *Bureaucracy and Society in Saudi Arabia* (PhD,
   University of Virginia, 1971).
Al-Elawy, Ibrahim S. Al-Abdullah, *The Influence of Oil upon Settlement in
   Al-Hasa Oasis, Saudi Arabia* (PhD, University of Durham, 1976).
al-Hasan, Hamza, *The Role of Religion in Building National Identity: Case
   Study: Saudi Arabia* (PhD, University of Westminster, 2006).
al-Nuaim, Mishary Abdalrahman, *State Building in a Non-Capitalist Social
   Formation: The Dialectics of Two Modes of Production and the Role of the
   Merchant Class, Saudi Arabia 1902–1932* (PhD University of California, 1987).
al-Saud, Faisal Bin Mishal, *Political Development in the Kingdom of Saudi Arabia:
   An Assessment of the Majlis Ash-Shura* (PhD, University of Durham, 2000).
al-Saud, Saʿad, *The Evolution of Local Government in the Kingdom of Saudi
   Arabia with Special Reference to the 1992 Reforms* (PhD, University of
   Reading, 2005).
Al-Shihri, Faez Saad, *Sustainable Development and Strategic Environmental
   Assessment (Sea) in the Planning Process: The Case of Al-Qatif Oasis and its
   Settlements* (PhD, University of Newcastle upon Tyne, 2001).

al-Shuaiby, Abdulla Mansour, *The Development of the Eastern Province with Particular Reference to Urban Settlement and Evolution in Eastern Saudi Arabia* (PhD, University of Durham, 1976).

al-Zekri, Muhammad A., *The Religious Encounter between Sufis and Salafis of East Arabia: Issue of Identity* (PhD, University of Exeter, 2004).

AlSayf, Tawfiq, *Religion and the Legitimation of the State: The Development of Political Thought in Contemporary Shi'ism (Case Study: Iran 1979–2004)* (PhD, University of Westminster, 2005).

Anderson, Gary, *Differential Urban Growth in the Eastern Province of Saudi Arabia: A Study of the Historical Interaction of Economic Development and Socio-Political Change* (PhD, Johns Hopkins University, 1984).

Babeair, Abdul-Wahab S., *Ottoman Penetration of the Eastern Region of the Arabian Peninsula, 1814–1841* (PhD, Indiana University, 1985).

Cancian, Alessandro, *La Hawza 'Ilmiyya: E la formazione dell' elite religiosa nei collegi teologici nello sciismo duodecimano: elementi dottrinali e indagine di campo* (PhD, Universita degli Studi di Siena, 2005).

Gleave, Robert, *Akhbari Shii Jurisprudence in the Writings of Yusuf B. Ahmad al-Bahrani (d.1186/1772)* (PhD, University of Manchester 1996).

Ibrahim, Fuad, *The Shiite Opposition in the Eastern Province from Revolution to Accomodation (Case Study: The Reform Movement in Saudi Arabia)* (PhD, SOAS, 2004).

Jones, Toby Craig, *The Dogma of Development: Technopolitics and the Making of Saudi Arabia 1950–1980* (PhD, Stanford University, 2006).

Keynoush, Azra Banafsheh, *The Iranian-Saudi Arabian Relationship: From Ideological Confrontation to Pragmatic Accommodation* (PhD, Tufts University, 2007).

Krimly, Rayed Khalid, *The Political Economy of Rentier States: A Case Study of Saudi Arabia in the Oil Era 1950–1990* (PhD, George Washington University, 1993).

Liu, Chang-Cheng, *Saudi-Iranian Relations, 1977–1997* (PhD, University of Durham, 2003).

MacEoin, Denis, *From Shaykhism to Babism: A Study in Charismatic Renewal in Shi'i Islam* (PhD, Cambridge University, 1979).

Matthiesen, Toby, *The Shia of Saudi Arabia: Identity Politics, Sectarianism and the Saudi State* (PhD, SOAS, 2011).

Samore, Gary Samuel, *Royal Family Politics in Saudi Arabia (1953–1982)* (PhD, Harvard University, 1983).

Solaim, Soliman A., *Constitutional and Judicial Organization in Saudi Arabia* (PhD, Johns Hopkins University, 1970).

Unpublished Master's Dissertations

Azoulay, Rivka, *Entre marchands, effendi et l'Etat: changement social et renouvellement des élites au sein de la communauté chiite koweitienne* (MA, Institute d'Etudes Politiques de Paris, 2009).

al-Jarbou, Mohammed A., *Regional and Municipal Administration in Saudi Arabia: Problems and Issues* (MSc, California State University, 1983).

Gweed, Fayhan, *Participation in Decision Making to Improve the Saudi Arabian Municipal System* (MA, Sangamon State University, 1987).

Opposition Publications and Pamphlets

Committee for the Defence of Legitimate Rights Communiqué no. 47, *Oppression and Persecution of the Shi'a*, London, 3 October 1996.

Press Release by International Committee for Human Rights in the Gulf and Arabian Peninsula, Washington, D.C., 29 July 1993.

Press Release by International Committee for Human Rights in the Gulf and Arabian Peninsula, Demonstrations in Saudi Arabia (n.d., Nashville).

Hizb al-'Amal al-Ishtiraki al-'Arabi fi al-Jazira al-'Arabiyya, *al-naft wa-l-mujtama' fi al-jazira al-'arabiyya "al-su'udiyya"* (Oil and Society in the "Saudi" Arabian Peninsula) (n.p.: al-Dar al-Lubnaniyya, 1984).

Ahdath november (muharram) 1979 fi al-su'udiyya (Events of November (Muharram) 1979 in Saudi) (n.p.: Manshurat al-Hizb al-Shuyu'i fi al-Su'udiyya, n.d.).

Ittihad al-Shabab al-Dimuqrati fi al-Su'udiyya, *watha'iq al-mu'tamar al-thani li-ittihad al-shabab al-dimuqrati fi al-su'udiyya 1986* (Documents of the Second Congress of the Union of Democratic Youth in Saudi) (n.p.: n.p, n.d.).

Munazzamat al-Thawra al-Islamiyya fi al-Jazira al-'Arabiyya, *Intifadat al-muharram fi al-mintaqa al-sharqiyya: al-halqa al-ula (watha'iq al-inti-fada)* (The Uprising of Muharram in the Eastern Province: The First Part (Documents of the Uprising) (n.p.: Munazzamat al-Thawra al-Islamiyya fi al-Jazira al-'Arabiyya 'al-Su'udiyya', 1979).

al-bayyanat al-lati sadarat khilal 'am 1400–1401A.H. (The Statements that were Published in the Year 1979/1980) (n.p.: n.d.).

Intifadat al-haram (The Uprising of the Sanctuary) (London: 1981).

kalimat al-haraka al-islamiyya fi al-jazira al-'arabiyya (The Word of the Islamic Movement in the Arabian Peninsula) (n.p.: 1986).

Munazzamat al-'Amal al-Islami fi al-'Iraq, *al-ta'sis al-sira wa-l-ahdaf* (The Foundation, the Path and the Goals), available on the Internet, www.iao-iraq.org.

rabi' al-su'udiyya wa-mukhrijat al-qama': du'at al-islah al-siyasi (The Saudi Spring and the Outcomes of Repression: A Call for Political Reform (Beirut: Dar al-Kunuz al-Adabiyya, 2004).

Arabic Reports

al-taqrir al-sanawi li-muntada al-'Awwamiyya: al-dawra al-ula 1.7.1426–30.6.1427A.H. (The Annual Report for the Awwamiyya Forum: The First Round 2005–2006) (n.p.: n.p., n.d.).

al-shi'a fi al-su'udiyya: al-waqi'a al-sa'b wa-tatalla'at al-mashru'a (The Shia in
    Saudi: Difficult Reality and Legitimate Aspirations) (n.p.: Rabitat 'Umum
    al-Shi'a fi al-Su'udiyya, 1991).
Infijar al-Khubar: dirasa tawthiqiyya mufasala li-tafjir mabnat sakan al-quwwat
    al-jawiyya al-amrikiyya fi madinat al-Khubar wa-l-ladhi waqa'a bi-tarikh
    25/6/1996 (The Khobar Bombing: A Detailed Documentary Study of the
    Explosion of the Residence Building of the American Air Forces in Khobar
    City that Took Place on 25/6/1996) (n.p.: Markaz al-Haramayn li-l-I'alam
    al-Islami, 2002), previously available on www.alhramain.com.

Secondary Sources

Reports

Amnesty International, *Saudi Arabia: Detention without Trial of Suspected
    Political Opponents* (London: 1990).
Article 19, *Silent Kingdom: Freedom of Expression in Saudi Arabia* (London:
    October 1991).
Center for Religious Freedom of Freedom House/Institute for Gulf Affairs, *Saudi
    Arabia's Curriculum of Intolerance: With Excerpts from Saudi Ministry of
    Education Textbooks for Islamic Studies* (Washington, DC, 2006).
Centre de Recherche sur les Menaces Criminelles Contemporaines, *Atlas Mondial
    de l'Activisme* (Paris, 1990).
Human Rights Watch, *Empty Reforms: Saudi Arabia's New Basic Laws* (New
    York: 1992).
    World Report 1992: Chapter Saudi Arabia.
    The Ismailis of Najran: Second-Class Saudi Citizens (2008).
    *Denied Dignity: Systematic Discrimination and Hostility toward Saudi Shia
    Citizens* (2009).
International Crisis Group, *Can Saudi Arabia Reform Itself?* (2004).
    Saudi Arabia Backgrounder: Who Are the Islamists? (2004).
    Bahrain's Sectarian Challenge (2005).
    The Shiite Question in Saudi Arabia (2005).
    Popular Protests in North Africa and the Middle East (III): The Bahrain Revolt
    (2011).
    *Popular Protest in North Africa and the Middle East (VIII): Bahrain's Rocky
    Road to Reform* (2011).
U.S. Department of State, Bureau of Democracy, Human Rights, and Labor,
    International Religious Freedom Report: Saudi Arabia (2001–11).

Books in Persian

Javadi, Ahmad Sadr Hajj, Kamran Fani, and Baha' al-Din Khorramshahi, eds.,
    dayerat al-ma'arif-i tashayyu' (Encyclopedia of Shiism), 12 vols. (Tehran:
    Nashr-i Shahid Sa'id Muhibbi, 1988–2007).

Montazeri, Ayatollah Hossein ʿAli, *khaterat* (Memoirs) 2 vols., available on the Internet, www.amontazeri.com, 2000.

Articles and Books in Arabic

al-tasawwuf fi al-suʿudiyya wa-l-khalij (Sufism in Saudi and the Gulf) (Dubai: Markaz al-Misbar li-l-Dirasat wa-l-Buhuth, 2011).
"ʿIndama absartu al-haqiqa: haqaʾiq la yasaʿ ahl najran jahlaha" (When I Saw the Truth: Facts Can not Help the People of Najran from their Ignorance), available on the Internet, http://maktabah.com/site/itemfiles/AndmaAbsartALhagigah.pdf.
ʿAbd al-Majid, Muhammad, *al-tamayyiz al-taʾifi fi al-suʿudiyya* (Sectarian Discrimination in Saudi) (n.p.: Rabitat ʿUmum al-Shiʿa fi al-Suʿudiyya, n.d.).
ʿAdnan, Ahmad, *al-sajin 32: ahlam Muhammad Saʿid Tayyib wa-hazaʾimhu* (Prisoner 32: The Dreams of Muhammad Saʿid Tayyib and his Defeats) (Beirut: Markaz al-Thaqafi al-ʿArabi, 2011).
al-Ahmad, Fuʾad, *al-shaykh Hasan ʿAli Al Badr al-Qatifi* (Beirut: Muʾassasat al-Baqiʿ li-Ihyaʾ al-Turath, 1991).
al-Ahmari, ʿAbd al-Rahman bin ʿAbdallah Thamir, *dawr sharikat al-zayt al-ʿarabiyya al-amrikiyya (Aramku) fi tanmiyyat al-mintaqa al-sharqiyya min al-mamlaka al-ʿarabiyya al-suʿudiyya: dirasa fi tarikh al-tanmiyya 1363–1384 AH/1944–1964* (The Role of the Arabian American Petroleum Company (Aramco) in the Development of the Eastern Province of the Kingdom of Saudi Arabia: A Study in the History of Development 1944–1964) (Riyadh: n.p., 2007).
al-Ahsaʾi, Muhammad Al ʿAbd al-Qadir al-Ansari, *tuhfat al-mustafid bi-tarikh al-Ahsaʾ fi al-qadim wa-l-jadid* (A Beneficial Masterpiece about the Old and New History of al-Ahsa), 2 vols. (vol. 1: Riyadh: Matabiʿ al-Riyyad, 1960; vol. 2: Damascus: 1963).
al-ʿAkri, ʿAbd al-Nabi, *al-tanzimat al-yasariyya fi al-jazira wa-l-khalij al-ʿarabi* (The Leftist Organisations in the Peninsula and the Arabian Gulf) (Beirut: Dar al-Kunuz al-Adabiyya, 2003).
al-ʿAli, Ahmad, *shaʿb al-Qatif fi al-qarn al-hadi wa-l-ʿashrin: dirasa tahliliyya li-hadir wa-mustaqbal al-mujtamaʿ al-islami al-shiʿi fi al-alfiyya al-thalitha* (The People of Qatif in the 21st Century: An Analytical Study of Present and Future of Shia Islamic Society in the Third Millenium) (n.p.: Dar al-ʿArab, 2007).
al-Amin, Muhsin, *mustadrakat aʿyan al-shiʿa: haqqaqahu wa-akhrajahu Hasan al-Amin* (Amelioration of Outstanding Men of the Shia: Checked and Published by Hasan al-Amin) 11 vols. (Beirut: Dar al-Taʿarruf li-l-Matbuʿat, 1986).
al-ʿAmir, ʿAbd al-Latif Muhammad, *al-haraka al-islamiyya fi al-jazira al-ʿarabiyya* (The Islamic Movement in the Arabian Peninsula) (n.p.: Munazzamat al-Thawra al-Islamiyya fi al-Jazira al-ʿArabiyya/al-Safa li-l-Nashr wa-l-Tawziʿ, 1408AH [1987/88]).
al-Athari, Abu ʿAbdallah, *"bahth tafsili ʿan rafidat al-madina al-nakhawila"* (A Detailed Study on the Nakhawila Rejectionists of Medina), available on the Internet, http://ar.islamway.net/book/99.

al-'Attar, 'Adnan, *al-harakat al-taharruriyya fi al-Hijaz wa-Najd: 1901–1973* (The Liberation Movements in the Hijaz and Najd: 1901–1973) (n.p.: n.p., 1973).

al-'Awwami, al-Sayyid Hasan, "al-qada' al-shi'i fi al-Qatif: al-waqi' wa-l-tumuh" (Shia Jurisprudence in Qatif: Reality and Future), *al-Waha* 20 (2001), 43–6.

    min wahi al-qalam: rasa'il jari'a fi tafa'il al-mujtama' wa-ta'sil al-wahda: al-halaqa al-thalitha (Of the Inspiration of the Pen: Daring Letters on the Activation of Society and the Rooting of Unity: Part Three) (Beirut: Dar al-Mahajja al-Bayda'/al-Waha li-l-Khadamat al-Thaqafiyya, 2005).

    min thamarat 'umri: hasila qira'at 70 'aman (Of the Fruits of My Life: Outcome of Readings of 70 Years), 2 vols. (Beirut: Mu'assasat al-Intishar al-'Arabi, 2008).

al-'Awwami, Muhammad, *tha'ir min ajl al-din: malamih min hayat al-'allama al-mujahid al-shaykh Muhammad bin Nasir al-Nimr* (A Revolutionary for the Sake of Religion: Features of the Life of the Learned Fighting Shaykh Muhammad bin Nasir al-Nimr) (London: Dar al-Jazira li-l-Nashr, 1987).

    al-za'im Ahmad bin Mahdi Nasrallah: hayatuhu wa-shi'ruhu (The Leader Ahmad bin Mahdi Nasrallah: His Life and His Poetry) (London: Dar al-Jazira li-l-Nashr wa-l-Tawzi', n.d.).

al-'Awwami, 'Ali Baqir 'Ali, "al-shaykh Abu 'Abd al-Karim al-Khunayzi," *al-Waha* 20 (2001), 53–66.

al-'Awwami, al-Sayyid 'Ali al-Sayyid Baqir, *al-haraka al-wataniyya fi al-su'udiyya 1953–1973* (The National Movement in Saudi 1953–1973), 2 vols. (Beirut: Riyyad al-Rayyis li-l-Kutub wa-l-Nashr, 2012).

al-'Ayyash, Hussayn, "al-hawza al-'ilmiyya bi-l-Ahsa' wa-tatalla'atuha al-mustaqbaliyya" (The Community of Learning and its Future Aspirations), in *al-mashad al-thaqafi fi al-Ahsa': muntada al-mu'ayli unmudhajan* (The Cultural Scene in al-Ahsa: The al-Mu'ayli Forum as an Example), ed. Salman bin Hussayn al-Hijji, vol. 1 (Beirut: Dar al-'Ulum li-l-Tahqiq wa-l-Tiba'a wa-l-Nashr wa-l-Tawzi', 2007), 215–74.

al-Badr, Ahmad 'Abd al-Muhsin, *shams al-shumus: ustadh al-maraji' ayatallah al-'uzma al-shaykh Muhammad al-'Ithan al-Ahsa'i* (The Greatest Sun: The Teacher of Maraji' Grand Ayatallah Shaykh Muhammad al-'Ithan al-Ahsa'i) (Beirut: Dar al-Mahajja al-Bayda', 2011).

al-Bahrani, Muhammad 'Ali bin Ahmad bin 'Abbas al-Tajir, *muntazim al-darrayn fi tarajim 'ulama' wa-udaba' al-Ahsa' wa-l-Qatif wa-l-Bahrayn (tahqiq Daya' Badr Al Sunbal)* (A Dictonary of the Pearls amongst the Biographies of the Clerics and Writers from al-Ahsa, Qatif and Bahrain), 3 vols. (Qum/Beirut: Mu'assasa Tayyiba li-Ihya' al-Turath, 2009).

al-Bahrani, Yusuf bin Ahmad, *lu'lu'at al-Bahrayn fi al-ijazat wa-tarajim rijal al-hadith* (The Pearl of Bahrain in the Licences and Biographies of the Men of Hadith) (Najaf: Matba'a al-'Uthman, 1966).

al-Bahrani, 'Ali al-Biladi, *anwar al-badrayn fi tarajim 'ulama' al-Qatif wa-l-Ahsa' wa-l-Bahrayn* (The Lights of the Two Moons in the Biographies of the Scholars of Qatif, al-Ahsa and Bahrain) (Beirut: Dar al-Murtada, 1991).

al-Darura, ʿAli bin Ibrahim, *tarikh al-ihtilal al-burtughali li-l-Qatif 1521–1572* (The History of the Portuguese Occupation of Qatif 1521–1572) (Abu Dhabi: Majmaʿ al-Thaqafi, 2001).

al-Dumayni, ʿAli, *zaman li-l-sijn: azmina li-l-hurriyya* (Time for Prison, Times for Freedom) (Beirut: Dar al-Kunuz al-Adabiyya, 2005).

al-Fadli, Fuʾad ʿAbd al-Hadi, ed., *qiraʾat fi fikr al-ʿallama al-duktur al-Fadli* (Readings in the Thought of the Learned Doctor al-Fadli) (al-Ahsa: al-Lajna al-Diniyya bi-l-Qara, 2008).

al-Faraj, Suʿud ʿAbd al-Karim, *al-ʿAwwamiyya bayn ʿaraqat al-ams wa-ibdaʿ al-yawm* (Awwamiyya: Between the Deep-Rootedness of the Past and the Creation of Today) (n.p.: n.p., 2008).

al-Fardan, Maytham, ed., *al-hiwar al-madhhabi wa-l-masar al-sahih: muhadarat al-shaykh Hasan al-Saffar wa-hafl takrimihi fi ithnayniyya al-shaykh ʿAbd al-Maqsud Khuja* (Confessional Dialogue and the Right Path: Lecture of Shaykh Hasan al-Saffar and a Celebration for him in the Monday Diwaniyya of Shaykh ʿAbd al-Maqsud Khuja) (Beirut: al-Intishar al-ʿArabi, 2008).

al-Hajiri, Yusuf, *al-baqiʿ: qissa tadmir Al Suʿud li-l-athar al-islamiyya fi al-Hijaz* (The Story of the Destruction of Islamic Archaeological Sites in the Hijaz by the Al Saud) (Beirut: Muʾassasat al-Baqiʿ li-Ihyaʾ al-Turath, 1990).

Hajlawi, Nur al-Din bin al-Habib, *taʾthir al-fikr al-nasiri ʿala al-khalij al-ʿarabi 1956–1971* (The Impact of Nasserist Thought on the Arabian Gulf 1956–1971) 2nd ed. (Beirut: Markaz Dirasat al-Wahda al-ʿArabiyya, 2010).

Hammada, Rashid, *ʿasifa fawq miyah al-khalij: qissa awwal inqilab ʿaskari fi al-Bahrayn 1981* (A Storm on the Waters of the Gulf: Story of the First Military Coup in Bahrain 1981) (London: al-Safa li-l-Nashr wa-l-Tawziʿ, 1990).

al-Hasan, Hamza, "al-muʿarada fi al-suʿudiyya: al-taʾarjuh bayn al-hawa al-iqlimi wa-l-wataniyya al-jamaʿa" (The Opposition in Saudi: Oscillation between Regional Sentiment and Comprehensive Nationalism), *al-Jazira al-ʿArabiyya* 18 (July 1992), 40–7.

al-shiʿa fi al-mamlaka al-ʿarabiyya al-suʿudiyya (The Shia in the Kingdom of Saudi Arabia), 2 vols. (Beirut: Muʾassasat al-Baqiʿ li-Ihyaʾ al-Turath, 1993).

al-wataniyya: hawajis al-wahda wa-l-infisal fi al-suʿudiyya (Nationality: Thoughts about Unity and Separatism in Saudi) (n.p.: Dar al-Multaqa, 2009).

al-ʿamal al-matlabi fi miʾa ʿam: tajribat ʿamal wujahaʾ al-shiʿa fi al-suʿudiyya (Hundred Years of Petitions: The Experience of Shia Notables' Work in Saudi) (n.p.: Dar al-Multaqa, 2010).

al-Hatlani, Ibrahim, *al-shiʿa al-suʿudiyyun: qiraʾa tarikhiyya wa-siyasiyya li-namadhij matlabiyya* (The Saudi Shia: A Historical and Political Reading of Sample Claims) (Beirut: Riyyad al-Rayyis li-l-Kutub wa-l-Nashr, 2009).

al-Hijji, Salman bin Hussayn, *sirat ayatallah al-shaykh Muhammad bin Salman al-Hajari* (The Biography of Ayatallah Shaykh Muhammad bin Salman al-Hajari) (n.p.: n.p., 2005/2006).

dirasa fi al-nizam al-mali wa-l-khadmati li-baʿd jamaʿiyyat al-hajj fi al-Ahsaʾ (A Study of the Financial and Service System of some Hajj Societies in al-Ahsa) (al-Ahsa: Matbaʿa al-Ahsaʾ al-Haditha, 2006).

ed., *al-mashad al-thaqafi fi al-Ahsa': muntada al-mu'ayli unmudhajan* (The Cultural Scene in al-Ahsa: The al-Mu'ayli Forum as an Example) vol. 1 (Beirut: Dar al-'Ulum li-l-Tahqiq wa-l-Tiba'a wa-l-Nashr wa-l-Tawzi', 2007).

hakadha wajadtuhum (This Is how I Found them) (Beirut: Jawatha li-l-Nashr, 2008).

ru'ia muhasibiyya li-l-khums wa-l-fara'id al-maliyya (An Accounting Perspective of the Khums and the Financial Duties) (Beirut: Mu'assasat Umm al-Qura li-l-Tahqiq wa-l-Nashr, n.d.).

al-Hirz, Muhammad, *al-shaykh Baqir Abu Khamsin: 'ilm wa-'ata' wa-adab* (Shaykh Baqir Abu Khamsin: Knowledge, Giftedness and Literature) (Beirut: Dar al-Khalij al-'Arabi li-l-Tiba'a wa-l-Nashr, 1999).

"al-qada' al-ja'fari fi al-Ahsa'" (Shia Jurisprudence in al-Ahsa), *al-Waha* 20 (2001), 19–38.

al-ta'lim al-taqlidi al-mutawwa' fi al-Ahsa' (The Traditional "Mutawwa" Education in al-Ahsa) (Beirut: Dar al-Mahajja al-Bayda', 2001).

"al-hawzat wa-l-madaris al-'ilmiyya fi al-Ahsa'" (The Hawzas and Religious Schools in al-Ahsa), *Rasid* (11 August 2005).

al-Hirz, Siba, *al-akharun* (The Others) (Beirut: Dar al-Saqi, 2006).

al-Ibrahim, Badr and Muhammad al-Sadiq, *al-hirak al-shi'i fi al-su'udiyya: tasyis al-madhhab wa-madhhabat al-siyasa* (The Shia Movement in Saudi: The Politicisation of Confession and the Confessionalisation of Politics) (Beirut: al-Shabaka al-'Arabiyya li-l–Abhath wa-l-Nashr, 2013).

Ibrahim, Fu'ad, *al-faqih wa-l-dawla: tatawwur al-fikr al-siyasi al-shi'i* (Cleric and State: The Development of Shia Political Thought) (Beirut: Dar al-Kunuz al-Adabiyya, 1998).

al-shi'a fi al-su'udiyya (The Shia in Saudi) (Beirut: Dar al-Saqi, 2007).

al-Ihqaqi, Mirza 'Abd al-Rasul al-Ha'iri, *qarnan min al-ijtihad wa-l-marji'iyya fi usrat al-Ihqaqi* (Two Centuries of Ijtihad and Marji'iyya in the al-Ihqaqi Family) (Kuwait: Maktabat al-Imam al-Sadiq al-'Amma, n.d.).

al-Jad'an, al-Shaykh Salih, *Ayatallah al-Shaykh Muhammad 'Ali al-'Amri: sira wa-'ita'* (n.p.: n.p., 2011).

al-Jishi, Jamil bin 'Abdallah, *turath al-ajdad: dirasa fi watha'iq 'a'ilat al-Jishi fi al-Qatif wa-l-Bahrayn (1200–1350AH)* (Heritage of the Forefathers: A Study of the Documents of the al-Jishi Family in Qatif and Bahrain (1786–1931)) (Jeddah: Dar al-Su'udiyya li-l-Nashr wa-l-Tawzi', 2007).

Al Jumay', Habib, *mu'jam al-mu'allafat al-shi'iyya fi al-jazira al-'arabiyya* (Bibliography of Shia Writings in the Arabian Peninsula), 3 vols. (Beirut: Dar al-Mahajja al-Bayda'/Mu'assasat al-Baqi' li-Ihya' al-Turath, vol. 1 1997, vol. 2, 2006, vol. 3, 2013).

al-Kandari, Faysal 'Abdallah, *al-hamla al-'uthmaniyya 'ala al-Ahsa' 'am 1871 min khilal al-watha'iq al-'uthmaniyya* (The Ottoman Campaign on al-Ahsa in the Year 1871 according to Ottoman Documents) (Kuwait: Markaz Dirasat al-Khalij wa-l-Jazira al-'Arabiyya, 2003).

al-Katib, Ahmad, *mudhakkirat Ahmad al-Katib: sirati al-fikriyya wa-l-siyasiyya ... min nazariyyat al-imama ... ila al-shura* (Memoirs of Ahmad al-Katib: My Intellectual and Political Biography ... from the Theory of the Imamate ... to the Shura), available on the Internet, www.alkatib.net.

al-marji'iyya al-diniyya al-shi'iyya … wa-afaq al-tatawwur: al-imam Muhammad al-Shirazi namudhajan (The Shia Religious Marji'iyya … and the Horizons of Evolution: Imam Muhammad al-Shirazi as an Example), 2nd ed. (Beirut: Arab Scientific Publishers, 2007).

Khalil, Muhammad Mahmud, *tarikh al-khalij wa-sharq al-jazira al-'arabiyya al-musamma iqlim bilad al-Bahrayn fi zill hukm al-duwaylat al-'arabiyya 469–963A.H./1076–1555m* (History of the Gulf and the East of the Arabian Peninsula Called 'Lands of Bahrain' Region in the Shadow of the Rule of Arab States 1076–1555) (Cairo: Maktaba Madbuli, 2006).

al-Khunayzi, 'Ali Abu al-Hasan ibn Hasan bin Mahdi, *al-da'wa al-islamiyya ila wahdat ahl al-sunna wa-l-imamiyya* (The Islamic Call for Unity of the People of the Sunna and the Imamiyya), 2 vols. (Beirut: Dar al-Fikr, 1956).

al-Khunayzi, Jihad, *ma'alim marji'iyyat al-imam al-Shirazi fi al-Qatif wa-adwa' 'ala tarikh al-'ulama' wa-l-marji'iyya fi al-Qatif* (Signposts of the Marji'iyya of Imam Shirazi in Qatif and Lights on the History of the Clerics and the Marji'iyya in Qatif) (Beirut: Dar al-Waha li-l-Tiba'a wa-l-Nashr wa-l-Tawzi'/ Dar al-'Ulum li-l-Tahqiq wa-l-Tiba'a wa-l-Nashr wa-l-Tawzi', 2002).

al-Khunayzi, Muhammad Sa'id al-Shaykh 'Ali, *khuyut min al-shams: qissa wa-tarikh* (Strands of the Sun: Story and History) 2 vols. (Beirut: Mu'assasat al-Balagh li-l-Tiba'a wa-l-Nashr wa-l-Tawzi', 1999).

al-'abqariyyu al-maghmur (The Unknown Genius) (Beirut: Mu'assasat al-Balagh li-l-Tiba'a wa-l-Nashr wa-l-Tawzi', 2003).

al-Khunayzi, Najib, "al-ihtifa' bi-l-shakhsiyya al-wataniyya al-bariza Mirza al-Khunayzi" (The Celebration of the Outstanding National Personality Mirza al-Khunayzi), *Rasid* (24 December 2009).

"al-nishat al-siyasi li-l-shi'a fi al-su'udiyya" (The Political Discourse of the Shia in Saudi), *Rasid* (25 October 2003).

al-Khunayzi, 'Abdallah, *dhikra al-imam al-Khunayzi* (Remembrance of Imam Khunayzi) 2nd ed. (Beirut: al-Mu'assasa al-'Alamiyya li-l-Kitab, 1998).

al-harakat al-fikriyya fi al-Qatif (The Intellectual Movements in Qatif), 3 vols. (Beirut: Mu'assasat al-Balagh li-l-Tiba'a wa-l-Nashr wa-l-Tawzi', 2002).

Abu Talib mu'min Quraysh: dirasa wa-tahlil (Abu Talib Believer of Quraysh: Study and Analysis) 6th ed. (Beirut: Mu'assasat al-Balagh li-l-Tiba'a wa-l-Nashr wa-l-Tawzi', 2005 [1st ed. 1961]).

Kurshun, Zakariyya, and Muhammad Musa al-Qarini, *sawahil Najd "al-Ahsa'" fi al-arshif al-'uthmani: Jabal Shammar – al-Qasim – al-Riyyad – al-Qatif – al-Kuwayt – al-Bahrayn – Qatar – Masqat* (The Oases of Najd "al-Ahsa" in the Ottoman Archives: Jabal Shammar – Qasim – Riyadh – Qatif – Kuwait – Bahrain – Qatar – Musqat) (Beirut: al-Dar al-'Arabiyya li-l-Mawsu'at, 2005).

al-Labad, 'Adil, *al-inqilab: bay' al-wahm 'ala al-dhat* (The Coup: The Selling of the Illusion to the Self) (Beirut: Dar al-Jamal li-l-Tiba'a wa-l-Nashr, 2009).

Mahfuz, Muhammad, *al-hiwar wa-l-wahda al-wataniyya fi al-mamlaka al-'arabiyya al-su'udiyya* (Dialogue and National Unity in the Kingdom of Saudi Arabia) (Beirut: Dar al-Saqi, 2004).

al-islah al-siyasi wa-l-wahda al-wataniyya: kayfa nabni watanan li-l-'aysh al-mushtarak (Political Reform and National Unity: How We Build a Homeland to Live Together) (Beirut: al-Markaz al-Thaqafi al-'Arabi, 2004).

Al Mahna, 'Ali 'Isa, *mun'ataf al-qarar: al-Fadli bayn 'Iraqayn* (The Turn of Decisions: al-Fadli between two Iraqs) (Beirut: Dar al-Mahajja al-Bayda', 2007).

al-Makarim, 'Abd al-Qadir al-Shaykh 'Ali Abu, *al-kisa' fi ma'arif al-umma al-islamiyya* (The Cloak: On the Knowledge of the Islamic Umma) (Beirut: Dar al-'Ulum li-l-Tahqiq wa-l-Tiba'a wa-l-Nashr wa-l-Tawzi', 2007).

Makki, 'Aliyya, *yawmiyyat imra' fi al-sujun al-su'udiyya* (Diary of a Woman in Saudi Prisons) (London: Al-Safa, 1989).

Makki, Yusuf, "hizb al-ba'th al-'arabi al-ishtiraki fi al-'arabiyya al-su'udiyya" (The Arab Socialist Baath Party in Saudi Arabia), in *al-ahzab wa-l-harakat wa-l-tanzimat al-qawmiyya fi al-watan al-'arabi* (The Nationalist Parties, Movements and Organisations in the Arab Homeland), ed. Muhammad Jamal Barut (Beirut: Markaz Dirasat al-Wahda al-'Arabiyya, 2012), 291–301.

"harakat al-qawmiyyin al-'arab fi al-khalij wa-l-jazira al-'arabiyya" (The Movement of Arab Nationalists in the Gulf and the Arabian Peninsula), in *al-ahzab wa-l-harakat wa-l-tanzimat al-qawmiyya fi al-watan al-'arabi* (The Nationalist Parties, Movements and Organisations in the Arab Homeland), ed. Muhammad Jamal Barut (Beirut: Markaz Dirasat al-Wahda al-'Arabiyya, 2012), 467–86.

"al-haraka al-nasiriyya fi al-'arabiyya al-su'udiyya" (The Nasserist Movement in Saudi Arabia), in *al-ahzab wa-l-harakat wa-l-tanzimat al-qawmiyya fi al-watan al-'arabi* (The Nationalist Parties, Movements and Organisations in the Arab Homeland), ed. Muhammad Jamal Barut (Beirut: Markaz Dirasat al-Wahda al-'Arabiyya, 2012), 672–80.

al-Maskin, 'Uqayl, "al-shaykh Sa'id Abu al-Makarim ba'd nisf qarn min al-khitaba al-diniyya" (Shaykh Sa'id Abu al-Makarim after Half a Century of Religious Preaching), *al-Waha* 20 (2001), 142–59.

al-Milad, Zaki, "al-shaykh 'Ali Abu al-Hasan al-Khunayzi: manhajiyyat al-hiwar al-islami" (Shaykh 'Ali Abu al-Hasan al-Khunayzi: A Methodology for Islamic Dialogue), *al-Waha* 3 (1995), 129–31.

min al-turath ila al-ijtihad: al-fikr al-islami wa-qadaya al-islah wa-l-tajdid (From Heritage to Independent Reasoning: Islamic Thought and the Issues of Reform and Renewal) (Beirut: al-Markaz al-Thaqafi al-'Arabi, 2004).

al-Mudayris, Falah 'Abdallah, *al-ba'thiyyun fi al-khalij wa-l-jazira al-'arabiyya* (The Baathists in the Gulf and the Arabian Peninsula) (Kuwait: Dar Qurtas li-l-Nashr, 2002).

al-harakat wa-l-jama'at al-siyasiyya fi al-Bahrayn 1937–2002 (The Political Movements and Groups in Bahrain 1937–2002) (Beirut: Dar al-Kunuz al-Adabiyya, 2004).

al-Mudarrisi, Hadi, *hiwar 'an al-mar'a* (Discussion of the Woman) (Beirut: Dar al-Ta'arruf, 1978).

al-Muhammad Salih, Ahmad 'Abd al-Hadi, *a'lam madrasat al-shaykh al-awhad fi al-qarn al-thalith 'ashr al-hijri* (Scholars of the School of the Unique Shaykh in the 13th Century A.H.) (Beirut: Dar al-Mahajja al-Bayda', 2006).

Al Mulham, Muhammad bin ʿAbd al-Latif bin Muhammad, *kanat ashbah bi-l-jamiʿa: qissat al-taʿlim fi muqataʿat al-Ahsaʾ fi ʿahd al-malik ʿAbd al-ʿAziz* (It Was like a University: The Story of Education in the al-Ahsa District in the Era of King ʿAbd al-ʿAziz) (Riyadh: Darat al-Duktur Al Mulham li-l-Nashr wa-l-Tawziʿ, 1999).

Al Mulla, ʿAbd al-Rahman bin ʿUthman, *tarikh hajar: dirasa shamila fi ahwal al-juzʾ al-sharqi min shibh al-jazira al-ʿarabiyya: al-Ahsaʾ, al-Bahrayn, al-Kuwayt wa-Qatar* (History of Hajar: A Comprehensive Study on the Situation of the Eastern Part of the Arabian Peninsula: al-Ahsaʾ, Bahrain, Kuwait and Qatar), 2. vols. (Hufuf: Maktabat al-Taʿawun al-Thaqafi, 1990).

Musa, Hussayn, *al-ahzab wa-l-harakat al-islamiyya fi al-khalij wa-l-jazira al-ʿarabiyya* (The Islamic Parties and Movements in the Gulf and the Arabian Peninsula) (Manama: n.p., 2004).

al-Mushaykhas, ʿAbd al-ʿAzim, *al-ʿAwwamiyya: majdun wa-aʿlam* (Awwamiyya: Honour and Symbols) (Beirut: Dar al-Khalij al-ʿArabi li-l-Tibaʿa wa-l-Nashr, 1999).

    al-Qatif wa-mulahaqatuha: abʿad wa-tatallaʿat (Qatif and its Surroundings: Dimensions and Outlooks), 2 vols. (Beirut: Sharikat al-Shaykh li-l-Tahqiq wa-l-Nashr, 2002).

al-Muslim, Muhammad Saʿid, *sahil al-dhahab al-aswad: dirasa tarikhiyya insaniyya li-mintaqat al-khalij al-ʿarabi* (Coast of Black Gold: A Historical-Humanitarian Study of the Arabian Gulf Region), 2nd ed. (Beirut: Manshurat Dar Maktabat al-Haya, 1962).

    al-Qatif waha ʿala difaf al-khalij (Qatif: An Oasis on the Shores of the Gulf) 2nd ed. (Riyadh: Matabiʿ al-Farazdaq, 1991).

al-Nakhli, Hasan bin Marzuq Rijaʾ al-Sharimi, *al-nakhawila (al-nakhliyyun) fi al-Madina al-Munawwara: al-takwin al-ijtimaʿi wa-l-thaqafi* (The Nakhawila in Medina: The Social and Cultural Formation) (Beirut: Muʾassasat al-Intishar al-ʿArabi, 2012).

al-Nasiri, al-Shaykh Ahmad al-ʿAmari, *qabilat bani Khalid fi al-tarikh* (The Bani Khalid Tribe in History) (Beirut: Dar al-Rafidayn li-l-Tibaʿa wa-l-Nashr wa-l-Tawziʿ, 2009).

al-Nimr, Muhammad, "qudat al-Qatif" (Judges of Qatif), *al-Waha* 21 (2001), 41–4.

al-Qahtani, Fahd, *zilzal Juhayman fi Makka* (Juhayman's Earthquake in Mecca) (London: Munazzamat al-Thawra al-Islamiyya fi al-Jazira al-Arabiyya, 1987).

    majzarat Makka: qissat al-madhbaha al-suʿudiyya li-l-hujjaj (Mecca Massacre: The Story of the Saudi Bloodbath of the Pilgrims) (London: al-Safa li-l-Nashr wa-l-Tawziʿ, 1988).

    shuyuʿiyyun fi al-suʿudiyya: dirasa fi al-ʿalaqat al-sufitiyya al-suʿudiyya (Communists in Saudi: A Study of Soviet-Saudi Relations) (n.p.: n.p., 1988).

al-Qarini, Muhammad Musa, *al-idara al-ʿuthmaniyya fi mutasarrifiyyat al-Ahsaʾ 1288–1331/1871–1913* (The Ottoman Administration in the al-Ahsa District 1871–1913) (Riyadh: Darat al-Malik ʿAbd al-ʿAziz, 2005).

al-Qasha'mi, Muhammad 'Abd al-Rizzaq, *al-kuttab al-su'udiyyun fi majallat (Sawt al-Bahrayn) 1369–1373* (The Saudi Writers in the Magazine, "Voice of Bahrain") (Riyadh: Dar al-Mufradat li-l-Nashr wa-l-Tawzi', 2010).

al-Rayyis, Riyyad Najib, *riyyah al-sumum: al-su'udiyya wa-du'ul al-jazira ba'd harb al-khalij 1991–1994* (Poisonous Winds: Saudi Arabia and the States of the Peninsula after the Gulf War 1991–1994) (Beirut: Riyyad al-Rayyis li-l-Kutub wa-l-Nashr, 1994).

Ra'uf, 'Adil, *al-'amal al-islami fi al-'Iraq bayn al-marji'iyya wa-l-hizbiyya: qira'a naqdiyya li-masirat nisf qarn (1950–2000)* (The Islamic Action in Iraq between the Marji'iyya and the Party System: A Critical Reading of the Voyage of Half a Century (1950–2000) (Damascus: al-Markaz al-'Iraqi li-l-I'lam wa-l-Dirasat, 2000).

Saban, Suhayl, *min watha'iq al-Ahsa' fi al-arshif al-'uthmani 1871–1913* (Some Documents on al-Ahsa in the Ottoman Archives) (al-Ahsa': Nadi al-Ahsa' al-Adabi, 2009).

  aradi al-Ahsa' wa-mazari'ha al-miriyya fi sajl al-khazna al-khasa raqm 4125 min sajalat al-arshif al-'uthmani (The Landholdings of al-Ahsa and its Agricultural Miri Gardens in the Special Register No. 4125 of the Ottoman Archives) (al-Ahsa': Nadi al-Ahsa' al-Adabi, 2010).

al-Saffar, Hasan, *al-imam al-mahdi: amal al-shu'ub* (Imam Mahdi: Hope of the People) (Beirut: Mu'assasat al-A'lami li-l-Matbu'at, 1979).

  al-jamahir wa-l-thawra (The Masses and the Revolution) (Qatif: n.p., 1981).

  al-mar'a mas'uliyya wa-mawqif (The Woman: Responsibility and Position) (Qatif: n.p., 1981).

  al-mar'a wa-l-thawra (The Woman and the Revolution) 2nd printing (Beirut: Mu'assasat al-A'lami li-l-Matbu'at, 1981).

  al-shaykh 'Ali al-Biladi al-Qudayhi (Beirut: Mu'assasat al-Baqi' li-Ihya' al-Turath, 1990).

  al-ta'addudiyya wa-l-hurriyya fi al-Islam: bahth hawla hurriyyat al-mu'taqad wa-ta'addud al-madhahib (Pluralism and Freedom in Islam: A Study on the Freedom of Belief and the Plurality of Confessions) (Beirut: Dar al-Manhal/ Dar al-Bayan al-'Arabi, 1990).

  al-Hussayn wa-mas'uliyyat al-thawra (Hussayn and the Responsibility of Revolution) 7th ed. (Beirut: Dar al-Bayan al-'Arabi, 1991).

  al-imam al-Shirazi: malamih al-shakhsiyya wa-samat al-fikr (Imam al-Shirazi: Features of the Personality and Attributes of the Thought) (Beirut: al-Amin li-l-Tiba'a wa-l-Nashr wa-l-Tawzi', 2002).

  al-nadi al-riyadi wa-l-mujtama' (The Sport Club and Society) (Khobar: Matabi' al-Raja', 2004).

  al-salafiyyun wa-l-shi'a: nahwa 'alaqa afdal (Salafis and Shia: Towards a Better Relationship), 2nd printing (Qatif: Atyaf li-l-Nashr wa-l-Tawzi'/Beirut: al-Intishar al-'Arabi, 2007).

  al-madhhab wa-l-watan: mukashafat wa-hiwarat sariha ma' samahat al-shaykh Hasan al-Saffar ajraha al-ustadh 'Abd al-'Aziz Qasim (The Confession and the Homeland: Revelations and Open Discussions with Shaykh Hasan al-Saffar Conducted by 'Abd al-'Aziz Qasim) (Beirut: al-Mu'assassa al-'Arabiyya li-l-Dirasat wa-l-Nashr, 2008).

Sayf, ʿAbdallah, *al-maʾtam fi al-Bahrayn: dirasa tawthiqiyya* (The Maʾtam in Bahrain: A Documented Study) (Bahrain: al-Matbaʿ al-Sharqiyya, 1995).

Al Sayf, ʿAbd al-ʿAli, "qarn min tarikh al-qadaʾ fi al-Qatif" (A Century of the History of Jurisprudence in Qatif), *al-Waha* 20 (2001), 14–18.

al-Sayf, ʿAbd al-Jalil, "al-Hajj Muhammad Taqi Al Sayf," *al-Waha* 47 (2007), 73–7.

> *mishwar fi durub al-watan: tajriba haya* (Errands on the Path of the Homeland: Experience of a Life) (Riyadh: n.p., 2008).

al-Sayf, Tawfiq, *nazariyyat al-sulta fi al-fiqh al-shiʿi* (The View of Political Power in Shia Jurisprudence) (Beirut: al-Markaz al-Thaqafi al-ʿArabi, 2002).

> *an takun shiʿiyan fi al-suʿudiyya: ishkalat al-muwatana wa-l-hawiyya fi mujtamaʿ taqlidi* (To be a Shia in Saudi: Questions of Citizenship and Identity in a Traditional Society), available on the Internet, http://talsaif. blogspot.co.uk, 2013.

al-Salih, Zaki ʿAli, *al-ʿAwwamiyya: tarikh wa-turath* (Awwamiyya: History and Heritage) 2nd ed. (Beirut: Dar al-Kunuz al-Adabiyya, 1998).

al-Saʿid, Nasir, *tarikh Al Suʿud* (The History of Al Saud) (Beirut: Ittihad Shaʿb al-Jazira al-ʿArabiyya, 1984).

> *haqaʾiq ʿan … al-qahr al-suʿudi* (Truths about … Saudi Oppression) (London: al-Safa li-l-Nashr wa-l-Tawziʿ, 1988).

al-Shaykh, ʿAbd al-Rahman, *al-masʾala al-filastiniyya fi al-manzar al-suʿudi* (The Palestinian Question in the Saudi View) (n.p.: Munazzamat al-Thawra al-Islamiyya fi al-Jazira al-ʿArabiyya, 1982).

al-Shaykh, ʿAbd al-Rahman, Salih al-Dukhayyil, and ʿAbdallah al-Zayir, *intifadat al-mintaqa al-sharqiyya 1400AH-1979m* (The Uprising of the Eastern Province 1979) (n.p.: Munazzamat al-Thawra al-Islamiyya fi al-Jazira al-ʿArabiyya, 1981).

al-Shaykh, Hasan, *al-raʾis al-ʿIthan: tarjuma li-l-shaykh Muhammad al-ʿIthan bi-munasibat al-dhikra al-miʾawiyya al-ula ʿala rahilihi* (The Leader al-ʿIthan: A Biography of Shaykh Muhammad al-ʿIthan on the Occasion of the Rememberance of his Hundredth Deathday) (n.p.: Dar al-Mahajja al-Baydaʾ/ Dar Kumayl, 2010).

al-Shaykh Yaʿqub, Ishaq, *wujuh fi masabih al-dhakira* (Faces of the Lamps of Memory), 4 vols., vol. 1 (Kuwait: Dar Qurtas li-l-Nashr, 2001), vol. 2 (Kuwait: Dar Qurtas li-l-Nashr, 2005), Vol. 3 (Kuwait: Dar Qurtas li-l-Nashr, 2007), vol. 4 (Beirut: Dar al-Farabi, 2011).

al-Shaykh, Tawfiq, *al-batrul wa-l-siyasa fi al-mamlaka al-ʿarabiyya al-suʿudiyya* (Oil and Politics in the Kingdom of Saudi Arabia) (London: Dar al-Safa li-l-Nashr wa-l-Tawziʿ, 1988).

al-Shakhs, Hashim Muhammad, *aʿlam hajar min al-madiyyin wa-l-muʿasirin* (Symbols of al-Ahsa from Past and Present), 4 vols. (Beirut: Muʾassasat Umm al-Qura li-l-Tahqiq wa-l-Nashr, 1996–2006).

al-Shammari, Abu Bakr Muhammad ʿAbdallah Ibrahim, *al-fihrist al-mufid fi tarajim aʿlam al-khalij, al-halaqa al-ula* (The Useful List of Biographies of Scholars of the Gulf: Part One) (Khobar: al-Dar al-Wataniyya al-Jadida li-l-Nashr wa-l-Tawziʿ, 1992/1993).

al-Shammasi, ʿAbdallah Rida, "taʿliq wa-idah" (Comment and Note), in al-Sayyid ʿAli al-Sayyid Baqir al-ʿAwwami, *al-haraka al-wataniyya fi al-suʿudiyya 1953–1973* (The National Movement in Saudi 1953–1973), 2 vols. (Beirut: Riyyad al-Rayyis li-l-Kutub wa-l-Nashr, 2012), vol. 1, 152–8.

al-Shurafaʾ, Muhammad ʿAli Salih, *al-mintaqa al-sharqiyya min al-mamlaka al-ʿarabiyya al-suʿudiyya: hadara wa-tarikh* (The Eastern Province of the Kingdom of Saudi Arabia: Civilization and History) (Dammam: Matabiʿ al-Madukhl, 1992).

al-Subayʿi, ʿAbdallah ibn Nasir, *al-haya al-ʿilmiyya wa-l-thaqafiyya wa-l-fikriyya fi al-mintaqa al-sharqiyya 1930–1960* (The Scholarly, Cultural and Intellectual Life in the Eastern Province 1930–1960) (Riyadh: al-Dar al-Wataniyya al-Jadida, 1987).

  iktishaf al-naft wa-atharuhu ʿala al-haya al-ijtimaʿiyya fi al-mintaqa al-sharqiyya 1933–1960 (The Discovery of Oil and its Influence on Social Life in the Eastern Province 1933–1960) (Riyadh: al-Dar al-Wataniyya al-Jadida, 1987).

  al-hukm wa-l-idara fi al-Ahsaʾ wa-l-Qatif wa-Qatar athnaʾ al-hukm al-ʿuthmani al-thani 1871–1913 (Government and Administration in al-Ahsa, Qatif and Qatar during the Second Period of Ottoman Rule 1871–1913) (Riyadh: Matabiʿ al-Jumʿa al-Iliktruniyya, 1999).

  al-qadaʾ wa-l-awqaf fi al-Ahsaʾ wa-l-Qatif wa-Qatar athnaʾ al-hukm al-ʿuthmani al-thani 1871–1913 (Judiciary and Religious Endowments in al-Ahsa, Qatif and Qatar during the Second Period of Ottoman Rule 1871–1913) (Riyadh: Matabiʿ al-Jumʿa al-Iliktruniyya, 1999).

  iqtisad al-Ahsaʾ wa-l-Qatif wa-Qatar athnaʾ al-hukm al-ʿuthmani al-thani 1871–1913 (The Economy of al-Ahsa, Qatif and Qatar during the Second Period of Ottoman Rule 1871–1913) (Riyadh: Matabiʿ al-Jumʿa al-Iliktruniyya, 1999).

Al Sulham, Hussayn bin Hasan bin Makki, *Sayhat wa-l-bahr: bahth tarikhi li-l-haraka al-milahiyya fi madinat Sayhat* (Saihat and the Sea: A Historical Study of Seafaring in the City of Saihat) (Beirut: Dar al-Mahajja al-Baydaʾ, 2000).

Sunaytan, Muhammad bin, *al-nukhab al-suʿudiyya: dirasa fi al-tahawwulat wa-l-ikhfaqat* (The Saudi Elites: A Study of Transformations and Failures) 2nd ed. (Beirut: Markaz Dirasat al-Wahda al-ʿArabiyya, 2005).

Al Sunbal, Luʾi Muhammad Shawqi, *al-ʿallama al-Khatti: taʾrikh mushriq* (The Most Learned al-Khatti: Shining History) (n.p.: n.p., 1998).

  al-shaykh al-Khunayzi: ʿaliman wa-zaʿiman (Shaykh al-Khunayzi: Cleric and Leader) (n.p.: Manshurat Dar Wahi al-Qalam, 2004).

  dhikra al-ʿallama al-khatti (Remembrance of the Most Learned al-Khatti) (Beirut: Dar al-Awliaʾ li-l-Tibaʿa wa-l-Nashr wa-l-Tawziʿ, 2005).

Al Suʿud, Jawahir Bint ʿAbd al-Muhsin bin Jiluwi, *al-amir ʿAbdallah bin Jiluwi Al Suʿud wa-dawruhu fi taʾsis al-dawla al-suʿudiyya al-thalitha* (Prince ʿAbdallah bin Jiluwi Al Saud and his Role in the Foundation of the Third Saudi State) (Dammam: Matabiʿ al-Nimri, n.d.).

Al al-Talaqani, Muhammad Hasan, *al-shaykhiyya: nashʾatha wa-tatawwurha wa-masadir dirasatha* (The Shaykhiyya: Its Emergence, Development and Sources of Studies) (Beirut: al-Amal li-l-Matbuʿat, 1999).

al-'Umar, Nasir ibn Sulayman, *waqi' al-rafida fi bilad al-tawhid* (The Situation of the Rejectionists in the Lands of Monotheism), available on the Internet, http://ar.islamway.net/book/3165.

al-'Umran, Faraj, *al-azhar al-arajiyya fi al-athar al-farajiyya* (The Aroma Blossoms of the Faraji Legacy), 2nd ed., 6 vols. (Beirut: Manshurat Dar Hajar, 2008).

   majmu'a mu'allafat al-shaykh Faraj al-'Umran (A Collection of Writings of Shaykh Faraj al-'Umran), vol. 1 (Beirut: Mu'assasat al-Khutt li-l-Tahqiq wa-l-Nashr, 2010).

al-'Uqayl, 'Abd al-Rahman Muhammad 'Umar, *ahdath al-'Awwamiyya wa-l-Qatif* (The Events of Awwamiyya and Qatif: From 10 February 2011 to 10 February 2012) (Riyadh: [leaked through www.awamia.net], 2012).

al-'Utaybi, Maryam bint Khalaf, *al-Ahsa' wa-l-Qatif fi 'ahd al-dawla al-su'udiyya al-thaniyya (1245–1288 AH)* (al-Ahsa and Qatif in the Era of the Second Saudi State 1830–1871) (Beirut: Jadawel, 2012).

al-'Uthaymin, 'Abdallah al-Salih, *tarikh al-mamlaka al-'arabiyya al-su'udiyya* (The History of the Kingdom of Saudi Arabia), 9th ed., 2 vols. (Riyadh: Obeikan, 1998).

al-Wahbi, 'Abd al-Karim bin 'Abdallah al-Munif, *banu Khalid wa-'alaqatuhum bi-Najd 1669–1794* (Bani Khalid and their Relationship with Najd 1669–1794) (n.p.: Dar Thaqif li-l-Nashr wa-l-Ta'lif, 1989).

Articles and Books in European Languages

Aba-Namay, Rashed, "The New Saudi Representative Assembly," *Islamic Law and Society* 5, no. 2 (1998), 235–65.

Abir, Mordechai, *Saudi Arabia in the Oil Era: Regime and Elites, Conflict and Collaboration* (London: Croom Helm, 1988).

   Saudi Arabia: Government, Society and the Gulf Crisis (London: Routledge, 1993).

AbuKhalil, Asad, *The Battle for Saudi Arabia: Royalty, Fundamentalism, and Global Power* (New York: Seven Stories, 2004).

al-Fahad, Abdulaziz H., "Ornamental Constitutionalism: The Saudi Basic Law of Governance," *Yale Journal of International Law* 30 (2005), 375–96.

al-Hamad, Turki, *Adama* (London: Saqi, 2003).

Alhasan, Hasan Tariq, "The Role of Iran in the Failed Coup of 1981: The IFLB in Bahrain," *The Middle East Journal* 65, no. 4 (2011), 603–17.

al-Herz, Seba, *The Others* (New York: Seven Stories, 2009).

al-Khoei, Yousif, "The Marja and the Survival of a Community: The Shia of Medina," in *The Most Learned of the Shia: The Institution of the Marja' Taqlid*, ed. Linda Walbridge (Oxford: Oxford University Press, 2001), 247–50.

al-Mani', Saleh, "The Ideological Dimension in Saudi-Iranian Relations," in *Iran and the Gulf: A Search for Stability*, ed. Jamal S. al-Suwaida (Abu Dhabi: Emirates Center for Strategic Studies and Research, 1996), 158–74.

al-Mdaires, Falah, "Shi'ism and Political Protest in Bahrain," *Domes* 11, no. 1 (Spring 2002).

al-Najjar, Muhammad Rajab, "Contemporary Trends in the Study of Folklore in the Arab Gulf States," in *Statecraft in the Middle East: Oil, Historical*

Memory, and Popular Culture, ed. Eric Davis and Nicolas E. Gavrielides (Miami: Florida International University Press, 1991), 176–201.

al-Rasheed, Madawi, "God, the King and the Nation: Political Rhetoric in Saudi Arabia in the 1990s," *The Middle East Journal* 59, no. 3 (1996), 359–71.

"Political Legitimacy and the Production of History: The Case of Saudi Arabia," in *New Frontiers in Middle East Security*, ed. Lenore G. Martin (London: Macmillan, 1998), 25–46.

"The Shia of Saudi Arabia: A Minority in Search of Cultural Authenticity," *British Journal of Middle Eastern Studies* 25, no. 1 (1998), 121–38.

A History of Saudi Arabia (Cambridge: Cambridge University Press, 2002).

Contesting the Saudi State: Islamic Voices From a New Generation (Cambridge: Cambridge University Press, 2007).

"Sectarianism as Counter-Revolution: Saudi Responses to the Arab Spring," *Studies in Ethnicity and Nationalism* 11, no. 3 (December 2011), 513–26.

A Most Masculine State: Gender, Politics, and Religion in Saudi Arabia (Cambridge: Cambridge University Press, 2013).

al-Rasheed, Madawi, and Loulouwa al-Rasheed, "The Politics of Encapsulation: Saudi Policy towards Tribal and Religious Opposition," *Middle Eastern Studies* 32, no. 1 (1996), 96–119.

al-Sayf, Tawfiq, *Islamic Democracy and its Limits: The Iranian Experience since 1979* (London: Saqi, 2007).

al-Shayib, Ja'far, "Saudi Municipal Councils and Political Reform," *Arab Reform Bulletin*, 20 November 2005.

"Saudi Local Councils Struggling to Produce Results," *Arab Reform Bulletin*, 18 October 2006.

Alshamsi, Mansoor Jassem, *Islam and Political Reform in Saudi Arabia: The Quest for Political Change and Reform* (New York: Routledge, 2011).

Amirahmadi, Hooshang, "Iranian-Saudi Arabian Relations since the Revolution," in *Iran and the Arab World*, ed. Hooshang Amirahmadi and Nader Entessar (London: Macmillan, 1993), 139–60.

Ammoun, Camille, "The Institutionalization of the Saudi Political System and the Birth of 'Political Personnel,'" in *Constitutional Reform and Political Participation in the Gulf*, ed. Abdulhadi Khalaf and Giacomo Luciani (Dubai: Gulf Research Center, 2006), 213–40.

Anderson, Benedict, *Imagined Communities: Reflections on the Origin and Spread of Nationalism*, 2nd ed. (London: Verso, 1991).

Anscombe, Frederick F., *The Ottoman Gulf: The Creation of Kuwait, Saudi Arabia, and Qatar* (New York: Columbia University Press, 1997).

"An Anational Society: Eastern Arabia in the Ottoman Period," in *Transnational Connections and the Arab Gulf*, ed. Madawi al-Rasheed (London: Routledge, 2004), 21–38.

Awad, Abdul Aziz M., "The Gulf in the Seventeenth Century," *Bulletin (British Society for Middle Eastern Studies)* 12, no. 2 (1985), 123–34.

Aziz, T. M., "The Role of Muhammad Baqir al-Sadr in Shii Political Activism in Iraq from 1958 to 1980," *International Journal of Middle East Studies* 25, no. 2 (1993), 207–22.

Badeeb, Saeed M., *The Saudi-Egyptian Conflict over North Yemen 1962–1970* (Boulder, CO: Westview Press, 1986).

Saudi-Iranian Relations 1932–1982 (London: Centre for Arab and Iranian Studies, 1993).

Barth, Fredrik, *Models of Social Organization* (London: Royal Anthropological Institute, 1966).

Ethnic Groups and Boundaries: The Social Organization of Culture Difference (Prospect Heights, IL: Waveland Press, 1998 [1st edition 1969]).

Batatu, Hanna, *The Old Social Classes and the Revolutionary Movements of Iraq: A Study of Iraq's Old Landed and Commercial Classes and of its Communists, Ba'thists, and Free Officers* (Princeton, NJ: Princeton University Press, 1978).

Beblawi, Hazem, "The Rentier State in the Arab World," in *The Rentier State*, ed. Giacomo Luciani and Hazem Beblawi (London: Croom Helm, 1987), 49–62.

Benhabib, Seyla, *The Claims of Culture: Equality and Diversity in the Global Era* (Princeton, NJ: Princeton University Press, 2002).

Bowen, Richard LeBaron, "Marine Industries of Eastern Arabia," *Geographical Review* 41, no. 3 (1951), 384–400.

"The Pearl Fisheries of the Persian Gulf," *The Middle East Journal* 5, no. 2 (1951), 161–80.

Bradley, John R., *Saudi Arabia Exposed: Inside a Kingdom in Crisis* (New York: Palgrave Macmillan, 2006).

Brass, Paul R., *Ethnicity and Nationalism: Theory and Comparison* (London: Sage, 1991).

Brown, Anthony Cave, *Oil, God, and Gold: The Story of Aramco and the Saudi Kings* (Boston: Houghton Mifflin, 1999).

Buchan, James, "Secular and Religious Opposition in Saudi Arabia," in *State, Society and Economy in Saudi Arabia*, ed. Tim Niblock (London: Croom Helm, 1982), 106–24.

Bulloch, John, and Harvey Morris, *The Gulf War: Its Origins, History and Consequences* (London: Methuen London, 1989).

Calabrese, John, *Revolutionary Horizons: Regional Foreign Policy in Post-Khomeini Iran* (New York: St. Martin's Press, 1994).

Carter, Robert, "The History and Prehistory of Pearling in the Persian Gulf," *Journal of the Economic and Social History of the Orient* 48, no. 2 (2005), 139–209.

Caskel, Werner, "Eine "unbekannte" Dynastie in Arabien," *Oriens* 2, no. 1 (1949), 66–71.

"'Abd al-Qays," *Encyclopedia of Islam*, 2nd. ed., ed. P. Bearman, Th. Bianquis, C. E. Bosworth, E. van Donzel and W. P. Heinrichs (Leiden: Brill Online).

Cetinsaya, Gökhan, "The Ottoman View of the Shiite Community of Iraq in the Late Nineteenth Century," in *The Other Shiites: From the Mediterranean to Central Asia*, ed. Alessandro Monsutti, Silvia Naef and Farian Sabahi (New York: Peter Lang, 2008), 19–40.

Chalcraft, John, *Monarchy, Migration and Hegemony in the Arabian Peninsula* (London: LSE Kuwait Programme on Development, Governance and Globalization in the Gulf States, 2010).

Champion, Daryl, *The Paradoxical Kingdom: Saudi Arabia and the Momentum of Reform* (London: Hurst, 2003).

Chaudhry, Kiren Aziz, *The Price of Wealth: Economies and Institutions in the Middle East* (Ithaca, NY: Cornell University Press, 1997).

Cheney, Michael Sheldon, *Big Oilman from Arabia* (London: Heinemann, 1958).

Chubin, Shahram, and Charles Tripp, *Iran and Iraq at War* (London: I. B. Tauris, 1988).

Iran-Saudi Arabia Relations and Regional Order: Iran and Saudi Arabia in the Balance of Power in the Gulf (London: Oxford University Press/International Institute for Strategic Studies, 1996).

Cole, Juan R. I., "Rival Empires of Trade and Imami Shiism in Eastern Arabia, 1300–1800," *International Journal of Middle East Studies* 19, no. 2 (1987), 177–203.

"Casting Away the Self: The Mysticism of Shaykh Ahmad al-Ahsa'i," in *The Twelver Shia in Modern Times: Religious Culture & Political History*, ed. Rainer Brunner and Werner Ende (Leiden: Brill, 2001), 25–37.

Commins, David, *The Wahhabi Mission and Saudi Arabia* (London: I. B. Tauris, 2006).

Cook, Michael, "Max Weber und islamische Sekten," in *Max Webers Sicht des Islams: Interpretation und Kritik*, ed. Wolfgang Schluchter (Frankfurt a. M.: Suhrkamp, 1987), 334–41.

Cordesman, Anthony H., *Saudi Arabia Enters the Twenty-First Century: The Political, Foreign Policy, Economic, and Energy Dimensions* (Westport, CT: Praeger, 2003).

Daftary, Farhad, *The Ismailis: Their History and Doctrines*, 2nd ed. (Cambridge: Cambridge University Press, 2007).

Dekmejian, Richard, "The Rise of Political Islamism in Saudi Arabia," *The Middle East Journal* 48, no. 4 (1994), 627–43.

"Saudi Arabia's Consultative Council," *The Middle East Journal* 52, no. 2 (1998), 204–18.

"The Liberal Impulse in Saudi Arabia," *The Middle East Journal* 57, no. 3 (2003), 400–13.

Determann, Jörg Matthias, *Historiography in Saudi Arabia: Globalization and the State in the Middle East* (London: I.B. Tauris, 2014).

Dinkelaker, Christoph, "Im Osten nichts Neues? – Zur Situation der Schia in Saudi-Arabien," in *Saudi-Arabien: ein Königreich im Wandel?* ed. Ulrike Freitag (Paderborn: Schöningh, 2009), 189–220.

Djalili, Mohammad-Reza, *Diplomatie Islamique: Stratégie Internationale du Khomeynisme* (Paris: Presses Universitaires de France, 1989).

Doumato, Eleanor Abdella, "Manning the Barricades: Islam according to Saudi Arabia's School Texts," *The Middle East Journal* 57, no. 2 (2003), 230–47.

Drewes, Frauke, "Das Nationale Dialogforum in Saudi-Arabien – Ausdruck politischer Reformen oder Stagnation?" in *Saudi-Arabien: ein Königreich im Wandel?* ed. Ulrike Freitag (Paderborn: Schöningh, 2009), 29–60.

Dunn, Micheal, "Until the Imam Comes: Iran Exports its Revolution," *Defense & Foreign Affairs* (July/August 1987), 43–51.

Ebert, Charles H. V., "Water Resources and Land Use in the Qatif Oasis of Saudi Arabia," *Geographical Review* 55, no. 4 (1965), 496–509.

Echagüe, Ana, and Edward Burke, "'Strong Foundations'? The Imperative for Reform in Saudi Arabia," *FRIDE Working Paper* 84 (2009).

Eickelman, Dale F., and James P. Piscatori, *Muslim Politics*, 2nd ed. (Princeton, NJ: Princeton University Press, 2004).

El-Shazly, Nadia El-Sayed, *The Gulf Tanker War: Iran and Iraq's Maritime Swordplay* (Houndmills, UK: Macmillan, 1998).

Ende, Werner, "Sunni Polemical Writings on the Shi'a and the Iranian Revolution," in *The Iranian Revolution and the Muslim World*, ed. David Menashri (Boulder, CO: Westview Press, 1990), 219–32.

   "The Nakhawila, a Shi'ite Community in Medina, Past and Present," *Die Welt des Islams* 37, no. 3 (1997), 264–348.

   "'Teilhaber an dem einen Vaterland': Die Petition saudischer Schiiten vom 30. April 2003," in *Iran und iranisch geprägte Kulturen: Studien zum 65. Geburtstag von Bert G. Fragner*, ed. Markus Ritter, Ralph Kauz and Birgitt Hoffmann (Wiesbaden: Ludwig Reichert, 2008), 336–44.

   "Steine des Anstoßes: Das Mausoleum der Ahl al-bayt in Medina," in *Differenz und Dynamik im Islam: Festschrift für Heinz Halm zum 70. Geburtstag*, ed. H. Biesterfeldt and V. Klemm (Würzburg: Ergon Verlag, 2012), 181–200.

Fandy, Mamoun, "From Confrontation to Creative Resistance: The Shia's Oppositional Discourse in Saudi Arabia," *Critique: Critical Middle Eastern Studies* 5, no. 9 (1996), 1–27.

   Saudi Arabia and the Politics of Dissent (Basingstoke, UK: Palgrave, 1999).

   "Saudi Opposition between Globalization and Localization," *Comparative Studies in Society and History* 41, no. 1 (1999), 124–47.

Fattah, Hala, *The Politics of Regional Trade in Iraq, Arabia, and the Gulf 1745–1900* (Albany: State University of New York Press, 1997).

Field, Michael, *The Merchants: The Big Business Families of Saudi Arabia and the Gulf States* (New York: Overlook Press, 1985).

Firro, Kais M., *Inventing Lebanon: Nationalism and the State under the Mandate* (London: I. B. Tauris, 2003).

Fischer, Michael M. J., *Iran: From Religious Dispute to Revolution* (Cambridge, MA: Harvard University Press, 1980).

Fox, John W., Nada Mourtada-Sabbah, and Mohammed al-Mutawa, "Heritage Revivalism in Sharjah," in *Globalization and the Gulf*, ed. John W. Fox, Nada Mourtada-Sabbah and Mohammed al-Mutawa (London: Routledge, 2006), 266–87.

Frankl, P. J. L., and K. Jopp, "Lieutenant Jopp's Report on a Visit to Hufuf, 1257/1841," *New Arabian Studies* 1 (1993), 215–27.

Franzén, Johan, *Red Star over Iraq: Iraqi Communism before Saddam* (London: Hurst, 2011).

Freitag, Sandria B., *Collective Action and Community: Public Arenas and the Emergence of Communalism in North India* (Berkeley: University of California Press, 1989).

Fuccaro, Nelida, *Histories of City and State in the Persian Gulf: Manama since 1800* (Cambridge: Cambridge University Press, 2009).

"Between Imara, Empire and Oil: Saudis in the Frontier Society of the Persian Gulf," in *Kingdom without Borders: Saudi Political, Religious and Media Frontiers* ed. Madawi al-Rasheed (London: Hurst, 2008), 39–64.

Fuller, Graham E., *The "Center of the Universe": The Geopolitics of Iran* (Boulder, CO: Westview Press, 1991).

Fuller, Graham E., and Rend Rahim Francke, *The Arab Shi'a: The Forgotten Muslims* (New York: St. Martin's Press, 1999).

Fürtig, Henner, *Der irakisch-iranische Krieg, 1980–1988: Ursachen, Verlauf, Folgen* (Berlin: Akademie, 1992).

Iran's Rivalry with Saudi Arabia between the Gulf Wars (Reading, UK: Ithaca Press, 2002).

Gause III., F. Gregory, *The International Relations of the Persian Gulf* (Cambridge: Cambridge University Press, 2010).

"Rageless in Riyadh," *Foreign Affairs*, March 16, 2011.

Gengler, Justin J., "Understanding Sectarianism in the Persian Gulf," in *Sectarian Politics in the Persian Gulf*, ed. Lawrence G. Potter (London: Hurst, 2013), 31–66.

Gerges, Fawaz A., *The Far Enemy: Why Jihad Went Global* (Cambridge: Cambridge University Press, 2005).

Gleave, Robert, "Khums," *Encyclopedia of Islam*, 2nd. ed., ed. P. Bearman, Th. Bianquis, C. E. Bosworth, E. van Donzel and W. P. Heinrichs (Leiden: Brill Online).

Goldberg, Jacob, "The 1913 Saudi Occupation of Hasa Reconsidered," *Middle Eastern Studies* 18, no. 1 (1982), 21–9.

"The Shi'i Minority in Saudi Arabia," in *Shi'ism and Social Protest*, ed. Juan R. I. Cole and Nikki R. Keddie (New Haven, CT: Yale University Press, 1986), 230–46.

"Saudi Arabia and the Iranian Revolution: The Religious Dimension," in *The Iranian Revolution and the Muslim World*, ed. David Menashri (Boulder, CO: Westview Press, 1990), 155–70.

Gresh, Alain, "Between Tradition and Demands for Change: Saudi Arabia: Reality Check," *Le Monde Diplomatique*, February 2006.

Habib, John S., "Wahhabi Origins of the Contemporary Saudi State," in *Religion and Politics in Saudi Arabia: Wahhabism and the State*, ed. Mohammed Ayoob and Hasan Kosebalaban (London: Lynne Rienner, 2008), 57–73.

Haddad, Fanar, *Sectarianism in Iraq: Antagonistic Visions of Unity* (London: Hurst, 2011).

Haidari, Ibrahim, *Zur Soziologie des schiitischen Chiliasmus* (Freiburg in Breisgau: Klaus Schwarz, 1975).

Hajrah, Hassan Hamza, *Public Land Distribution in Saudi Arabia* (London: Longman, 1982).

Hakken, B. D., "Sunni-Shia Discord in Eastern Arabia," *The Moslem World* 23 (1933), 302–5.

Halbwachs, Maurice, *La topographie légendaire des Évangiles en Terre Sainte: Étude de memoire collective* (Paris: Presses Universitaires de France, 1941).
On Collective Memory (Chicago: The University of Chicago Press, 1992).
Halliday, Fred, "Iranian Foreign Policy since 1979: Internationalism and Nationalism in the Islamic Revolution," in *Shi'ism and Social Protest*, ed. Juan R. I. Cole and Nikki R. Keddie (New Haven, CT: Yale University Press, 1986), 88–107.
Arabia without Sultans, 2nd ed. (London: Saqi Books, 2002).
Halm, Heinz, *Die Schiiten* (München: C. H. Beck, 2005).
Hamilton, Jennifer, Ulf Hansson and John Bell (et. al.), *Segregated Lives: Social Division, Sectarianism and Everyday Life in Northern Ireland* (Belfast: Institute for Conflict Research, 2008).
Hamza, Fuad, "Najran," *Journal of The Royal Central Asian Society* 22, no. 4 (1935), 631–40.
Haydari, Ibrahim, "The Rituals of Ashura: Genealogy, Functions, Actors and Structures," in *Ayatollahs, Sufis and Ideologues: State, Religion and Social Movements in Iraq*, ed. Faleh A. Jabar (London: Saqi Books, 2002), 101–13.
Heard-Bey, Frauke, *Die arabischen Golfstaaten im Zeichen der islamischen Revolution* (Bonn: Europa Union Verlag, 1983).
Hegghammer, Thomas, "Deconstructing the Myth about al-Qa'ida and Khobar," *CTC Sentinel* 1, no. 3 (2008), 20–2.
Jihad in Saudi Arabia: Violence and Pan-Islamism since 1979 (Cambridge: Cambridge University Press, 2010).
Hegghammer, Thomas, and Stéphane Lacroix, "Rejectionist Islamism in Saudi Arabia: The Story of Juhayman al-'Utaybi Revisited," *International Journal of Middle East Studies* 39, no. 1 (2007), 103–22.
Hertog, Steffen, "Segmented Clientelism: The Political Economy of Saudi Economic Reform Efforts," in *Saudi Arabia in the Balance: Political Economy, Society, Foreign Affairs*, ed. Paul Aarts and Gerd Nonneman (New York: New York University Press, 2005), 111–43.
"The New Corporatism in Saudi Arabia: Limits of Formal Politics," in *Constitutional Reform and Political Participation in the Gulf*, ed. Abdulhadi Khalaf and Giacomo Luciani (Dubai: Gulf Research Center, 2006), 241–75.
"Petromin: The Slow Death of Statist Oil Development in Saudi Arabia," *Business History* 50, no. 5 (2008), 645–67.
Princes, Brokers, and Bureaucrats: Oil and the State in Saudi Arabia (Ithaca, NY: Cornell University Press, 2010).
Holden, David, and Richard Johns, *The House of Saud* (London: Sidgwick and Jackson, 1981).
Hourani, Albert, "Ottoman Reform and the Politics of Notables," in *The Modern Middle East: A Reader*, ed. Albert Hourani, Philip S. Khoury and Mary C. Wilson (London: I. B. Tauris, 2004), 83–110.
Hudson, Michael C., "Arab Regimes and Democratization: Responses to the Challenge of Political Islam," in *The Islamist Dilemma: The Political Role of Islamist Movements in the Contemporary Arab World*, ed. Laura Guazzone (Reading: Ithaca, 1995), 217–45.

Ibrahim, Ferhad, *Konfessionalismus und Politik in der arabischen Welt: Die Schiiten im Irak* (Münster: LIT-Verlag, 1997).

Ibrahim, Fouad, *The Shi'is of Saudi Arabia* (London: Saqi Books, 2006).

Ilhan, Mehmet Mehdi, "The Katif District (Liva) During the First Few Years of Ottoman Rule: A Study of the 1551 Ottoman Cadastral Survey," *Belleten (Türk Tarih Kurumu)* 51, no. 200 (1987), 780–98.

Ismail, Raihan, "The Saudi Ulema and the Shi'a of Saudi Arabia," *Journal of Shi'a Islamic Studies* 5, no. 4 (2012), 403–22.

Jabar, Faleh A., *The Shi'ite Movement in Iraq* (London: Saqi Books, 2003).

Jones, Justin, *Shi'a Islam in Colonial India: Religion, Community and Sectarianism* (Cambridge: Cambridge University Press, 2012).

Jones, Toby, "Violence and the Illusion of Reform in Saudi Arabia," *Middle East Report Online*, November 13, 2003.

"Seeking a "Social Contract" for Saudi Arabia," *Middle East Report* 228 (2003), 42–8.

"The Iraq Effect in Saudi Arabia," *Middle East Report* 237 (2005), 20–5.

"Rebellion on the Saudi Periphery: Modernity, Marginalization, and the Shi'a Uprising of 1979," *International Journal of Middle East Studies* 38 (2006), 213–33.

"Saudi Arabia's Not So New Anti-Shi'ism," *Middle East Report* 242 (2007), 29–32.

Embattled in Arabia: Shi'is and the Politics of Confrontation in Saudi Arabia (Combating Terrorism Center at West Point, 2009).

Desert Kingdom: How Oil and Water Forged Modern Saudi Arabia (Cambridge, MA: Harvard University Press, 2010).

Kapiszewski, Andrzej, "Saudi Arabia: Steps toward Democratization or Reconfiguration of Authoritarianism?" *Journal of Asian and African Studies* 41, no. 5/6 (2006), 459–82.

Katz, Mark N., *Russia and Arabia: Soviet Foreign Policy toward the Arabian Peninsula* (Baltimore: Johns Hopkins University Press, 1985).

Katzman, Kenneth, *The Warriors of Islam: Iran's Revolutionary Guard* (Boulder, CO: Westview Press, 1993).

Kechichian, Joseph A., *Succession in Saudi Arabia* (New York: Palgrave Macmillan, 2001).

Keddie, Nikki R., *Modern Iran: Roots and Results of Revolution* (New Haven, CT: Yale University Press, 2006).

Khalaf, Samir, *Civil and Uncivil Violence in Lebanon: A History of the Internationalization of Communal Conflict* (New York: Columbia University Press, 2002).

Khalaf, Sulayman, "The Nationalisation of Culture: Kuwait's Invention of a Pearl-Diving Heritage," in *Popular Culture and Political Identity in the Arab Gulf States*, ed. Alanoud Alsharekh and Robert Springborg (London: Saqi, 2008), 40–70.

Khuri, Fuad I., *Tribe and State in Bahrain: The Transformation of Social and Political Authority in an Arab State* (Chicago: The University of Chicago Press, 1980).

Imams and Emirs: State, Religion and Sects in Islam (London: Saqi Books, 1990).

Khuri-Makdisi, Ilham, *The Eastern Mediterranean and the Making of Global Radicalism, 1860–1914* (Berkeley: University of California Press, 2010).

Kornrumpf, Hans-Jürgen, "Neuere Beschreibungen von al-Hasa in amtlichen osmanischen Veröffentlichungen," *Der Islam* 55, no. 1 (1978), 74–92.

Kostiner, Joseph, "Shi'i Unrest in the Gulf," in *Shi'ism, Resistance, and Revolution*, ed. Martin Kramer (Boulder, CO: Westview Press, 1987), 173–86.

Kramer, Martin, "Syria's Alawis and Shi'ism," in *Shi'ism, Resistance, and Revolution*, ed. Martin Kramer (Boulder, CO: Westview Press, 1987), 237–54.

Arab Awakening and Islamic Revival: The Politics of Ideas in the Middle East (New Brunswick, NJ: Transaction, 1996).

Kwarten, Leo, *Why the Saudi Shiites Won't Rise Up Easily* (Conflicts Forum, 2009).

Lacey, Robert, *Inside the Kingdom: Kings, Clerics, Modernists, Terrorists and the Struggle for Saudi Arabia* (London: Penguin, 2009).

Lackner, Helen, *A House Built on Sand: A Political Economy of Saudi Arabia* (London: Ithaca Press, 1978).

Lacroix, Stéphane, "Between Islamists and Liberals: Saudi Arabia's New Islamo-liberal Reformist Trend," *The Middle East Journal* 58, no. 3 (2004), 345–65.

"Islamo-Liberal Politics in Saudi Arabia," in *Saudi Arabia in the Balance: Political Economy, Society, Foreign Affairs*, ed. Paul Aarts and Gerd Nonneman (Washington Square, NY: New York University Press, 2005), 35–56.

Awakening Islam: The Politics of Religious Dissent in Contemporary Saudi Arabia (Cambridge, MA: Harvard University Press, 2011).

"Is Saudi Arabia Immune?" *Journal of Democracy* 22, no. 4 (October 2011), 48–59.

Lacroix, Stéphane, and Steffen Hertog, "Dissidenz und Institutionalisierung: Die zweischneidige Debatte der Modernisierung," *inamo* 42 (2005).

Leverrier, Ignace, "L'Arabie Saoudite, le pèlerinage et l'Iran," *Cahiers d'Études sur la Méditerranée Orientale et le Monde Turco-Iranien* 22 (1996), 111–47.

Litvak, Meir, *Shi'i Scholars of Nineteenth-Century Iraq: The 'Ulama' of Najaf and Karbala'* (Cambridge: Cambridge University Press, 1998).

"The Finances of the Ulama Communities of Najaf and Karbala, 1796–1904," *Die Welt des Islams* 40, no. 1 (2000), 41–66.

Long, David E., "The Impact of the Iranian Revolution on the Arabian Peninsula and the Gulf States," in *The Iranian Revolution: Its Global Impact*, ed. John L. Esposito (Miami: Florida International University Press, 1990), 100–15.

Louër, Laurence, *Transnational Shiite Politics: Religious and Political Networks in the Gulf* (London: Hurst, 2008).

"Shi'i Identity Politics in Saudi Arabia," in *Religious Minorities in the Middle East: Domination, Self-empowerment, Accommodation*, ed. Anh Nga Longva and Anne Sofie Roald (Leiden: Brill, 2012), 221–43.

"The State and Sectarian Identities in the Persian Gulf Monarchies: Bahrain, Saudi Arabia, and Kuwait in Comparative Perspective," in *Sectarian Politics in the Persian Gulf*, ed. Lawrence G. Potter (London: Hurst, 2013), 117–42.

Luciani, Giacomo, "Allocation vs. Production States: A Theoretical Framework," in *The Rentier State*, ed. Giacomo Luciani and Hazem Beblawi (London: Croom Helm, 1987), 65–84.

Mackie, J. B., "Hasa: An Arabian Oasis," *The Geographical Journal* 63, no. 3 (1924), 189–207.

Makdisi, Ussama Samir, *The Culture of Sectarianism: Community, History, and Violence in Nineteenth-Century Ottoman Lebanon* (Berkeley, CA: University of California Press).

Mandaville, Jon E., "The Ottoman Province of al-Hasa in the Sixteenth and Seventeenth Centuries," *Journal of the American Oriental Society* 90, no. 3 (1970), 486–513.

Marschall, Christin, *Iran's Persian Gulf Policy: From Khomeini to Khatami* (London: RoutledgeCurzon, 2003).

Masters, Bruce, *Christians and Jews in the Ottoman Arab World: The Roots of Sectarianism* (Cambridge: Cambridge University Press, 2001).

Matthiesen, Toby, "The Shiʿa of Saudi Arabia at a Crossroads," *Middle East Report Online* (May 6, 2009).

"Diwaniyyas, Intellectual Salons and the Limits of Civil Society in Saudi Arabia," in *Viewpoints: Saudi Arabia 1979–2009: Evolution of a Pivotal State* (Washington, DC: Middle East Institute, 2009), 13–15.

"Hizbullah al-Hijaz: A History of the Most Radical Saudi Shiʿa Opposition Group," *The Middle East Journal* 64, no. 2 (Spring 2010), 179–97.

"Saudi Arabia: The Middle East's most Under-Reported Conflict," *The Guardian*, 23 January 2012.

"Sable Rattling in the Gulf," *Foreign Policy*, July 10, 2012.

"A "Saudi Spring?": The Shiʿa Protest Movement in the Eastern Province 2011–2012," *The Middle East Journal* 66, no. 4 (Autumn 2012), 628–59.

"Saudi Royal Family Politics and the Arab Spring," *Foreign Policy*, January 14, 2013.

"Syria: Inventing a Religious War," *New York Review of Books Blog*, 12 June, 2013.

Sectarian Gulf: Bahrain, Saudi Arabia, and the Arab Spring that Wasn't (Stanford, CA: Stanford University Press, 2013).

"The Local and the Transnational in the Arab Uprisings: The Protests in Saudi Arabia's Eastern Province," in *The Silent Revolution: The Arab Spring and the Gulf States*, ed. May Seikaly and Khawla Matar (Berlin: Gerlach Press, 2014), 105–143.

"Mysticism, Migration and Clerical Networks: Ahmad al-Ahsaʾi and the Shaykhis of al-Ahsa, Kuwait and Basra," *Journal of Muslim Minority Affairs* 34, no. 4 (2014).

"Between Communism, Nationalism and Islam: Labour Movements and Opposition Groups in Saudi Arabia, 1950–1975," *International Review of Social History* 59, no. 3 (Autumn 2014).

"Shiʻi Historians in a Wahhabi State: Identity Entrepreneurs and the Politics of Local Historiography in Saudi Arabia," *International Journal of Middle East Studies* 47, no. 1 (2015).

"Center-Periphery Relations and the Emergence of a Public Sphere in Saudi Arabia: The Municipal Elections in the Eastern Province, 1954–1960," *British Journal of Middle Eastern Studies* (forthcoming).

McGuire, Meredith B., *Religion, the Social Context*, 4th ed. (Belmont, CA: Wadsworth, 1997).

Meijer, Roel, "Reform in Saudi Arabia: The Gender Segregation Debate," *Middle East Policy* 17, no. 4 (Winter 2010), 80–100.

Meijer, Roel, and Joas Wagemakers, "The Struggle for Citizenship of the Shiites of Saudi Arabia," in *The Dynamics of Sunni-Shia Relationships: Doctrine, Transnationalism, Intellectuals and the Media*, ed. Brigitte Maréchal and Sami Zemni (London: Hurst, 2013), 117–38.

Mervin, Sabrina, "Sayyida Zaynab, Banlieue de Damas ou nouvelle ville sainte chiite?" *Cahiers d'Études sur la Méditerranée Orientale et le Monde Turco-Iranien* 22 (1996), 149–62.

"Ashura: Some Remarks on Ritual Practices in Different Shiite Communities (Lebanon and Syria)," in *The Other Shiites: From the Mediterranean to Central Asia*, ed. Alessandro Monsutti, Silvia Naef and Farian Sabahi (New York: Peter Lang, 2008), 137–47.

Moin, Baqer, *Khomeini: Life of the Ayatollah* (London: I. B. Tauris, 1999).

Montagu, Caroline, "Civil Society and the Voluntary Sector in Saudi Arabia" *The Middle East Journal* 64, no. 1 (2010), 67–83.

Munif, Abdelrahman, *Cities of Salt* (London: Vintage, 1994).

Murray, Bill, *The Old Firm: Sectarianism, Sport, and Society in Scotland* (Edinburgh: John Donald Publishers, 1984).

Nakash, Yitzhak, "The Conversion of Iraq's Tribes to Shiism," *International Journal of Middle East Studies* 26, no. 3 (1994), 443–63.

The Shiʻis of Iraq, 2nd ed. (Princeton, NJ: Princeton University Press, 2003).

Reaching for Power: The Shiʻa in the Modern Arab World (Princeton, NJ: Princeton University Press, 2006).

Nasr, Vali, *The Shia Revival: How Conflicts Within Islam Will Shape the Future* (London: W. W. Norton & Company, 2007).

"International Politics, Domestic Imperatives, and Identity Mobilization: Sectarianism in Pakistan, 1979–1998," *Comparative Politics* 32, no. 2 (2000), 171–90.

Navias, Martin S., and E. R. Hooton, *Tanker Wars: The Assault on Merchant Shipping during the Iran-Iraq Conflict 1980–1988* (London: I. B. Tauris, 1996).

Nawwab, Ismail I., Peter C. Speers and Paul F. Hoye, eds., *Saudi Aramco and its World: Arabia and the Middle East* (Dhahran: The Saudi Arabian Oil Company (Saudi Aramco), 1995).

Nevo, Joseph J., "Religion and National Identity in Saudi Arabia," *Middle Eastern Studies* 34, no. 3 (1998), 34–53.

Nischan, Bodo, *Lutherans and Calvinists in the Age of Confessionalism* (Aldershot: Ashgate, 1999).

Nonneman, Gerd, *Iraq, the Gulf States & the War* (London: Ithaca Press, 1986).

Okruhlik, Gwenn, "Rentier Wealth, Unruly Law, and the Rise of Opposition: The Political Economy of Oil States," *Comparative Politics* 31, no. 3 (1999), 295–315.

"Making Conversation Permissible: Islamism and Reform in Saudi Arabia," in *Islamic Activism: A Social Movement Theory Approach*, ed. Quintan Wiktorowicz (Bloomington, IN: Indiana University Press, 2004), 250–69.

"The Irony of Islah (Reform)," *Washington Quarterly* 28, no. 4 (2005), 153–70.

Omar, Farouk, "Urban Centres in the Gulf during the Early Islamic Period: A Historical Study," *Bulletin (British Society for Middle Eastern Studies)* 14, no. 2 (1987), 156–61.

Onley, James, *The Arabian Frontier of the British Raj: Merchants, Rulers, and the British in the Nineteenth-Century Gulf* (Oxford: Oxford University Press, 2007).

Özbaran, Salih, "Ottomans and the India Trade in the Sixteenth Century: Some New Data and Reconsiderations," *Oriente Moderno* 25, no. 86 (2006), 173–79.

Palgrave, William Gifford, *Personal Narrative of a Journey through Central Arabia* (London: Macmillan and Co., 1868).

Pampanini, Andrea H., *Cities from the Arabian Desert: The Building of Jubail and Yanbu in Saudi Arabia* (Westport, CT: Praeger, 1997).

Patterson, Henry, *Class Conflict and Sectarianism: The Protestant Working Class and the Belfast Labour Movement 1868–1920* (Belfast: Blackstaff Press Limited, 1980).

Pelly, L., *Report on a Journey to Riyadh in Central Arabia 1865* (Cambridge: Oleander Press, reprinted 1978).

Peskes, Esther, *Muhammad b. 'Abdalwahhab (1703–92) im Widerstreit: Untersuchungen zur Rekonstruktion der Frühgeschichte der Wahhabiya* (Beirut: Orient-Institut, 1993).

Peterson, J. E., *Historical Dictionary of Saudi Arabia* (Metuchen, NJ: Scarecrow Press, 1993).

Philby, H. St John, *Sa'udi Arabia* (London: Benn, 1955).

Philipp, Hans-Jürgen, *Geschichte und Entwicklung der Oase al-Hasa (Saudi Arabien)* (Saarbrücken: Breitenbach, 1976).

Piscatori, James P., ed., *Islamic Fundamentalisms and the Gulf Crisis* (Chicago: The American Academy of Arts and Sciences, 1991).

"Managing God's Guests: The Pilgrimage, Saudi Arabia and the Politics of Legitimacy," in *Monarchies and Nations: Globalisation and Identity in the Arab States of the Gulf*, ed. P. Dresch and J. Piscatori (London: I. B. Tauris, 2005), 222–45.

Pritzke, Herbert, *Bedouin Doctor: The Adventures of a German in the Middle East* (London: Weidenfeld and Nicolson, 1957).

Prokop, Michaela, "The War of Ideas: Education in Saudi Arabia," in *Saudi Arabia in the Balance: Political Economy, Society, Foreign Affairs*, ed. Paul Aarts and Gerd Nonneman (Washington Square, NY: New York University Press, 2005), 57–81.

Quandt, William B., *Saudi Arabia in the 1980s: Foreign Policy, Security, and Oil* (Washington: The Brookings Institution, 1981).

Ramazani, Rouhollah K., "Shi'ism in the Persian Gulf," in *Shi'ism and Social Protest*, ed. Juan R. I. Cole and Nikki R. Keddie (New Haven, CT: Yale University Press, 1986), 30–54.

   Revolutionary Iran: Challenge and Response in the Middle East (Baltimore, MD: Johns Hopkins University Press, 1988).

   "Iran's Export of the Revolution: Politics, Ends, and Means," in *The Iranian Revolution: Its Global Impact*, ed. John L. Esposito (Miami: Florida International University Press, 1990), 40–62.

Raphaeli, Nimrod, "Demands for Reforms in Saudi Arabia," *Middle Eastern Studies* 41, no. 4 (2005), 517–32.

Reiche, Danyel, "War Minus the Shooting? The Politics of Sport in Lebanon as a Unique Case in Comparative Politics," *Third World Quarterly* 32, no. 2 (2011), 261–77.

Reichert, Horst, *Die Verstädterung der Eastern Province von Saudi Arabien und ihre Konsequenzen für die Regional- und Stadtentwicklung* (Stuttgart: Krämer, 1980).

Rentz, G., "al-Qatif," *Encyclopedia of Islam*, 2nd. ed., ed. P. Bearman, Th. Bianquis, C. E. Bosworth, E. van Donzel and W. P. Heinrichs (Leiden: Brill Online).

Rihani, Ameen Fares, *Ibn Sa'oud of Arabia: His People and His Land* (London: Constable, 1928).

Sadlier, George Forster, and Patrick Ryan, *Diary of a Journey across Arabia from el Khatif in the Persian Gulf, to Yambo in the Red Sea, during the Year 1819* (Bombay: Education Society's Press, Byculla, 1866).

Salameh, Ghassane, and Vivian Steir, "Political Power and the Saudi State," *MERIP Reports* 91 (1980), 5–22.

Samin, Nadav, "Dynamics of Internet Use: Saudi Youth, Religious Minorities and Tribal Communities," *Middle East Journal of Culture and Communication* 1, no. 2 (2008), 197–215.

Scott, James C., *Domination and the Arts of Resistance: Hidden Transcripts* (New Haven, CT: Yale University Press, 1990).

Seale, Patrick, *Asad of Syria: The Struggle for the Middle East* (London: I. B. Tauris, 1988).

Sedgwick, Mark J. R., "Saudi Sufis: Compromise in the Hijaz, 1925–40," *Die Welt des Islams* 37, no. 3 (1997), 349–68.

Shaery-Eisenlohr, Roschanack, *Shi'ite Lebanon: Transnational Religion and the Making of National Identities* (New York: Columbia University Press, 2008).

Shambayati, Hootan, "The Rentier State, Interest Groups, and the Paradox of Autonomy: State and Business in Turkey and Iran," *Comparative Politics* 26, no. 3 (1994), 307–31.

Shariati, Ali, *Hajj* (Bedford, OH: Free Islamic Literature, 1977).

Shirlow, Peter and Brendan Murtagh, *Belfast: Segregation, Violence and the City* (London: Pluto Press, 2006).

Sindawi, Khalid, "The Shiite Turn in Syria," *Current Trends in Islamist Ideology* 8 (June 23rd, 2009), 82–107.

Skocpol, Theda, "Rentier State and Shi'a Islam in the Iranian Revolution," *Theory and Society* 11, no. 3 (1982), 265–83.

Solomon, John, "Saudi Arabia's Shiites and their Effect on the Kingdom's Stability," *Terrorism Monitor* 4, no. 15 (2006).

Sreberny, Annabelle, and Ali Mohammadi, *Small Media, Big Revolution: Communication, Culture, and the Iranian Revolution* (Minneapolis: University of Minnesota Press, 1994).

Steinberg, Guido, "The Shiites in the Eastern Province of Saudi Arabia (al-Ahsa') 1913–1953," in *The Twelver Shia in Modern Times: Religious Culture & Political History*, ed. Rainer Brunner and Werner Ende (Leiden: Brill, 2001), 236–54.

Religion und Staat in Saudi-Arabien: Die wahhabitischen Gelehrten 1902–1953 (Würzburg: Ergon Verlag, 2002).

"Jihadi-Salafism and the Shi'is: Remarks about the Intellectual Roots of Anti-Shi'ism," in *Global Salafism: Islam's New Religious Movement*, ed. Roel Meijer (London: Hurst, 2009), 107–25.

"The Wahhabiyya and Shi'ism, from 1744/45 to 2008," in *The Sunna and Shi'a in History: Division and Ecumenism in the Muslim Middle East*, ed. Ofra Bengio and Meir Litvak (New York: Palgrave Macmillan, 2011), 163–82.

Sugden, John Peter, and Alan Bairner, *Sport, Sectarianism and Society in a Divided Ireland* (Leicester: Leicester University Press, 1993).

Sunayama, Sonoko, *Syria and Saudi Arabia: Collaboration and Conflicts in the Oil Era* (London: I. B. Tauris Academic Studies, 2007).

Takriti, Abdel Razzaq, *Monsoon Revolution: Republicans, Sultans, and Empires in Oman 1965–1976* (Oxford: Oxford University Press, 2013).

Talhamy, Yvette, "The Fatwas and the Nusayri/Alawis of Syria," *Middle Eastern Studies* 46, no. 2 (2010), 175–94.

Taylor, Charles, and Amy Gutmann, eds., *Multiculturalism: Examining the Politics of Recognition* (Princeton, NJ: Princeton University Press, 1994).

Teitelbaum, Joshua, "Saudi Arabia's Shi'i Opposition: Background and Analysis," *Policy Watch* 225 (Washington: Washington Institute for Near East Policy, November 14, 1996).

Holier than Thou: Saudi Arabia's Islamic Opposition (Washington: Washington Institute for Near East Policy, 2000).

"Dueling for Da'wa: State vs. Society on the Saudi Internet," *The Middle East Journal* 56, no. 2 (2002), 222–39.

"The Shiites of Saudi Arabia," *Current Trends in Islamist Ideology* 10 (2010).

"Sunni vs. Shiite in Saudi Arabia," *Jerusalem Issue Briefs* 10, no. 23, 16 January 2011.

Totten, Don E., *Erdöl in Sa'udi-Arabien* (Heidelberg: Keyser, 1959).

Trofimov, Yaroslav, *The Siege of Mecca: The Forgotten Uprising* (London: Allen Lane, 2007).

Valeri, Marc, "High Visibility, Low Profile: The Shi'a in Oman under Sultan Qaboos," *International Journal of Middle East Studies* 42, no. 2 (2010), 251–68.

Van Dam, Nikolaos, *The Struggle for Power in Syria: Sectarianism, Regionalism and Tribalism in Politics 1961–1978* (London: Croom Helm, 1979).

Vassiliev, Alexei, *The History of Saudi Arabia* (London: Saqi, 2000).

Vidal, F. S., "Date Culture in the Oasis of al-Hasa," *The Middle East Journal* 8 (1954), 417–28.

The Oasis of al-Hasa (n.p.: Arabian American Oil Company, 1955).

Vitalis, Robert, *America's Kingdom: Mythmaking on the Saudi Oil Frontier*, 2nd ed. (London: Verso, 2009).

Vogel, Frank E., *Islamic Law and Legal System: Studies of Saudi Arabia* (Leiden: Brill, 2000).

Wahba, Hafiz, *Arabian Days* (London: Arthur Barker, 1964).

Weber, Max, "Kirchen und Sekten," in *Schriften 1894–1922*, ed. Dirk Kaesler (Stuttgart: Alfred Kröner, 2002), 227–42.

Wehrey, Frederic, *The Forgotten Uprising in Eastern Saudi Arabia* (Carnegie Endowment for International Peace, June 14, 2013).

Sectarian Politics in the Gulf: From the Iraq War to the Arab Uprisings (New York: Columbia University Press, 2014).

Weiss, Max, "Institutionalizing Sectarianism: The Lebanese Ja'fari Court and Shi'i Society under the French Mandate," *Islamic Law and Society* 15, no. 3 (2008), 371–407.

"The Historiography of Sectarianism in Lebanon," *History Compass* 7, no. 1 (2009), 141–54.

In the Shadow of Sectarianism: Law, Shi'ism, and the Making of Modern Lebanon (Cambridge, MA: Harvard University Press, 2010).

Wiley, Joyce N., *The Islamic Movement of Iraqi Shi'as* (Boulder, CO: Lynne Rienner, 1992).

Wilson, Bryan R., *Religion in Sociological Perspective* (Oxford: Oxford University Press, 1982).

Winder, R. Bayly, *Saudi Arabia in the Nineteenth Century* (London: Macmillan, 1965).

Woodward, Peter N., *Oil and Labor in the Middle East: Saudi Arabia and the Oil Boom* (New York: Praeger, 1988).

Wright, Robin B., *Sacred Rage: The Crusade of Modern Islam* (London: Andre Deutsch, 1986).

Yassini, Ayman, *Religion and State in the Kingdom of Saudi Arabia* (Boulder, CO: Westview Press, 1985).

Yisraeli, Sarah, *The Remaking of Saudi Arabia: The Struggle between King Saud and Crown Prince Faysal, 1953–1962* (Tel Aviv: Moshe Dayan Center for Middle Eastern and African Studies, 1997).

Yodfat, Aryeh Y., *The Soviet Union and the Arabian Peninsula: Soviet Policy towards the Persian Gulf and Arabia* (London: Croom Helm, 1983).

Index

CPSIA information can be obtained
at www.ICGtesting.com
Printed in the USA
LVHW080827170721
692966LV00014B/1172